www.wadsworth.com

wadsworth.com is the World Wide Web site for
Wadsworth Publishing Company and is your direct
source to dozens of online resources.

At *wadsworth.com* you can find out about
supplements, demonstration software, and
student resources. You can also send e-mail to
many of our authors and preview new publications
and exciting new technologies.

wadsworth.com
Changing the way the world learns®

FROM THE WADSWORTH SERIES IN SPEECH COMMUNICATION

Babbie *Basics of Social Research* (with InfoTrac)

Babbie *The Practice of Social Research*, Eighth Edition

Barranger *Theatre: A Way of Seeing*, Fourth Edition

Campbell *The Rhetorical Act*, Second Edition

Campbell/Burkholder *Critiques of Contemporary Rhetoric*, Second Edition

Cragan/Wright *Communication in Small Groups: Theory, Process, Skills*, Fifth Edition

Crannell *Voice and Articulation*, Fourth Edition

Freeley *Argumentation and Debate: Critical Thinking for Reasoned Decision Making*, Tenth Edition

Govier *Practical Study of Argument*, Fourth Edition

Hamilton *Essentials of Public Speaking*

Hamilton/Parker *Communicating for Results: A Guide for Business and the Professions*, Sixth Edition

Jaffe *Public Speaking: Concepts and Skills for a Diverse Society*, Second Edition

Kahane/Cavender *Logic and Contemporary Rhetoric: The Use of Reason in Everyday Life*, Eighth Edition

Larson *Persuasion: Reception and Responsibility*, Eighth Edition

Littlejohn *Theories of Human Communication*, Sixth Edition

Lumsden/Lumsden *Communicating in Groups and Teams: Sharing Leadership*, Third Edition

Lumsden/Lumsden *Communicating with Credibility and Confidence*

Miller *Organizational Communication: Approaches and Processes*, Second Edition

Peterson/Stephan *Complete Speaker: An Introduction to Public Speaking*, Third Edition

Rubin et al. *Communication Research: Strategies and Sources*, Fifth Edition

Rybacki/Rybacki *Communication Criticism: Approaches and Genres*

Samovar/Porter *Intercultural Communication: A Reader*, Ninth Edition

Samovar/Porter/Stefani *Communication Between Cultures*, Third Edition

Trenholm/Jensen *Interpersonal Communication*, Fourth Edition

Ulloth/Alderfer *Public Speaking: An Experiential Approach*

Verderber *The Challenge of Effective Speaking*, Eleventh Edition

Verderber *Communicate!*, Ninth Edition

Verderber/Verderber *InterAct: Using Interpersonal Communication Skills*, Eighth Edition

Wood *Communication Mosaics: A New Introduction to the Field of Communication*

Wood *Communication in Our Lives*, Second Edition

Wood *Communication Theories in Action: An Introduction*

Wood *Gendered Lives: Communication, Gender, and Culture*, Third Edition

Wood *Interpersonal Communication: Everyday Encounters*, Second Edition

JULIA T. WOOD

UNIVERSITY OF NORTH CAROLINA – CHAPEL HILL

Relational Communication

Continuity and Change in Personal Relationships

SECOND EDITION

Wadsworth Publishing Company

I(T)P® An International Thomson Publishing Company

Belmont, CA • Albany, NY • Boston • Cincinnati • Johannesburg
London • Madrid • Melbourne • Mexico City • New York
Pacific Grove, CA • Scottsdale, AZ • Singapore • Tokyo • Toronto

ASSISTANT EDITOR: Megan Gilbert

EXECUTIVE EDITOR: Deirdre Cavanaugh

PROJECT EDITOR: Cathy Linberg

PRINT BUYER: Barbara Britton

PERMISSIONS EDITOR: Susan Walters

PRODUCTION: Vicki Moran, Publishing Support Services

COPY EDITOR: Jennifer Gordon

TEXT & COVER DESIGNER: Andrew Ogus ■ Book Design

COVER IMAGES: © 1999 PhotoDisc, Inc.

COMPOSITOR: Publishing Support Services

TEXT & COVER PRINTER: Webcom Limited

This book is printed on acid-free recycled paper.

Printed in Canada
2 3 4 5 6 7 8 9 10

Wadsworth Publishing Company
10 Davis Drive
Belmont, CA 94002

International Thomson Publishing Europe
Berkshire House
168-173 High Holborn
London, WC1V 7AA, United Kingdom

Nelson ITP, Australia
102 Dodds Street
South Melbourne
Victoria 3205 Australia

Nelson Canada
1120 Birchmount Road
Scarborough, Ontario
Canada M1K 5G4

International Thomson Editores
Seneca, 53
Colonia Polanco
11560 México D.F. México

International Thomson Publishing Asia
60 Albert Street #15-01
Albert Complex
Singapore 189969

International Thomson Publishing Japan
Hirakawa-cho Kyowa Building, 3F
2-2-1 Hirakawa-cho, Chiyoda-ku
Tokyo 102, Japan

International Thomson Publishing Southern Africa
Building 18, Constantia Square
138 Sixteenth Road, P.O. Box 2459
Halfway House, 1685 South Africa

Library of Congress Cataloging-in-Publication Data
Julia T. Wood
    Relational communication: continuity and change in personal
relationships / Julia T. Wood —2nd ed.
      p. cm. —(Wadsworth series in speech communication)
    Includes bibliographical references and index.
    ISBN 0-534-56160-8
      1. Interpersonal communication. 2. Interpersonal relations.
3. Intimacy (Psychology) I. Title. II. Series.
BF637.C45W66 1999   98-46235
158.2—dc21

"We assume that relationships need both continuity and change to remain viable and that too much of either can destroy the relationship."

—Werner et al

I dedicate this book to the people with whom I am most close

ROBBIE
*The great love of my life, Robbie is my partner in love,
friendship, and life, with whom I've shared
26 years of adventure, challenges, and joy*

CAROLYN
*Sister by birth, friend by choice, whose life and history
are intricately intertwined with my own*

NANCY
*Confidante, companion, and conversationalist
extraordinaire, whose creativity in composing her life
and herself inspires me*

LINDABECKER
*Both friend and family, LindaBecker teaches me
the meaning of loyalty and commitment through her
life choices*

ABOUT
THE AUTHOR

JULIA T. WOOD is a professor of Communication Studies at the University of North Carolina at Chapel Hill. Since completing her Ph.D. (Pennsylvania State University) at age 24, she has conducted research and written extensively about communication in personal relationships and about gender, communication, and culture. In addition to publishing over 60 articles and chapters, she has authored or co-authored 15 books and edited or co-edited 6 others. The recipient of seven awards for outstanding teaching and seven awards for distinguished scholarship, Professor Wood divides her professional energies between writing and teaching.

Professor Wood lives with her partner, Robbie Cox, who is also a professor of Communication Studies at the University of North Carolina and is actively involved with the national Sierra Club. She also lives with Madhi-the-Wonder-Dog and two cats, Sadie Ladie and Ms. Wicca. When not writing and teaching, Professor Wood enjoys traveling, legal consulting, and spending time talking with students, friends, and family.

CONTENTS

CHAPTER 3

Communication: The Central Dynamic in Personal Relationships 48

PART TWO

THE EVOLUTION OF PERSONAL RELATIONSHIPS 129

CHAPTER 6

Launching Personal Relationships 130

CHAPTER 7

Committing to Personal Relationships   155

CHAPTER 9
Transforming and Ending Personal Relationships   213

CHAPTER 10

Summing Up: Communication, Choice, Commitment, and Change in Personal Relationships 244

ACKNOWLEDGMENTS

EVEN THOUGH I AM LISTED as the author of *Relational Communication*, this book reflects perspectives other than my own. Like all of us, who I am and how I interpret life reflect my interactions with others who have been and are significant in my life. From start to finish, the professionals at Wadsworth have supported me with insights, gentle guidance, and generous investments of time and encouragement. At the top of that list is Deirdre Cavanaugh, who is a remarkably gifted editor and a generous collaborator. Megan Gilbert is another member of the Wadsworth family who has assisted me greatly with her insights and her uncanny ability to solve any problem that arises. Andrew Ogus is the talented artist who designed the book's cover and interior. I am also indebted to Vicki Moran for her creativity and extraordinary skill in managing production of the book.

My work also benefits from intimate relationships in my life. My partner Robbie, my sister Carolyn, and my friends Nancy and LindaBecker, have influenced this book by discussing ideas and by testing theories and research about personal relationships against the reality of their lived experiences. Moreover, I am indebted to them for their unflagging support and their belief in the value of my work.

Relational Communication reflects the perspectives of many scholars who took the time to read early drafts of the book and offer generous suggestions for improving the final version. Specifically, I am grateful to the following individuals for their intellectual support of the first edition of this book: Mary Ann Fitzpatrick, University of Wisconsin, Madison; Robert Martin, Ithaca College; Paul A. Mongeau, Miami University; Kristi A. Schaller, Georgia State University; Joe Walther, Northwestern University; and Lynne Webb, Memphis State University. I am also indebted to individuals who worked with me on the second edition of the book: Mara Adelman, Seattle University; Krystyna S. Aune, University of Hawaii at Manoa; Mary A. Banski, University of Houston; Shereen Bingham, University of Nebraska at Omaha; Melanie Booth-Butterfield, West Virginia University; Patrice M. Buzzanell, Northern Illinois University; Stanley O. Gaines, Jr., Pomona College; Pamela Kalbfleisch, University of Wyoming; and Virginia T. Katz, University of Minnesota, Duluth.

Finally, I acknowledge the key contributions that my students made to this book. They have enlightened me in ways that surface in the chapters that follow. Always, they teach me at least as much as I teach them. They prod and challenge what I think, refine my understandings of relationships, and help me realize how the circumstances of their lives, in some ways so different from my own, reverberate into relationships. Because my students have taught me so much, I've included many of their insights and reflections in this book. Punctuating its pages are entries from their journals in my classes. In these journal passages they share their experiences, concerns, hopes, and questions about the ways we human beings relate to others. I hope that you will find their reflections as wise, stimulating, inspiring, and valuable as I do.

INTRODUCTION

KEY CONCEPTS

communication

gender

sex

RELATIONAL COMMUNICATION is about how communication affects the personal relationships we create, sustain, revise, and sometimes dismantle. In this opening sentence, I suggest several key themes of this book.

THEMES OF RELATIONAL COMMUNICATION

Personal Relationships Are Distinct

First, *Relational Communication* is not concerned with the entire range of human relationships—those we have with our neighbors, colleagues, and casual friends. Instead, it focuses specifically on romantic relationships and, to a lesser extent, close friendships. These special relationships are distinct from the gamut of human associations. For instance, with close friends and romantic partners, we hope for more caring, understanding, and investment than we expect from casual buddies. In our most important relationships, we also expect to give more of ourselves than we do to the majority of relationships in our lives.

Personal relationships are central to our individual identity and to our well-being. You probably realize that personal relationships have impact on your emotional health. You may be less aware of their importance to your physical health. In a recent study of 122,859 people, the National Center for Health Statistics found that people who lived with a romantic partner (either in marriage or cohabitation) were sick fewer days and had fewer health problems than people who lived alone (Sheehan, 1996). Further, researchers who have reviewed studies on the effects of intimacy conclude that social isolation is as great a danger to physical health as smoking, high blood pressure, or obesity (Crowley, 1995). Because intimate connections are unique in their importance and impact on our lives and in how they operate, we will concentrate solely on understanding what they are and how they work—or fail to.

Human Choices Influence Personal Relationships

The sentence that opened this Introduction also indicates that human communication is a primary influence on how we create, sustain, and uniquely tailor our personal relationships. Too often we think of relationships as things that happen apart from our personal actions and choices. For instance, people often say, "We fell in love," "The relationship came apart," "It wasn't strong enough to last," or "Our marriage didn't work anymore." Each of these statements implies that what happens in relationships is independent of choices that individuals make. Obviously, many factors beyond individuals have an impact on relationships, and we need to be aware of how circumstances and external events influence friendships and romantic bonds.

Yet, we make decisions and engage in activities that influence the course of intimacy. We are choice-making agents who can substantially affect the quality and endurance of commitments we make. When we do not recognize our agency and the responsibilities it entails, we are likely to make choices that are less informed and less effective than they could be. This book should enlarge your personal agency in two ways. First, by making you aware of the fact that your choices do affect what happens, *Relational Communication* invites you to assume an active stance in charting your intimate relationships. Second, by providing you with research findings on a range of choices open to you and the possible effects of these, this book provides knowledge that empowers you to make more informed choices—ones that take into account various options and their probable consequences.

Communication Is a Primary Influence on Personal Relationships

A third theme of *Relational Communication* is that communication is central to personal relationships. Clearly, communication is not the only influence on personal relationships, because they are also shaped by social forces and events and by individuals' personalities, histories, feelings, needs, conflict styles, and values. Although relationships are made up of and affected by multiple phenomena, communication is particularly important for two reasons.

First, communication is the primary way we express ourselves, learn about others, and work out issues in relationships. In other words, communication is not simply a mechanical process that transmits preexisting information. Instead, in the process of interacting with others, we discover similarities and differences, create the unique character of particular relationships, deal with concerns and conflicts, and celebrate closeness. The pivotal role of communication in shaping and continuously reshaping human connections reminds us that **communication*** is a generative process that *creates* understandings between people, defines relationships and partners' identities, composes rules for interaction, and establishes the overall climate of intimacy.

Communication is also the primary way through which we create meaning as individuals and as partners in personal relationships. Relying on communication, we symbolize ourselves to others, symbolize others to ourselves, define what we and others are doing, and decide what it means. We also use communication to describe to ourselves and others what is happening in interaction—do we call ourselves dates, girlfriends and boyfriends, or just friends? If John punches Eric in the arm, what does it mean? Is it a friendly form of play between buddies, or an invitation to fight, or John's way of declaring that he dominates Eric? The act of punching means nothing in and of itself. Like all feelings, thoughts, and actions, punching gains meaning only as we interpret it and assign significance. How we symbolize ourselves, our relationships, and specific interactions, then, creates their meaning for us. For this reason, communication is a primary influence on our experience of personal relationships.

Personal Relationships Are Processes

Finally, the sentence with which I opened this book implies that personal relationships develop and change over time, and this is a central theme of *Relational Communication*. Intimacy seldom arises suddenly in full bloom; likewise, relationships do not usually decline all at once. The creation, transformation, and deterioration of intimacy usually (although not always) take place over time. Thus, relationships must be understood as processes, not static entities. Throughout its life course, an intimate connection is characterized by change and continuity. Independently and in tandem, change and continuity contour what happens between partners. We set up routines and patterns that confer on each relationship a persisting rhythm and character. At the same time, we instigate and respond to changes that may be large or small, subtle or obvious. Hence, to understand personal relationships, we need to learn both how we sustain a sense of continuity with intimates and how relationships change over time and circumstance.

As processes, relationships are always in flux—changing, evolving, moving, becoming more or less close, refining goals and patterns of interaction. Personal relationships change in response to individuals' growth, dynamics between inti-

---

***Boldfaced terms** appear in the Glossary at the end of the book.

mates, and interaction between relationships and the contexts in which they are embedded. As individuals change, so do their goals for personal relationships and the ways they behave in them. For instance, what you considered an ideal best friend when you were 8 years old differs from what you seek in a close friend today. Relationships also evolve as a result of what happens between partners—the ways they communicate and how they think about and interpret each other and their relationship.

Within all relationships, change is brought about by tensions between contradictory desires, called dialectics. One dialectic involves the companion urges to be both an autonomous agent and deeply connected to another person. Both of these are normal human needs, and both must be accommodated in intimate relationships. How partners manage the dialectic of autonomy/connection is one of the ongoing challenges of long-term relationships. It is also important to understand that relationships are not isolated enclaves, immune to outside influences. Instead, they interact with and evolve in relation to other systems, including work situations, families, friends, and society as a whole. Thus, what happens in personal relationships and what they mean depends on individuals, communication between partners, and interaction with people and influences outside of the relationship itself.

OVERVIEW OF RELATIONAL COMMUNICATION

These four themes introduce the framework for *Relational Communication* in which we explore personal relationships as evolving processes that are defined, understood, and experienced in relation to individuals' choices about how to communicate with each other and themselves.

The Chapters That Follow

The ten chapters in this book cover a range of topics that help us understand personal relationships as processes that evolve through communication. Chapter 1 introduces the study of personal relationships. In it, we will define key concepts and establish an initial framework for thinking about personal relationships and how they operate. Chapter 2 introduces theoretical frameworks that help us understand the complexities of human connections. Chapter 3 explores the central role of communication in personal relationships. In addition to describing the complex process of communication, we will consider how the process functions to create meaning. Chapter 4 discusses relational culture, the private world partners create that is the nucleus of intimacy. Here we will see how interaction between partners fosters a distinctive relationship that is sustained by and reflected in particular patterns of thought, feeling, and communication. Chapter 5 completes Part One of the book by placing personal relationships in the larger context of social communities and society. We will see how social rules, expectations, and values, as well as emerging social trends, affect our efforts to build and sustain intimacy.

Part Two includes five chapters. In Chapter 6 we begin tracing the evolutionary course that is typical of most romantic relationships. There we will learn about some of the more common issues and turning points in the early stages of intimacy. In Chapter 7 we explore how feelings of love and passion are sometimes transformed into abiding commitment, which is a cornerstone of enduring intimacy.

Following this is Chapter 8 in which we examine ways that intimate partners sustain connections over time. Here we will concentrate particularly on everyday processes and routines that interweave partners' lives and identities. More so than big occasions like anniversaries and major declarations such as "I love you," the day-in, day-out processes between partners are what sustain the fabric of intimacy. We will also identify ways that partners repair relationships that have become stale or gone seriously awry. Chapter 9 considers how people end or transform personal relationships that have become unsatisfying. We will point out factors that precipitate relational distress and symptoms of deteriorating intimacy so that you have the knowledge to diagnose problems should they occur in your own relationships. We will also trace the typical course of relational decline and note a range of ways partners respond to it by ending, suspending, or transforming personal relationships. Finally, Chapter 10 summarizes the major themes that weave through the preceding chapters.

Gender and Sex in Personal Relationships

Throughout all ten chapters, we consider how gender and sex affect how individuals think, feel, and act in personal relationships. Within Western culture, gender is especially pronounced, affecting everything from how people dress and the roles they assume to personal senses of identity and expectations of intimate relationships. Given this, it is hardly surprising that gender and sex influence how people think and act in personal relationships. Your own experiences with women and men probably inform you of a number of general differences, although of course not all women or all men conform to every gender pattern. You might have noticed, for example, that women generally talk about relationships more than men do and that women tend to feel close when they talk with intimates, whereas men more often experience closeness through doing things together. These and

EMAIL: RSTROMOSKI@AOL.COM

NON SEQUITUR ©1998 Rick Stromoski, Washington Post Writers Group. Reprinted with permission.

other gender differences reflect the distinct socialization women and men typically receive in our society.

In recent years, both scholars and laypersons have become increasingly interested in how sex and gender influence relationships. Consequently, studies of sex differences appear regularly in academic journals, and popular bookstores feature titles such as *You Just Don't Understand. Women and Men in Conversation* (Tannen, 1990) and *Men Are from Mars, Women Are from Venus* (Gray, 1992). Burgeoning proclamations of differences between women and men should not necessarily be accepted, because popular topics are sometimes transient fads without much substance to support them. Hence, we need to reflect carefully on the extent to which claims about women, men, and the differences between them are substantiated by sound evidence.

Some scholars think differences between the sexes are very small. For instance, Dan Canary and Kimberly Hause (1993), two communication researchers, reviewed hundreds of studies and concluded that "sex differences in social interaction are small and inconsistent" (p. 140). Some communication scholars have reported small or no gender differences in specific types of communication. For example, researchers argue there are only minor sex differences in self-disclosure (Dindia & Allen, 1992), helping behavior (Eagly & Crowley, 1986), and leadership (Eagly & Johnson, 1990; Eagly & Karau, 1991). Still other researchers suggest that limited investigations conducted to date have not yet yielded persuasive evidence of strong general differences between women and men (Canary & Dindia, 1998; Ragan, 1989).

On the other hand, many scholars are convinced that substantial differences between men and women exist and that they have a major impact on personal relationships. Based on years of empirical research, Sandra Brehm (1992) asserted that gender is probably the single greatest influence on relationships. Along the same line, Deborah Tannen (1990), a linguistics scholar, declared that women and men live in such different worlds that talk between the sexes is like cross-cultural communication. Marital counselors John Gottman and Sybil Carrère (1994) document distinctly gendered patterns in marital communication and show that these patterns affect spouses' satisfaction with the marriage. Although I did not initially believe that sex and gender exert major influence on relationships, over the past decade my own research as well as my reading of that by others has convinced me that women and men do differ generally in many of the ways they think about and communicate in relationships. Obviously, what happens between intimate friends and romantic partners is not determined by sex or gender alone; yet, among the many influences on relationships, sex and gender are important ones. This conclusion is reflected in *Relational Communication*, which presents research demonstrating the impact of sex and gender on relational processes ranging from conflict strategies to sources of satisfaction to styles of loving.

To decide for yourself whether men and women differ substantially in their approaches to intimacy, you might read some of the articles cited earlier in this section and in the chapters that follow. To supplement your critical evaluation of scholarly reports, you might test claims of sex differences made in this book and elsewhere against your own experiences and observations. Attention to research and reflection on personal experience should provide you with a reasonable basis for forming your own opinion of the credibility of claims about differences between women and men.

You may have noticed that I've referred to both sex and gender in the foregoing paragraphs. I've done this to call your attention to an important distinction between the two concepts. **Sex** is a category based on genetic and biological characteristics. *Boys, men,* and *males* are sex terms that refer to people who have XY, XXY, or XYY chromosomes and who have male internal and external genitalia such as penises and testes. *Women, girls,* and *females* are sex terms that refer to people who have XX, XO, or XXX chromosomal structures and who have female genitalia such as ovaries and labia majora. **Gender,** on the other hand, is a category based on socially prescribed meanings for the sexes. *Feminine* and *masculine* are gender terms that describe social expectations attached to being female and male, respectively. Currently, gender expectations in the United States are that men should be ambitious, assertive, aggressive, in control, and successful and that women should be caring, cooperative, and emotionally sensitive (Basow, 1992; Wood, 1994d, 1995, 1999).

Because gender socialization is pronounced in our culture, a majority of males do learn and enact masculine styles of thought, feeling, and action, and a majority of females do adopt feminine modes of thought, feeling, and action. Yet, these are generalizations, not absolutes about human behavior, so not all women are feminine and not all men are masculine. In other words, sex is not equivalent to gender, because both females and males can be masculine or feminine or some of each. For example, recent research indicates men and women both can be violent, but gender differences are evident in both proclivity toward violence and the reasons for it (Jacobson & Gottman, 1998). Both women and men with masculine orientations are more prone toward using violence to control or dominate than women and men with feminine orientations (Campbell, 1993; Goldner, Penn, Scheinberg, & Walker, 1990). Similarly, social structures and practices place women more often than men in caregiving roles; thus, caring for others is widely associated with femininity (Wood, 1994d). Yet, research demonstrates that men are equally capable of learning and enacting caregiving (Risman, 1989). Recognizing the distinction between sex and gender is important if we are to understand some of the dynamics in close friendships and romantic intimacy. Although this distinction is unfortunately blurred in much existing research, in *Relational Communication* we will respect the difference between the two concepts.

A final point to keep in mind is that findings from research provide information about sex and gender *in general.* Studies can yield generalizations about women and men and about masculine and feminine behaviors. What social scientific investigations cannot tell us is how any individual woman or man thinks, feels, acts, or communicates. Consequently, when you read, for instance, that "women are generally more attentive than men to relationship dynamics," you should not assume all women are sensitive to interpersonal issues and no men are. That would be an erroneous conclusion for two reasons. First, there is considerable variation within each sex, so not every woman and every man will match generalizations about women and men. Second, there is overlap between the sexes in interpersonal sensitivity and other areas. Thus, although it may be true that women in general have greater relational awareness than men in general, this does not mean that only women have this quality or that all men entirely lack it. Rigidly polarized views of the sexes and their capacities are simply not supported by research (Canary & Hause, 1993; Duck & Wright, 1993).

In sum, although not all researchers agree that women and men differ significantly in their interpersonal styles, currently a majority of scholars regard sex and gender as important influences on personal relationships. In this book, you'll encounter evidence of these influences that you should recognize as qualified generalizations, not as uniform descriptions of the sexes. Further, you should subject this material to your own critical scrutiny to decide how credible you find it.

A PERSONAL INTRODUCTION

When I was an undergraduate student taking classes as you are now, I often wondered about the people who had written my textbooks. I wanted to know something about the individuals whose ideas I was expected to study. Now that I write books, I want to do what I wished authors of my textbooks had done—tell you a little about myself so that you may understand how my identity influences what you will read.

I am a 47-year-old woman who has been in a committed relationship for 26 years. I am Caucasian, heterosexual, and middle class. I live on two acres of wooded land, where deer appear outside my den window most mornings and birds of all sorts enchant me with their songs, while fascinating and frustrating my two cats. For 24 years I have been on the faculty of the Department of Communication Studies at the University of North Carolina at Chapel Hill, where I conduct research and teach about communication in personal relationships and gender, communication, and culture.

I have focused my career on communication because I believe that it is central to human life. Our ability to communicate allows us to participate in a world of meaning and significance. In both my research and my life, I have found that the ways we communicate profoundly influence the quality of connections we build and how others respond to us. I focus my teaching and writing on relationships because I believe our connections with others are vital to human growth and contentment and because I believe we can learn to communicate in ways that enhance our personal relationships.

Who each of us is in any moment reflects the relationships in which we have been and are involved. Further, healthy, affirming friendships and romantic relationships provide contexts in which we can develop personally and contribute to the development of others. My marriage and my friendships have encouraged me to develop intellectually, emotionally, and spiritually. My intimates have celebrated life's pleasures with me and cushioned its pains; together we have encountered problems, had conflicts, experienced moments of genuinely magical connection, and dealt with risk and loss. In all of these experiences, communication has figured prominently, shaping my perceptions of what was happening and allowing understanding to be crafted between me and those with whom I am closest. Because communication in relationships has been and continues to be so central to my own life, I wanted to write a book that might open others' eyes to the wonder and power of relational communication.

By telling you a little about who I am, I underline the fact that *Relational Communication*, like all books, is a human construction. Although we commonly regard books as sources of information and objective knowledge, this is only part of the picture. It is true that textbooks are informed by findings from research and other sources. The hundreds of articles and books that I drew on to write this book represent a wealth of research on how intimate relationships operate. Yet, a book is more than a collection of findings or a detached summary of information. It is also a personal creation that reflects a particular author's values, experiences, and perspective. Thus, this book is shaped by my beliefs that relationships are important to our lives, that communication is a primary means by which we create and sustain them, and that individuals can and do make choices that influence the quality of their relationships. The topics I choose to focus on and the ways I discuss them reflect my views and values, as well as the substantial research produced by interdisciplinary study of human relationships. I hope that you will find value in both the information in this book and the personal perspective I bring to it.

Julia T. Wood
The University of North Carolina at Chapel Hill
January 1999

Conceptual Foundations for Studying Personal Relationships

Communication and Personal Relationships

Janna feels guilty because Mike wants to go away for a long weekend with her, and she craves time alone. Janna feels she should want to be with Mike and wonders whether her desire for private time means she doesn't love him.

Eric is confused about his relationship with Miranda. They started seeing each other five months ago, and for the last two weeks he's felt practically giddy about her. But this week he's started having second thoughts and noticing things about Miranda that bother him. Does this mean he's fallen out of love?

Lucy is frustrated and so is her friend, Charles. Every time she tries to talk to him about her concerns, he either spouts advice or suggests they go out and do something. Lucy thinks Charles's responses are uncaring. Charles, on the other hand, is frustrated that Lucy doesn't appreciate his efforts to get her mind off her troubles. When she's down, he always makes time for her and tries to suggest a way to solve a problem or something they can do to cheer her up. That's what his buddies do for him when he's having a rough time, so why does Lucy get bent out of shape when he does that for her?

CHANCES ARE YOU'VE HAD EXPERIENCES like one or more of these. You're in a relationship that is really special, yet somehow something seems not quite right. You cannot put your finger on any specific problem, but things just aren't running smoothly. Maybe, like Janna, you're unsure whether what you are feeling is normal or whether it signals a problem in your commitment. Possibly you've felt the frustration Lucy and Charles are experiencing when a tension repeatedly surfaces in your interaction with a partner. Or perhaps, like Eric, you find your feelings about a partner are changing, and you don't know what that means.

What do you do in such moments? If you are like a lot of people, you feel mystified. Sometimes things get better, sometimes not; maybe you and your partner figure out what is amiss, maybe not. It may seem that random, erratic forces beyond your control determine what happens. Yet, relationships do not defy human understanding, and they are not immune to our efforts to guide them. Researchers and clinicians have discovered a great deal about why relationships work, why they sometimes flounder, and what individuals can do to affect the quality of their friendships and romances.

Close relationships—friendships and romantic bonds—are important to our physical health and psychological well-being. Researchers have consistently found that being in good relationships is associated with physical and mental health (Bolger & Eckenrode, 1991; Bolger & Kelleher, 1993) and, conversely, that social isolation and lack of intimates are correlated with increased problems in physical and psychological well-being (Cohen, 1988; House, Umberson, & Landis, 1988). This seems especially the case for men, who are consistently found to derive more benefits from marriage than women (Bolger & Kelleher, 1993; Dickson, 1995; Mirowsky & Ross, 1986). One reason for the discrepancy is that in general women are more attentive than men to other people and relationships, so they tend to provide more emotional support than men (Chodorow, 1978, 1989; Gilligan, 1982; Wood, 1993b, d, 1994a, b, d, 1996, 1999). In the chapters that follow, we will discuss this sex tendency and explore its causes and implications. Sex differences in benefit notwithstanding, healthy, close relationships enhance the well-being of most people.

DANA

I sure identify with feeling helpless in relationships. There's this one thing that really drives me crazy with my boyfriend. He says he's committed to our relationship, but he doesn't act that way. Like he never does half of the chores in our apartment—I do them or we'd live in a pig sty. He's told me I need to interview with companies in New York, since that's where he wants to locate, but when I asked him to interview with some firms in California where my best prospects are, he said no way. If he's committed, why am I supposed to make all the compromises? Is that an equal relationship? And how could anything I do change things?

Actually, we are not as helpless as Dana thinks when it comes to influencing our personal relationships. We don't have to resign ourselves to the fates and furies and simply hope for the best. In fact, there's a great deal we can do to build close relationships that are stalwart and satisfying and to make effective choices about corrective action when difficulties do arise.

ABOUT THIS BOOK

Relational Communication grows out of my conviction that the choices we make can influence, though not entirely control, what happens in our relationships. Choices imply that we have options, that there is more than one way we can act in a given situation. For example, Dana could accept her boyfriend's assumption that she will follow him and adjust her career to his. On the other hand, she could refuse to do that and look for a job in California. She might also propose that they have a long-distance relationship so each person can work where jobs are best. Or she could propose that one of them follow the other now and agree that in five years they will move to maximize the career options for the person who follows now. Each of these choices will affect how the relationship evolves.

Choices, of course, may be wise or unwise, well informed or naive, effective or ineffective. The best interpersonal choices are usually based on knowledge about how relationships work and what personal, contextual, and interpersonal factors influence what happens in them. The knowledge presented in this book comes from over 600 sources of information about relationships. Many of the references are articles reporting original investigations. In addition, I've relied on a number of books and chapters in edited works that summarize areas of study or extensive programs of empirical research. Finally, I've drawn on the rich insights of counselors whose knowledge of relationship issues derives from their work with individuals and couples. The research and theories discussed in *Relational Communication* should enhance your understanding of how relationships work and of probable consequences associated with various choices you might make in your life.

Theory and research are relevant to practical life because they pertain to everyday activities. Thus, Part One of the book provides a conceptual framework for thinking about personal relationships. The chapters composing Part One focus on theories and research that illuminate what personal relationships involve and how they develop through communication. Animating these chapters are examples and students' reflections, illustrating how theoretical knowledge applies to everyday life.

Part Two of *Relational Communication* extends the conceptual foundations of the first part to trace processes by which we build, sustain, transform, and sometimes disassemble intimate connections with others. We will discuss turning points that change the direction or intensity of relationships. We will also pay particular attention to communication processes, because these are a primary generative dynamic of intimacy. In and through communication, individuals launch and escalate commitment, develop and sustain a shared sense of who they are, adapt intimacy over time, and end or refashion personal relationships to fit changing needs and circumstances. In tandem, Parts One and Two advance understanding of personal relationships and enhance your ability to make informed choices about your own communicative encounters with others.

As a foundation for the book, this chapter introduces concerns and themes that weave through the pages that follow. In it we will define personal relationships and identify key influences on them. We will also draw on your experiences to gain initial insights into the workings of personal relationships. Later chapters elaborate the issues introduced by exploring in depth how close relationships develop, evolve, and change over time.

DEFINING PERSONAL RELATIONSHIPS

Social by nature, we enter into a great many relationships throughout our lives. You probably have a number of casual acquaintances with whom you regularly engage in small talk and activities. These relationships may be with roommates, neighbors, classmates, members of sport teams, and peers with whom you work. Add to this members of your family with whom you may have closer relationships: parents and stepparents, siblings, children if you have any, and other relatives with whom you are close. You probably also have some special friends, and you may have been involved in one or more serious romances. Of all of these relationships, only a few profoundly affect you. Those are our personal relationships, which are the specific concern of this book. To begin our study, we will define what they are, clarify how they differ from other types of human connections, and identify factors that influence intimate patterns, processes, and outcomes.

Personal relationships* are voluntary commitments that are continuously in process and are marked by continuing, significant interdependence between particular individuals who are irreplaceable. Let's look more closely at the terms in this definition so that we have a clear understanding of personal relationships.

Continuing, Significant Interdependence

Although personal relationships aren't necessarily permanent, they do endure over a substantial period of time. For instance, you might really like someone you meet at a rally or on an airplane. Unless interaction extends beyond the initial encounter, however, your influence on each other's life is limited. Partners in personal relationships significantly affect each other over extended periods of time. Because they are continuing and important presences in each other's life, partners in personal relationships become interdependent on one another.

***Boldfaced terms** appear in the Glossary at the end of the book.

Interdependence means that partners count on each other. There are many forms of interdependence, and not all personal relationships include all of them. Partners may establish **behavioral interdependence, in which case each person's behaviors affect the other** (Berscheid & Peplau, 1983). For example, I count on my partner, Robbie, to do our laundry each week, and he counts on me to shop for groceries. If he doesn't do the laundry, then I'll be inconvenienced when I don't have clean clothes to wear. If I fail to shop for groceries, Robbie may be disappointed when he doesn't have juice for breakfast. Of course, intimates count on each other for many things more significant than juice and laundry. Assistance, support, time, disclosure, concern, and remembering things are among the many expectations that friends and romantic partners consider important (Beck, 1988; Duck & Wright, 1993; Wegner, Raymond, & Erber, 1990).

Companionship is another way in which intimate partners usually depend on each other. We expect someone we love to spend time with us, make trips with us, join us for concerts, movies, dinners, and so forth. Spending time together and engaging in joint activities allow intimates to enhance experiences by sharing them: What did you think of that movie? Does this remind you of our trip to Mexico? The chow mein here isn't as good as what we get at the Jade Chrysanthemum, is it? Do you think this play is a rehash of the last one this director did? Experiences tend to seem more full and more real if they are shared and discussed with another person (Berger & Kellner, 1975). We count on intimates as companions who help us structure time and enhance experiences by sharing them.

Partners may also have **emotional interdependence** in several ways. Perhaps the most common kind of emotional interdependence between close partners is mutual feelings of love, affection, and attachment (Beck, 1988). Based on extensive research, Beverly Fehr (1993) reports that among North Americans there is a widely shared conception that the emotional nucleus of love consists of five expectations: trust, caring, honesty, respect, and friendship. These core elements of widely held views of love suggest that caring and being cared for are key emotional needs intimates expect each other to meet (Weiss, 1969). Partners assume they will share each other's joys and empathize with each other's defeats and sorrows. They assume they will help each other out in difficult times and during illness. To varying degrees, we depend on our intimates to accept, comfort, and care for us and to allow us to do the same for them.

Fehr's research (1993) also identifies respect as a common form of emotional interdependence between partners in personal relationships. Many couples, particularly dual-worker ones, regard respect as a cornerstone of their connection. They count on each other to adjust daily schedules to accommodate work demands, not begrudge evenings and weekends devoted to professional activities, support career growth, and treat each other as equals in making decisions. One of the specific ways in which the expectation of equality shows up is in the division of responsibilities for household chores and child care. According to a series of studies (Belsky, Lang, & Huston, 1986; Hochschild with Machung, 1989; Thompson & Walker,

1989), tension and discontent often arise in dual-worker families when partners make inequitable contributions to home life. When one partner shoulders most of the responsibilities for homemaking and child care, relationship satisfaction often declines (Eckenrode & Gore, 1989; Silberstein, 1992). For interdependence to be gratifying, partners need to communicate their needs and expectations clearly and collaborate to work out agreements that honor both individuals.

Emotional interdependence may also take the form of tacit agreements to divide relationship responsibilities between partners (Scarf, 1987). One person may be in charge of the practical, organizational matters for both of them while the other looks out for the couple's affective needs. Both of them depend on the organizer to negotiate for cars and homes, keep household records, coordinate family members' schedules, and organize joint activities. The affective specialist is expected to safeguard the emotional climate for the couple, and both partners rely on her or him to furnish the bulk of nurturing, notice when there is tension between partners, and initiate efforts to resolve problems. Each counts on the other to provide something important for their joint well-being.

Exemplifying emotional interdependence is a couple in which one partner is an introvert and the other an extrovert. The extrovert typically provides the sociality, encourages interaction with people outside the couple relationship, and integrates the couple into social and family networks. Meanwhile, the introvert focuses more intensely on the couple's private world and provides a willing audience for the extrovert. From years of counseling intimate partners, Maggie Scarf (1987) identified some types of emotional interdependence that may promote unhealthy relationships. For instance, in some couples one person is in charge of expressing emotions for both partners whereas the other specializes in rationality. The person in the unemotional role seldom shows anger, rapture, or other intense feelings, and is rarely capricious, impulsive, or illogical. Instead, the person cast as the emotional one expresses strong emotions for both partners. Each has disowned one part of herself or himself, and the other is expected to enact that part for both of them.

Similarly, some partners strike an implicit bargain whereby one person assumes the role of adult/parent and the other takes the role of child. The parent is expected to take care of the child, and the child is supposed to depend on the parent for guidance and protection. When such roles are too extreme or when one person abandons a role she or he previously played, the relationship may become strained. Then couples either renegotiate roles or risk erosion in satisfaction. Lisa's reflections on her parents' marriage provide a case in point.

LISA

My parents were emotionally interdependent in a pretty traditional way. Mom stayed home and took care of us and the house, and Dad worked to make an income. Until I was about 16, Mom was totally dependent on Dad for everything. She didn't make any important decisions on her own, and when he announced something she went along, even if she didn't like it. But then she went back to college to finish her degree, and you could just see the changes starting in her. She got more sure of herself and started doing things on her own without his advice. Then there was this huge blowup when he came home one day and announced he'd accepted a transfer to another location. Mom got all over him for not consulting her first, and that just flabbergasted Dad. He asked since when did he have to consult her about family decisions, and she said, "Since now, that's when." Then she refused to move. The next couple of years were really rough as she found a job and got more and more confident in herself and insisted on more equality in the marriage. Right now they're in marital counseling to try to work things out.

Becoming interdependent with another means you are no longer entirely autonomous. Instead, you count on another for certain things, and you allow that person to count on you. Each of you influences and is influenced by what the other expects, does, and feels. Whether interdependence is behavioral, emotional, or both, intimates link their lives, which means they affect and are affected by each other (Lederer, 1981).

Between Particular Individuals

Relationships may be thought of as existing on a continuum from impersonal to highly personal, and most of our relationships cluster around the continuum's midpoint. The relationships closer to the impersonal end tend to be casual and to involve superficial conversation. The interaction you have with most sales clerks and restaurant workers is impersonal. Those relationships in the middle of the continuum are social ones that tend to follow norms and to involve friendly but not highly personal communication. You may have social relationships with some classmates and members of groups to which you belong. Those relationships at the personal end of the continuum are tailored to the specific individuals in your life who create personal roles and a unique relational culture with you. Personal relationships also involve more intimate communication. Because each personal relationship reflects particular individuals, it is unique and not interchangeable with any other relationship.

The vast majority of our relationships are not personal. We form social relationships with friends, acquaintances, and colleagues. **Social relationships** are

FIGURE 1.1

Relationship Continuum

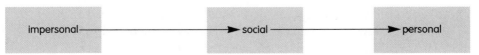

ones in which participants interact primarily according to social norms and roles but are not significantly interdependent on each other as unique individuals. For instance, you might exchange assistance and support with a colleague for many years. Likewise, you might count on a neighbor for a weekly tennis match and look forward to exchanging political views with another acquaintance. In each of these cases, the person we rely on could be replaced by someone else in the same role. If the colleague retires, you could find another work associate; if your neighbor moves away, you could round up a new tennis buddy; if the person with whom you discuss politics dies, you could find a different crony. In these relationships, specific people are less relevant to the association than the roles they fulfill for each other. We engage in **social comparison** (Festinger, 1954) with these people, but the value of such relationships lies more in what participants do than in who they are, because a variety of people could replace the particular individuals.

In personal relationships, however, the particular people, as well as what they do, define the connection. I don't share my life with just anybody who could be replaced by someone else in the same role. I share it with Robbie, because of the unique person that he is and the particular ways in which we have fitted ourselves together. He is not simply filling a role in my life; he is the unique man, Robbie, whose personal character and choices significantly define our relationship. Intimate partners cannot be replaced by others. When a partner leaves or dies, that relationship ends. We may later form intimate ties with other people, perhaps even marrying more than once in a lifetime, but a second spouse or second best friend will not be a facsimile of the former one. A personal relationship ends when partners cease to be primary in each other's life. Unlike the majority of relationships, then, personal ones are unique and partners are irreplaceable. That is one reason personal relationships are so special in our lives.

Voluntary Commitment

Our study of personal relationships is confined to those that are voluntary. Partners engage in them out of choice, not convenience, chance, or necessity. Unlike many of our associations with others, most of our personal relationships are voluntary (Rubin, 1985). An exception is personal relationships with family members such as parents, siblings, and other relatives with whom we have biological and historical connections. At least during the early years of life, relationships with members of our family are important, although they aren't entirely free choices. However, we voluntarily elect to sustain and enlarge intimacy with some family members and not others, and it is in those chosen relationships that we voluntarily invest ourselves. You may feel very close to one of your siblings and may make time to see her or him and to share your innermost thoughts with her or him. Perhaps you feel distant from or even hostile toward other siblings, and you don't visit them or share your feelings with them.

Personal relationships are also not dictated by proximity or other circumstantial factors, although clearly circumstances influence whom we meet and with whom we interact (Allan, 1993). Affiliations with neighbors and co-workers arise because they are nearby, and we run into them regularly. We may choose to develop more personal ties with some, but whether or not we do, we have to interact with them to some degree on a social level.

Voluntary personal relationships are connections we choose to form and sustain and to define as important in our lives. Romantic commitments and friendships are the primary voluntary relationships in our lives; friendships, however, are often considered the exemplar of intimacy (Allan, 1993; Rubin, 1985). Although marriages are easier to end today than they were years ago, they involve a great deal of interdependence and intimate communication, and thus, they are more enduring than most other personal relationships.

Continuously in Process

The final feature in our definition highlights the processual character of personal relationships. To say that personal relationships are processual means that they are always in motion, changing, evolving. They are not static or fixed once and for all. Steve Duck refers to personal relationships as "unfinished business" (1990). By this he means that our most intimate relationships are never settled, resolved, or stable. Instead, they are always in motion, moving to new forms and meanings. Partners develop new patterns and discard old ones; adjust interaction times and styles to fit changes in their lives and family; revise rules for managing conflict; redefine the relationship's identity and meaning in response to births of children, deaths of parents, and partners' changing needs and abilities; and realign their individual and couple goals.

Processes of change do not happen around relationships: Rather, relationships *are* processes. Through interaction, partners engage in the never-ending adventure of creating and re-creating personal relationships. Whatever patterns, organization, or understandings a relationship has at time$_1$ will not be identical to those it has at time$_2$ or time$_x$. Because personal relationships are processes, partners endlessly engage in creating and re-creating intimacy.

By now it should be clear that personal relationships are a very specific type of connection. We've defined them as marked by changes and ongoing interdependence between particular individuals who choose to create, invest in, and continuously revise their connection. These qualities make close friendships and romantic relationships extremely intense, important, and challenging.

The foregoing discussion has pointed out that intimacy profoundly affects individuals. To understand more fully the diverse ways in which intimacy influences our lives, let's consider what our own experiences teach us about personal relationships.

FIRST INSIGHTS INTO PERSONAL RELATIONSHIPS

From the moment you were born, you've been engaged in relationships with others. As an infant, your parents nurtured you and helped you as you struggled to figure out who you were. Your needs and your activities also influenced how your parents interacted and how your family operated. By participating in family life, you extracted basic ideas, or **working models,** about relationships (Duck, 1993a,b). As a child, of course, you didn't realize you were learning rules of relating, and even today you are probably not fully aware of your many assumptions about how to interact with others. Nonetheless, your family is one source of many of your tacit beliefs about how relationships work. These beliefs, even if you aren't fully conscious of them, influence how you think, feel, and interact with others.

Over the years you've formed many friendships from which you've learned a lot about relationships and yourself. Interacting with friends allows us to crystallize identities, clarify values and beliefs, discover activities we enjoy, develop individual interests, and refine interpersonal skills. You may also have entered into one or more romantic relationships and discovered the unique pleasures and frustrations they involve. Your history of relationship experiences shapes how you see yourself, how you think about close connections, and how you interact with others. We'll discuss three insights we can glean from our experiences in relating to others.

Personal Relationships Vary

A first insight is that personal relationships are not all the same. They vary considerably. Some seem effortless; others are difficult. Some seldom encounter snags; others seem plagued by problems. Some are deeply satisfying; others are often frustrating and disappointing. Some adapt to changes in partners' lives and continue over time; others come apart when partners change or move, so they are relatively short-lived. The extent to which personal relationships satisfy us, progress smoothly, and endure is not random. Researchers have identified a number of factors that influence the quality and stability of relationships. Of these, several are at least partially subject to human control, so you can use these studies to guide your efforts to sculpt strong, long-lasting connections. In addition, findings from research can help you diagnose when a relationship is not healthy or should not be continued. The chapters that follow highlight choices open to you as you engage in the extended process of building and sustaining intimate friendships and romances. As you read, consider the specific choices that you can and do make at different moments in the life of personal relationships.

Personal Relationships Affect Identity

A second basic insight is that each meaningful relationship in your life has significantly affected who you are. Our intimate connections profoundly influence our identities and the quality of our lives. Healthy, gratifying relationships tend to enrich us by affirming our basic worth as human beings and enlarging our sense of personal competence and confidence (Canary & Stafford, 1994; Satir, 1967). Conversely, enmeshment in unhealthy relationships tends to diminish and demoralize us, making us less than we have potential to be (Beck, 1988; Jacobson & Gottman, 1998; Scarf, 1987). When we are involved in negative attachments, self-concept is on the line. We may feel unsure of our value, lose sight of our possibilities, and develop a negative outlook on life in general (Crowley, 1995; Sheehan, 1996). In later chapters we will probe complex interactions between identity and personal relationships to see how profoundly relationships with family, friends, and romantic partners have shaped your current sense of who you are. We'll also trace how your current identity contours your goals, expectations, and beliefs about relationships, as well as your behavior within them.

Personal Relationships Share Common Features

Reflecting further on the relationships you've experienced, you may arrive at a third insight: You may realize that although each relationship is unique, there are also themes, issues, and patterns that recur in most or all of them (Lederer & Jackson, 1968). For instance, each relationship has its own distinctive challenges, but encountering difficulties is common to all relationships. Similarly, partners in relationships develop alternative ways of coping with the inevitable problems: Some confront and work through tensions constructively, others deny problems and avoid discussing them, and still others engage in hurtful, unproductive forms of conflict. These distinctions notwithstanding, common to every relationship are some relatively consistent modes of responding to difficulties. In a similar manner, all friends and romantic partners generate rules for how to make decisions, what topics are off limits, how to signal emotions, and how to negotiate needs for autonomy and togetherness. The rules may differ from relationship to relationship, but every relationship operates by rules the partners establish.

This book discusses theories and research that explain themes, patterns, rules, and processes in personal relationships—commonalities that exist despite idiosyncrasies that make each intimate bond unique. This knowledge can inform your thinking about relationships in general and your own in particular. Increasing understanding of how personal relationships work should help you clarify what you want and how various courses of action facilitate or impede your goals. In addition, learning about processes that compose relationships will sharpen your ability to diagnose and deal effectively with inevitable tensions.

As you begin your formal study of personal relationships, you already have insights based on your experiences. Three initial insights derived from your experiences are that personal relationships vary in nature, quality, and endurance; intimate connections deeply affect who we are; and personal relationships involve common issues and forms, along with unique content.

We've noted that personal relationships are unique. Perhaps you are wondering whether there are any general qualities of satisfying, enduring intimacy. Most people would say love is essential, yet research indicates other factors may be at least as important as love for personal relationships to survive and flourish over time. Important though love may be, it is seldom sufficient to ride out the strains, problems, and changes that punctuate all relationships (Beck, 1988; Lederer, 1981; Scarf, 1987). Let's consider some of the important general influences on personal relationships.

INFLUENCES ON PERSONAL RELATIONSHIPS

In addition to love, sustaining intimacy requires four things: assuming agency; acting on knowledge about yourself, others, and relationships; ensuring mutual commitment and investment; and dealing with uncertainty. *Relational Communication* directly addresses these requirements. Throughout the book, you'll be encouraged to take responsibility for individual choices that affect relationships and to acquire knowledge about yourself and relationships. You'll also learn what commitment is (as distinct from love) and how to cultivate it in your personal relationships. Finally, you'll discover that uncertainty is a natural and inevitable part of all personal relationships, and you'll gain some knowledge of how to understand and deal with the uncertainty that punctuates your personal relationships.

Assuming Agency

The attitudes individuals have about themselves and their relationships greatly affect what they say, do, and feel (Duck & Pond, 1989; Fletcher, Rosanowski, & Fitness, 1992; Honeycutt, 1993). One of the most important ways you can influence what happens in your relationships is to realize you are an active agent whose choices affect who you become and how your relationships evolve or dissolve (Seligman, 1990). This doesn't mean that simply by exerting our will we can control anything and everything around us. That would be naive to assume. Although our actions aren't the *only* influence on what happens in relationships, they are among the most important ones over which we have control. To assume **agency** is to recognize that you make choices, rather than reacting passively to events and people around you.

Along with agency comes responsibility for the consequences of our choices on ourselves, our partners, and our relationships. People who do not view themselves as agents assume what happens in relationships is beyond their control; a belief that can become a self-fulfilling prophecy. At the same time, it would be imprudent to think that individuals have total control because many factors other than personal choices affect relationships. Yet, within certain constraints humans

NON SEQUITUR © 1998 Wiley Miller / dist. by The Washington Post Writers Group. Reprinted with permission.

have a substantial latitude of freedom to choose how they will act, who they will be, and what kinds of relationships they will create and sustain.

Our choices are not entirely free or unrestricted. Instead, they are relatively free within the limits imposed by social and biological forces that shape lives and opportunities (Allen, 1989). Hence, latitudes of choice and the very kinds of choices we perceive are always and inevitably framed by individual histories and resources, social values and trends, and cultural structures and practices.

Existential philosophers (Binswanger, 1963; Heidegger, 1927/1962) refer to the arbitrary conditions that influence individuals as "thrownness." For instance, if you had been thrown into Salem Village in the late 1600s as a woman with extrasensory perception, you might well have been accused of being a witch and burned at the stake. If you were thrown into the United States in 1965 as a Black male, your chances of being drafted to fight in the Vietnam War would have been greater than had you been thrown in as a White male. If you had been thrown into Sweden in 1990 as a gay man, your sexual orientation would have received greater social approval and legal protection than had you been thrown into the southern United States. How we are thrown into the world is beyond our control, yet what we do with our thrownness is up to us. The challenge for each of us is to create a meaningful life given the constraints of our situation, abilities, and opportunities. This view of agency assumes personal choices are both significant and bounded, which implies that agency and responsibility are important but are not the only factors affecting relationships.

Defining ourselves as agents whose actions matter influences the choices we make in forming and sustaining connections with others. In one of the examples that opened this chapter, Lucy and Charles were frustrated by their different views of how friends support each other. If they assume there's nothing they can do to make their friendship more satisfying, it's unlikely either of them will attempt to alter an unpleasant and recurrent pattern that blemishes their friendship.

On the other hand, Charles and Lucy might exert agency to improve their interaction and, thus, their friendship. What would this mean? Lucy might realize she has some responsibility for the existence of the problem. The first few times she disclosed personal concerns to Charles and he offered advice or suggested diversionary activities, she didn't inform him that she didn't appreciate those responses. By saying nothing she implicitly ratified the way he responded. Lucy might further realize that she still has the option to explain to Charles what she wants from him—a sympathetic ear and willingness to talk extensively about issues that matter to her. She might initiate a change in the friendship by saying

> "Charles, it doesn't help me when you offer advice or try to get my mind off my problems. What I'd really like is for you to just listen and let me know you understand what I'm going through."

Charles, too, might assume agency by inviting Lucy to tell him what she wants from him. He might, for instance, ask her,

"How can I help? I care about you, and I know that what I'm saying is frustrating you, but I don't know why. Can you tell me what I can say or do that would make this easier for you?"

If either or both of them inaugurate this kind of dialogue, they open the possibility of understanding each other more fully. In turn, better understanding of each other should lead to more mutually satisfying communication and a richer friendship.

The example of Charles and Lucy is a relatively simple one, yet it illustrates how easy it is for us not to assume active responsibility for our relationships. A number of current trends in our culture undercut our sense of agency. We hear and read a great deal about things we cannot control: the economy, accidents at nuclear facilities, carcinogens in our foods, downsizings and layoffs, shootings in schools, and other acts of senseless violence. Constantly bombarded by reports of forces that defy personal influence, we may falsely conclude that we cannot affect what happens in our lives. Yet, within the realm of personal relationships, we have substantial agency. Exercising it is one of the most important choices you can make if you wish to create and sustain enriching personal relationships.

The choices open to us in relationships and the ones we actually make are not always obvious. In fact, they are often so subtle that we can fail to recognize them. We tend to be most aware of choices our culture has defined as pivotal issues: whether to marry, to move an ailing parent into our home, to have children, or to divorce. Yet many choices—the vast majority—are neither obvious nor socially recognized as significant. Instead, most choices are small and can easily escape our notice and, thus, any consciousness that we are even making choices. Should you spend time comforting a friend when you are behind in your own work? Do you ask what a partner means when she or he suggests being closer, or do you assume closeness means the same thing to you and your partner? Do you consider alternative ways to manage conflict and the different outcomes they yield, or do you just act on impulse? Do you tell a friend you want a different kind of support than he or she is providing, or do you let the friendship erode because of dissatisfaction you don't express? It is through such small choices—ones we often fail to perceive—that we weave the basic fabric of personal relationships. Far more than special moments and major events, subtle, everyday choices define the quality of intimacy.

Acting on Knowledge

A second prerequisite for sustaining good personal relationships is acquiring and acting on knowledge about ourselves, others, and interaction patterns and processes, including communication. Reading this book and taking a course in communication in personal relationships are primary ways to increase your knowledge of these matters. Understanding ourselves allows us to recognize our needs and to monitor our tendencies in interaction. Insight into others and relationship dynamics enhances our capacity to interpret what is going on and to make informed choices about how we participate in interaction. We might suggest that Dana should look over the history of her relationship to figure out how she and her partner ratified the norm that she makes more compromises than he does. She might also ponder why she has accommodated so often and whether she has been honest in communicating about the imbalance she perceives. By recognizing recurrent patterns, Dana will gain insight not just into the structure of her relationship but also into the processes through which she and her partner have developed and normalized that structure.

Responsible agency involves more than exerting personal will; it requires making *informed* choices about how to influence relationships. Informed choices grow out of knowledge about who you are and what you need, what others generally expect and want, and how various processes and dynamics contour intimacy. The more you understand yourself and others, the greater will be your insight into how you can collaborate with them to create satisfying personal relationships. Also, knowledge of yourself helps you identify and, when appropriate, reconsider some of your assumptions about how to relate to others. For example, it's useful to know about working models of relationships that shape how individuals perceive and act in relationships. Learning about working models opens the possibility of editing your own if it is not constructive for you. In the chapters that follow, we'll discuss working models and other factors that affect identity and personal relationships.

Effective participation in personal relationships is also facilitated by knowledge of interpersonal dynamics. We need to learn from research that shows how interpersonal processes and practices shape patterns, rules, and quality in relationships. The research that we will discuss in the following chapters will help you understand some of the ways in which personal relationships evolve and the reasons for different paths that relationships take.

Ensuring Mutual Commitment and Investment

A third prerequisite for good relationships is mutual commitment and investment by both partners. One partner alone can neither make nor break an intimate relationship—whatever happens always involves all participants (Lederer, 1981; Lederer & Jackson, 1968). Again, Dana's comments are instructive here. She feels her partner is less committed to the relationship than she is. She might discover otherwise if they talk about their patterns and the discrepancy she perceives in their investments. If she can help him understand how she feels and if he is committed to a joint future, then they might be able to alter what they do or how they interpret each other. On the other hand, focused communication about this problem may reveal that Dana really is more committed than her partner and that he is interested in continuing the relationship only if she continues to make compromises. If this is the case, Dana will have to decide whether her partner is committed enough, even if not as much as she, and whether she is willing to stay with him, knowing her dedication exceeds his. That choice will depend, in part, on knowing herself well enough to recognize her bottom line and knowing enough

about relationships to make an informed assessment of the consequences of unequal commitment by partners.

Personal relationships are not individual creations; they reflect both partners
as well as the communication between them and all that grows out of their interaction. Each of us makes choices that influence how our partners perceive us and
themselves, how relationships operate, how satisfying they are, and how well they
endure. In addition to initiating actions, we respond to those of our partners, who
are simultaneously responding and adapting to what we do. Thus, relationships are
not simply the sum of what individuals contribute. Instead, they arise out of interactions, which shape the expectations, interaction patterns, satisfaction, and stability of personal relationships.

Satisfaction. The most satisfying relationships tend to be those in which partners
feel they are relatively equal in their levels of commitment. One research team
studied influences on satisfaction of dating couples (Fletcher, Fincham, Cramer,
& Heron, 1987). Not surprisingly, they found the happiest couples were those in
which both partners felt they contributed equally to the relationship. Other
researchers have reported similar findings about both dating and married couples
(Hecht, Marston, & Larkey, 1994; Rook, 1987). These studies indicate that couples
cherish feeling they are equally involved in creating and nurturing their relationship. Mutuality of commitment seems to be a more pivotal influence on satisfaction than the sheer amount of pleasure or benefit individuals receive. For instance,
people who believe they get more out of a relationship or invest less in it than their
partners tend to feel uncomfortable about the discrepancy. Guilt usually accompanies feeling a relationship benefits us more than our partner. On the other hand,
perceiving that our partner is benefiting more than we are often fosters anger and
resentment (Gottman & Carrère, 1994; Rook, 1987; Schafer & Keith, 1980).
Either way, when partners perceive their investments are unequal, satisfaction is
endangered. In addition to influencing satisfaction, mutuality of investments per-
tains to relationship stability, or continuity.

RANDALL

*I really don't know which is worse—getting more than you deserve in a rela-
tionship or less than you deserve. I've been in both situations, and neither was
very pleasant. Once I was going with this girl who was crazy about me, but I
was just lukewarm about her. Well, she did everything she could to please me,
gave into anything I wanted, the whole thing, but I just felt I was using her,
since I didn't feel as strongly. Then another time I fell hard for this girl who
kind of strung me along. Anytime I didn't do exactly what she wanted, she'd
say maybe we should stop seeing each other. It was really a power thing I
think. But for a long time I kept bowing down to her to keep her happy.
Then I finally got angry at her and at myself for being such a wimp. From*

my experience at least, feelings have to be mutual or somebody is unhappy, and maybe both somebodies are.

Continuity. You may have noticed this discussion has focused more on commitment than love. This calls attention to an important distinction between love and commitment. **Commitment** refers to an intention or a decision to continue a relationship. **Love** is a strong and positive feeling toward another person. Obviously, the ideal is to have both love and commitment, but the two are discrete phenomena and they don't always go together.

For various reasons, we may love someone we don't see as part of our future. Sometimes we fall in love when we are not ready to settle down, or we love a person who is unavailable, whose religion differs from ours, or who doesn't seem stable enough to be a partner for life. In such cases we may choose not to commit. Conversely, we may remain committed to people we no longer love because of factors such as children ("They need both parents"), financial dependence ("I can't support myself on what I earn"), public image ("My constituents expect politicians to be solid family people"), and even convenience ("It's too much of a hassle to move and divide our property").

The importance of commitment and its distinction from love are highlighted in a landmark study conducted by Mary Lund (1985). Seeking to discover what holds a relationship together, Lund reasoned that the glue would be most evident during times of change and transition in partners' lives. Since prior research had shown that college students' relationships are most likely to break up at the end of academic years, Lund selected 129 heterosexuals who were graduating seniors, and she measured their commitment and love both in February and in the summer following graduation. Two of her findings deserve special attention. First, she discovered commitment better predicts a relationship's continuation than love, so intentions may eclipse feelings in determining whether a couple endures. Second, Lund found that making investments in a relationship enhanced commitment more than feelings of love or the perception that a relationship is rewarding. Summing up her findings, Lund wrote: "Although love usually accompanied commitment, commitment and investments alone told more about the likelihood of a relationship lasting over time" (pp. 17–18). She reasoned that investments increase our commitment because they represent personal choices, whereas loving and being loved do not result from acts of will. It makes sense that we are more dedicated to relationships we have freely chosen and to which we devote time, energy, thought, and so forth.

Lund's work suggests that investing tends to increase commitment. Conversely, individuals who are unwilling to make investments of time, energy, and accommodation are less likely to be highly committed. Dana may be wise to doubt her partner's commitment because he seems unwilling to make substantial investments. In considering your own relationships, it is prudent to ask how much you and your partner invest. If only one person is investing or if there is serious disparity between how much each invests, then commitment and, ultimately, continuity may be dubious.

Dealing with Uncertainty

Finally, partners' ability to sustain a vital personal relationship depends on their capacity to accept and deal with uncertainty. There are many kinds of uncertainty that affect close relationships. One kind is luck, good and bad, that can make relationships more easy or more difficult. Recognizing the influence of luck or circumstances is not inconsistent with assuming agency, because intimate relations are affected by both personal choices and conditions beyond our control. One couple may break up when too many stresses assault it, and another couple that is no more or less intrinsically strong may stay together under more favorable conditions. Thinking again of Dana, if she locates a good job in her field in New York, the fact that her partner wouldn't interview in California may be less important—at least in the short term. However, Dana should realize that a potential long-term consequence of deferring to him is possibly ratifying an uneven power structure between them.

Circumstances beyond our control affect intimacy because relationships are not isolated from the rest of the world (Allan, 1993; Baxter, 1993). For instance, when the economy is precarious and people lose jobs or have to accept reductions in salary, there are personal consequences (Bolger & Kelleher, 1993). Relationships that progress satisfactorily when money is no problem may be strained if finances become tight. Being unemployed or seeing your income shrink can damage self-concept, so a partner experiencing career difficulties may become depressed, hostile, or otherwise unhappy and unpleasant. Because partners are interdependent, one person's unhappiness reverberates throughout a relationship.

LUKE

It's really true that luck can affect a relationship. When I was a sophomore I met this wonderful girl, and we really clicked. I mean right from the start, Pam and I just fit together. I never felt so close to anyone before, and I know she felt the same way. I began to think about long-term stuff, even though we'd only been dating a couple of months. Then my life fell apart. My dad got laid off, so the money for my college ran dry and I had to take a job. I was working about 25 hours a week, which really cut into the time I could spend with Pam. Then my kid brother got into a little bit of trouble, and I felt I had to spend time with him and kind of run interference for him with Mom and Dad. So that cut more into the time for Pam and me. Then I started having really bad headaches all the time, and that made me grouchy and hard to get along with. So even when we were together, I guess you could say I wasn't much fun. I guess Pam tried to be understanding, but I think we didn't have enough of a foundation to survive all of this at once. Later I found out a food allergy was causing the headaches, so now I don't have them, but it's too late for the relationship with Pam. I guess I'll always wonder if Pam and I would have made it if every bit of bad luck in the world hadn't fallen on us so early.

Health is another factor that can have a major impact on our relationships. Severe and prolonged psychological conditions, such as depression or obsessive compulsive disorders, take heavy tolls on relationships and may even result in co-dependency (Wright & Wright, 1995). Likewise, physiological problems can interfere with relationship satisfaction and stability. Prolonged illness and debilitating conditions create serious challenges for personal relationships (Lyons & Meade, 1995). For example, a couple I know, Ken and Denise, camped, trekked, and engaged in rugged outdoor activities during their courtship and the first four years of their marriage. Then Ken was in a car accident that left him moderately disabled. Although he could walk with some difficulty, he no longer had the muscular strength and control to engage in outings. Satisfaction waned and eventually they divorced because a change in Ken's health impaired an essential foundation of their union. Although you might conclude that Ken and Denise had a shallow basis for their marriage, the relationship worked until an act beyond their control eroded a critical foundation for their shared life. Both routine and extraordinary strains—from children, parents and in-laws, and job demands—also affect personal relationships (Bolger & Kelleher, 1993; Silberstein, 1992). They have an impact on individual partners and on interaction between them. Thus, a number of factors we cannot fully control impinge on private relationships.

Another type of uncertainty that laces personal relationships is how each partner will grow and change over time. Two people who come together at one point will not stay the same. As partners develop in ways that cannot be foreseen, their expectations and needs will shift. What they want from each other and what they feel able to give will vary. Relationships that survive over time tend to involve many adjustments and accommodations to changes in individual partners.

Although we cannot predict or control all of the circumstances that can affect our relationships, we can exercise some choice in how we respond to them. Some marriages dissolve when besieged by external pressures, yet others grow stronger as partners collaborate to deal with problems. Some families fall apart when a child is killed; others gain depth by weathering the tragedy together. Whether external stresses defeat or strengthen personal relationships depends on many complex factors, some of which partners can shape.

One of the most important elements within partners' control is communication. Couples who establish healthy, supportive, and honest communication patterns are able to talk with each other, share concerns, explore options for dealing with bad luck, and—in general—accompany each other through life. Without open lines of communication, partners are less likely to be able to work through individual and joint problems and to remain close to each other. So, although you cannot direct all happenings in life, you can usually exert some influence on how you build your relationships and whether you respond to chance in ways that are more or less constructive for intimacy. By taking responsibility for creating your relationships and for how you respond to circumstances, you do a lot to safeguard your close connections.

SUMMARY

This chapter introduced themes and concepts central to *Relational Communication*. We have seen that voluntary personal relationships are ongoing, ever-changing processes marked by continuing interdependence between individuals who cannot be replaced by others. We've also taken a first look at four influences on the satisfaction and endurance of close connections. In the chapters that follow we'll explore in more detail how relationships work so that you can choose actions that encourage favorable patterns and processes and avoid those that are unproductive. In addition, you'll learn more about what it means to be a conscious, active agent who takes some responsibility for what happens in your interactions with others. As you understand more about yourself, others, and relationship dynamics, you'll gain insight into how to assess whether someone you care about is also committed and willing to invest so that you can gauge the likelihood of an enduring bond with that person. Finally, you'll learn more about options for responding to life's surprises, even if you cannot always control what they are.

Gratifying personal relationships enrich our lives when other things are going well, and they buffer and fortify us when we encounter problems, stresses, and disappointments. They stimulate growth and change in us and allow us to be part of others' growth. In short, they make an enormous difference in the quality of our lives. Thus, your decision to study personal relationships is a wise investment in your health and future.

FOR FURTHER REFLECTION AND DISCUSSION

1. Have you created more close relationships with some members of your family than others? Describe differences between family members to whom you've voluntarily made commitments and those to whom you have not. How did you build intimacy with some members of your family?

2. Describe the forms of interdependence in one of your personal relationships. Try to explain what you expect from a romantic partner or friend and what you think she or he expects from you. If you're really adventurous, get your partner to do this also and then compare notes.

3. The author claims that both luck and personal choices affect what happens in relationships. Are these two factors inconsistent? Think about the impact of luck and choice in your own personal relationships. How much has each influenced them? Is it reasonable to believe both influence intimacy?

4. Do you agree that commitment is as important as love for satisfying and enduring friendships and romantic relationships? Have you had experiences in which one, but not the other, was present? Reflect on how relationships that were committed differ from ones that were not.

5. Consider your thrownness. How do circumstances beyond your control affect your identity and the opportunities available and not available to you as an individual and in relation to others in the present era? With others in your class, discuss how factors such as race, sex, class, and affectional preference affect identity and options in life.

RECOMMENDED READINGS

Beck, A. (1988). *Love is never enough.* New York: Harper & Row.

Canary, D., & Stafford, L. (Eds.). (1994). *Communication and relational maintenance.* New York: Academic Press.

Lund, M. (1985). The development of investment and commitment scales for predicting continuity of personal relationships. *Journal of Social and Personal Relationships, 2,* 3–23.

Vanzetti, N., & Duck, S. (Eds.). (1996). *A lifetime of relationships.* Belmont, CA: Brooks-Cole.

CHAPTER TWO

Theoretical Insights
into Personal Relationships

Doria, who was raised in a traditional Italian family and community, is talking with her boyfriend Mark, who grew up in Kansas. She shouts at him, "You have to talk to me about your relationship with Malissa. I need to know about it." For emphasis, Doria slams the book she was reading on the floor. Mark tells her, "My relationship with Malissa has nothing to do with us. It's history and it's private." "No," roars Doria, "it's not private because we're together now. We have to understand each other's history." Her arms gesticulate wildly as she adds, "Besides, what happened that's so secret you can't tell me?" "Nothing so secret happened," Mark says in a self-composed, soft tone. He wishes she would lower her voice—what must the people in the next apartment think is going on? He says, "It's just private—that's all." Doria storms across the room, then turns back to Mark and exclaims, "I hate it when you just sit there, acting so detached. Why can't you get involved in this issue?" "I am involved," he says coolly, "but that doesn't mean I have to scream and be irrational."

WHAT IS HAPPENING BETWEEN MARK AND DORIA? Is she acting irrationally? Is he un-involved? Why won't Mark tell Doria about his prior relationship? Why does Doria feel she needs to know about a past relationship? Should Mark be concerned about neighbors overhearing their argument?

Although we cannot know for sure why Doria and Mark communicate as they do, we can be sure that both of them have reasons for communicating this way. We can also be sure that each of them will strive to describe and explain what is happening between them and predict what it means for their future. When they try to describe, explain, and predict their relationship, they enter the realm of theorizing.

Many people think theories are removed from real life. Yet, actually, you and each of us use theories every day to make sense of the relationships and experiences in our lives. You make theoretical statements when you say, "What's involved here is . . ." (a description), or "You did that because . . ." (an explanation), or "If we don't find a way to handle this, then . . ." (a prediction). Each of us thinks theoretically as we try to make sense of our relationships.

Theory is a way to describe, explain, predict, and control something. Our interest here is personal relationships, so the theories that concern us are ones that effectively describe, explain, predict, and control personal relationships. Sound theories help us understand the complex dynamics of relationships—what relationships involve, why certain things happen and where those events lead, what influences occurrences in relationships, what we might do to control interaction and what it implies for the future.

In this chapter, we will introduce a number of theories that shed light on the structure and dynamics of personal relationships. To understand how our most intimate connections operate, we will need to discuss theories at several levels. The broadest theory is symbolic interactionism, which helps us understand how society influences individuals' identities and the ways they perceive and act in personal relationships. At the next level are theories focusing on social communities—such as families and gender and ethnic groups—that distinctively shape the individual identities of members of those communities. Third, we'll consider constructivism, which sheds light on how individuals interpret others and their communication. Finally, we'll look at theories that give us insight into the dynamic processes that shape and reflect intimate relationships. Table 2.1 previews these theories at each level of explanation. The aim of this chapter is to introduce the theories, not to examine them in detail. At the end of the chapter you should have a general appreciation of what each theory contributes to an overall understanding of personal relationships. In later chapters, we'll revisit these theories in more depth.

THEORIZING SOCIETY

Although many theories about society exist, one is particularly useful to us because it focuses on communication. **Symbolic interaction theory** (or **symbolic interactionism**) regards communication as the primary means by which individuals inter-

TABLE 2.1
Theories Relevant to Understanding Personal Relationships

SOCIETY	SOCIAL COMMUNITIES	INDIVIDUALS	RELATIONSHIP PROCESSES
Symbolic interactionism	Standpoint theory Attachment theory	Constructivism	Systems theory Social exchange theory Dialectical theory Turning points

nalize and use social values to guide how they see themselves and others and how they interact.

Symbolic interactionism was formulated by George Herbert Mead, who taught at the University of Chicago in the early 1900s. Since Mead's original theorizing, others have extended his work (Blumer, 1969; Hochschild, 1975; Wood, 1992, 1994a) to gain insight into human interaction and social life. One reason for this theory's persisting prominence is that it offers an unusually rich analysis of how communication forms personal identity and makes social life possible. At the heart of symbolic interactionism is the idea that humans have minds and selves, both of which arise in interaction with others.

Mind

Mead thought that an individual has neither a mind nor a self at birth but acquires both in the process of communicating with others. **Mind** is the ability to use significant symbols, which are symbols that have common social meanings. For example, members of a society have functionally similar meanings for words such as *home, democracy, engagement, marriage,* and *divorce.* Although each of us has some unique meanings for the words, as members of the same society we share sufficiently similar meanings to allow us to communicate with one another.

Language allows us to reflect on ourselves and our world because we can use symbols to indicate ideas to ourselves, hold them in our thoughts, and share them with other symbol users. Initially, infants interact with others only by behaving and responding to others' behaviors. With language, however, ideas can replace behavior. Instead of crying for food, a child says "food." Rather than scowling at a child who is about to have a temper tantrum, a parent can warn, "If you start crying, you won't get dessert." With the ability to use symbols, ideas—not just behaviors—have meaning. We don't just act, but we think about acting and use symbols to express our thoughts to others. Language ushers humans into the realm of ideas and meaning. Within symbolic interactionism, this is what it means to have a mind.

Self

Like mind, self is not present at birth but is acquired in interaction. Mead defined **self** as the ability to take the self as an object. By this he meant we have the unique capacity to be both the subjects and the objects of our experiences. In other words, we act as subjects and also observe ourselves as objects. Learning to observe ourselves starts early in life. How others act toward us as infants initiates our first sense of self and the ability to use others' perspectives to view ourselves. As we come to view our own actions from the perspectives of others, we learn to conceive of ourselves, assess alternative ways we could act, think about how others perceive us and particular actions, and envision potential versions of ourselves.

Mead described the self as consisting of two complementary parts. First, there is the **I**, who is a performer, doer, or actor—the subject of our actions. The **ME** is a critic, analyst, or socially conscious part of the self that reflects on us as an object. The I is impulsive, creative, and largely unconstrained by social rules and norms, which is why the I is the source of individuality and creativity. The ME is analytical, reflective, and socially aware, which enables the ME to edit I's impulses. ME evaluates I's actions using perspectives derived from interacting with others. So, for instance, while eating at a restaurant you impulsively kiss your date, then think, "I shouldn't have been so demonstrative in public." Your I acted spontaneously, and your ME critiqued I's behavior from a social perspective. In the scenario that opened this chapter, Mark's ME was concerned about how others would perceive Doria's shouting.

KATE

I never heard the terms "I" and "ME" before, but that really describes something that happens to me all the time. I'll do something, and then inside my head will be these thoughts about it that I've heard from others. I have a short fuse, and I often chew somebody out first and think afterward that I shouldn't have done it. Honestly, every time I blow up at somebody I get down on myself, and what I'm thinking is "It's not nice for girls to be outspoken" or "It's not ladylike to show anger." I know exactly where I got that because my parents were always trying to get me to tone down my temper. But the funny thing is that it's not them criticizing me now. It's me. Their views really are in me so that I see myself through their eyes.

Although Mead recognized the individual aspect of self he called the I, his primary interest was the ME, which uses social understandings to direct and evaluate the self. Because we internalize others' ways of interpreting people, situations, and ourselves, our perspectives are intrinsically social. By extension, the self is necessarily social because we rely on the perspectives of others to reflect on ourselves.

Our understandings of ourselves and the social world are shaped by the perspectives of others around us—both specific individuals and society as a whole. Initially, we internalize the views of specific individuals who are significant to us (Mead's "significant others")—parents and siblings, for instance. Throughout life we continue to enlarge our outlook as we interact with others and society as a whole and import multiple perspectives into ourselves.

The Generalized Other

Yet others' perspectives do not remain only a collection of individual pieces. Instead, we organize them into what Mead called the **perspective of the generalized other,** which is the viewpoint of society as a whole. We learn society's overall perspectives as we attend school and religious gatherings, engage in social activities, watch television and films and read newspapers and magazines, and observe people around us. The generalized other is "a composite of rules, roles, and attitudes endorsed by the whole social community of which an individual is part" (Wood, 1992, p. 164). Internalizing the generalized other's perspective allows us to understand and participate effectively in social life (Mead, 1934). Thus, we sometimes adopt the perspective of a specific person to reflect on ourselves or situations, and at other times we adopt the viewpoint of the generalized other. Either way, self-reflection is inevitably social reflection, because it involves others' perspectives.

Symbolic interactionism gives us a broad understanding of how individuals develop mind and self. It explains that we learn how to see ourselves and the world in the process of interacting with others. Through communication we gain perspectives to use in reflecting on experiences and ourselves. Although Mead explains how societies endure and how individuals are socialized into common values, he does not account for divergencies among social groups. Why, for instance, does family mean different things to various ethnic groups? How do we explain gender variations in views of relationships? To answer these questions, we need to consider theories that focus on social communities.

THEORIZING SOCIAL COMMUNITIES

Two theories shed light on how membership in specific social groups fosters differences in how individuals perceive and use communication in personal relationships.

Standpoint Theory

Standpoint theory extends symbolic interactionism by noting that the particular social groups to which individuals belong affect how they perceive people and relationships and how they communicate.

Standpoints reflect social locations. The basic premise of standpoint theory is straightforward: The social, material, and symbolic circumstances of a social group shape how members perceive, interpret, and act toward events, situations, others, and themselves. Every social group invites some experiences and precludes others, teaches specific roles and not others, and selectively emphasizes particular values and viewpoints. Thus, social locations affect how members of groups understand everything from money to relationships (Wood, 1994b). For example, people's views and expectations of marriage are patterned by economic, ethnic, educational, and employment factors (Allan, 1993; O'Connor, 1992; Parke & Kellam, 1994;

Wellman & Wellman, 1992). More wealthy individuals are likely to think of families as involving only one full-time wage earner, but working-class people generally assume both partners will work full-time.

Perhaps the first inklings of standpoint theory emerged from the German philosopher Georg William Fredrick Hegel. Writing in 1807, he suggested that the different positions of slaves and masters result in distinct views of social life. Although slaves and masters belong to a common society, their different social positions constrain what each perceives. Hegel argued that slaves' perspectives are more complete, and therefore more accurate, because their survival depends on understanding both their views and those of their masters, but masters have no parallel need to appreciate slaves' points of view. Patricia Hill Collins (1986) argued that African American women academics are "insider-outsiders." Professionally, they are inside academe, yet their race and often their economic class define them as outsiders. Collins claims that insider-outsiders have a dual consciousness that enriches insight.

FRANK

Standpoint theory helps me understand why Cheryl, my fiancé, and I disagree about our wedding. I want a simple ceremony, but she wants a big society affair with all the trimmings. I'd rather take the money a fancy wedding would cost and save it as a nest egg for us. But I come from a farming family in a small town. Cheryl's family is upper-crust, old-money types. When I was a kid my birthdays were homemade cakes and friends Mom called to invite. Cheryl's Mom sent out written invitations to her friends, ordered specialty cakes from a bakery, and hired an entertainer for her birthday parties. She had a coming-out party and was a debutante. I guess the circumstances that she was brought up in make her think that a wedding should be very extravagant and formal. The way I was raised, fancy to-dos are stuffy and ostentatious.

As Hegel's and Collins's analyses indicate, standpoint theory is directly concerned with circumstances common to most members of social groups. Every culture develops criteria to differentiate social groups. Among Hindus, caste is used to assign people to groups, and in the United States, sex, race, ethnicity, sexual orientation, and class are used to designate social placement. Further, groups are not defined as just different but as differently valuable. Standpoint scholars have shown that Western society assigns radically disparate rights, roles, experiences, and opportunities to members of different social groups (Haraway, 1988; Harding, 1991; Hartsock, 1983).

Differences among groups are produced and reproduced by cultural structures and practices that confer and withhold privilege based on the value society assigns to various groups (Collins, 1986; Harding, 1991). Once distinct groups are specified, a culture prescribes specific roles that involve disparate activities, which distinctively shape how members perceive themselves and social life. By regulating members' experiences, a culture reproduces distinctions among the groups it constructs. Through this process, societies sustain social hierarchies and, with those, distinct standpoints of individuals in different groups.

Standpoints yield situated views of personal relationships. Our views of relationships reflect the standpoints fostered by the social groups to which we belong. For instance, Stanley Gaines (1995) reports that individualism is more pronounced among middle-class European Americans than among some other ethnic groups. He demonstrates that Hispanics have a strong familial orientation in which loyalty to family and its welfare eclipses individuality. Among African Americans, Gaines identifies a collective orientation that inclines partners to see themselves as belonging not only to their immediate families but also to extended families and the whole Black culture. Other research shows that many Blacks generally prioritize interdependence, whereas many Whites tend to emphasize autonomy (Bellah, Madsen, Sullivan, Swindler, & Tipton, 1991). An African American student of mine reported an experience that shows how different standpoints can foster misunderstandings. He wanted to leave school for a week to be with a critically ill aunt, but several of his White instructors refused to excuse his absence because they did not consider aunts immediate family. Among African Americans, aunts are often considered immediate family (Wood, 1998b).

Standpoints influence communication. The particular experiences of a social group lead to group-specific communication patterns. Because an individual social group develops a unique way of communicating, it is called a **speech community** (Labov, 1972). A speech community exists when members of a social group understand and use communication in ways that are not shared by those outside the group. Scholars have identified a number of speech communities, including gay, elderly, African American, Hispanic, lesbian, Native American, people with disabilities, and gender (Samovar & Porter, 1997). Each speech community has specific perspectives on why, when, and how to communicate. Although there are individual variations, members of groups usually share many understandings about communication.

Among speech communities studied so far, gender has received particularly substantial attention, because it is primary to how Western societies organize themselves (Bem, 1993; Janeway, 1971; Miller, 1986; Wood, 1993d, 1994a,b, 1995, 1997, 1998b, 1999). Despite changes in social attitudes and women's and men's activities, males and females in our society still tend to be socialized primarily in sex-segregated groups (Johnson, 1989, 1996; Wood, 1996, 1999), which cultivate distinct standpoints on communication and relationships.

Most girls are socialized into feminine values, understandings, and codes of conduct. Thus, they acquire a feminine standpoint that regards communication as

SALLY FORTH reprinted with permission of King Features Syndicate.

a primary way to build and sustain relationships. Boys, who are generally social-ized into masculine standpoints, more typically view communication as an instru-mental activity to accomplish tasks and attain personal status (Chodorow, 1978, 1989; Wood, 1996, 1999). Differences in masculine and feminine speech commu-nities may help us understand why Doria felt it was important for her and Mark to talk about his past relationship, and why Mark did not feel that way.

> ### SALINA
>
> *I've always wondered why Black women are so much more self-confident and assertive than White women. All of my friends are strong, and we sometimes talk about how unassertive White girls are, especially around guys. Black women have always had to be strong and rely on themselves. It's not just that a lot of Black families don't have fathers, either. Even in those that do have fathers, the woman is strong too. And Black girls are taught to be indepen-dent and self-sufficient. I was told from day one to learn to take care of myself. I have a Black standpoint on women's identity, and that's different from a White woman's standpoint.*

What are the pragmatic implications of standpoint theory for personal rela-tionships? It suggests that how we interpret communication reflects our own stand-points, which may be incongruent with those of others. The converse is also true: How others interpret our communication may not parallel our meanings for it. This implies intimates should explain their standpoints to each other and learn to understand each other's standpoint.

In sum, standpoint theory highlights how social locations and the roles, expe-riences, and understandings entailed in them shape individuals' thoughts, feelings, and actions. Although not denying individuality, standpoint theory insists that so-cial groups are important contexts that shape how individuals perceive others and relationships and how they communicate.

Attachment Theory

Family is another social group that profoundly influences individuals' expectations of relationships and communication. Developed by clinicians, **attachment theory** claims that individuals' orientations toward intimacy are shaped by very early relationships with caregivers, usually parents. Like symbolic interactionism and standpoint theory, attachment theory assumes interaction is the primary process through which individuals learn about relationships, others, and themselves. It extends other theories by clarifying how early, formative communication in families fashions initial working models of relationships.

Styles of attachment. Originally developed by John Bowlby (1973, 1988), attachment theory claims that our earliest experiences decisively influence how we view ourselves, others, and relationships. Writing in 1993, Judi Miller explained that the first significant relationship is particularly influential because it establishes expectations for later ones. The initial bonding between a child and its primary caregiver, usually the mother, is the first and an especially formative influence on individuals' views of relationships (Ainsworth, Blehar, Waters, & Wall, 1978), and this initial view is generally established by the age of 1 (Miller, 1993).

Based on interaction with its initial caregiver in early life, an infant forms a working model that consists of its views of self-worth and the worth of others in terms of their responsiveness, trustworthiness, and caring (Bartholomew, 1993; Bartholomew & Horowitz, 1991; Simon & Baxter, 1993). The infant then extends this model to relationships in general (Bowlby, 1977; Early bonding, 1993). Children whose caregivers are consistently warm and responsive tend to feel positive about themselves and others. Conversely, when a caregiver is distant or rejecting, infants may assume people in general are uncaring and relationships are danger zones.

There are three working models of attachment, which yield four distinct styles of attachment (Ainsworth et al., 1978; Bartholomew, 1993; Miller, 1993; Putallaz, Costanzo, & Klein, 1993). The **secure attachment model** is the most common and the most likely to promote positive conceptions of self and others (Kobak & Sceery, 1988; Miller, 1993). As the name implies, this model reflects a caregiver who consistently responds to a child in a loving, reassuring, and supportive way. For instance, one investigation showed that mothers who hold babies more closely and tenderly tend to have children who grow up with secure attachment styles (Main, 1981). When responsive caring typifies the first critical relationship, a child tends to develop a positive, secure view of self and others and to feel confident, affectionate, resilient, and open to new experiences and people.

We know of at least two influences on the likelihood that a primary caregiver will be loving, attentive, and nurturing. First, standpoint theory reminds us that the circumstances of different social groups vary in the extent to which they promote parental availability and responsiveness. For instance, couples who are middle or upper class are likely to have the financial resources to ensure that a caregiver is consistently available to a child: Either one partner's salary is sufficient to allow the other partner to stay home with the child or the parents can afford good day care. Parents in less economically privileged social groups often can neither live on a single salary nor afford the best day care (Burns & Scott, 1994). Second, ongoing research on attachment has shown that parents tend to replicate the patterns they experienced with their first caregiver, because those frame the parents' own working models (Putallaz, Costanzo, & Klein, 1993).

The **anxious-avoidant attachment model** tends to develop when a caregiver is consistently negative, disinterested, rejecting, or, in extreme cases, abusive. For instance, a caregiver might ignore a child's crying, fail to reassure a child who is frightened, or punish a child harshly. From this treatment, a child deduces that others are not caring, that she or he is not worthy of love, or both. The working model constructed from this pattern defines close relationships as either unnecessary or unattainable.

Although initially researchers treated all people with avoidant working models as a single group, recent studies have shown that this model yields two distinct profiles or attachment styles. The first, fearful attachment style, is based on a low self-image and a low evaluation of others. People with this style are likely to believe they are unworthy of love and others are incapable of providing it, which may make them dependent on others for self-worth but fearful that others will not provide validation (Bartholomew, 1993; Simon & Baxter, 1993). It is not uncommon for people with fearful attachment styles to be perfectionistic (Kaplan & Main, 1985), perhaps hoping that if they are good enough others will love them. A fearful attachment style also seems linked to the tendency to be easily discouraged in seeking goals (Erickson, Stroufe, & Egeland, 1985). Thus, this attachment style may beget a sense of powerlessness in relationships.

A different response to the anxious-avoidant model is a dismissive attachment style in which individuals think well of themselves and poorly of others. They may deny wanting relationships and avoid contact. As you might expect, people with this style tend to resist support and comfort even when they need it. They have learned to believe others are not caring, and thus, they convince themselves that it's safer not to depend on others and not to form strong attachments. This response appears to be a defensive effort at self-protection (Bartholomew, 1993).

Avoidant models may be promoted if caregivers are truly uncaring people or if their circumstances preclude the skills or resources necessary for loving, attentive engagement with children (Okin, 1989). Thus, people with limited finances, educations, or both have diminished opportunity to be optimum caregivers. Cultural values and the social practices they authorize also affect caregiving styles. Hewlett (1986, 1991) has shown that societies that value family life have national policies mandating substantial paid leave for family matters. The United States remains the only developed country that has no national policy guaranteeing paid leave to all parents (Wood, 1994d, 1999). Even the Family and Medical Leave Act of 1993 falls short of enabling everyone to meet family responsibilities, because it covers only about 50 percent of workers and does not guarantee compensation for family leaves. Thus, this act is least helpful to people who most need support for caregiving. In addition, adults who were rejected as infants are likely to have anxious-avoidant working models that guide their own caregiving. Therefore, parents who were abused are more likely to abuse their own children than parents who had positive bonds (Chodorow, 1978; Mills & Rubin, 1993; Putallaz, Costanzo, & Klein, 1993).

The most complex pattern is the **anxious-resistant attachment model.** Unlike the other two, which reflect consistent styles of caregiving, the anxious-resistant model grows out of inconsistent and unpredictable responses. Sometimes the adult is compassionate and involved, at other times indifferent or cruel. The caregiver may even respond variably to the same actions at different times, which may lead children to see relationships as unstable and unsafe.

Family circumstances may cause inconsistent responses to a child. If there are many young children in a family, a caregiver cannot always be responsive to each one. Similarly, parents who juggle jobs, family, and other pressures may lack the physical and psychological energy for nurturing. Loving caregivers may be forced away, leaving an infant feeling abandoned by the person it trusted to be available (Bowlby, 1988; Early bonding, 1993).

Children who experience inconsistent caring early in life may respond by developing preoccupied attachment patterns that are based on negative views of self and positive views of others. Hence, they assume they aren't worthy of caring, but they know that others can be loving sometimes, even if not to them. A preoccupied attachment style may result in obsessiveness about relationships and overdependence on others' evaluations of personal worth. Similarly, people with preoccupied patterns may be highly self-critical, mirroring the caregiver's treatment of them (Kaplan & Main, 1985). Figure 2.1 represents how views of self and others create the four different attachment styles.

According to John Bowlby (1988), patterns of attachment tend to persist because the core of a working model serves as a blueprint that guides views of relationships later in life. This blueprint shapes what individuals expect of others and relationships. For instance, a person with a secure attachment style would expect others to be friendly and, thus, would *be* friendly, thereby evoking amiable

FIGURE 2.1
Attachment Styles

	Positive View of Self	Negative View of Self
Positive View of Others	Secure	Preoccupied
Negative View of Others	Dismissive	Fearful

responses from others. Individuals with secure attachment styles engage in more prosocial communication than people with dismissive, fearful, or preoccupied styles (Simon & Baxter, 1993).

A number of researchers have found consistent positive associations between attachment styles formed in infancy and those in adult relationships (Belsky & Pensky, 1988; Franz, McClelland, & Weinberger, 1991; Ognibene & Collins, 1998). For instance, people with anxious-avoidant working models tend to select unresponsive partners, who reinforce those models (Bartholomew & Horowitz, 1991). Other attachment styles also show up in adult romantic relationships (Collins, 1991; Collins & Read, 1990; Harrison-Greer, 1991; Senchak & Leonard, 1992).

The working models we form as infants tend to persist *unless* they are disconfirmed by later experience. *Unless* is a key word, because working models are not set in stone. We can revise limiting models by disputing their validity and by choosing partners who are loving and responsive to us (Seligman, 1990).

GLENN

I think I learned to be anxious-avoidant because my folks divorced right after I was born. Mom was very depressed and also had to take a job to support us, so she didn't have much emotional energy for a new baby. I remember growing up feeling she didn't want me around, so I learned not to want her. That's how I was with others too until Beth and I got together. First it was like all my other relationships in that I didn't expect her to be there for me and I didn't count on her. But when I was withdrawn or even nasty, she just stayed right by me. No matter how I acted, she was loving. I really don't know why, but she stayed by me. It's been two years now, and I've learned that she is going to love me, no matter what. I trust her, so I don't withdraw as much or do hostile things when I feel down. Maybe I don't need to show her that I don't need her, because I've learned that it's safe to count on her.

Glenn's reflection illustrates several important points about working models. First, his experiences exemplify how working models develop. When Glenn was born, his mother was so overwhelmed by her own circumstances that she couldn't be emotionally available and nurturing, so he became anxious about attachment and learned to avoid it. Glenn created a self-fulfilling prophecy by withdrawing and resisting closeness, which provoked others to rebuff him and, thus, to reinforce his working model. This is consistent with theory and research (Caspi & Elder, 1988; Hazen & Shaver, 1987; Swann, 1987). Yet Beth's constant acceptance prompted Glenn to revise his working model. Moving toward a more secure working model is consistent with research that shows we are more likely to move toward healthy working models than unhealthy ones (Hazen & Shaver, 1987; Main & George, 1985).

THEORIZING INDIVIDUALS

So far, we've discussed theories that focus on how society and specific social communities affect our views of and our actions in personal relationships. Complementing these theories is work that describes, explains, and predicts individual thought, or cognition.

Constructivism or Social Cognition Theory

Building on Mead's symbolic interactionism, George Kelly (1955, 1969) focused on cognitive processes humans use to create meaning. **Constructivism,** the theory Kelly formulated, maintains that individuals develop and use cognitive structures to organize and make sense of experience (1955). Like Mead before him, Kelly believed individuals learn ways of thinking, or cognitive structures, in the process of interacting with others.

In the four decades since this theory emerged, it has been expanded to include multiple cognitive structures that individuals use to interpret themselves, others, and relationships. Both Mead and Kelly, as well as those influenced by their theories, accord symbols a central role in explanations of human conduct. The reason for this is that above all else, symbols are the doorway to meaning, and meaning is at the heart of human life and human relationships. Symbols allow us not just to engage in experience as it concretely exists but to imbue it with significance.

Knowledge schemata. Kelly (1955) considered personal constructs to be the building blocks for individuals' interpretations of experience. Since his original work, scholars have identified three additional cognitive structures, called schemata, that organize perception and thought about others and relationships. Figure 2.2 defines and illustrates the four schemata.

Prototypes are the broadest knowledge structure we use to interpret others. Beverly Fehr (1993) defines a prototype as the clearest case or best example of a category. A **prototype** is an exemplar of some category of people, events, concepts, objects, or situations. We evaluate other people or situations we have placed in the same category according to how closely they measure up to the prototype. For example, your prototype of a really great date would be the person who is the clearest example of the whole class of great dates. Fehr (1993) identified five features that make up most North Americans' prototype of love: trust, caring, honesty, friendship, and respect.

Although important to some people, more passionate qualities are not widely regarded as definitive of love (Button & Collier, 1991; Fehr & Russell, 1991; Luby & Aron, 1990). Thus, the prototype of love in Western society focuses on companionate features of relationships.

Kelly defined **personal constructs** as mental yardsticks that allow us to measure something along particular dimensions of judgment. Personal constructs are bipolar dimensions of judgment that are cognitive tools we use to define how specific people measure up on particular qualities. For example, when you go out with someone for the first time, you compare the person to others you have dated. You might ask if she or he is intelligent or unintelligent, interesting or uninteresting, attractive or unattractive. Intelligence, interestingness, and attractiveness are constructs or mental yardsticks you use to evaluate that person relative to others you have dated. Whereas prototypes tell us in which category to place something (friend or date), personal constructs let us interpret something in greater detail by assessing it along specific dimensions that matter to us (Trenholm & Jensen, 1992).

DOREEN

I think being friends and being able to trust are what's most important in loving someone. It's not that I don't like hearts and flowers and fireworks, because I do. But those aren't the real foundation of love. I can remember my mother telling me that you can feel butterflies and sparks with a lot of people, but those don't last, so you have to build a relationship on something more solid. That's friendship and trust to me.

The third knowledge structure that influences meaning is stereotypes. Like prototypes, **stereotypes** are generalizations about people or experiences. Prototypes, however, stop at the level of description—they allow us to compare someone or some experience to the best example of its category. Stereotypes go beyond clas-

FIGURE 2.2
Knowledge Schemata

Prototype	The exemplar of a category	Best friend Romantic setting
Personal Construct	Bipolar dimension by which we assess people	Confident–not confident Moody–not moody Attractive–unattractive
Stereotype	Predictive generalization based on how we perceive the group into which we place people	Attractive women are conceited. Wealthy people are conservative.
Script	Guide to action in specific situation	Engage in small talk with clerks. Avoid major disclosures on first dates. Keep friends' confidences.

sification to predict behaviors of a person or object we have classified within a particular group (Trenholm & Jensen, 1992). Therefore, when we stereotype another person we predict what she or he will do based on our beliefs about the group into which we classify the person: All lawyers are out to make money; all fraternity brothers drink; all conservatives are opposed to abortion.

Researchers have shown that members of a culture tend to hold some common stereotypes. For example, one study (Dion, Berscheid, & Walster, 1972) demonstrated that Westerners generally believe physically attractive people are sensitive, interesting, sociable, outgoing, sexually responsive, and kind. At the same time, attractive women are thought to be conceited (Dermer & Thiel, 1975), and attractive men are presumed to be unintelligent (Byrne, London, & Reeves, 1968). Accurate or not, stereotypes affect personal relationships. We may refuse to form relationships or be rebuffed by others because of stereotypes that aren't accurate.

Finally, individuals rely on scripts to organize interpersonal knowledge. As the name implies, **scripts** are guides to action. They are our views of what is an expected or appropriate sequence of activities in particular situations. We have scripts for many of our daily routines: how to talk to a professor, greet friends, make conversation with clerks, and so forth. Likewise, we have scripts for dating that identify appropriate behaviors for each person and the order in which they should occur. There is wide agreement among college students about the normal sequence of dating events and which things women and men should do (Pryor & Merluzzi, 1985). The consensus on how to enact a first date suggests scripts reflect broad social understandings and norms. Because individuals internalize the generalized other's perspective, however, it becomes a personal guide for belief and action.

We also have broader scripts about relationships. For instance, Steve Duck and Paul Wright (1993) reviewed decades of study on friendship and surveyed over 1,700 people to find out whether there are general expectations for enacting friendship. They discovered that both women and men regard talking together as the most frequent activity between friends, working together on a project as a fairly regular occurrence, and discussing personal and relationship problems as appropriate but less frequent. Adding to this, Leslie Baxter (1992) found that playfulness and "hanging out" with no particular purpose are generally considered important activities between friends. Broadly endorsed scripts for being friends are qualified by sex differences. Specifically, women more than men express emotions overtly and talk explicitly about feelings, and both sexes seem to see expressive communication as more appropriate for women than men (Duck & Wright, 1993). Notice that this sex difference concerns how the sexes tend to *express* caring and support, not whether they care equally about friends. Research does not support the idea that men are less caring than women—only that there may be masculine and feminine modes of expressing care (Monsour, 1992; Wood, 1998b; Wood & Inman, 1993).

Most individuals also have scripts regarding the normal path to romantic intimacy. James Honeycutt (1993) reports high consistency among individuals on what should happen in progressing toward intimacy. Probably reflecting society's influence on individuals' scripts, Honeycutt also found general agreement regarding when various things should occur. Serious personal disclosure, for example, is regarded as inappropriate on a first date but appropriate when a couple begins to get serious.

Changes in Scripts

Scripts vary across time and contexts. Broad agreements about what friends do and how intimacy progresses reflect current social views. Time affects scripts in two ways. First, individuals change throughout their lives, so what behaviors they regard as appropriate also vary (Allan, 1993). Think about your relationship with your parents: Probably you thought it was appropriate for them to establish rules and direct you when you were 5 or 10, but it is less acceptable now that you are more adult. As people advance in their careers, engaging in more assertive behaviors and exercising greater authority become more appropriate (Epstein, 1981). Time also affects scripts in the sense that social norms change over the years. For example, in the 1950s there was general agreement about the script that nice girls don't kiss on first dates. When Western society strongly disapproved of divorce, few people considered it part of the script for a respectable life.

These scripts have changed, as has the once ubiquitous script that children are necessarily part of a good marriage. Individuals' ages and values endorsed by society affect their scripts for relationships.

> A N N A
>
> *Mike and I had been together about four months when we had our first fight. He got mad because I fussed at him for forgetting his mother's birthday, and then I got upset about how defensive he was toward me. After we'd been at it a while he got real quiet, so I started trying to pull him out. The more I tried to get him to talk about what he was feeling, the quieter he got. Finally, he took me back to my place and said he'd call later. And he did—after two days—and then we talked about our argument and he told me what he'd been feeling at the time. He also said that when he gets angry he withdraws because otherwise he's likely to say stuff he doesn't mean, and he'd rather cool down before talking. We had a couple more incidents like this, and I figured out that he really will talk about issues between us, but he needs a cooling-off period first. So now when we have a fight, I know not to try to get him to talk right away because he can't. But I can trust him to talk about issues when he's ready. That's not my style—or at least it wasn't before—but it's the only way Mike can deal with problems.*

Anna's reflection highlights the process by which intimate partners develop viable scripts through interaction. Partners have to figure out how to coordinate individual scripts into ones that work for them as a couple (Wood, 1982). Over time, partners develop a number of scripts to guide them through recurrent episodes in their relationship: how to greet each other each morning and after work each day, how to engage in an argument, how to plan a vacation. Initially, friends and romantic partners have no script for having a disagreement. In any relationship that progresses beyond a superficial level, however, disagreements occur. What individuals do and say in their first few disagreements will influence how they construct a joint script for disagreeing. Thinking back to Doria and Mark, we see that they haven't yet developed a mutually satisfying script for arguing. Perhaps growing up in an Italian community, Doria learned to argue emotionally and energetically. Mark's Midwestern background may have taught him a script that calls for calm, rational discussion. If they are to deal effectively with their current disagreement, as well as ones that will come later, they need to work out a joint script for how to argue.

Scripts develop and change over time in long-term relationships. Partners revise them when initial scripts become dysfunctional because partners change or circumstances affect the relationship. When a couple has a child, for example, new scripts must be devised for many daily activities. The newborn's arrival disrupts prior patterns of communication. Likewise, when a partner changes jobs, the new responsibilities and schedule often necessitate adjustments in scripts for interacting. Developing joint or compatible scripts facilitates closeness because they coordinate partners in a world governed by shared understandings.

We've considered how individuals use prototypes, personal constructs, stereotypes, and scripts to organize thinking and action in friendships and romantic relations. These four schemata, or knowledge structures, clarify how we interpret and make sense of relationship experiences, as well as how we decide the way we should communicate in specific situations. In the final section of this chapter we consider theories about relationship dynamics that add to our understanding of personal relationships.

THEORIZING RELATIONSHIP DYNAMICS

Like the other theories we've examined, theories about relationships provide descriptions, explanations, and predictions. These theories, however, focus specifically on how relationships operate, or the key dynamics of interaction in human relationships. We'll introduce four relationship-focused theories here and elaborate on them in later chapters.

Systems Theory

To understand how social and personal contexts affect personal relationships, many scholars draw on **systems theory** (Lederer, 1981; Watzlawick, Beavin, & Jackson, 1967). A system is a group of interrelated elements that interact in ways that influence one another and the system as a whole. Personal relationships are systems because they involve interacting parts that affect one another. Viewing personal relationships as systems leads to four insights into how they operate.

Parts of relationships influence one another. When we defined personal relationships in Chapter 1, we noted that they involve interdependence between partners. Another way to say this is that partners are parts of a system, so they are interrelated and affect each other. Likewise, other features interact, so physical settings (quiet restaurant, shopping mall, home), communication patterns, social communities, and individual cognitions affect one another. Within personal relationships, all features are interdependent. This means that what Doria does influences what Mark does and vice versa. Further, the knowledge schemata that each of them relies on affect how they interpret and respond to each other.

All aspects of personal relationships must be understood within their contexts. Because parts of a system are interrelated, we cannot understand any part removed from the whole. We must, instead, view it within contexts. It will do us little good, for instance, to focus just on Doria or just on Mark if we want to understand what is going on in their relationship. We have to understand the society and social communities in which Doria and Mark grew up, as well as those they participate in today. We must take all of the interlinked parts of the relationship into consideration in order to comprehend how any single part operates.

Because relationships are located within multiple contexts, or other systems, what happens between two people is influenced by physical, psychological, cultural, familial, professional, and personal systems. For example, a sense of urgency characterizes a society when it is readying for war, so people often feel impelled to form commitments. Similarly, the stress and uncertainty of war cultivate a hunger for stability when peacetime returns. Given this, it is not surprising that the national mood in the United States in the 1950s emphasized family stability and growth and elevated family life to unprecedented prominence. Systems logic tells us that the postwar salience of families was not an individual phenomenon, but one influenced by the broad cultural mood of the time.

Personal relationships are organized wholes. Marcia Dixson and Steve Duck (1993) note that "there is a curiosity about relationships. They are composed of individuals, yet are more than the sum of their parts (p. 176)." That something more is what transpires *between individuals*—the processes and results of interaction. As individuals interact, new phenomena emerge. Trust, commitment, and shared meanings do not exist in individuals prior to a relationship; instead, they arise directly out of and because of communication between people. Further, as new phenomena emerge, the whole relationship changes. Because systems are organized, interconnected wholes, a change in any feature reverberates throughout an entire system.

When I first came to college, I was really lonely. None of my friends came to school here, and I hadn't made any new friends. I met this guy who wasn't that great or anything, but he was interested, and I got involved fast—too fast. It wasn't like me, and ever since I've thought I was stupid. But now I understand that the unfamiliar context made me feel I needed to belong with somebody.

Consider an example to grasp how any single change can infuse the entire system of a personal relationship. If one partner loses his job, that clearly will affect his personal identity. Yet the consequences go beyond just the individual person. Perhaps his self-concept is bruised, and he becomes depressed. This affects how he talks with his girlfriend—maybe he becomes reticent and withdraws into himself. In turn, the change in his interaction style affects how his girlfriend communicates with him—at first she tries to draw him out, but then she gives up and seeks engagement with him less and less. The decline in both quality and quantity of communication between partners affects their satisfaction with the relationship. Feeling uncomfortable in the relationship, the woman increases the time she spends with other friends. Noticing she is enjoying and seeking contact with others leads her boyfriend to feel more dejected and depressed, so he withdraws further. And on and on. When any part of a relationship changes, the entire system alters. Whether changes are small and subtle or abrupt and obvious, they always reverberate through an entire system.

Relationships strive for but cannot maintain complete balance or stability. This can be a tricky point to understand because it involves two contradictory ideas. On the one hand, personal relationships struggle to achieve equilibrium or a balance point. Couples develop regularities—routines, rituals, and taken-for-granted understandings—to order their lives. Over time, these patterns come to feel comfortable and right. Yet, because relationships are dynamic, change is inevitable and continuous. Permutations in partners, contexts, society, and so forth occur, and relationships adapt to accommodate them. Because personal relationships are always in process, they continuously seek new points of equilibrium that cannot be rigidly maintained.

Last year my fiancé graduated and took a job that is 300 miles away; meanwhile, I'm here completing school. We tried to keep things just as they were by calling and writing all the time and one or the other of us driving to visit the other every weekend. But things weren't the same. They can't be when you've always lived by each other and now live 300 miles apart. My grades were dropping, and he wasn't concentrating on making a good impression in his new job. So both of us were starting to resent the relationship, and that affected how we were with each other. Finally, we had a long talk about what each of us needed and how we could manage that and still keep the relationship. We decided to cut calls to just a couple a week and to visit only if we had vacations or breaks. That took a lot of pressure off us and made the relationship work in our new situation, but we surely did fight making the changes, as if they would be bad for us. If you ask me, inertia is the first principle of relationships, and change is the second.

In sum, systems theory highlights the holistic, interrelated, contextual character of personal relationships and the constant tension between impulses to achieve a steady state of balance and to instigate change or adjust to external currents and events.

Social Exchange Theory

A second theory that focuses on interpersonal dynamics is **social exchange theory** (see Brehm, 1992, for a summary), which claims relationships operate according to economic principles. For instance, exchange theorists argue that partners seek to minimize costs and maximize rewards in relationships. According to this theory, each of us seeks relationships that give us many rewards (good companionship, financial security, personal support) and does not involve heavy costs (time, money, effort). Exchange theorists assume that partners conduct, perhaps unconsciously, cost-benefit analyses to see whether they are getting enough rewards in exchange for what the relationship costs them and whether they and partners are being equally or equitably rewarded by the relationship.

A number of scholars regard social exchange theory as very useful in describing key relationship issues (costs and rewards) and in explaining why people do things (to gain rewards, to create or restore equity) and why people stay with or leave relationships (the net outcome of cost-benefit analysis). Bernard Murstein (1997), for instance, claims that exchange principles govern and explain personal

SALLY FORTH reprinted with permission of King Features Syndicate.

relationships. Undoubtedly, we have some self-interested motivations for what we do for others and for our decisions to remain with or end relationships.

Social exchange theories are also valuable in highlighting several key dynamics in personal relationships that are less prominent in other theories of how relationships operate. From social exchange theorists, we've gained insight into how to judge the quality of a current relationship. Research suggests that many of us do this by comparing a specific relationship to a general standard for personal relationships (called the comparison level or CL) and by comparing the current relationships to alternatives that are perceived to be available (called the comparison level of alternatives or CL_{alt}). These two standards offer a convincing explanation of the process by which individuals decide how rewarding a given relationship is and whether it is worth continuing.

Social exchange theory has also focused attention on the critical importance of equity in relationships. Most of us want relationships that are relatively equitable. Thus, we are unhappy when we feel we are investing far more than a partner. We may also feel guilty if we are in a relationship in which our partner invests substantially more than we do. In both cases, the relationships are inequitable and, thus, less satisfying than a more balanced relationship would be. In later chapters of this book, we'll discuss CL, CL_{alt}, and equity in greater detail. For now, recognize that these are useful concepts advanced by social exchange theories.

Despite the intuitive appeal of social exchange theory, some scholars think economic terms and metaphors are inappropriate for describing, explaining, and predicting what happens between intimates (Bochner, 1984; Lannaman, 1991; Mills & Clark, 1982). Steve Duck (1993a) argues vigorously that personal relationships are not motivated by marketplace logic, a claim I have also advanced on several occasions (Wood, 1993a, 1994c, 1998a; Wood, Dendy, Dordek, Germany, Varallo, 1994; Wood & Duck, 1995). Some scholars also think that because personal relationships are based on feelings for particular people, it is impossible to conduct objective analyses of costs and benefits. Intimacy may involve forms of satisfaction that cannot be fully captured by the quantification, comparison, and discreteness that exchange theories assume. Further, in intimate friendships and romances, each partner's rewards and costs are intertwined with those of the other. If you love someone, what is rewarding to him or her is often also rewarding to you. Hence, it may not make sense to think of strictly individual rewards, costs, and net outcomes (Wood, 1998a).

Perhaps the most balanced assessment of exchange theory is that it does shed light on some motives and decisions regarding relationships, but it isn't sufficient to account for all of the feelings and actions in personal relationships and all of the reasons people choose to stay with or end relationships. The same criticism could be made of each of the theories discussed in this chapter. No single theory offers a comprehensive account of how we create and sustain personal relationships. This suggests that the best, the most complete understanding of relationships is informed by multiple theories, each of which provide important insights.

YVONNE

I don't see how anybody could say people who love each other sit around calculating what they get and what they give up and asking whether it is a "fair bargain." That's just not how people think about really intimate relationships. I mean, sure, I sometimes ask if I'm having to give too much, or I think a guy I'm with isn't doing his share. I guess you could call that thinking about rewards and costs, but that's not really what's happening. In that situation, it's more like I'm asking about whether he really cares and is as committed as I am or committed enough. It may be true that nobody likes to be taken advantage of or to make too many sacrifices, but that still isn't how we think about love relationships. At least it isn't how I think about them.

Dialectical Theory

Further insight into how relationships work comes from **dialectical theory.** The most prominent dialectical theorist is Leslie Baxter, who is on the communication faculty at the University of Iowa. She emphasizes that process and contradiction are the two central principles underlying dialectical theory. These two principles resonate well with the processual complexity and evolutionary character of personal relationships. Attention to process clarifies ongoing dynamics that affect how relationships develop and change over time. The emphasis on contradiction highlights interdependency and interaction among competing needs, desires, and feelings.

According to dialectical theory, in most, if not all, personal relationships, partners have to deal with three contradictions (Baxter, 1988, 1990, 1993; Baxter & Montgomery, 1996). The first dialectic is **autonomy and connection.** Every human needs both autonomy (independence or individual identity) and connection with others (closeness or interdependence). In addition to striving to satisfy both of these needs for each individual, partners try to build a relationship that accommodates individual and couple preferences for closeness and independence.

The second dialectic, **novelty and predictability,** identifies tension between desires for stimulation (novelty) and routine (predictability). All of us like a certain amount of habit, because it provides security, comfort, and predictability in our lives. At the same time, we like experiences that are challenging and unexpected. The third dialectic is **openness and closedness.** This tension arises out of companion desires to share thoughts, feelings, and experiences, and also to preserve some personal privacy and boundaries, even with intimates. These three dialectics seem primary to explanations of relational culture, commitment, satisfaction, and stability.

Dialectics are sometimes misunderstood as competing demands that partners choose between. To avoid this confusion, we should realize dialectics are continually in process, not necessarily resolved by simple balances. We should also realize that, although dialectics involve contradiction between oppositional needs, they work in a complementary fashion—each relies on the other. For example, novelty is meaningless unless we also experience routine; being open means something because we understand being closed; we enjoy time alone and independent identity in contrast to time with others and connectedness.

Dialectics are *ongoing relational processes*. They are not settled permanently. We resolve them at given times, but only for that time, and each and every resolution is subject to change. We should also realize that dialectics seldom achieve a homeostatic balance in which a couple maintains a stable equilibrium between contradictory needs. Instead, dialectics are contradictions that generate tension; they instigate action and change, which allows relationships to progress.

Both individuals and personal relationships benefit from preserving both of the needs that make up each dialectic. For instance, a desire for personal privacy qualifies the affiliated need for openness. Without privacy as its companion, the desire for openness could diminish individual identities in a relationship, not to mention creating psychological overload from having to know every aspect of another's life. Likewise, without a desire for openness, seeking privacy could promulgate secrecy and distance between partners. So, it's not always constructive to quell one of the companion needs in dialectics. It seems more constructive to find ways to satisfy both needs and grow from the tension cultivated by their mutual existence. As needs change over time, partners continuously negotiate and renegotiate contradictory desires that infuse and animate their relationships.

Dialectical theory is suited to the intrinsically processual, changeable character of personal relationships. For this reason, it is particularly helpful in understanding, explaining, and predicting the ongoing processes through which intimates create, define, and constantly redefine themselves and their connection. In Chapter 7 we'll discuss dialectical theory further.

REGGIE

The idea of dialectics explains how I feel with my girlfriend. Shirley and I are really tight, and that's not going to change, but my feelings do sometimes. Like for a while I want to be real close and do everything together, and then I just feel really smothered and need to get away from her and the relationship, so maybe I go camping or something for a weekend. I could never understand how I could want to be with her so much one minute and then just want her out of my hair the next. But thinking about how everybody likes to be with others and away from them too helps me see that my feelings are normal.

Turning Points

Finally, we want to consider a relatively new perspective on dynamics in personal relationships. In recent years, a number of scholars have focused on **turning points** that shape intimate relationships (Barge & Musambira, 1992; Graham, 1997; Huston, Surra, Fitzgerald, & Cate, 1981; Kelley, 1997; Siegert & Stamp, 1994). Leslie Baxter and Connie Bullis (1986) define a turning point as "any event or occurrence that is associated with change in relationships" (p. 470).

Turning point research has yielded some interesting insights into how personal relationships progress. For example, Baxter and Bullis (1986) identified 26 turning points in romantic relationships; they reported that, on average, individuals identified nine to ten key turning points in a particular relationship. Other researchers are less interested in the range of turning points than in how specific ones shape relationships. John Siegert and Glen Stamp (1994), for example, focused on the first big fight as a milestone in romantic relationships, and they explored why some couples survived their first major conflict and others did not.

The research that has been done in this area suggests there are four distinct types of turning point events that shape the course of intimacy (Surra & Huston, 1987). *Intrapersonal/normative turning points* occur when one partner or the relationship is assessed against some ideal or widely accepted social standard (he's too old for me; this relationship has too much conflict). *Dyadic turning points* arise directly out of interaction between partners (self-disclosing, making love). *Social network turning points*, as the term implies, involve the influence of one or more individuals in either or both partners' social networks (parents who disapprove of the relationship, friends who like a partner). Finally, *circumstantial turning points* occur when there is influence from factors over which partners have little control (job relocation, natural disasters). Each kind of turning point shapes how a relationship progresses—or dissolves.

SUMMARY

In this chapter, we've taken a first look at some of the main theories that provide insight into personal relationships. As we've seen, understanding how intimate relationships grow and operate requires knowledge of broad cultural contexts, social communities, individuals, and relationship dynamics. Working together, the different theories we've introduced provide an overall framework that allows us to analyze personal relationships.

As I noted early in this chapter, you shouldn't expect to have a detailed knowledge of all of the theories at this time. For now, you should have a basic grasp of each theory and how it works with other theories to help us appreciate the complexities and dynamics of intimate connections. In the chapters that follow, we'll gain a more thorough understanding of specific theories.

FOR FURTHER REFLECTION AND DISCUSSION

1. Prior to this class, you had personal theories that you used to understand, explain, and predict your relationships. What is one theory you did or do apply to friendships? Did or do you apply the same theory to romantic relationships?

2. In your personal relationships, have you experienced the three dialectics discussed in this chapter? Did you find the contradictory needs in each dialectic complemented one another?

3. Discuss the dialectic of novelty/predictability and relationships' tendency to strive for, yet never fully achieve, dynamic equilibrium.

4. Theories covered in this book are based largely on research on middle-class, White, heterosexual Westerners. To appreciate the extent to which theories are culture-specific, discuss how key issues in theories we've considered might differ in cultures where marriages are arranged and in which extended family ties are more the norm than for Whites in the United States.

5. What knowledge schemata do you use when assessing a new acquaintance? Do they differ if you perceive the person as a potential friend or a potential romantic partner?

6. Return to the scenario between Doria and Mark that opened this chapter. How does each theory we have discussed contribute to our understanding of the interaction between them?

RECOMMENDED READINGS

Baxter, L., & Montgomery, B. (1996). *Relating: Dialogues and dialectics.* New York: Guilford.

Collins, P. H. (1986). Learning from the outsider within: The sociological significance of black feminist thought. *Social Problems, 33,* 514–532.

Scarf, M. (1987). *Intimate partners: Patterns in love and marriage.* New York: Random House.

Watzlawick, P., Beavin, J., & Jackson, D. (1967). *Pragmatics of human communication: A study of interactional patterns, pathologies, and paradoxes.* New York: Norton.

Wood, J. T. (1998). *But I thought you meant . . .: Misunderstandings in human communication.* Mountain View, CA: Mayfield.

Wood, J. T., & Inman, C. C. (1992). In a different mode: Masculine styles of communicating closeness. *Journal of Applied Communication Research, 21,* 279–295.

Communication:

The Central Dynamic

in Personal Relationships

Communication difficulties are probably the most common type of problem encountered in couples who seek assistance to improve their interpersonal relationships. Among the frequently heard complaints are that partners argue, quarrel, nag, insult, or put each other down; that they talk past each other, don't say what they mean, mislead, talk out of both sides of their mouths, or lie; that they can't or won't understand what is said, or ignore each other; that they talk too much, too little.

RELATIONSHIP COUNSELOR EDWIN THOMAS (1977, p. 1) made this statement based on years of working with couples who were having difficulties in their relationships. Thomas is correct in noting that communication has a major impact on what happens in relationships and on how we feel about them. Many scholars, in fact, regard communication as the primary process that creates and sustains intimacy (Baxter, 1988; Berger & Kellner, 1975; Bochner, 1984; Duck & Pond, 1989; Shotter, 1993; Wood, 1982, 1992, 1998b). Marital therapists (Gottman & Carrère, 1994; Walsh, 1993) concur and note that teaching communication skills is a cornerstone of marital therapy.

This chapter focuses on communication, which is the heart of intimacy. Drawing on theories and research introduced in Chapter 2, we will explore how communication between partners constructs the meaning of intimacy and influences the structure and satisfaction of relationships. To launch our discussion, we will first define communication in some detail. Building on that, we will discuss seven premises about communication that will give us a rich appreciation of this process and its importance.

The importance of communication in personal relationships is not restricted to especially challenging situations such as conflict. Actually, the closeness and satisfaction partners feel is based primarily on casual conversation and undramatic moments. How partners communicate on a day-to-day, moment-to-moment basis is critical to the quality of the relationships they create. Steve Duck (1990) asserts that the routine talk between intimate partners—the often mundane small talk—*is* the real relationship. Communication, then, is a central, generative process of intimacy that profoundly shapes what we experience as relationships.

Clearly, relationships involve more than communication. Not all problems are communication problems, and communication won't solve every challenge partners face. However, there are at least two reasons why understanding communication and becoming proficient in it are critical to the process of building and sustaining intimacy. First, many tensions between intimates do result from ineffective communication, and these can be avoided or diminished by learning how particular interaction patterns tend to enrich or damage relationships. Second, even problems that do not result directly from communication are compounded when intimates lack the insights and skills to communicate competently. In other words, even problems that are not inherently communication problems can be managed when partners know how to communicate in competent, affirming ways.

DAMIAN

We learned the hard way that you have to be able to communicate to keep a marriage together. My wife, Janene, and I talked past each other all the time. We just didn't understand each other, so we were always getting hurt or angry or frustrated when we tried to discuss things. Because we were both in graduate school, we qualified for free counseling at the university. What we found out was that we had really different communication styles. She liked to talk through a problem and analyze it a lot more than I found useful, so after a point I'd tune her out and she'd be hurt. My style was to identify a problem and move straight to solutions without lingering on all of the details about it, and to her that felt like I was shortchanging our marriage and her. Our counselor helped us identify what each of us needed from the other, and we learned to hear each other. Now we understand each other better, and we can talk about things, even tough issues. Our marriage is a lot stronger now.

COMMUNICATION AS SYMBOLIC INTERACTION

Recalling Chapter 2's preliminary discussion of symbolic interaction, you'll remember that communication is the process of creating meaning by interacting with and through symbols. As we interact with and through symbols, we develop and share meanings for ourselves and our actions, others and their actions, and relationships. Viewing communication as symbolic interaction highlights the importance of symbols to humans and the relationships they form. Symbols are the doorway to **meaning,** which is central to human life. Meaning is constructed as individuals use symbols—verbal and nonverbal—to interpret and share experiences with one another.

Through interaction with symbols we define ourselves, others, and relationships. We interact with others through symbolic exchanges that allow us to express our feelings, thoughts, needs, and understandings and to coordinate ours with those of others. Finally, if communication is a process of constructing meaning, then it is both dynamic and systemic, qualities we discussed in Chapter 2. To recap, because communication is dynamic, it is an ongoing, ever-evolving process. Because it is systemic, it both is a holistic system and embedded within other systems, or contexts, that influence what occurs and how individuals interpret experiences. This means that our symbolic interactions with others are always, inevitably unfinished—ongoing, ever changing, eternally open to further **interpretation.**

Symbols

Because symbols are the nucleus of communication, we need to understand what they are and how they work. A number of philosophers (Burke, 1968; Cassirer, 1944; Langer, 1953, 1979) believe that what most clearly distinguishes us from nonhuman creatures is our advanced capacity to use symbols. In an interview, Alfonso Caramazza, a neuroscientist who specializes in symbolic activity, said, "Language is quintessentially the thing that makes us different from the animals" (Bishop, 1993, p. A1). Our capacity to symbolize enriches our lives immeasurably, making it possible for us to reflect on ourselves, dream, plan, remember, evaluate, and consider options to our present, concrete situation. At the same time, symbolizing complicates our lives because it compels us to analyze and consider alternative interpretations of ourselves and our experiences, to perceive selectively, and to be frustrated by discrepancies between what we have or are and what we can envision having or being. To better understand how our symbolic abilities influence relationships, we'll define symbols and then explore their critical impact on our lives.

A **symbol** is an arbitrary, ambiguous, and abstract representation of something else such as a person, event, thought, feeling, or object (Wood, 1992). All language and much nonverbal behavior is symbolic, but not all symbols are words or nonverbal communication. Nonlinguistic symbols such as art and music may also represent moods, feelings, and experiences. A symbol might stand for a person (a pet name for a buddy), an object (a photo of a wedding), a process (the arrows on highway signs direct traffic), an event (a birthday gift), a relationship (a wedding band), or anything else. Because many difficulties in communication arise out of the arbitrary, ambiguous, and abstract character of symbols, we'll probe these further.

Symbols are arbitrary. Something is **arbitrary** if there is no necessary or absolute association between it and what it represents. There is no direct connection between the actual process of communicating and the word *communication*. We might as easily symbolize the process with the word *buzzing* or *tango*. Further, because communication is systemic, the meaning of a symbol varies from one context to another. For example, we speak of communication between people, computers, and networks; we speak of mass communication, interpersonal communication, nonverbal communication, and intercultural communication. The meaning of the symbol "communication" varies in each usage.

The arbitrariness of symbols has implications for personal relationships. Words such as *marriage* and *love* have no natural relationship to any referents. The association between symbols and what they symbolize is a matter of convention and agreement: We agree to use the term *marriage* to designate a specific arrangement between heterosexual people and *love* to refer to an intense and positive feeling. Agreeing to use words in consistent ways is convenient. Indeed, as George Herbert Mead realized, it would be impossible to have a society or to share meanings with others if we didn't have agreements about what symbols mean. However, this should not obscure the fact that the particular symbols we agree to use are always arbitrary. Other symbols would work as well if everyone used them consistently.

In relationships, the way we label experiences affects how we perceive and feel about them (Fincham, Bradbury, & Scott, 1990; Harvey, Weber, & Orbuch, 1990). Calling a friend "insensitive" is likely to cause hurt and arouse defensiveness. On the other hand, saying "I don't feel you're paying attention to my concerns" lays the foundation for a constructive conversation about what is happening. The label we choose affects how we think about the friend and how the friend perceives and responds to us. Aaron Beck (1988), a distinguished cognitive therapist, maintains that the language we use in describing relationships and partners is a primary influence on how we experience them. Beck reports that partners in distressed relationships tend to use far more negative symbols to refer to their relationships and each other than do partners in healthy relationships.

Beck's clinical observations are amply supported by empirical research that reveals a link between relationship dissatisfaction and negative symbolization of the relationship (Bradbury & Fincham, 1990; Fincham & Bradbury, 1987; Gottman, 1979; Gottman & Carrère, 1994). Negative labels promote dissatisfaction because we react to the label we have used, not to the concrete person or behavior we label. In counseling, Beck advises partners to question negative labels and to practice using more positive words to refer to each other and relationship matters.

Symbols are ambiguous. If something is **ambiguous,** its meaning is unclear, open to more than one interpretation. Symbols are ambiguous because what they mean is not clear-cut. Unlike natural signals, such as red berries that indicate a plant is poisonous, symbols don't have uniform, unvarying meanings. For example, the word *marriage* means different things to different people. To one person marriage may symbolize a sacred, religious joining of lives, yet to another it is a legal contract devoid of spiritual significance. To some people marriage is an ideal state; to others, it is something to be avoided. In cultures where marriages are arranged, love is not presumed to be necessary for marriage.

Because individuals' experiences vary so widely, they often attribute different meanings to the same symbols. Individuals with secure attachment styles, for example, are likely to regard intimacy as desirable. Yet people with fearful or preoccupied styles may perceive intimacy as dangerous or even as impossible (Harrison-Greer, 1991). For a person who learned the word *love* in the context of hearing it used by his father who battered him and his mother, love may be linked to abuse (Gelles & Loeseke, 1993). For someone whose parents were tender with each other, the word *love* is unlikely to be associated with abusive behavior. Current research indicates that some battered women and battering men may regard abuse as part of normal relationships between men and women (Barnett & LaViolette, 1993; Goldner, Penn, Scheinberg, & Walker, 1990; Jacobson & Gottman, 1998).

Think about the many ways we use the word *love*: I love my partner; I love my cat; I love broccoli; I love my job; I love America. Even in the context of personal relationships, love means different things. A number of years ago a psychiatrist (Meerloo, 1952) identified a variety of things love means to different people: I love you because you love me; I want something you can offer that I cannot provide for myself; I want you to let me take care of you; I want you to take care of me; I desire a sexual relationship with you.

Although meanings clearly vary among individuals, within a given society there is usually a range of meanings people share for most verbal and nonverbal symbols. As symbolic interaction theory points out, we are socialized into a common social world that includes general agreements about what things mean. Through the process of communicating with others, we learn the social meanings on which our culture has agreed, and this makes it likely that the majority of people will share basic meanings for ideas and experiences that are important in their society. To these social meanings we each add unique twists that reflect our individual experiences (Duck, 1994a). This explains why Beverly Fehr (1993) found that people in the United States generally agree on the core elements that define love (trust and support, for example) and also that individuals augment the social view with more idiosyncratic understandings, based on their unique experiences. Thus, symbols have both shared social meanings and personal ones.

Misunderstandings between people often arise because symbols are ambiguous (Wood, 1998b). First, friends and romantic partners may communicate vaguely with the result that meanings are unclear (Beck, 1988). For example, if someone asks you a question and you say, "I don't know," you may be indicating that you don't know the answer, don't care about it, aren't interested in having a conversation, or are angry and giving the silent treatment. If a wife says to her husband, "Please help out more around the house," what does it mean? Does it mean cooking half of the meals, doing more housekeeping chores, or cleaning out the overstuffed closets? Researchers report that husbands and wives in dual-worker families often have different understandings of what a fair share of homemaking and child care means. Does it mean that each partner should do exactly half of the work? Many women think it does, but many men perceive "doing a fair share" as doing more than their fathers did (Hochschild with Machung, 1989; Wood, 1998b). Without further clarification, women use themselves and men use their fathers as the standard for what "doing a fair share" means. Stress is likely to result, because inequity in homemaking tasks is a major source of marital discontent and divorce (Fowers, 1991; Suitor, 1991; Zietlow & Sillars, 1988).

Somewhat less obvious is a second way that ambiguity may foster relationship snarls. Words and nonverbal behaviors are intrinsically imprecise, yet we often act as if what they mean to us is *the true* meaning. I recall being hurt some time ago when a friend didn't give me a gift for Christmas. As she opened my present to her and had none for me, I felt she didn't value our friendship or me very highly. Several months afterward when she gave me a gift not tied to any occasion, I learned she dislikes giving on an external, obligatory schedule and prefers to give spontaneously. Another incident during the opening years of my marriage further illustrates the ambiguity of symbolic activities. Having been brought up to believe politeness demanded writing thank-you notes for gifts, I dutifully wrote to thank my in-laws for presents they gave us, and I wondered why they didn't send thank-you notes to us. Later I discovered they considered notes stilted and, thus, inappropriate among family members. Although amusing in retrospect, neither incident was humorous at the time. Both illustrate the human tendency to assume others share *our* meanings, a fallacy underlying much misunderstanding.

DENISE

I've been seeing this guy for a while and he's pretty cool in most ways, but he's kind of conservative about men's and women's roles. He always expects me to do the cooking and clean up afterward, or whenever I say something about athletics he laughs and says, "What do you know about sports?" Well, I finally got fed up with this a couple weeks ago and told him I wished he wouldn't be so chauvinistic. Then I noticed that he stopped opening car doors for me and quit leaving these cute little notes for me to find. When I asked him why he'd stopped all of these nice things, he told me I was the one who told him to quit being a chauvinist. I guess he thought I didn't want him to open a door or send romantic cards, but that wasn't what I meant at all. Now that we've talked he understands what I meant, but he still hasn't cooked anything!

Effective communication requires realizing that symbols are ambiguous and mean different things to different people. In turn, this suggests two guidelines for interaction: First, it's unwise to assume our symbols mean to others what they do to us. Second, it's equally imprudent to think we automatically understand what our intimates mean by their words and actions. Whether expressing ourselves or listening to others, we need to check on the correspondence between meanings.

Symbols are abstract. A third quality of symbols is that they are abstract, which means that they stand for ideas, people, events, and objects, but they are not themselves the things they represent. They are abstracted from what they represent. Some symbols are more abstract than others. Love, for instance, is highly abstract, because it refers to a broad class of phenomena; romantic love is less abstract, because it refers to one kind of love; the love between two specific partners is even less abstract.

As symbols become more abstract, the potential for misunderstanding expands. In personal relationships, partners sometimes say they want to be "closer" or "more in touch with each other." The concrete experiences we have in mind when we use such phrases, however, are less than clear. Research indicates that men tend to experience closeness by doing things with others, whereas women more typically create closeness through intimate dialogue (Inman, 1996; Johnson, 1996; Wood, 1986, 1994a, 1996, 1998b, 1999; Wood & Inman, 1993). Thus, "I'd like to be closer" may lead to misunderstanding between women and men.

Another communication behavior tied to the abstractness of symbols is overgeneralization, which Aaron Beck considers one of the most troublesome problems in intimacy (1988). Because symbols are abstract, they allow us to classify and generalize experiences (Wood, 1992). Although useful in many respects, generalizing may also cause problems. For instance, a broad conclusion based on one or two incidents is usually inaccurate. Negative overgeneralizations are particularly damaging to relationships: "You always ignore my wishes," "You never do what I want," "He's chronically irresponsible," "She's never on time."

Abstracting both directs and limits perception. On the one hand, we heighten awareness of particular phenomena by abstracting them from the flow of experience and labeling them for our attention. At the same time, the labels we impose suppress perception of all that we have not symbolized. For instance, if Leon forgets his girlfriend Minada's birthday, she might say to herself, "He's not a caring person." Defining him as uncaring shapes Minada's perceptions of Leon and the relationship. Research indicates, for instance, that she will be likely to notice other behaviors that could be interpreted as uncaring because her label makes them salient to her (Brehm, 1992; Fincham & Bradbury, 1987). At the same time, because she has abstractly symbolized Leon as uncaring, she's not likely to recall he skipped a big game to help her move, gives her gifts when there is no special occasion, and in other ways shows he cares about her. The symbols we use powerfully direct and limit our perceptions of others and relationships (Shotter, 1993).

Realizing that symbols are abstract and ambiguous reminds us that misunderstandings between people are bound to occur. To compensate for the abstractness of symbols, intimates may clarify expressions of feelings and ideas. Consider the difference between saying to a partner, "I want you to quit being so inconsiderate" and "I wish that you would check with me before you make plans for both of us." The former statement is quite abstract, which leaves it open to various interpretations and fails to specify what is wanted. The second statement is more concrete, so partners are more likely to ascribe similar meanings to it. Because abstract statements invite misunderstanding, communication scholars Bobby Patton and Kurt Ritter (1976) advise intimates to make communication specific, saying, "I feel put down when you look away when we talk," instead of "You always ignore me."

Symbols and Meaning

In sum, human communication is a highly complex symbolic process. Because we symbolize, we are able to lift ourselves out of merely physical existence and into the human world of meaning (Cassirer, 1944). For this reason, Jonathan Shotter (1993) argues that we construct our realities through language. The language partners use to talk about themselves and each other shapes their perceptions of each other and their shared relationship. Our reliance on symbols also moves us into a realm teeming with potential misunderstanding. Because symbols are abstract, arbitrary, and ambiguous, individuals rarely, if ever, assign identical meanings to words and nonverbal behaviors. Thus, a principle of effective relationship communication is to monitor correspondence of meanings between partners.

In most enduring relationships, partners gradually figure out each other's personal vocabularies and develop a number of common understandings that allow them to inhabit a shared world of meaning. This transpires over time through an extended process of talking, listening, clarifying, and negotiating meanings. Yet even serious efforts to understand each other will not yield absolutely equivalent meanings, because partners remain unique individuals whose personal experiences shape what things mean to them. Thus, the potential for misunderstanding is constant, as is the need to keep checking on each other's interpretations.

PREMISES ABOUT COMMUNICATION

Our discussion of symbols makes it clear that communication is not simply a straightforward exchange of information. As we communicate in personal relationships, we try to understand others' meanings and make our own meanings clear to them. We also work out values, identities, patterns of interacting, and goals for our relationships. Communication, then, makes things happen — it generates meanings, relationship structures, and partners' identities. In the pages that follow, we'll discuss ten premises that help us unravel the process by which intimate partners use symbols to create meaning for themselves and their relationships. Table 3.1 summarizes the premises we will discuss.

1. Communication Is Rule Guided

Although communication may seem to flow freely in personal relationships, actually it is structured by what scholars call communication **rules.** This means that we tend to follow rules about how, when, where, and to whom to communicate. The fact that rules guide our communication does not mean that rules *determine* our communication. When we say that communication is rule guided, we mean that people generally choose to follow rules but not that they must or that they always adhere to rules. This reminds us that we exercise choice in deciding how to communicate.

The rule-guided character of communication implies that communication is not completely idiosyncratic or spontaneous. Instead, there are observable regularities in how people interact within particular cultures or speech communities (Argyle & Henderson, 1985; Argyle, Henderson, Bond, Iizuka, & Contarello, 1986; Fisher, 1987). For example, most of us follow turn-taking rules in conversation: We understand when we are supposed to speak and when we should let others talk. Similarly, there are rules for greeting rituals, so when a casual acquaintance says, "How ya doing?" we know better than to respond, "I feel awful, my work is out of control, and I just broke up with my partner." Regardless of how we really feel, we're likely to say, "Fine; how are you?" or something equally polite. We also have rules that guide when, to whom, and how much to self-disclose.

Regulative rules. Researchers have identified two kinds of rules that guide how we engage in and interpret communication. The first is **regulative rules,** which regulate interaction by specifying sequences for developing topics, taking turns in conversation, not interrupting, and so forth. Regulative rules tell us when it is okay and not okay for us to speak (do not talk during class); when responses are called for (reply to a direct question unless it is a rhetorical question); what kinds of responses are acceptable (sass peers but not elders); and with whom it is appropriate and inappropriate to talk about particular things (talk to friends but not parents about partying; don't introduce controversial or unpleasant topics during dinner).

Regulative rules reflect both personal and social influences. When you were a child, perhaps your parents told you, "*Please* and *thank you* are magic words." If so, you may have a regulative rule that tells you to use those words when you ask for and get things. If your parents argued in front of you, you may have a regulative rule that says it is appropriate to engage in conflict in public settings. Do your

TABLE 3.1

Premises About Communication in Personal Relationships

1. Communication is rule guided.

2. Communication involves two levels of meaning.

3. Individuals punctuate communication.

4. Contexts of communication affect meanings.

5. Meanings are not necessarily shared by partners.

6. Listening is at least as important as talking.

7. Metacommunication can improve relationships.

8. Dual perspective is critical for effective communication in personal relationships.

9. Communication is not always consistent.

10. In personal relationships, partners affect each other.

friends routinely interrupt each other during conversations? Within masculine speech communities, interruptions aren't usually perceived as impolite. Within feminine speech communities, however, interruptions are often considered impolite unless they function to show interest in what the speaker is saying (Tannen, 1990; Wood, 1998b).

Regulative rules also reflect broadly shared understandings within a particular society. Because Western culture encourages individualism and assertiveness, most Westerners consider it appropriate to say no to others who make proposals that don't interest them. Japanese culture, on the other hand, emphasizes commitment to groups and avoiding directly refusing others because that would make them lose face (Cathcart & Cathcart, 1997). Even within a single society, different speech communities may operate according to distinct regulative rules. Many African Americans are socialized to be more communal than many European Americans. This emphasis on community explains the call-and-response pattern in Black churches and Black community gatherings. Janice Hamlet (1994), a scholar of intercultural communication, explains that when a preacher preaches or a speaker speaks in a Black community, the listeners are expected to answer back vocally. This is considered positive involvement within the particular speech community.

Regulative rules are especially evident in the cultural script for romance. A 1989 study (Rose & Frieze) found nearly unanimous agreement among college students on rules for what men and women should do on a first date: Both sexes expected men to initiate and plan activities, women to facilitate dialogue, and women to defer to men except on sexual activities. The fact that most people operate by the same rules regarding dating reflects Mead's idea that through interaction, members of a society develop and act on shared understandings.

Constitutive rules. The second type of rule is the constitutive rule. **Constitutive rules** define the meaning of communication by indicating what counts as what. For instance, two people in a romantic relationship may count disclosing personal information as increasing intimacy. They might also count asking about each other's day as showing interest.

A communication philosopher named John Searle (1976) referred to the concrete things that we say and do as brute facts. Distinct from brute facts are the meanings for actions and words, which are guided by the constitutive rules that tell us how to interpret brute facts. Constitutive rules, just like regulative ones, reflect both personal and social experiences. If you grew up in a family that displayed physical affection, you may have a constitutive rule that says hugs and kisses count as affection. However, if your family of origin was not physically demonstrative, then you may have a constitutive rule that says hugs and kisses are imposing or inappropriate. Some families teach us the constitutive rule that meals count as the time for people to share their lives and thoughts. In other families, meals count as the period to watch the evening news.

Cultures and speech communities also influence our constitutive rules. Many people who grow up in Jewish communities learn to engage in a ritual form of griping called kvetching. Kvetching is not serious complaining or requests for assistance in dealing with problems. Thus, it is inappropriate to suggest solutions to the issues a person kvetches about. Instead, members of Jewish speech communities understand kvetching is a means of venting frustrations that don't require analysis or solutions.

The rules governing communication are *relatively* stable, not absolutely fixed. Like everything else in relationships, the rules guiding communication are in process and subject to change. Until a rule that partners are using creates problems, however, it tends to be followed. For example, friends have regularized greeting rituals: hugs, slaps on the back, handshakes, or just jumping into conversation. Although the content of greeting patterns varies, regularized patterns of greeting are constant across friendships. Similarly, intimates devise rules for managing conflict (Burgess, 1981; Honeycutt, Woods, & Fontenot, 1993), making decisions, and

SALLY FORTH reprinted with permission of King Features Syndicate.

expressing affection (Argyle & Henderson, 1984; Beck, 1988; Fitzpatrick, 1988; Jones & Gallois, 1989; Thomas, 1977).

Rules typically followed in social relationships differ in an important way from those that partners use to guide interaction in a personal relationship. As symbolic interactionism points out, we're socialized into cultural values and patterns that exist prior to any individual. These rules are primarily external and established, and we have to learn them to participate competently in the social world. In intimacy, however, partners have greater freedom to create rules that suit their personal needs and preferences (Phillips & Wood, 1983). In intimacy, or what is often called "the private zone," we can be creative in developing patterns that may depart from social norms (Berger & Kellner, 1975; Wood, 1982).

For instance, because both my partner and I work a great deal in our home, we have an understanding that we don't interrupt each other in our dens unless there is an emergency. When my mother lived with us in the final 14 months of her life, she initially found this odd, because she was used to free interaction among family members in the home. Her rule had been functional in my family of origin where work and home were separate. After living with us for several months, Mom commented that our rule made sense to her, because she saw that work and home merged in our lives.

Particularly important in our understanding of how rules guide meaning in intimate interaction is realizing that we do not have to be aware of rules and regularities to follow them. In fact, for the most part we're not conscious of rules—until they are violated, at which point we realize we had an expectancy (Argyle & Henderson, 1985; Honeycutt, Woods, & Fontenot, 1993). In a 1991 study, Victoria DeFrancisco found clear patterns in which husbands interrupt wives and discourage topics wives initiate, and wives continue to suggest topics until one is found that husbands want to discuss. Couples were unaware of these rules and the relationship patterns they sustain. Learning to recognize our rules and the patterns of interaction they sustain enables us to alter those that do not serve us well. Sean illustrates this point in an entry from his journal.

S E A N

Bob and I have been buddies since high school, and we hang out together all the time. But this one thing keeps happening. I'll tell him something good that happened to me like I did well on a test or got accepted into Stanford's law school. And he always says something like, "I really aced all my exams too" or "I got accepted at Brown." No matter what I say, he has to best me. So then I say, "Well, Brown has lower standards than Stanford." And it keeps going from there. The rule I see now is that each of us competes to better the other, and each move one of us makes provokes the countermove from the other. I wanted to change this pattern between us so I didn't take the bait the last time Bob and I were talking. I mentioned I'd made the cut to finalists for a scholarship I want, and, sure enough, Bob came back by saying he'd gotten a financial aid package from Brown. Instead of trying to top him, I said, "That's great, Bob." A little later he said to me he was pleased I was a finalist.

Sean's insight is important: When we learn to identify rules, we empower ourselves to alter ones that we find unhealthy or undesirable. Counselors point out that couples rarely recognize communication rules that pattern how they handle conflict (Beck, 1988; Gottman & Carrère, 1994; Gottman & Levenson, 1988; Gottman, Markman, & Notarius, 1977; Schaef, 1981; Thomas, 1977; Watzlawick, Beavin, & Jackson, 1967). John Gottman (1979) found clear, consistent differences between conflict patterns of distressed and satisfied couples. Most notably, partners in distressed relationships tended to focus on themselves and to respond to complaints with countercomplaints. Satisfied couples were more likely to acknowledge partners' complaints (which isn't always agreeing) and to focus on each other and the relationship as well as themselves. Similarly, Bobby Patton and Kurt Ritter (1976) note that healthy relationships are promoted by rules that validate partners and accept responsibility for one's own feelings.

2. Communication Involves Two Levels of Meaning

A number of years ago, a group of therapists working with troubled families (Watzlawick, Beavin, & Jackson, 1967) realized that many interpersonal problems result from difficulties in communication. Analysis of these problems led them to discover that there are two levels of meaning in all communication. The first level of meaning, which we're all aware of, is referred to as the **content level of meaning.** This refers to the literal or denotative meaning of communication. For instance, assume that Shelley tells her boyfriend Joe that she's frustrated that her roommate is sloppy, and he replies, "You need to tell her to clean up her stuff." The content level of Shelley's message is that she is frustrated that her roommate is sloppy. The content meaning of Joe's reply is his suggestion that Shelley tell her roommate to clean up. Content meaning is the literal, informational content of a message.

Although we tend to be less aware of the second level of meaning, it generally has greater impact on relationships. Called the **relationship level of meaning,** it defines partners and the relationship between them. The relationship level of meaning has to do with the interpersonal significance of messages. There are three dimensions of relationship level meaning (Mehrabian, 1981). The first is power: Our messages can suggest that we feel superior, equal, or inferior to others. The second dimension is affection or liking: Messages can express friendliness, love, distance, or hostility. Third, relationship level meanings may indicate responsiveness: Messages may show we are attentive or inattentive to others (Figure 3.1).

Let's look back at the exchange between Shelley and Joe. On the relationship level, the meaning of Shelley's communication was that she wanted to share her feelings with Joe. To her, Joe's advice may feel like a lack of responsiveness to her feelings because he didn't express empathy. Further, she might interpret advice as meaning he feels superior in knowing how to handle the situation and presuming to advise her.

Because the relationship level of meaning reflects and affects how people feel about each other, it often guides how we interpret content. For example, if you tell a friend who's been ribbing you to "get lost" and grin as you say it, the relationship level of meaning makes it clear not to take the content level seriously. Your friend would know that you do not literally mean for him to go away but that you are joking. "You shouldn't have gotten me such an extravagant gift," said by someone smiling widely, suggests the relationship meaning is "I am touched you cared so much about me," which is clearly not the content meaning. Similarly, when an intimate snarls, "Nothing's wrong," the clear relationship level meaning is that something is *very* wrong indeed!

Nonverbal communication is especially powerful in conveying relationship level meanings (Brehm, 1992; Burgoon, Buller, Hale, & deTurck, 1988; Fletcher & Fitness, 1990; Sallinen-Kuparinen, 1992). Smiles, frowns, or dancing eyes indicate how we feel about another and what is happening between us. Similarly, vocal qualities such as volume and pitch convey warmth or coldness, equality or superiority, and responsiveness or distance, all of which are messages about the relationship (Patterson, 1988). Particularly interesting is the recurrent finding that unhappy partners sustain negative relationship climates by reciprocating negative nonverbal behaviors such as frowns and glares (Gottman & Levenson, 1988; Halford, Hahlweg, & Dunne, 1990). Relatedly, spouses in happy marriages exchange fewer negative and more positive nonverbal behaviors than do dissatisfied spouses (Gottman, Markman, & Notarius, 1977; Noller, 1982, 1985).

Gendered standpoints also influence how we interpret and enact nonverbal behaviors. In a study mentioned earlier in this chapter, Victoria DeFrancisco (1991) found that failure to respond or a delayed response to a partner's communi-

FIGURE 3.1

Dimensions of Relationship Level Meaning

Power	Affection	Responsiveness
Superiority: I know what's best. Equality: Let's work together to solve this problem. Inferiority: I'll defer to you.	Friendliness: I want to spend more time with you. Distance: Stay away from me. Hostility: You irritate me.	Attentiveness: I'm listening; Tell me more. Inattentiveness: I don't have time to listen to you. I didn't catch what you said.

cation was often interpreted on the relationship level as meaning the nonrespond-ing person was uninterested and felt superior to the person initiating communica-tion. In her study, husbands accounted for 68 percent of failures to respond and 70 percent of delayed responses. Not only are men generally less responsive than women, but they also tend to take less initiative in maintaining conversation and connection by asking others what they think (Canary & Stafford, 1992; Dainton & Stafford, 1993).

Relationship level meanings, which Aaron Beck (1988, p. 75) calls "hidden meanings" in intimate dialogue, are typically more important to the emotional tone of a relationship and feelings between partners than content meanings. It is on the relationship level of meaning that we indicate we do or don't care about others, we are or aren't interested in what they say, we do or don't understand their feelings, and we do or don't regard them as equals. These hidden meanings chart the emotional climate of intimacy.

3. Individuals Punctuate Communication

You learned about punctuation in English composition classes. Just as we use com-mas, periods, and other punctuation marks to divide written language into units, we punctuate oral communication by marking in our minds when it starts and stops (Watzlawick, Beavin, & Jackson, 1967). **Punctuation** is our perception of the beginnings and endings of communicative encounters.

We cannot tell what something means until we first establish its bound-aries—where it starts and stops. In communication, we do this by defining the onset and conclusion of particular interactions. For example, arriving home from work, Mike approaches Susan, his wife, holding a large box of gourmet truffles and says "a gift for you." What has Mike communicated, and what does it mean? Al-though on first glance it seems obvious he's expressing affection for Susan, we can-not interpret this interaction until we establish its boundaries. Perhaps Mike battered Susan last night, and it's just the latest episode in a long history of abuse. Every time he beats her, he follows up with apologies and gifts for days afterward. Known as the honeymoon period (Wood, 1999), attentiveness in the wake of abuse is typical of the battering syndrome. So Susan perceives the truffles as an act of re-pentance, not love (notice she is applying a constitutive rule to decide what his ac-tion means). She doesn't smile or accept the gift because she thinks that would indicate she forgives him. Notice she punctuates the communication as starting long before this moment when Mike appears with the truffles. In this case, she may also punctuate the end of the interaction as further episodes of abuse, because more battering has previously followed the honeymoon phase.

A second possibility is that Mike brought the truffles only two days after he and Susan had a long talk about wanting to treat themselves better and to include more luxuries in their daily life. In the context of that conversation, Susan sees his gift as a follow-through on their pledge to make themselves feel special. Thus, she might apply a constitutive rule that says the truffles count as affirmation of a jointly made commitment to enrich their relationship. What this or any communication means depends on how we punctuate it.

There is no right punctuation; it's a matter of interpretation, and that, as we've seen, depends on individuals' experiences, cognitive tendencies, and working models. Many misunderstandings between friends and romantic partners arise because they do not realize their divergent punctuations lead them to attribute different meanings to interactions. One of the most common examples of this is the demand-withdraw or pursuer-distancer pattern (Bergner & Bergner, 1990; Christensen & Heavey, 1990; James, 1989; Napier, 1977) in which one partner attempts to create closeness and the other strives for distance. The more the pursuer demands intimacy, the more the distancer withdraws; the more the distancer retreats, the harder the pursuer tries to escalate closeness. Each punctuates interaction as starting with the other's action and sees her or his behavior as a response. Thus, the pursuer punctuates this way: "I keep pushing for closeness because you withdraw," and the distancer punctuates this way: "I retreat because you pursue me" (Figure 3.2).

Which punctuation is correct? This interaction, like most, is a cycle, and there is no clearly correct punctuation. Becoming conscious of punctuation reminds us that we actively create meaning through patterns we impose. Relatedly, we should realize that others may punctuate differently than we do, and that there is no absolutely right way to punctuate.

Becoming aware of how you punctuate and the arbitrariness of any person's punctuation encourages you to explore how others might punctuate and, consequently, how they might interpret the meaning of communication.

FIGURE 3.2

The Pursuer-Distancer Pattern of Communication

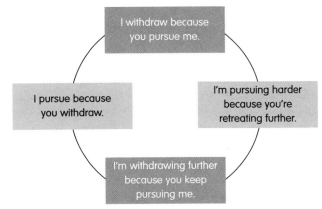

4. Contexts of Communication Affect Meanings

A fourth important premise about communication is that contexts affect meanings. To appreciate how settings influence meaning, let's elaborate on previous discussions of various contexts that influence our interpretations.

Cultural contexts. One major context of all communication is culture, which establishes normative expectations for close relationships and interaction within them. Social structures and practices define which forms of intimacy are socially authorized, who counts as family, what roles women and men are expected to assume, and so forth. In our society, only heterosexuals can marry and receive social and legal recognition of their commitment. Traditionally, the term *family* has referred to blood relatives or people related by marriage. Yet, in her 1991 book *Families We Choose*, Kath Weston argued that families can also be defined as people we care about and who care about us, regardless of whether the connections are legally recognized.

ELLEN

Anne and I have been together for seven years, longer than most of my straight friends have stayed with anyone. Three years ago we had a commitment ceremony, and we gave each other gold rings. When one of us is sick, the other cares for her. We coordinate our time off so we can vacation together. We own property jointly, and we listed each other as beneficiary on our insurance policies. The law may not recognize our commitment, but we are as married and as much family as anyone could be.

Cultural trends such as mobility and technology also contribute to the context for personal relationships, making it more likely that intimates will be separated for periods of time and, simultaneously, increasing the ways they may stay in touch. Social diversity is also part of the contemporary context for intimacy. Interethnic romances were less common and less socially approved in 1970 than they are today. Even if partners deviate from normative prescriptions, cultural values nonetheless shape the environment in which we conduct our relationships.

Personal contexts. Personal contexts also affect how individuals perceive and interpret interaction, as well as their working models of intimacy. Each of us has internalized others' perspectives from our interactions with family, friends, past and current romantic partners, and professional associates. We rely on these perspectives to interpret what happens in our lives, including our personal relationships. Maggie Scarf (1987) points out that a good deal of tension early in marriages results from the fact that the constitutive and regulative rules each spouse learned in their families often conflict. To fashion a satisfying marriage, partners have to work out joint rules to pattern how they interact and how they interpret one another.

HARRISON

It was so weird spending Christmas at my girlfriend's house last year. My family always opens presents on Christmas eve so that we can sleep in the next day. Then we have a huge brunch on Christmas. But Meggan's family opens presents on Christmas morning and the big meal is turkey served midafternoon. I wonder how we'll do Christmas after we're married.

Physical contexts. Communication is also affected by physical environments. Quiet restaurants with private booths invite more lingering, personal engagement than do fast-food eateries (Mehrabian, 1976). Accompanying meals with television or videos discourages conversation between partners. New environments tend to be more stimulating than familiar ones, but familiar ones may be more comfortable. We often feel more cheerful and optimistic on sunny days than on overcast ones. Rooms with chairs placed close to one another invite conversation more than rooms with chairs separated by distance.

Personal physiology. How we communicate and how we interpret our partners are also influenced by personal physiology. Most people tend to be less friendly and responsive when they are tired, stressed, or sick. When we're in pain we are likely to be less understanding and quicker to anger than when we are feeling good physically. Depression also affects how individuals interact with others and how they interpret others' responses to them (Coyne, Burchill, & Stiles, 1990; Segrin, 1993).

Personal biorhythms are yet another context influencing communication. For example, I often awake between 3 and 4 A.M., and I am ready to interact as soon as I arise. Both my partner and my best friend are evening people who wake up slowly and dislike interaction first thing in the morning. I've learned to let Robbie have a cup of coffee and read the paper before launching into any conversations with him. With my friend Nancy, I've learned not to call her before 10 A.M., and she's learned not to call me after 11 P.M. In both relationships, we've worked out ways to accommodate our disparate temporal rhythms.

Individuals' communication changes as they enter new contexts and encounter new perspectives. For instance, a number of studies demonstrate that people who are unassertive become confident communicators when they enter professions that cultivate assertiveness (Epstein, 1968, 1981, 1982; Gordon, 1991; Hatcher, 1991; Hochschild, 1975; McGowen & Hart, 1990). Similarly, Barbara Risman (1989) found that men who were primary caregivers of young children developed skill in nurturing and attending to others. This reminds us that communication—as well as individuals, relationships, and contexts—is an evolving process. Being aware that contexts, ranging from society to personal biorhythms, influence interaction enables intimates to take into account the multiple contexts that influence what occurs and what it means.

5. Meanings Are Not Necessarily Shared by Partners

A fifth premise about communication follows from ones we've already discussed: Intimates don't necessarily share meanings for their communication. Misunderstandings occur when people don't share meanings. Misunderstandings are compounded when people don't realize that they have different meanings for their communication. In the earlier example of a conversation between Shelley and Joe, he thought her comment was a request for him to help her figure out how to deal with a sloppy roommate. Shelley, however, meant the comment as a request for him to acknowledge that she was feeling frustrated. When he offered advice, he meant to be helpful, but she perceived his suggestion as condescending and unfeeling. If neither realizes that they have different meanings, they're likely to feel hurt, confused, or offended.

Personal sources of misunderstandings. Many misunderstandings result from differences in communicators' backgrounds, experiences, values, and constitutive and regulative rules. In my family of origin, bantering and friendly insults were forms of play and connection. (By my family's constitutive rules, bantering counted as affection.) Robbie's family, however, didn't engage in routine teasing and jesting insults. When he and I began dating, he was frequently hurt by my playful barbs and sarcasm, and I was disappointed that he wouldn't play the game with me. (By Robbie's family's constitutive rules, bantering counted as insulting.) Eventually, he learned not to take my verbal jabs literally, and he has even become adept at playing the game. And I learned to curb some of the sharpness of my tongue and to find other ways of playing and showing affection.

Social sources of misunderstandings. Misunderstandings also arise because individuals were socialized in different societies or speech communities. We've already discussed several examples of misunderstanding that reflect cultural differences. Another example is in storytelling style. Deanna Hall and Kristen Langellier (1988) reported that generally women employ a less linear form of storytelling than men. Women are more likely than men to add details and side comments and to invite others to interact in the process of telling a story. Men more typically tell a story in straightforward linear fashion, moving from one major event to another and not adding details beyond the bare bones of the story. Given these differences, it's not surprising that men and women are sometimes frustrated by each other's style of storytelling. Frank is frustrated when he asks Margaret about her day and she replies with a detailed account including lots of comments he considers entirely extraneous and irrelevant. He wishes she would just get to the point. Margaret, on the other hand, perceives Frank as being closed to her because he tells her about his day by summarizing events without saying anything about his feelings and what else was going on. The misunderstandings reflect their respective socialization in masculine and feminine speech communities.

Across cultures, too, there are differences that can lead to misunderstandings. What is considered a comfortable conversational distance in Arabic cultures is perceived as intrusive in Western culture (Samovar & Porter, 1997). The amount of casual, social touching that most Westerners perceive as normal is regarded as unacceptable by some citizens of the United Kingdom. Germans do not share Americans' penchant for small talk, so a German might interpret an American's small talk as meaning the American lacks substance or is impolite.

The value of misunderstandings. Although misunderstandings can be unpleasant, they also can enrich us and our relationships (Wood, 1998b). Misunderstandings offer us opportunities to clarify our own perspectives and to enhance self-knowledge. If Shelley **monitors** her interaction with Joe, she may gain insight into what she wants when she mentions problems to him. Consequently, she may be able to communicate her needs more clearly when she talks to Joe and others in the future. Perhaps she could introduce complaints about her roommate by saying, "I don't need help solving this problem. I just want a sympathetic ear."

Misunderstandings also provide valuable insight into others. When others don't understand what we mean, or we don't understand what others mean, it's a clue that we have more to learn about each other. When I saw that Robbie seemed hurt by what I meant as playful bantering, I knew I didn't have full insight into him. This led us to talk about our communication styles and, after that, about interaction dynamics in our respective families. We learned not only how each of us interpreted banter but also about our respective early years in our families. What we learned from that conversation enlarged our insight into each other and, thus, strengthened our relationship.

However uncomfortable misunderstandings can be, they are opportunities to grow as individuals and to enrich our personal relationships. Misunderstandings between people are inevitable. When recognized as opportunities to enhance ourselves, others, and relationships, misunderstandings can cultivate healthy, enduring connections based on awareness of and respect for individual meaning systems.

6. Listening Is at Least as Important as Talking

When you think about communication, what comes to mind? If you're like most Westerners, talking is the first thing you think of. Yet, communication—at least when it's effective—involves at least as much listening as talking. Listening is especially important in personal relationships. It's impossible to know another person intimately if we don't listen carefully and sensitively to what she or he says. Listening allows us to learn about another person's perspective—the thoughts, feelings, values, goals, fears, hopes, and secrets that make that person unique.

Listening is not the same as hearing. We hear whenever sound waves hit our ears. Hearing is a physiological process that requires no special effort. Listening, on the other hand, is a complex activity, and it requires active effort on our part.

Listening is defined as a complex process of attending to, receiving, perceiving, organizing, interpreting, responding, and remembering messages. As this definition suggests, listening is not a single activity but a complex group of activities. Communication scholars agree that listening involves at least five activities, and some scholars include seven activities in the full process of listening (Table 3.2).

The foundation of effective listening is becoming *mindful*, which is choosing to be fully attentive to what is happening in the hear and now. When you attend mindfully to another person, you don't think about what you did before this moment and you don't let your mind wander to what you plan to do later. You don't focus on your own experiences and feelings. Instead, you immerse yourself in the present moment and what another is saying.

Mindfulness is a choice. It requires a conscious decision to attend fully to another. In fact, *not* being mindful is our more normal state. Typically, we're doing more than one thing at once, thinking about our own issues while communicating with others, sorting information and feelings as we interact. To be mindful, we have to disrupt our normal pattern of mindlessness and choose consciously to focus our full attention on another person.

There are gender differences in listening style (Beck, 1988; Hall, 1987; Tannen, 1990). People who are socialized in feminine speech communities (a majority of women and a minority of men) tend to build on others' ideas, respond actively to what others say, and invite others into conversations. Pamela Fishman (1983) terms this style of listening the "maintenance work" of interaction because it functions to maintain communication by including and responding to others. Feminine communicators are more likely than masculine ones to show they are listening by nodding, keeping eye contact, and gesturing in response to messages.

Individuals who are socialized in masculine speech communities (a majority of men and a minority of women) generally learn to be less emotionally expressive. Thus, they give less verbal and nonverbal feedback when listening. They are more likely to give minimal response cues ("uh huh," "yeah") than more elaborate responses ("Wow!" "Really?" "I know just how you feel." "I can't believe you did that." "Go on—I want to hear more.").

ANNIE

My boyfriend drives me crazy with his way of listening. I'll be telling him about something that happened to me and I'll see he's not looking at me while I'm talking. He never gives me any feedback that shows he's following or interested. And then I'll get mad and say, "I'm going to quit talking since you aren't listening," and he'll recite back to me everything I said. He really is listening, but it just doesn't feel like it.

Annie's journal entry reminds us not to make the mistake of thinking a particular style of listening is the only, or best, style. Masculine and feminine social-

TABLE 3.2

The Listening Process

1. Becoming mindful	Focusing on another person and the present moment; giving full attention
2. Physically receiving messages	Receiving a message, either through audio signals and sound waves or through other means such as seeing nonverbal communication or American Sign Language
3. Selectively perceiving	Selecting aspects of noise or messages for focus; distinguishing what's important from what is not
4. Organizing what has been received	Grouping information together; noting connections among ideas; linking this message to previous knowledge
5. Interpreting	Assigning meaning to the selected and organized material; drawing conclusions about what the communication means
6. Responding	Demonstrating interest and attention through verbal and nonverbal feedback; asking questions, giving responses, encouraging elaboration
7. Remembering	Retaining what we consider the most important parts of messages and the meanings we've assigned to them

ization teach us different ways of listening and expressing ourselves. The lack of explicit displays of involvement from many men does not necessarily reflect lack of listening. People who don't show signs of interest and attention may well be listening intently. Yet, the fact that someone is listening intently is not the same thing as communicating that she or he is listening. This suggests that the listening style many men learn may not be effective in showing that they are involved in conversations. Finding ways to indicate your attentiveness is advisable if you want your relationship partners to know that you are listening and that you care about what they say.

What we have discussed suggests two guidelines for effective listening in personal relationships. First, we should recognize and respect different listening styles and not judge any specific style as inherently better than others. Partners in personal relationships should learn how to interpret each other on an individual basis. This means that we should work to understand how our particular partner listens and not necessarily hold him or her to external standards. Second, relationships are enhanced when partners learn to adapt their listening style to each other's expectations. For example, if you tend not to give overt signs of interest when listening and your partner feels you aren't involved in the conversation, then you may want to learn to show attention in ways your partner understands and appreciates. The bottom line is that listening is a critical part of communication in personal relationships, and partners should work together to develop listening habits that satisfy both of them.

7. Metacommunication Can Improve Relationships

Metacommunication is communication about (from the root term *meta*) communication (Watzlawick, Beavin, & Jackson, 1967). When we metacommunicate, we comment on our communication. Sometimes metacommunication is verbal: "What I meant when I said that was . . ." "Don't take this too seriously." "I can't believe we're arguing about this." Metacommunication can also be nonverbal: demonstrating displeasure by grimacing when someone interrupts us, nodding to indicate we like where a conversation is going.

Metacommunication can enhance partners' insight into each other. To assure Annie that he is listening to her, Annie's boyfriend might have said, "I may not give a lot of visible signs that I'm listening, but I am." By commenting on his listening style, he clarifies what it means and helps Annie realize he is attending to her. Metacommunication may also take the form of questions that lead to enlarged understanding between people: Do you realize that you keep interrupting me? Did you understand what I meant when I said. . . ?"

Metacommunication also allows intimates to monitor patterns in their communication and to change ones they perceive as undesirable or unhealthy. Ben might say to Kim, "It seems like all we talk about anymore is small stuff and coordinating our schedules. Do you miss the kind of talk we used to have?" Ben's comment calls attention to a pattern in his communication with Kim, so the two of them can consider whether it is a problem. Partners in personal relationships may metacommunicate to increase their awareness of communication patterns associated with constitutive and regulative rules, casual conversation, decision making, and conflict. By metacommunicating, partners communicate about how they communicate. In turn, this allows them to exert active control over the quality of their communication and, ultimately, their relationship.

8. Dual Perspective Is Critical for Effective Communication in Personal Relationships

Dual perspective is cognitive awareness of both our own and others' perspectives and ideas. If you have dual perspective with a friend or romantic partner, then you can recognize how she or he might interpret experiences, situations, actions, and so forth. Dual perspective is not a synonym for empathy. **Empathy** is the capacity to feel what someone else feels. Because each of us has unique experiences, cognitive schemata, and so forth, how a person feels about anything is highly individualistic. Sometimes we can understand what we would feel if we were in another's situation, but that's not necessarily the same thing as what that person feels, because we are not that person. Dual perspective, by contrast, is a cognitive process of understanding both your own and another person's views or ideas.

When partners adopt dual perspective, they demonstrate understanding and respect for each other. In addition, adopting dual perspective acknowledges the interdependence that exists between partners in personal relationships. People who do not engage in dual perspective act egocentrically. They think only in their own terms and interpret others in their terms, not those others use. Thus, they are not truly connecting with others, and they are not acknowledging others' meanings.

George Herbert Mead considered the capacity to engage in dual perspective as critical to human relationships, because it allows us to understand how others see things and to adapt our actions accordingly. Even if Marsha thinks birthdays are unimportant, she's likely to give her boyfriend a birthday gift if she understands that birthdays really matter to him. Marsha doesn't have to abandon her own viewpoint to understand that birthdays matter to her boyfriend. In fact, it would be just as unconstructive to suppress your own perspective as to ignore that of another person with whom you have a relationship. Dual perspective means two perspectives—yours and that of another person.

Dual perspective grows gradually and only if we are committed to understanding others. We gain dual perspective as we listen to others express their ideas, feelings, hopes, concerns, and so forth. With a serious commitment to understanding others, we gradually gain insight into how they perceive things and what things mean to them. Then we are able to engage in dual perspective so that in our communication we acknowledge and adapt to their perspective. This is affirming, especially on the relationship level of meaning. The result is enriched communication and equally enriched personal relationships.

9. Communication Is Not Always Consistent

Has anyone ever told you that something you said was inconsistent with what you said a week ago? Have you ever felt that someone you are close to seemed to say one thing at one time and something totally different at another time? If so, then welcome to the real world. Consistency may be the darling of formal logicians, but it is not always present in human nature or in personal relationships.

Many people dislike inconsistent communication, especially in personal relationships. Inconsistencies can be frustrating, because they hinder our ability to predict what others will say, do, feel, want, and expect. When we cannot predict what our friends and romantic partners will say, then we may understandably feel out of control and unsure of others and our own appropriate behaviors. Although we may not like it when we perceive others as inconsistent, most of us aren't willing to relinquish our own right to change our minds or to have conflicting desires and feelings.

There are several reasons for inconsistent communication in personal relationships. The most obvious is that few people are wholly consistent in their values, actions, beliefs, and desires. You might want both to be with someone and to have time alone (autonomy/connection dialectic). When thinking about a vacation, part of you might want to return to a favorite beach and part of you might want to go somewhere new and exciting (novelty/predictability dialectic). Sometimes you simultaneously want to disclose private information and you feel it would be safer not to do so (openness/closedness dialectic). You may both like and dislike the same person, feel like pulling someone closer and pushing him or her away. You may want to commit to a person and, yet, also have reservations about giving up your solo lifestyle. When we experience different, even contradictory, feelings, we are likely to send mixed messages to others. Conflicting desires and feelings are part of all of us, and they naturally show up in inconsistencies in our communication.

Another reason for inconsistency in communication is that relationships do not always progress in a smooth, predictable manner (Surra & Huston, 1987). Some relationships heat up quickly, then cool down just as quickly. Others cycle through periods of intense closeness and distance. Some escalate to intimacy and then level off for a period of time before either escalating again or deteriorating. And in still other cases relationships progress along a fairly steady trajectory until some conflict or major external event intrudes. When a relationship is escalating, we are likely to communicate high degrees of closeness and desire. If the relationship hits rough waters, we may communicate feelings of intimacy.

A third reason for inconsistency is different perceptions of communication. For example, you might say to a friend that you need to work more hours and watch what you spend so you can pay your bills. Later, you might say that you're buying a $200 suit for interviewing. Are these statements inconsistent? They might seem so to the person who is listening, because one statement seems to say you cannot spend money and the other states that you are going to buy an expensive suit. Perhaps to you, however, the first statement concerns personal spending habits and the second one concerns preparing for professional life. If you punctuate them as two separate statements about two distinct realms of your life, they don't seem inconsistent to you. If your friend perceives them as part of a single episode of interaction, they may seem highly inconsistent. Inconsistency, then, is a matter of perception—not objective truth. If messages seem inconsistent to you, it's a good idea to ask others how they perceive these same messages.

Inconsistencies are normal and inevitable in humans and the relationships they create. Letting go of rigid expectations for consistency allows you to be more comfortable with the natural ebb and flow of relationships and the normal incongruities in others (and yourself). Perceived inconsistencies are also opportunities for partners to explore relationships and learn about each other. By talking about apparent contradictions, partners may enlarge their insight into each other's complex, unique self.

10. In Personal Relationships, Partners Affect Each Other

This is a summary premise that grows out of the nine that we have discussed. The implication of each of the other premises is that people who are committed to a personal relationship inevitably affect each other. The more intense the commitment, the greater the impact they have on each other.

In the 1960s a popular phrase was "Do your own thing." It was a claim for radical individualism and a denial of impact on others. Most people who came of age in the 1960s quickly learned that it is impossible to do your own thing when you are affected by others and others are affected by you. Especially in personal relationships, we must recognize that we profoundly affect others. Our communication with them affects how they see and feel about themselves. It also affects how they feel about us and the relationship. There is no way to be intimately involved with another and not affect and be affected by that other person.

You'll recall that personal relationships involve interdependence. This implies that partners cannot be independent of each other. Although each person can and should retain individuality, the choice to form a relationship is a choice not to be wholly independent. This reminds us that the choice to commit to another person is accompanied by the responsibility of acknowledging interdependence and its implications.

Although most people want loving relationships with others, they are not always eager to accept the responsibility of interdependence. In his book *Love and Will*, Rollo May (1969) argues that love without will is false, empty, irresponsible. He urges us to accept the fullness of what it means to be committed to and interdependent with another person. What would it mean to do this? It would mean an end to statements such as "This is your issue, not mine," "What you feel has nothing to do with what I said, so don't blame me," and "I don't want to be involved in this issue." Following May's advice would also mean that we resist the urge to describe others' behaviors as if they were independent of us. For instance, we couldn't honestly say "You never tell me what you're feeling" without examining how our own communication might create barriers to disclosure. Do we seem uninterested or judgmental or critical when the other person expresses feelings? Do we share our feelings with the other person?

It's important to distinguish between recognizing interdependence and abdicating personal responsibility for our choices. We can realize that others affect us without holding others responsible for what we say and do. At the same time, we can and should distinguish between being responsible *to* another person, which is what May encourages, and being responsible *for* another person, which is not a desirable goal in adult relationships.

SUMMARY

This chapter has focused on communication, which is a central dynamic of personal relationships. Our ability to use symbols to communicate ushers us into the human world of meaning. At the same time, because symbols are arbitrary, abstract, and ambiguous, human communication is never transparent. What it means depends on perceptions, interpretations, and active efforts to construct meaning.

The ten premises we discussed in this chapter shed light on how we actively work to create meaning out of the symbolic exchanges that are so much a part of our everyday lives. We began by noting that communication in personal relationships is guided by regulative rules that tell us when, where, with whom, and how to communicate and by constitutive rules that define what specific communication counts as, or means. We also noted that communication has both relationship and content level meanings. The third premise is that how individuals punctuate communication influences the meanings they assign to particular messages and groups of messages. Next, we examined multiple contexts that affect communication in personal relationships.

Building on the first four premises, we explored the nature and value of misunderstandings and inconsistencies that punctuate communication in personal relationships. We also called attention to the valuable roles of listening, metacommunication, and dual perspective in helping relationship partners monitor and control the quality of their communication. Finally, we concluded the chapter by focusing on the inevitability of interdependence between people who are involved in a personal relationship.

Effective, satisfying communication doesn't just happen automatically. It requires an understanding of how communication works; skills in listening, speaking, metacommunicating; and a commitment to using conceptual understandings and skills continuously to keep relationships vibrant and mutually satisfying.

FOR FURTHER REFLECTION AND DISCUSSION

1. Can you recall experiences in which you and an intimate friend or romantic partner had different meanings for words? What happened? How did you discover the discrepancies?

2. Have you experienced sex or gender differences in your friendships and romantic relationships? Are your personal experiences consistent with those reported in research summarized in this and the previous chapter?

3. Our society does not generally emphasize the effects of physiology on relationships, yet the ways our bodies operate clearly affect how we interact with others. How do your personal biorhythms affect your communication style and your interactions with others? If you have or have had a serious handicap, how did that affect your relationships and your interaction style?

4. Watch a television program or film and notice relationship and content levels of meaning and different ways characters punctuate interaction.

5. Identify several communication contexts that you regularly inhabit: for instance, your home, a classroom, your dorm or apartment, and a campus gathering spot. How does each context affect your communication?

6. Deliberately enter an unfamiliar context in which you know nobody. How is your sense of yourself affected by your surroundings? Do you communicate differently than usual?

RECOMMENDED READINGS

Beck, A. (1988). *Love is never enough.* New York: Harper & Row.

Duck, S. (1994). *Meaningful relationships.* Thousand Oaks, CA: Sage.

Fitzpatrick, M. A. (1988). *Between husbands and wives: Communication in marriage.* Newbury Park, CA: Sage.

Martin, J., & Nakayma, T. (1997). *Intercultural communication in contexts.* Mountain View, CA: Mayfield.

Weston, K. (1991). *Families we choose.* New York: Columbia University Press.

Wood, J. T. (1998). *But I thought you meant . . .: Misunderstandings in human communication.* Mountain View, CA: Mayfield.

CHAPTER
FOUR

Relational Culture:
The Nucleus of Intimacy

KEY CONCEPTS

buffer zone

complementary structure

neutralization

parallel structure

reframing

relational culture

selection

separation

symmetrical structure

ANGIE

When I met Drew, it was like I'd found my other half. Our relationship is like my anchor that totally supports me. It helps me get through bad times and makes me feel good about who I am. I wouldn't be the same person without our relationship.

JAKE

Lindsay and I have built a great relationship. It is a source of strength and faith for both of us, and it makes both of us better people than we were without it.

JAKE AND ANGIE DESCRIBE THEIR relationship as having independent existence and the capacities of agents. They say, "It's a source of strength and faith for both of us," "It supports me," and "It makes both of us better people." What is the "it" to which Angie and Jake refer? How do people create identities for their relationships? To explore that question, this chapter focuses on a foundation for understanding personal relationships. We will probe the nature and value of relational culture, which is the nucleus of intimacy. We'll explore what it is, how it comes into being, and how it evolves over time in the process of communication between partners.

A hint about relational culture comes from Steve Duck (1992), who notes that "relationships have their permanence in the mind" (p. 86) because their reality arises from meanings we confer on what happens between us and our intimates. Individuals quite literally talk relationships into existence by naming them, defining what they mean, attaching value to interaction within them, and giving them symbolic significance. Leslie Baxter (1987), in fact, says, "Relationships can be regarded as webs of significance" (p. 262) that are spun by partners' communication. Thinking of relationships as webs of significance created by communication is a good starting point for discussing relational culture and the dynamics that create, uphold, and express it.

RELATIONAL CULTURE

Nearly two decades ago (Wood, 1982), I introduced the term *relational culture* to name the subjective reality of a relationship that close friends and romantic partners create. Although in 1982 there was no agreed-on term for this, many scholars had realized that something is created in the process of intimate interaction—something different and beyond individual partners that held a relationship together. Some researchers (McCall, 1970; McCall & Simmons, 1966) described relationships as social orders, world views, and cultures. One scholar (Lewis, 1972) referred to shared culture and noted that this is what binds intimates together. Peter Berger and Hansfried Kellner (1975) discussed the private sphere and private world view of intimates; and MaryAnn Fitzpatrick and Patricia Best (1979) emphasized the private culture of marriages. Using varying terminology, all of these scholars were pointing to the importance of a system of meanings that weaves partners together and confers reality on their personal relationship.

Defining Relational Culture

Relational culture is processes, structures, and practices that create, express, and sustain personal relationships and the identities of partners. The processes, structures, and practices organize interaction and coordinate meanings for individuals' identities, the relationship, and individual and joint interactions with external systems. All of these are realized in communication, which is the genesis of relational culture.

THE MARITAL CONVERSATION

The re-construction of the world in marriage occurs principally in the course of conversation. . . . Now, this conversation may be understood as the working away of an ordering . . . [in which] each partner ongoingly contributes his [or her] conceptions of reality, which are then "talked through," usually not once but many times. . . . The subjective

reality of this world for the two partners is sustained by the same conversation . . . concretized over and over again, from bed to breakfast
table, as the partners carry on the endless conversation that feeds on
nearly all they individually or jointly experience.

> *Source:* Peter Berger & Hansfried Kellner. (1975). Marriage and
> the construction of reality. In D. Brissett & C. Edgely (Eds.), *Life as*
> *theatre* (p. 226). Chicago: Aldine.

Structures are ways of organizing personal relationships, and practices are
activities and routines in which partners engage to express and sustain the values
and identities they have created. Processes are ongoing dynamics that underlie
both structures and practices; specifically, they include three basic dialectics that
shape intimacy: autonomy and connection, novelty and predictability, and openness and closedness. Each of these dialectics shapes and is reflected in the particular ways friends and romantic partners understand and interact with each other
and organize their relationships.

Just as a culture consists of processes, structures, and practices that reflect
and sustain the values of a society, relational culture is processes, structures, and
practices that reflect and sustain the values of a relationship. Like any culture, a
relational culture is not simply tangible objects and events such as homes or a wedding ring (Wood, 1982). Instead, it is the system of interpretations and significance
for objects, events, and so forth. These interpretations sustain intimates' views of
themselves and their relationship by guiding ongoing activities in ways that recon-
firm the view of the relationship that partners desire. In less abstract terms, relational culture is intimates' meanings for each other and their joint life.

Leslie Baxter (1987) observed that "to claim that a relationship is a culture is
to argue, quite simply, that it is a system of meanings created and maintained by its
parties" (p. 262). Thus, the essence of relational culture is neither the activities in
which partners engage nor legal, economic, and social definitions of a relationship. Instead, it is the meanings partners assign to activities, interactions, and symbols that make up their relationship. According to another scholar (Oring, 1984),
"Objects and experiences are not in themselves significant or insignificant. Significance is something bestowed" (p. 21). This reminds us that experience has no
intrinsic meanings; instead, humans create meanings for experiences, including
communication and personal relationships. For this reason, relational cultures are
extraordinarily creative enterprises—we compose initial meanings for intimacy
and then spend the duration of relationships expressing, clarifying, refining, affirming, and transforming the original meanings.

Features of Relational Culture

Discussing five properties of relational culture will help us understand what it is
and how it works to unite partners in a shared world of meaning and value.

Unique content. The content of each relational culture is unique. It embodies and expresses the particularities of partners, their specific forms of interacting, and the unique nature of the personal relationship they collaboratively create. Even the various relational cultures in which one individual participates are different, each reflecting the particularities of how she or he is *in relation* to another specific person. In one friendship you may engage in a great deal of personal disclosure, whereas in another friendship you participate in joint activities and you and your friend are companions more than confidantes. We are witty and spontaneous with some people, reflective and serious with others, and argumentative with still others. Even if we do the same things with different people, the meanings we assign vary, and as they do, they particularize the respective relational cultures.

Systemic character. Relational cultures are systems. You may recall from our previous discussions of systems that systems are interdependent wholes in which all parts interact and interrelate to affect one another. The structures, processes, and practices constituting relational cultures are interactive such that each is connected to all others. Hence, a relationship's structure, communication practices, decision-making styles, and modes of conflict work together as a whole. For example, MaryAnn Fitzpatrick and Patricia Best (1979) found an association between partners' autonomy and amounts of shared and private space in living quarters, as well as in the extent to which they interacted. Observing that couples create different physical contexts for their relationships by how they arrange and furnish their homes, Carol Werner and her colleagues (Werner, Altman, & Oxley, 1985; Werner & Haggard, 1985) found that different physical environments reflect and sustain variable degrees of autonomy in relationships.

In *Public Places, Private Spaces*, Albert Mehrabian (1976) analyzed how spaces are arranged and decorated to invite or discourage interaction between people. Chairs that face each other invite engagement, whereas chairs far apart or positioned in front of a television deter interaction. A particularly interesting study examined how couples who are divorcing and remarrying restructure living spaces to reflect changes in their relationships (Eiduson & Zimmerman, 1985). When spouses divorce, whoever stays in the formerly shared home often redecorates to reclaim the home as personal, not pair, territory. In remarriage, space is often redefined to make room for the new partner and to create an environment that includes her or him. Each aspect of relational culture that we alter sends ripples of change throughout the entire system. For example, changing how rooms are furnished and decorated may foster different kinds of interaction and different degrees of autonomy and connection.

Processual nature. Relational cultures are processes that develop and change over time. The processual quality of relational cultures is manifest in two ways. First, relational cultures do not spring forth full blown in one moment; instead, they evolve gradually as partners implicitly and explicitly define who they are and how they function. Relational culture grows directly out of partners' communication about everything from life philosophies to coordination of daily activities to the meaning of the relationship itself (Acitelli, 1988; Duck, 1980; Duck & Pond, 1989), as well as through retrospections (Acitelli, 1993; Duck & Pond, 1989) and memories (Honeycutt, 1989). Because creating and sustaining a shared sense of a private world is a process, relational culture evolves over time as partners interact.

The second sense in which relational culture is a process is that even after a clear and shared sense of the relationship is formed, it changes. People do not stay the same, nor do their needs, goals, contexts, and values. As we change, we revise our relational cultures to reflect who we have become or want to be. Sometimes we make changes deliberately and consciously; sometimes we don't realize we are transforming our relational culture. Dual-worker couples, for example, may decide to have one partner leave the paid work force when a baby is born. Choosing to move a sick parent into their home will alter partners' interaction patterns as well as how home space is defined (Stein, 1993). Reducing the amount of time partners spend communicating may alter satisfaction, commitment, and closeness. Because relational cultures are embedded in other systems, changing any part reverberates throughout the whole relationship.

Reciprocal influence. Relational cultures and the partners who compose them are involved in reciprocal influence (Berger & Kellner, 1975; Wood, 1982, 1992). This means that they are both created by partners and, at the same time, creative of partners and the relationship. In other words, relational cultures act back on their creators. Norman Denzin (1970) observes that intimates accord to their relationships the right to govern individual conduct. For instance, if partners establish open communication as a facet of their relational culture, they are then compelled to be open even if in particular moments they prefer not to be. The value of openness, once ratified as part of the relational culture, has authority over partners. Thus, relational cultures can make demands on us and impose constraints on individual conduct "for the good of the relationship" (Wood, 1982, p. 77). When the relational culture specifies that partners will support each other, they may be called on to provide time, help, and so forth, whether or not that is convenient (Schwarzer & Leppin, 1991). Similarly, if a relational culture includes a pledge that each partner will be there for the other in times of need, then the culture is structured to entitle each partner to ask for the other's time and availability (Wiseman, 1986). In sum, whatever partners ratify as their relational culture takes on a life of its own and influences the activities and identities of those who created it. Relational cultures have a moral authority, originally defined by partners yet now beyond them as individuals.

Healthy or unhealthy. It would be a mistake to assume relational cultures are necessarily healthy or constructive for partners. A good deal of research indicates that people who have close relationships are often more psychologically and physically healthy (Cohen, 1988; Reis, 1984) and more successful in careers (Dillard & Miller, 1988). In addition, considerable research indicates that close relationships frequently cushion people from both normal and extraordinary stresses in life (for a summary, see Bolger and Kelleher, 1993). These findings indicate that relational cultures can enrich our happiness and well-being.

At the same time, relational cultures can sustain patterns that are highly unsatisfying and, in some cases, even dangerous. Violence between intimates is unfortunately common. Neil Jacobson and John Gottman (1998) have spent years studying violence in personal relationships, and they conclude that it is sadly common. Violence comes in many forms, all of which are damaging. Emotional violence relies on communication that humiliates, degrades, or insults another person. Physical violence includes everything from slapping to brutal batterings and even murder. Relationships that include violence have relational cultures that allow and in some cases normalize the violence as part of the relationship (Goldner et al., 1990). Thus, we need to be mindful that relational cultures may be healthy or unhealthy. What makes a relationship healthy or unhealthy, however, is not self-evident; not even clinicians agree on all matters relevant to personal and interpersonal health. Even so, some relationships are clearly emotionally or physically damaging, or both.

BRENDA

I can verify that relationships can be unhealthy. My first marriage was. He was real nice and considerate when we were dating, but after we got married that all changed. At first he was just not very attentive, but then he started putting me down a lot—making fun of me because I was pregnant and not attractive and telling me I was stupid and all. Before long it progressed to violence, hitting me at first and then doing worse. Looking back, what's amazing is that I took it. I even supported him in a way. Once I told him I would leave if he kept hitting me, and he reminded me we had promised to stay together forever. Then he talked about saying "for better or worse" in God's eyes. And so I quieted down for a long time. It's like those rules had power over me.

Paul Wright and Katy Wright (1995) incisively analyzed dynamics that sustain co-dependent relationships in which one partner has a problem that affects others (drinking or drugs, for instance) and others collaborate, however unconsciously, to sustain the problem and an acceptable identity for the person who has it. Relationships in which elderly people, children, or spouses are battered occur when relational cultures legitimate or excuse abuse and abusers (Brock-Utne, 1989; Duck, 1991; French, 1992; Mahlstedt, 1992; Thompson & Walker, 1989). Also, families that overburden one person with caregiving contribute to the burnout common in caregivers (La Gaipa, 1990; Wood, 1994d). Unhealthy relational cultures harm or fail to support the well-being of at least one member of a relationship.

Summing up, we've defined relational cultures as meanings that emerge from processes, structures, and practices that sustain intimates' coordinated views of themselves, their relationship, and what it means. Distinguishing features of relational cultures are that they are unique, systemic, in process, reciprocal in influence, and neither inherently healthy nor unhealthy. We're now ready to consider more closely the communication dynamics that constitute, uphold, and express relational cultures.

CENTRAL DYNAMICS OF RELATIONAL CULTURE

Relational cultures are created, maintained, and altered through an intricate system of interconnected processes, structures, and symbolic practices that define and normalize identities for partners and patterns of interaction between them. We'll examine each of these features.

Relational Dialectical Processes

In Chapter 2, we introduced the idea that three fundamental dialectics infuse intimacy. We're now ready to elaborate on these to discover how they shape and express relational culture. You'll recall from the previous discussion that dialectics are tensions between contradictory impulses. The two root ideas of dialectics are *contradiction* and *process* (Cornforth, 1968). In each dialectic there are two dynamics that are contradictory, yet also productively interdependent, in satisfying different human needs and generating change in relationships (Baxter, 1988, 1990, 1993; Baxter & Montgomery, 1996; Stamp, 1992). The essence of dialectics is not the impulses themselves but the tension between them. Leslie Baxter (1990) argues that dialectics are not something we resolve but are continuous processes that infuse and affect intimacy.

Three dialectics within relationships have been identified. The first is the tension between needs for autonomy and connection—we want a sense of ourselves as separate, independent agents yet also desire intimacy with others. The second dialectic involves tension between needs for novelty and predictability—we seek both spontaneity and familiar routines. Tension between desires for openness and closedness constitutes the third dialectic—we like to be open and expressive with others, and we also value privacy. Individually and in tandem, these tensions propel much of the evolution in close relationships. The character of any relational culture is shaped, in large measure, by how partners work out dialectics and linkage among them. Further, how we feel about each dialectic and the tension between them varies over individual and relational life cycles.

Initially, studies of relational dialectics (Baxter, 1988, 1990; Baxter & Dindia, 1987; Lloyd & Cate, 1985; Rawlins, 1992; Wood et al., 1994) described them as

TABLE 4.1

Internal and External Forms of Dialectics

	DIALECTIC OF INTEGRATION/ SEPARATION	DIALECTIC OF STABILITY/ CHANGE	DIALECTIC OF EXPRESSION/ PRIVACY
INTERNAL FORM	Connection/ Autonomy	Predictability/ Novelty	Openness/ Closedness
EXTERNAL FORM	Inclusion/ Seclusion	Conventionality/ Uniqueness	Revelation/ Concealment

processes only within relationships. In 1993, however, Leslie Baxter extended discussion to include both dialectics within a relationship and between it and external systems such as friends and society. The basic dialectics are the same for both internal and external tensions, yet discrete needs and different relationship issues accompany the internal and external forms of dialectics. Table 4.1 represents the dialectics and their internal and external profiles (Baxter, 1993).

Integration/separation. The crux of this dialectic is tension between desires to be part of something beyond ourselves and to be separate or distinct from others. Internally, this dialectic is experienced as a struggle between merger and differentiation of individual partners. According to Maggie Scarf (1987), a marriage counselor, "The question of how to be one's own self (autonomous) and yet remain close to the marital partner (intimate) is the major marital dilemma . . . and must be addressed and readdressed continually" (p. 22). Other clinicians concur that perhaps the most central friction in intimacy is satisfying needs for both autonomy and connection (Karpel, 1976; Lidz, 1976; Sager, 1976; Wexler & Steidl, 1978). Further, scholars and clinicians note that healthy intimacy depends on both preserving individuality and creating unity (Askham, 1976, 1984; Baxter & Simon, 1993; Goldsmith, 1990; Rawlins, 1989; Sager, 1976; Wood, 1993b).

In its external form, the integration/separation dialectic involves interdependent desires to include the relationship in larger contexts and to seclude the relationship from social networks. Friends and romantic partners often want to feel a part of the community and seek connections with civic life and friends and family (Allan, 1993; Montgomery, 1992; Werner, Brown, Altman, & Staples, 1992). At the same time, friends, spouses, and lovers need private time to nurture and celebrate their closeness (Baxter, 1993; McCall, 1970). Robert Bellah and his colleagues (1985) found that our desire to be part of a community and at the same time distinct from it is a paradox rooted in Western cultural values that esteem both. Devising ways to be involved with and separate from others is an ongoing challenge, and how this is done varies among intimates and across specific partners over time.

Stability/change. At the heart of this dialectic is tension between desires for routine, stability, or familiarity, on the one hand, and stimulation, novelty, and change, on the other. Within a relationship, this dialectic shows up as a tension between savoring the comfort of familiar routines, patterns, and experiences and desiring spontaneity and unpredictability (Altman, Vinsel, & Brown, 1981; Baxter, 1988, 1990, 1993; Baxter & Simon, 1993). For relationships to function, considerable stability is needed, so partners settle into routines, interaction patterns, and expectations (Askham, 1984; Yerby, 1992). Yet relationships that are too stable can be rigid and boring, so novelty is sought. People differ in how much stability and change they desire and in the contexts for which each is considered appropriate, but all intimates develop ways to meet these interdependent needs. Further, desires for stability and change are influenced by other aspects of partners' lives. For example, after taking a new job and moving, a person may crave routine in relationships, whereas someone who is bored with work may heighten novelty in friendships. This suggests that dialectical tensions and responses to them vary over time and circumstance.

The external form of this dialectic is expressed in a tension between partners' desire to conform to conventional patterns and roles for relationships and their desire to assert the uniqueness of their relationship (McCall, 1970). Acceptance by others and public recognition of a relationship require substantial conformity to prevailing norms, so partners may comply with many social conventions. Yet as Baxter (1993) points out, "Carbon copy relationships do not provide couples with the sense of uniqueness so central to their intimacy" (p. 143). Sharing this view is William Foster Owen (1984), who reported that intimates regard their uniqueness as central to pair identity.

Expression/privacy. The final dialectic consists of tension between wanting expressiveness, on the one hand, and privacy, on the other. Within a relationship this dialectic is experienced as friction between partners' desire to be open and their need to have some parts of self that are closed, even to intimates (Baxter, 1988, 1990; Baxter & Simon, 1993; Petronio, 1991). In part, we may want privacy to reserve a purely personal aspect of ourselves and our lives that is not shared with

SALLY FORTH reprinted with permission of King Features Syndicate.

anyone. In addition, revealing ourselves to others makes us vulnerable to others' criticism and judgment, so a sense of self-protectiveness may also motivate the quest for privacy (Baxter, 1990).

Sometimes close relationships are idealized as totally honest and open. Popular advice books are prone to advise intimate partners to be completely open and honest with each other in order to create a "genuine relationship." Yet, total expressiveness really is not tolerable. Some parts of our lives are not of interest or concern to our partners, so talking about them would be an imposition. Also, expressing some private thoughts could be hurtful and pointless. Hence, a degree of discretion and reserve is healthy. At the same time, too much privacy tends to foster distance between partners. Thus, intimates continuously renegotiate this dialectic over the course of their relationship.

The external version of this dialectic is a tension between desires to reveal the relationship to outsiders and to conceal it from them. To gain social recognition and support we have to announce a relationship. Yet, once others know about it, they can interfere, as Romeo and Juliet discovered! Others may disapprove or offer unwelcome advice. Relationships such as affairs that are taboo may heighten needs for concealment. Also, intimates may be particularly prone to shroud problems from outsiders, because they are embarassed or because they fear disapproval or intervention (Klein & Milardo, 1993; Prins, Buunk, & Van Yperen, 1993). Understandable though this is, concealment may sustain problems by closing the relationship to others and the help they might provide.

The fundamental tensions that lace internal and external dialectics are interdependent. With other features of relationships, they make up a holistic system, and thus, they affect one another (Baxter, 1993; Werner et al., 1992; Werner, Altman, Brown, & Ginat, 1993). Friends who are extremely open are also likely to be very connected, because they've woven together many aspects of their lives (Aries, 1987; Johnson, 1989; Wood, 1994a). Partners who do not discuss feelings openly may form stronger ties with friends than do partners who satisfy each other's need for expressiveness (Rubin, 1985). In relationships that privilege autonomy, partners may also seclude themselves from family and friends more than partners who elevate connection over autonomy. Pointing out another probable interlinkage

SALLY FORTH reprinted with permission of King Features Syndicate.

between dialectics, Leslie Baxter (1993) hypothesizes that "highly conventional-ized relationships will probably find internal predictability easier to achieve than internal novelty; by contrast, relationships characterized by limited conventional-ity will probably experience the reverse pattern, with internal novelty easier to achieve than internal predictability" (p. 164).

C O N N I E

My mother was an alcoholic when I was in high school. Daddy told us not to talk to others about her, because family matters are private. Maybe so, but it seems then that families should try to solve them. We didn't. Nobody did any-thing to get help for Mom. When the counselor at school asked me why I was having trouble, I couldn't tell her, and I couldn't do anything to change the sit-uation. I couldn't ever invite friends home because I never knew what shape Mom would be in. People asked me why she never came to meetings for par-ents or never showed up for my recitals. What was I supposed to say? We had a code of secrecy in the family, and it destroyed Mom and ruined the whole family.

Responding to Dialectics

There is no single or best way to satisfy the interdependent needs making up each dialectic. Rather, different relational cultures reflect distinct styles of accommodat-ing the dialectics. Yet, how partners manage them is not entirely idiosyncratic because researchers have shown there are response tendencies across relationships. As part of her ongoing study of dialectics, Leslie Baxter (1990) investigated how partners respond to different internal dialectics and how different responses affect satisfaction. Focusing on premarital romantic dyads, she interviewed 106 under-graduates to find out how they dealt with dialectical tensions in their relationships.

She discovered four basic ways couples respond to dialectics. First, partners may engage in **selection,** in which they satisfy one of the two needs in a particular dialectic and do not satisfy the other. For example, couples may prioritize connec-tion and deny needs for autonomy. Second, partners may use a **separation** strategy, in which they assign each dialectical need to specific spheres, issues, or times. Friends might, for instance, choose to be very open about their work lives and social interests but be closed about politics and family relations. Many dual-worker couples are very connected about relationship issues but highly autonomous in the work sphere. The third response Baxter found is **neutralization,** which involves compromising so that both needs in a dialectic are met to a degree, but neither is fully satisfied. Thus, in discussing all issues, partners might be somewhat expres-sive but not completely open. Another way to neutralize is to disqualify certain issues or spheres from a general pattern that applies to all others. Some partners, for instance, are very open in all topics they discuss, yet certain subjects are off limits for discussion. Finally, Baxter noted that partners sometimes use **reframing**, which she defined as "a perceptual transformation . . . such that the two contrasts are no longer regarded as opposites" (p. 73). An example of this occurred in a study I and my students (Wood et al., 1994) conducted, in which we found that some couples defined preserving differences between them as enriching their connection; thus, they reframed the dialectic so that autonomy and intimacy were not experienced as opposites.

Baxter (1990) discovered a number of interesting patterns in responses to dialectics. First, she found that they tend to prevail at different times in relationships. The openness/closedness tension was most pronounced early in relationships when partners were negotiating how much to reveal to each other. In relationships of greater length, the autonomy/connection and novelty/predictability dialectics became more prominent. As far as managing the dialectics, autonomy/connection was most often managed by alternately emphasizing one, then the other—a cyclic separation response. Separation was also the most frequent strategy for managing openness/closedness, yet with this dialectic the separation was generally achieved by designating some topics as ones requiring openness and others as ones that allowed some reserve. Predictability/novelty was also most often managed by separation, defining some areas of a relationship as realms of spontaneity and others as more routinized.

Although satisfaction was not related to the presence or intensity of any dialectics, it was associated with different responses to them. Satisfaction was positively correlated with managing predictability/novelty through separating and reframing, and it was negatively correlated with the selection response. Satisfaction was also positively correlated with reframing and negatively associated with selection in response to the autonomy/connection dialectic. This suggests that squelching either need in these two dialectics may foster discomfort in relationships. The least satisfactory response to the openness/closedness dialectic was disqualification, indicating that intimates find areas of secrecy undesirable.

In her 1990 study, Baxter commented that reframing is an underused strategy for managing dialectical tensions. This makes sense, because transforming apparent contradictions into nonoppositions is considerably more sophisticated and difficult than selecting one or the other need, designating areas for each, or compromising between them. Reframing is a highly creative act, one that is difficult yet also extremely promising in its potential to generate new ways of sustaining closeness (Baxter, 1993).

Before leaving our discussion of dialectics as processes that define and regulate intimacy, we should note that what the dialectics mean, how partners manage them, and what impacts they have vary in relation to time and circumstances. Existing research indicates that relationships are constantly in flux (Baxter, 1990, 1993; Duck, 1990; Lidz, 1976). As they evolve, different dialectics assume and recede from prominence, and alternative modes of response emerge. In part, this occurs because of the tensions inherent in dialectics—they generate change because they resist resolution in a final-and-forever form. Partners who prioritize autonomy over connection may reverse the emphasis during a crisis when they need each other. A couple that experiences novelty accidently (for instance, getting lost on a trip) may discover that they enjoy the excitement of the unknown and seek more of it in the future. Over the course of a relationship, dialectics are continuously negotiated. Each new configuration evolves through communication and is woven into the fabric of a relationship in the ongoing conversation that constitutes intimacy. As partners vary in how they experience and manage dialectics, they revise the interlinked structures and practices of their relational culture.

Organizing Structures

The second element of relational culture is structures that organize personal relationships. All cultures are ordered, and those of relationships are no different. Just as the broad culture has a basic structure that is supported by customs and laws that define acceptable and objectionable conduct, so too do relationships have structures that are buttressed by themes and rules that prescribe and prohibit particular attitudes, feelings, and actions. Personal relationships are organized by structures and rules. We'll discuss structures first and then turn our attention to rules.

Structures. Structures order a relationship in terms of power and interdependence (Phillips & Wood, 1983), which regulate how partners fit together. Three basic organizational forms have been identified, although many relationships are blends, rather than a pure type (see Figure 4.1).

A **complementary structure** involves unequal power and high interdependence. This organization was traditional in the United States for many years, and males typically held the position of greater social power, so they had more authority regarding where families lived, who did what, how money was spent, and so forth. Power differentials in relationships are affected by surrounding contexts,

FIGURE 4.1

Relationship Structures

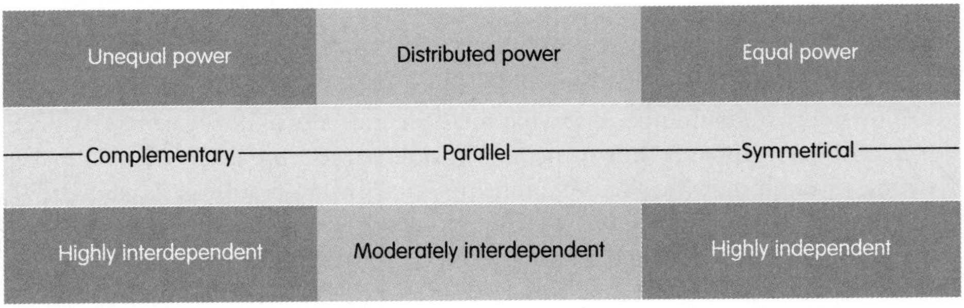

Unequal power	Distributed power	Equal power
——— Complementary ———	——— Parallel ———	——— Symmetrical ———
Highly interdependent	Moderately interdependent	Highly independent

especially by society's assignment of status to various activities. For instance, our society accords higher prestige to wage-producing labor than to reproductive labor (Okin, 1989; Wood, 1994d), so the breadwinner role carries greater social prestige than the role of homemaker and caregiver. Gender prescriptions in Western culture also stipulate that women should be less powerful than men (Christensen & Heavey, 1990; Lakoff, 1990; Schneider & Gould, 1987), so complementary heterosexual relationships typically array power along gendered lines (Riessman, 1990; Wood, 1999). Perhaps for this reason, men's preferences tend to prevail over women's, a pattern that holds true for preferences ranging from how to divide household tasks to how often to engage in sexual activities (Hiller & Philliber, 1986; Hochschild with Machung, 1989; Paul & White, 1990; Szinovatz, 1984; Thompson & Walker, 1989). Because relationships exist within larger social contexts, cultural values seep into intimate arrangements (Wood, 1993b, 1995).

The word *complementary* implies two or more things combining in ways that support one another. Each part offers something the other needs, making interdependence important for effective functioning. Teachers cannot teach without students, leaders cannot lead without followers, and vendors cannot sell without buyers. In complementary relationships, each role requires the other. The same is true in personal relationships with complementary structures. Partners define distinct roles and activities, which encourage interdependence and reliance on each other.

In studying different ways marital partners organize themselves, scholars (Fitzpatrick, 1988; Fitzpatrick & Best, 1979) report that complementary structures are very stable. Because partners are interdependent, separating is difficult. In addition, satisfaction and cohesion are high in complementary relationships, indicating this can be an effective structure for those who are comfortable with interdependence and distinct roles in personal relationships (Fitzpatrick & Best, 1979).

A **symmetrical structure**, as the name suggests, is based on sameness and equality between partners. Each person has the same amount of power and status and assumes equal responsibilities. Further, in symmetrical arrangements, partners tend to have more independent interests and schedules (Fitzpatrick, 1988; Fitzpatrick & Best, 1979; Johnson, Huston, Gaines, & Levinger, 1992). The sameness of status and rights that is the crux of symmetrical relationships explains why partners are less intertwined than in other structures: Each person has autonomous interests and is not highly dependent on the other for resources, assistance, and companionship.

Independent by design, symmetrical structures prioritize each partner's independence and often root their connection in a shared ideology emphasizing equality and a commitment to change (Fitzpatrick, 1988; Fitzpatrick & Best, 1979). Spouses who adopt a symmetrical structure tend not to have high consensus on most issues, because they stress independence in thinking as well as action (Fitzpatrick & Best, 1979). Satisfaction with the relationship is also lower for spouses in symmetrical relationships than for other types of couples (Fitzpatrick & Best, 1979). This may not signal problems, however, because it is possible that the relationship is less salient to partners' overall well-being than is the case for couples who emphasize their connection. This interpretation gains credence when we realize that symmetrical structures do not necessarily impair cohesion, because partners can be deeply connected by shared ideological commitments (Fitzpatrick & Best, 1979). Couples with independent interests and equal power are least likely to have children (Johnson et al., 1992), which may explain why they have more time together than do more functionally interdependent, traditional couples (Johnson et al., 1992).

Symmetrical structures are perhaps the most common organization for friendships (Rubin, 1985). Equality between friends and autonomous interests and other relationships are typically assumed in our society, so this becomes the presumptive structural pattern. Although friends count on each other and value their connection, typically there are limits on expectations of loyalty, support, and time (Rubin, 1985; Strikwerda & May, 1992).

Finally, a **parallel structure** has moderate interdependence and distributed power. Within parallel structures, partners define themselves as equal overall, but each has more authority in defined realms of the relationship. For example, one partner might be responsible for earning income and the other for raising children with the understanding that the caregiver role is no less valuable and confers no less authority in matters affecting the family. Spouses who define themselves this way must invest extra effort to sustain a definition that departs from the views of the society in which they and their marriage are situated (Okin, 1989; Wood, 1994b, 1999). Because partners divide responsibilities but not overall power, they are more interdependent than symmetrical partners and less so than complementary ones.

VINCE

I think any of the structures we discussed describes me and my buddy Mike. He and I are really what you'd call interdependent, like we go everywhere together and check out everything with each other. Yet, we're also very independent in how we think. We may ask each other's opinion on anything and everything, but we don't always agree, and that's not a problem.

ZOE

Power is a funny thing. What looks like power may not be. My parents have a very traditional marriage where Dad is the breadwinner and Mom is a full-time homemaker and mother. He has the status, and he "rules the roost" at home. Yet, Mom really makes most of the decisions and then leads him to them so that he thinks he's in charge. She's the one who decides we need a new car or it's time to move or they should finance my coming to this school.

Then she asks Dad his opinion on the issue and just leads him to the answer she has already figured out. So it looks like they have a complementary relationship, but really it's pretty symmetrical, since she has just as much real authority.

Vince and Zoe are right in noting that some relationships don't fit neatly into one of the three types we've discussed. As Vince points out, the structures we've identified are pure types and many relationships are blends. Further, individuals constantly experiment with new ways to structure intimate connections, so whatever forms exist today will be supplanted by new ones partners devise to meet their evolving needs and preferences. Parallel structure, for instance, is an innovation couples pioneered when the choice between complementarity and symmetry proved too limiting. As women and men continue to revise their roles and as new kinds of relationships emerge, we may see additional experiments with relationship structures.

The structure of a relationship is not static. Like other facets of interpersonal life, how we organize our intimacies is a process that changes over time. Romantic partners often move from relatively symmetrical to more parallel or complementary structures if they have children or if one becomes unemployed. Changes in how a relationship operates are necessary for partners to adapt to shifts in other aspects of their lives, as well as in the goals of the relationship, which also are subject to revisions. Relationship structures may also adjust to accommodate changes in individual partners. An egalitarian power structure with high independence, for example, may become impractical if one partner suffers disease or injury that renders her or him less independent. Friendships, too, may shift structures. For example, one of my close friends is a woman I first knew as a student, so initially our power and status were unequal. Now, however, we operate as peers, a shift that gradually evolved and reconfigured other features of our relationship.

Rules. Relationships are also structured by rules that define acceptable and unacceptable codes of thought, feeling, and conduct. In Chapter 3 we identified two types of rules that operate in relationships. You'll recall that constitutive rules stipulate what counts as what: A kiss counts as affection, eating meals together counts as a commitment to the family, being late without calling counts as rudeness. Regulative rules, on the other hand, regulate interaction by defining appropriate sequences and patterns. For example, masculine speech communities socialize men to be assertive and to wrest the talk stage from others (Maltz & Borker, 1982; Tannen, 1990; Wood, 1993b, 1998b).

One regulative rule associated with this conversational style is interrupting, which is more typical of males than females (DeFrancisco, 1991; Dindia, 1987; West & Zimmerman, 1983). Between male friends, interrupting is a normal part of interaction as are delayed responses and long periods without conversation

(Beck, 1988; Strikwerda & May, 1992; Tannen, 1990; Wood, 1999). Yet those socialized in speech communities cultures may find interruptions, delayed responses, and lack of interaction unsettling. Between women and men, regulative rules for conversation differ. This may explain, at least in part, why many people feel it's easier to communicate with same-sex intimates than with those of the other sex (Aries, 1977, 1987; Beck, 1988; Inman, 1996; Johnson, 1996; Rubin, 1985; Tannen, 1990).

Partners need to develop shared constitutive and regulative rules to coordinate their relationship and to understand each other. In the early stages of a relationship, partners tend to abide by widely endorsed social rules for communication—ones most members of a society know and share (Knapp & Vangelisti, 1992). As closeness grows, communication is progressively less constrained by social norms, and partners work out private rules. Sometimes they actually discuss constitutive and regulative rules (though these labels are seldom used), which allows them to understand and learn to speak each other's language. Explicit discussion of rules, in fact, is encouraged by clinicians who realize that many tensions in relationships result from incompatibilities in rules that cannot be resolved until they are understood (Beck, 1988; Bergner & Bergner, 1990; Lederer & Jackson, 1968; Thomas, 1977).

Yet most friends and romantic partners don't explicitly discuss rules. More often, these are implicitly negotiated in the process of interaction. Jeff rebukes Andy for not supporting him, saying, "Hey, I thought we were friends, but friends stick up for each other." Thus, Andy learns one of Jeff's constitutive rules for friendship. Cheryl explains to her boyfriend that she feels he isn't listening when he doesn't ask questions about what she's saying and fails to interject "ums," "uh-huhs," and other responses that she counts as signs that he is interested. He thus learns that Cheryl interprets listening noises as a sign of involvement. Through these tacit negotiations, partners work out constitutive and regulative rules to organize everything from trivial to important matters: how to talk and listen; how much time to spend alone and together; about which areas to be open; how to discipline children; how to manage money, including who keeps accounts and whether funds are separate, joint, or both; how to greet each other; and so on.

Rules also include "shalt nots." All relational cultures include prohibitions, or specifications of what is not allowed or not approved (Argyle & Henderson, 1985). Some common prohibitions in romantic commitments concern violence, abuse of substances, and fidelity. Yet every relationship also has more unique prohibitions that designate things the particular partners do not want or will not tolerate. Many families have a rule that nice people don't fight, so conflict is suppressed or denied, which may be unhealthy if it leaves feelings and issues unresolved (Lederer & Jackson, 1968; Sager, 1976; Thomas, 1977). Some couples have a rule that they do not express affection in public, whereas other couples regard public demonstrations of closeness as appropriate. Friends and spouses may agree not to attack each other's weaknesses, even in the midst of heated conflict, or not to criti-

TABLE 4.2
Relationship Symbols

Behavioral actions	Routines for interacting, such as using private language and starting the coffee in the morning
Prior events and times	Special occasions such as trips together, anniversaries, close moments, and celebrations of achievements
Physical objects	Tangible symbols of love or the relationship itself, such as gifts expressing affection and shared possessions
Special places	Settings that hold special meaning for partners, such as "our" restaurant, the place where they got engaged, or the church or synagogue or temple where they were wed
Cultural artifacts	Objects produced by the culture that are given special meaning within a relationship, such as a favorite song or movie

cize each other in front of others. Because they demarcate boundaries for partners, the shalt nots are as important in structuring a relationship as rules that stipulate what is allowed, expected, and desired.

Symbolic Practices

The dialectical processes and structure of a relationship are expressed through and reinforced by partners' symbolic practices. On the one hand, practices may be thought of as performances that express a relational culture, because they reflect its values, structure, rules, and dialectics. At the same time, practices are generative, because engaging in them creates and affirms partners' meanings for their relationship. Thus, symbolic practices both generate and embody relational cultures.

Symbolic practices include a range of phenomena. In a pioneering study of relationship symbols, Leslie Baxter (1987) identified five kinds of symbols that friends and romantic partners consider important to closeness. These are presented in Table 4.2.

In Baxter's study the only difference between symbols in friendships and romantic relationships was that more physical object symbols were associated with romances and more behavioral actions and event/time symbols with friendships. Each of these symbolic practices enriched partners' perceptions of closeness and their sense that their relationship was unique. Drawing on this study and others, we'll consider four ways intimates use symbols to define and express personal relationships.

Daily rituals. The basic fabric of a relationship is how partners interact with each other on a day-to-day basis (Bolger & Kelleher, 1993; Duck, 1994a; Duck, Rutt, Hurst, & Strejc, 1991). Interestingly, many if not most of our daily rituals are not necessary for survival or even comfort. Instead, intimates invent an amazing array of rituals and meanings for them to confirm over and over again the reality of their relationship and its place in or separation from larger contexts. We set tables certain ways to reflect social customs, say grace before eating to link our meal and relationship to spiritual values, have a predinner cocktail on weekend nights to demarcate them from the rest of the week, plant shrubs, weed lawns, decorate rooms, do laundry on Saturday and grocery shopping on Monday, and make enough coffee for two in the morning. Each of these rituals affirms that a relationship exists and that people in it are aware of and take care of each other.

The extent to which partners who live together interact throughout the day varies and is one indicator of how they manage the autonomy/connection dialectic (Fitzpatrick, 1988; Fitzpatrick & Best, 1979; Johnson et al., 1992). Similarly, the extent to which partners discuss feelings and individual activities reflects alternative responses to the openness/closedness dialectic (Fitzpatrick, 1988; Fitzpatrick & Best, 1979; Wood, 1993b). Power balance between partners may be expressed by who yields in arguments and who is allowed to neglect relationship responsibilities. Researchers have identified a pattern whereby after a trying day of work away from the home, some husbands default on domestic tasks and wives assume the husbands' responsibilities as well as their own (Bolger, DeLongis, Kessler, & Wethington, 1989; Repetti, 1989, 1992). Human relations specialists Ann Crouter and Heather Helms-Erickson (1997) describe this pattern as one in which husbands, but not wives, have a **buffer zone,** which is an allowance for not doing the usual household chores and child care. This particular ritual defines the relationship in which there is latitude for one partner to relax at the other's expense. Like it, all daily rituals are symbolic practices that express and perpetuate particular meanings in relational cultures. They also reflect partners' choices of who and how they will be.

MARY CATHERINE BATESON

We enact and strengthen our relationships by performing dozens of small practical rituals, setting the table, making coffee, raking the lawn. . . . Couples rely on real tasks and shared effort or, lacking these, they invent endless elaborations of unnecessary tasks to assure themselves that their relationship and their need for each other is real, to knit it together from day to day. . . . Relationships need the continuity of repeated actions and familiar space almost as much as human beings need food and shelter. . . . When people live together, the high purposes of that common living . . . become expressed in very concrete details. . . . Specific everyday tasks can be life-giving, binding individuals to each other and to the past.

Source: Mary Catherine Bateson. (1990). Composing a life (pp. 121–131). New York: Penguin/Plume.

Many of the daily routines in personal relationships operate as scripts, which, you'll recall, are expected sequences of action that follow constitutive and regulative rules that have been agreed upon, tacitly or otherwise. For instance, friends' scripts for arguing are informed by rules about listening, fair and unfair fighting, whether disagreement counts as lack of support or not, and so on (Argyle & Henderson, 1984). Similarly, couples' scripts for interacting with friends and members of their families are guided by rules that define how much time should be spent with others and which aspects of their private lives can be shared with others.

Many couples have a script for catching up each day. Often while partners fix dinner they share the important events of their days. Equally important, they may share some of the minor events and happenings to keep each other woven into the fabric of their lives. Partners in long-distance relationships generate alternative rituals for staying in touch. E-mail is a favorite way that couples stay in touch across the miles, and some partners agree to write at a specific time each day so that they are temporally together and focused on the relationship when they are communicating with each other. When Robbie or I travel, the one who is away always calls the other first thing in the morning. Usually we don't have big news to share, but we fill each other in on any family news, the latest mischief of our pets, and what we've been doing since we last talked. These daily calls allow us to feel we are still in touch and together despite our temporary separation.

In her investigation of symbols that friends and dating partners use to define their relationships, Leslie Baxter (1987) found that interaction rituals were a very important relational symbol, especially in friendships. Many of the rituals partners described are meaningful because they symbolize intimacy, or because they express the couple's uniqueness, or both. For instance, consider this excerpt from one of Baxter's respondents (p. 265):

> It all started on Valentine's Day when I gave him some stuffed hearts. We started hiding them from each other to find in strange places; it's like a game. I'll hide them in surprising places and he'll gradually find them without purposely looking for them—they'll just be somewhere. Then he'll do the same back to me.

Many, perhaps most, of intimates' daily rituals are unremarkable, even humdrum on the surface. Their importance lies in the relationship level of meaning that communicates partners care about each other and their connection. It's hardly exciting that Robbie brings me a cup of steaming coffee most mornings, a routine he initiated early in our marriage when he learned how I look forward to the first cup of coffee each day. The first few times he did it, I was touched by the show of affection, but after over 9,000 repetitions of the morning coffee ritual, it is commonplace. Even so, it still communicates to me that Robbie cares about me, and that is anything but commonplace! Likewise, our script for talking as we prepare dinner is well worn and not thrilling as a concrete sequence of behaviors. Yet, like other daily rituals, it expresses our involvement in each other's life and symbolizes our history and continuing connection. Engaging in familiar routines ratifies relationships and weaves partners together day by day. Practices are how intimates live out and nourish relational cultures, expressing them over and over again in daily life.

VALENTINE'S DAY

We all know that February 14 is the day to send valentines to those we love, but the origins of Valentine's Day are unclear. According to Lawrence Cunningham, chair of the theology department at the University of Notre Dame, there are two theories of how Valentine's Day got started.

One theory is that Valentine's Day grew out of the ancient Roman Feast of Lupercalia, which took place in the middle of February. This feast was a pagan fertility celebration in which maidens wrote love notes and placed them in an urn. The Roman men would take notes from the urn and then court the maidens whose notes they picked.

A second theory claims that Valentine's Day began because European people in the Middle Ages believed that birds mated on February 14 and people wanted to emulate the birds, who were revered for their beauty and agility.

Source: Lawrence Cunningham. (1996, February 15). Valentine's Day: A short history. *Bottom Line*, p. 12.

Special routines. Members of relationships also develop routines for special occasions (Werner et al., 1992, 1993), and these, too, express and sustain the relational culture. Some intimates emphasize major holidays such as Hanukkah, Christmas, and Thanksgiving, regarding these as times to celebrate togetherness. For others, official holidays are less salient. Whether couples celebrate holidays on their own or with extended families reveals how they manage the inclusion/seclusion dialectic. Intimates may also invent occasions that they uniquely wish to commemorate. For instance, my sister Carolyn and I were close to our parents so each year on the days of their deaths we call each other to remember them together and to remind each other that our parents and our family continue in the closeness between us. When I was a child of 7, my ever-imaginative father told me that if all of us children were very good over Christmas Santa would return and leave a New Year's stocking for us. That tradition has continued in my family: Each year Robbie and I give each other New Year's stockings and my sister Carolyn's children also get second stockings on New Year's morning. When Robbie treks in Africa or the Himalayas of Nepal, before he leaves we agree on a specific time that we will think about each other, and we set a special clock in the home and a second watch Robbie takes to each other's time zone.

What occasions we choose to notice and how we commemorate them often reflect and sustain cultural values. For instance, Western culture celebrates marriage by focusing on the couple, which is consistent with Western ideology's emphasis on romantic love. In other countries, such as Taiwan, marriage is an event that links families, and celebrations typically emphasize contracts between kin and community more than love between the couple (Harrell, 1982; Schak, 1974; Werner et al., 1992). In addition, ways of commemorating special occasions express partners' management of dialectics and their constitutive rules for what counts as appropriate acknowledgment of events.

Placemaking. Another interesting practice that expresses and fortifies relational cultures is placemaking. Commenting on this, Carol Werner and her colleagues (1992) observed, "Relationships require places to be viable. Couples cannot exist and grow independently from places; they create places, live in places" (p. 412). Also struck by how physical setting affects relationships, Mary Bateson (1990) noted, "The homes we create for ourselves are far more than physical shelters; the homeless lack far more than homes" (p. 119). Existing research tells us that intimates differ in how much territory they define as shared and private (Fitzpatrick, 1988; Fitzpatrick & Best, 1979; Mehrabian, 1976). How much space is common and how much time is spent in shared zones directly reflects and affects couples' relational cultures. How we arrange space and behavioral patterns in our homes also encourage more or less intimate conversation; personal talk is more likely when chairs are nearby and televisions and VCRs are off.

In *Composing a Life*, Mary Catherine Bateson (1990) chronicles how individuals engage in the ongoing process of creating their lives. Recurrently, she notes the importance of physical environments that reflect and support particular modes of relating. Similarly, Carol Werner and her colleagues (1992) regard "the ways in which dyads create and use a dwelling or home site as an intricate aspect of their relationship" (p. 428). Couples who live in neighborhoods where homes are close with an urban area nearby are responding differently to the dialectic of autonomy/connection than couples whose homes are removed from cities and located on large lots that provide distance between neighbors.

Relationships and interaction between partners also take place in physical settings not designed by partners. Yet, even here we see expressions of diverse relational cultures. People choose locations that are more or less private, intimate, and so forth. For example, a close friend and I get together weekly, allegedly for brunch, but our real agenda is to share the comings and goings of our lives. The personal talk in which we routinely engage is most comfortably conducted in relatively private settings, so it's not surprising that we meet in restaurants with generous space between tables and an unhurried pace. We deliberately choose places that support how we define our friendship.

Finally, places are important relationship symbols. In a study of symbols of friendships and romances that we discussed earlier in this chapter, Leslie Baxter

(1987) found that of the five symbols friends and romantic partners used to identify their relationships, 16 percent involved places. Often a place is important because of what occurred there — friends first met each other there, good conversations always occur there, a marriage proposal was made and accepted there (Baxter, 1987). Favorite vacations and important shared experiences may also be tied to places that symbolize times of special closeness.

Expressions of memory. Each year on the date of my father's death, Robbie brings me a single red rose. My father was not a great fan of flowers, but he did often say that he thought a single red rose was very dignified. At my father's funeral, each member of the family lay a single red rose on his casket. The rose that Robbie gives me each year is a way for him to communicate to me that he remembers my father. It is also a way that he tells me he loves me and understands that I still remember and miss my father. In an important way, my father remains alive for me as long as Robbie and I remember him with the rose, and my sister Carolyn and I remember him with our phone calls and the daddy stories they allow.

Memory is a big part of our lives. Memories keep us connected with who we have been, who we have known, what we have done and thought and felt. Through memory we weave our past into our present, making our lives and identities more coherent. You would feel greatly impoverished if suddenly you could not remember your past because, in a very real sense, you would have lost part of yourself.

Relationships, like individuals, are nourished by memories. Closeness is fostered when partners remember together where they've been and what they've done. In her studies of long-lasting marriages Fran Dickson (1995) has discovered that satisfied couples remember important times in their lives. She writes that "they tell their stories as if they are jointly owned by both partners . . . [with] frequent overlapping of dialogue . . . [and they] repeat the last few words of their partner's statement many times during storytelling" (p. 36). Many stories of past times *are* jointly owned by partners in a personal relationship. And past times stay real and alive, just as my father does, as partners tell their stories over and over again. The following is a dialogue that my parents-in-law engaged in during a recent visit:

Jimmie: *We sure didn't have much money when we were first married, did we?*

Julie: *No, we couldn't even put doors inside the house after we finally got enough together to build it.*

Jimmie: *Remember how we bought one bag of cement each week when I was paid until we had enough to make the basement floor?*

Julie: *And then we got pregnant again, just when we were getting a little ahead. Remember that?*

Jimmie: *Remember that? How could I forget it! We didn't know how we'd manage, but we weren't ever hungry or cold. We did all right for ourselves.*

Julie: *We did more than all right. Those were good years. We were rich in lots of ways other than money.*

Notice in this dialogue how Julie and Jimmie repeat each other's phrases and pick up on the ideas each other introduces. Together they are remembering the first years of their marriage, and sharing that memory links their lives together as a seamless whole. Remembering how poor they once were also increases their appreciation of the material comfort they enjoy today.

Steve Duck (1982, 1994a) points out another way in which memory functions to define personal relationships. He notes that when a relationship ends, partners often edit their memories to save face (I never really cared about her) or to account for why the relationship should have ended (There were a lot of problems, right from the start). If a romantic relationship ends, partners are more likely to remember what was negative about it than what was positive (Weber, 1983), especially if partners weren't friends before they became romantically involved (Metts, Cupach, & Bejlovec, 1989).

Expressing memories, engaging in daily rituals and special routines, and placemaking are symbolic activities that express and continuously re-create the relational culture that defines the meaning of a personal relationship and the identities of partners in relation to each other.

SUMMARY

In this chapter, we've focused on the nucleus of intimacy: relational culture. Just as a culture consists of processes, structures, and practices that reflect and sustain the values of a society, relational culture is processes, structures, and practices that define, express, and sustain intimacy and the identities of partners. Relational processes, structures, and practices work interdependently to order relationships, structure interaction, and create understandings of who partners are and what the relationship is—in private and in relation to outside contexts.

Relational cultures arise directly out of communication—small and large conversations through which individuals weave their lives together. As partners interact, they manage internal and external dialectical processes that, because of the tensions they entail, instigate change. The second component of relational culture is structures that organize relationships and define power and interdependence between partners. Relationships are further ordered by rules that specify what counts as what and how to engage in particular interactions. Taken together, organizational patterns and rules provide the infrastructure for personal relationships. Finally, symbolic practices express and fortify the relational culture partners have talked into existence and affirm the reality and significance of their connection. Practices that punctuate daily interaction concretely express and uphold the meanings intimates fashion for themselves and their relationships.

FOR FURTHER REFLECTION AND DISCUSSION

1. Describe the relational cultures in two of your close friendships. How are they alike and different?

2. Reflect on spatial arrangements in the home of your family of origin. To what extent was there shared and private space? How was furniture arranged, and how did that affect interaction between people? Where did the greatest amount of interaction occur, the most intimate talk? Why?

3. Describe how you ensure both spontaneity and stability in one personal relationship and how that relationship both conforms to social norms and is unique.

4. How did your family of origin manage dialectical tensions? Do your current individual tendencies reflect those of your family of origin?

5. Can you classify your responses to dialectics in terms of the four responses Baxter identified in her research: selection, separation, neutralization, and reframing? Are the consequences of your responses consistent with those Baxter reported?

6. Identify shalt not rules in one of your personal relationships. What did or would happen if your partner violated one of the shalt nots?

7. Reflect on daily rituals and special routines in one of your personal relationships. Describe the purposes they serve for the relationship. How did they develop?

8. What are the value and functions of small talk and everyday routines in intimacy? Why do they matter?

RECOMMENDED READINGS

Bateson, M. C. (1990). *Composing a life*. New York: Penguin/Plume.

Baxter, L. A. (1987). Symbols of relationship identity in relationship cultures. *Journal of Social and Personal Relationships, 4*, 261–279.

Crouter, A., & Helms-Erickson, H. (1997). Work and family from a dyadic perspective: Variations in inequality. In S. Duck (Ed.), *Handbook of personal relationships* (2nd ed., pp. 487–503). West Sussex, England: Wiley.

Dickson, F. (1995). The best is yet to be: Research on long-lasting marriages. In J. T. Wood & S. Duck (Eds.), *Understanding relationship processes, 6: Understudied relationships: Off the beaten track* (pp. 22–50). Thousand Oaks, CA: Sage.

The Social Context
of Personal Relationships

"IT WAS THE BEST OF TIMES, it was the worst of times," wrote Charles Dickens in *A Tale of Two Cities*. We might say the same for personal relationships in our era. We relish having greater options and opportunities than our parents. At the same time, many of us feel immense anxiety in the face of so many possibilities and no clear way to choose among them. We have access to far more experiences—virtual and real—than did our parents, and this begets both freedom to expand ourselves and frustration over not having clear-cut anchors for identity. The information age gives us nearly infinite ways to communicate with others, but we may feel unable to keep up with all of the technology available to us.

In this chapter we will explore culture as a context for, and influence on, personal relationships. This chapter will not prescribe right choices, because no single answer could fit the experiences and needs of people with diverse standpoints, attachment styles, and cognitive schemata that sculpt their identities and views of relationships. Instead, our goal is to explore the complex cultural context for intimate relations in our era. Because relationships exist within larger systems that influence what they mean and how they operate, we need to understand how the systems in which relationships are embedded affect our opportunities and options. Reflecting on cultural currents that complicate and enrich intimacy should help you make informed, albeit not certain, choices in your own life.

THE BEST AND WORST OF TIMES

In many ways our era is favorable for personal relationships. Increasing mobility means that you will meet more people and have greater choices for intimates than your parents did. In addition, social views of relationships have expanded considerably, so we have options not available in former eras. The contemporary smorgasbord of romantic relationships includes long-distance relationships (Rohlfing, 1995), cohabitation (Allan, 1993; Cunningham & Antill, 1995), communal arrangements, celibacy, child-free couples, gay and lesbian partnerships (Huston & Schwartz, 1995, 1996), single parenthood (Burns & Scott, 1994), divorce (Guttman, 1993), and what Kenneth Gergen (1991) calls "microwave relationships" that heat up fast. Today we have a cornucopia of options for personal relationships.

Yet the range of relationships open to us doesn't necessarily give us security. We realize that the relationships we choose may not be as likely to endure as they were in previous eras. Lifelong friendships are increasingly rare in our mobile society. The once assumed permanence of romantic relationships has also been eroded. In a national poll, only 58 percent of people said they considered it likely they would stay married to the same person for life (Indulgent "boomers," 1993). During their lifetimes, over 96 percent of men and 94 percent of women in the United States will marry at least once (Sher, 1996), and all but 4 percent of college students say they expect to marry (Rubinson & DeRubertis, 1991).

Although a majority of people expect to marry, not all of them will stay married. After rising steadily for 20 years, the divorce rate has evened off, but it is still high. For every two marriages in the United States each year, there is one divorce (Footlick, 1990; Guttman, 1993; Notarius, 1996; Sher, 1996), and nearly a fourth of those who divorce will do so in the first seven years of marriage (Cherlin, 1992). Divorce, however, isn't typically a permanent state for Americans. Many people marry two, three, or more times. In fact, over four-fifths of people who divorce remarry (Norton, 1987; Norton & Moorman, 1987). Table 5.1 summarizes statistics on remarriage from the National Center for Health Statistics (Rosewicz, 1996).

Exciting as boundless options are, they can also be unsettling. When roles and relationships were more uniform, people knew what was expected and they had blueprints for their lives. Although standard cultural prescriptions stifled some individuals, they also provided the comfort of clear guidelines. Today, even as we relish unprecedented liberty to sculpt our personal relationships in unique ways, we may simultaneously feel daunted by the sheer number of options and by con-

TABLE 5.1

Remarriage Rates over the Years

	FIRST MARRIAGE		SECOND MARRIAGE		THIRD MARRIAGE	
	1970	1990	1970	1990	1970	1990
BRIDES	76.4%	64.8%	19.4%	26.5%	4.1%	8.7%
GROOMS	76.1%	65.1%	20.1%	26.4%	3.8%	8.5%

flicts among them. You believe one parent should stay home with young children, but neither you nor your partner wants to sacrifice career advancement. You want long-term friendships, but professional success requires frequent moves.

Noted futurist Alvin Toffler (1970) coined the term **overchoice** to describe feeling overwhelmed by uncertainty in the face of mushrooming choices. Christy's journal entry mirrors the sense of overchoice many people feel today.

CHRISTY

I get so confused about how to plan my life. I know I want a career, so I'm majoring in accounting to get a good job when I graduate. But I also want a family—at least three children. I don't know if I can have both. I don't believe in sticking kids in day care, but should I have to abandon my career to take care of them? The guy I'm serious about won't even consider sharing childrearing. He says he will support us if I want to stay home with our children, but he won't take time off from his job to do that. My mother says I need to start my family early because it gets harder to have children later. She's always telling me horror stories about older women at the clinic where she works who are going through extreme treatments to get pregnant. But working women I know tell me that if I want to have a career, I need to put that first and get established before I even consider having a family. Sometimes I really think it was a lot easier when there weren't so many choices!

Like Christy, many of us don't know how to choose among or harmonize the multiple goals we value. We're uncertain how to compose our lives: Is there time for friendships if you're on the career fast track? How do couples decide where to locate when different places offer the best opportunity for each partner? If your parents need help, can you care for them if you also have a career and children (Wood, 1994d; Zarit, Pearlin, & Schaie, 1993)? Can your decisions be *right* if others you respect make different ones? How can you make a marriage work if your parents divorced? In the grip of overchoice, any choice may seem risky, because it might foreclose other, better alternatives. Perched on the edge of the new millennium, many people are bedazzled by boundless freedom, and ambiguity and anxiety-laced daily life.

It's important to realize that Christy and the rest of us are not alone in feeling both excited and confused by our array of choices. Our feelings are not strictly individual, because they arise out of the particular time and society in which we live and create ourselves and our relationships. This means that to understand our relationships today we need an awareness of the overall culture and social trends that influence what they mean and how they operate.

CULTURE AS A CONTEXT OF INTIMACY

At the outset we must realize that terms like *culture* are misleading in suggesting there is a homogeneous social world that everyone experiences identically. We know that standpoints are shaped by diverse material, social and symbolic circumstances available to different social groups. Despite various standpoints and family backgrounds, however, within Western society there are general patterns that have impact on personal relationships (Allan, 1993).

A **culture** consists of structures and practices that uphold a social organization by perpetuating and normalizing particular values, expectations, meanings, and patterns of thought, feeling, and action (Weedon, 1987). Structures are institutions that reflect and support a society's values. Examples of structures are the military, the legal system, churches and synagogues, schools, and families. Practices are recurring routines and activities that embody and reproduce cultural values. Practices include everything from norms in organizations to communication rituals in families. Thus, a culture is composed of intricately interconnected structures and practices that individually and collectively sustain a particular social order. As we'll see, these structures and processes deeply affect personal relationships.

Cultures Legitimate Only Some Personal Relationships

Cultures define which relationships are and are not socially legitimate (Allan, 1993). Western culture currently approves marriage between women and men and denies equal social standing to commitments between homosexuals and cohabiting heterosexuals. Cultural approval of marriage is evident in inheritance laws, tax filing status, and property laws. Cultural approval of heterosexuality is evident in prevailing laws and religious codes that recognize only marriages between women and men.

Marriage. Our society defines marriage between women and men as the normal and preferred lifestyle and links it to personal worth, maturity, and responsibility. Thus, married people are considered better risks for automobile and health insurance and positions of professional and civic responsibility. People in the United States are more likely to marry and to do so at younger ages than are Europeans (Brehm, 1992). Through communication, society inculcates into most individuals the idea that marriage is the preferred lifestyle and that being unpaired is a sign of personal failure or inadequacy.

JARRAD

If I don't have a date on the weekend, I get a lot of grief about not being able to get one. When I break up with a girl, the first thing my buddies do is try to hook me up with other girls, like it's wrong if I don't have somebody. But one thing I've noticed is that the pressure to pair is a lot stronger for girls than guys. For all the ribbing I get, nobody thinks there's anything really wrong with me if I'm not dating, and a lot of people do think girls are losers if they're unattached. I told my friends about this one girl I thought was cute, and one of the guys said something was probably wrong with her because he'd never seen her with a guy. And some of the girls I'm friends with get all torn up if they don't have a guy.

As Jarrad points out, in our culture, being single may have different connotations for the sexes. Because society defines women in relation to men, single women violate cultural prescriptions. Men, however, aren't so strongly defined by their relationships, so single men don't upset the social order: Unmarried women are spinsters or old maids, but unmarried men are playboys or bachelors. News stories routinely mention women's but not men's marital status (Foreit et al., 1980), and prime-time programs feature women more often than men in relationship roles, even if female characters work and male ones have families (Dow, 1996; Faludi, 1991; Lott, 1989).

Gay and lesbian relationships. Current estimates are that at least 10 percent of adults in the United States are gay or lesbian (Sher, 1996; Wood, 1998b). Like heterosexuals, many gays and lesbians seek long-term committed relationships. Contrary to the stereotypes of gays and lesbians as flitting from one relationship to another, a majority of gays and lesbians build relationships that are as stable and enduring as those of heterosexuals. In a study of 560 gay couples the average length of the relationship was seven years, and fully 76 percent of the men said they were committed for life (National survey results, 1991). Similarly, a survey of lesbian couples found that the average length of the relationship was five years, and 18 percent of them had been together for at least eleven years (National survey results, 1991).

JAY

There may never be a time when Joe and I can "marry" in the legal sense, but we've been married in spirit for 15 years. From the first time we got together, both of us knew the other was the one for life. What we feel for each other is no different than what a man and a woman who are in love feel. We take care of each other when we're sick. We help each other out financially. We support each other emotionally. We work through problems together. We dream about the future and growing old together. If that's not a marriage, I don't know what is.

As Jay's journal entry makes clear, present laws limit social and legal rights of gays and lesbians, which deprives them of privileges that heterosexuals enjoy—joint tax filing status, housing, insurance for partners, hospital visiting privileges for next of kin, and pension and inheritance rights (Issacson, 1989).

In recent years social attitudes and legal provisions have reflected increasing acceptance of gay and lesbian relationships. Around the nation, many localities recognize gay and lesbian relationships. Some members of the clergy perform commitment ceremonies for same-sex couples, a growing number of corporations provide domestic partner benefits, and many states have passed civil rights laws to ensure that same-sex partners have rights such as including each other on insurance policies.

Cohabitation. Cohabitation is an increasingly popular relationship form for many heterosexuals. In the early 1980s 39 percent of women under age 44 reported cohabiting; in 1998 53 percent of women in the same age group said they had cohabited (Hamilton & Wingert, 1998). Some people view cohabitation a way to test marriage. In the United States and Canada, cohabitation is widely accepted, especially among people under 30 (Carlozo, 1995). Cohabitation is also growing in popularity in other countries. One-third of students from India, a traditional society, who attend U.S. universities reported wanting to live with someone before marrying (Davis & Singh, 1989). Even the U.S. Census Bureau recognizes cohabitation as a sufficiently common type of household to merit its own title: POSSLQ, which stands for "persons of the opposite sex sharing living quarters."

Although many people think cohabitation is a way to try out marriage, that may not be an accurate assumption. Psychologists John Cunningham and John Antill (1995) caution that cohabitation doesn't really serve as a trial marriage. In fact, cohabiting before marrying reduces the likelihood that marriage will endure (Bumpass & Sweet, 1989; Hamilton & Wingert, 1998). One reason for this finding may be that marriage involves a firm commitment and cohabitation is a more tentative connection that can be abandoned with less difficulty than marriage.

Not all couples who live together see cohabitation as leading to marriage. For many people cohabitation is a preferred alternative—not a forerunner—to marriage. For these couples, marriage is not a goal. Some care enough about each other to want to live together, but they aren't willing to make the total commitment that marriage entails. Researchers have found that a significant number of people who are cohabiting expect to marry later but do not think they will marry the person with whom they are currently living (Cunningham & Antill, 1995; Landale & Fennelly, 1992). For these individuals, cohabitation is an ideal because it allows greater intimacy than dating but less than marriage.

Other cohabiting couples perceive their relationship as a permanent commitment, but they dislike the institution of marriage. For them, cohabitation is a way to define their commitment in ways that don't reflect the roles and expectations associated with marriage.

MAGGIE

There's no doubt in my mind that I love Bill, but marriage is a long, long way off for me. There's so much I want to do before I settle down. But I care more about Bill than any of the other guys I've dated—enough that I want to live with him for now. I'm just not serious enough to think about marrying him.

LIZETTE

I just don't see the point of marriage. Jeff and I have lived together for eight years, and we both assume we'll live together forever. What would a piece of paper and a preacher's words add to the pledge we've made to each other? Heck, I know a lot of people who marry and don't stay together eight years!

Despite the growing popularity of cohabitation, social institutions and practices make it difficult for people who cohabit to rent or own property, obtain loans, or qualify for family insurance. Further, if a cohabiting couple separates, partners have few legal rights, because laws safeguard only those who form relationships that the culture approves. Thus, an array of cultural institutions and practices support heterosexual marriage and deny rights and social legitimacy to other couples.

BETSY

I learned the hard way what happens to people who violate society's views of proper relationships. Alan and I were together for ten years in a committed, monogamous relationship. We split up three years ago, but while we were together we were entirely faithful to each other, which is more than I can say for a lot of married people. When we split up, Alan didn't want to pay any child support or finance my return to college, even though I worked to put him through law school. I petitioned the court but learned I have no rights to child support or a settlement or alimony to compensate me for what I invested in him and our relationship. I am totally unprotected. But a friend of mine just left her husband, and the court awarded her half of their assets plus ordered him to pay for her B.A. in education. And they were married less than a year!

Minority families. U.S. society also discriminates against families that do not fit the middle-class Caucasian model. As we saw in Chapter 2, African American and Hispanic families are often more extended than Caucasian ones, so immediate family may include grandparents, aunts, and cousins as well as children not formally adopted (Gaines, 1995). Yet existing laws define immediate family as spouses, parents, and biological or formally adopted children. More than a legal abstraction, this definition has a concrete impact on people's lives (Ingrassia, 1993). One major result is that many people who aren't Caucasian are unable to insure all members of their families, because only those legally recognized as immediate family are eligible for coverage. Further, existing laws define only children and spouses as "class A heirs," whose inheritances are tax-free up to a maximum level. Laws generally reflect the standpoint of the dominant group and ignore and disadvantage other social groups.

Sex Roles in Relationships

Also deeply ensconced in our culture are prescriptions for women, men, and relationships between them. Although a majority of both women and men work outside the home, broadly held social views still define men as breadwinners and women as homemakers. Despite laws prohibiting discrimination on the basis of sex, social practices continue to subordinate women to men. Only in 1993 did my state, North Carolina, enact a law making it illegal for a husband to force sexual activity on his wife, and it passed only after prolonged debate in which some legislators protested that a law prohibiting marital rape would give wives power over husbands. This argument assumes it is preferable for a man to have the power to impose sex than for a woman to have the power to refuse or seek redress. Some states still lack laws against marital rape.

Embodying the cultural view that women are subordinate to men is the practice of women's giving up their birth names on marrying. Although some women retain their names and some couples hyphenate last names, the majority of modern spouses adopt a single symbolic identity—his (Stafford & Kline, 1996). Families, which are major socializing institutions, further reproduce gendered identities by encouraging sons to be independent and assertive and daughters to be deferential and responsive to others (Basow, 1992; Bruess & Pearson, 1996; Stern & Karraker, 1989). The pattern continues in schools, where girls are rewarded for quietness and dependence and boys for independence and assertion (Krupnick, 1985; Sadker & Sadker, 1994; Sexism in the schoolhouse, 1992; Wood & Lenze, 1991). Such practices reproduce autonomy in males and dependence in females. From children's cartoons (Carter, 1991) to MTV (Texier, 1990), media reinscribe cultural views of women as thin, beautiful, and deferential and men as rugged, aggressive, and domineering (Faludi, 1991).

Social institutions and practices bolster expectations that women and not men should take care of others (Cancian, 1987; Miller, 1986; Okin, 1989; Tavris, 1992; Thompson & Walker, 1989; Wood, 1994d; Zarit, Pearlin, & Schaie, 1993). Workplaces play a pivotal role in sustaining gendered expectations of caregiving. Company policies allowing leave for maternity but not paternity communicate that women and not men are primary parents, which reflects and reinforces society's prescription that caregiving is a feminine activity.

Institutional structures make it difficult for men to be as involved in parenting as many would like to be. In a 1996 Princeton survey, men reported increasing commitment to fathering. More than half of the fathers surveyed said that being a parent is more important to them than it was to their fathers. Fully 70 percent of fathers surveyed said they spend more time with their children than their fathers spent with them (Adler, 1996). Yet men in this survey also stated that work policies make it far more difficult for them (than for women) to assume substantial roles in child care. The equation between women and caring is further reflected in custody practices that accord strong presumption to women. Even if a father is more willing or able to be a parent, he is disadvantaged by a legal system that defines women as caregivers (Database, 1993).

Cultural views of women, and not men, as caregivers are also reflected in expectations that daughters, more than sons, will care for elderly and/or ailing parents and parents-in-law (The daughter track, 1990; Wood, 1994d). This expectation was brought home to me between 1982 and 1991 when I cared for each of my parents during their final years. Shortly after a second stroke my father said, "I used to wish I had sons, but now I'm glad I had daughters, because I couldn't ask a man to put me before his work." In that moment I realized that both of us had assumed I would rearrange my career and marriage to care for him, which exemplifies Mead's insight that individuals internalize cultural values into their own perspectives.

Changes in Cultural Views of Relationships

Because cultures are highly dynamic, cultural values change over time. There have been many shifts, some fairly fundamental, in cultural views of personal relationships (Allan, 1993). For example, many of the most odious practices of sexual and racial discrimination are now prohibited by laws and policies. Thus, women and people of color are entitled to fair consideration in admission to schools, hiring, and promotion, which affords them greater (though still not equal) opportunities for personal and professional development. Heterosexism and homophobia have also diminished somewhat. Although structures and practices that disadvantage lesbians and gays still riddle social life, there is growing acceptance of their commitments and rights. A number of cities and towns recognize domestic partnerships and provide partners with benefits long enjoyed by heterosexuals (Seligmann, 1990). Cohabiting couples, as well, are increasingly winning social recognition (Allan, 1993; Cunningham & Antill, 1995). Palimony suits that punctuated the 1980s forced society to deal with cohabitation, and some localities now provide limited rights to cohabiting partners. It is likely that we will see more changes in social attitudes and laws regarding cohabitation in the years ahead.

Social views of marriage have shifted markedly in a number of ways. In the 1950s the average age of a first marriage was 20.2 years for women and 22.6 years for men. By the mid-1990s the average ages were 24.5 and 26.5 years, respectively (Carlozo, 1995). Whereas only one in three married women was in the paid labor force in the 1940s, over 50 percent of married women today work outside the home. Social condemnation of divorce has waned precipitously, as has the equation between marriage and parenting. Nine percent of young women today plan to be child-free, and most others want only two children (More women consider,

1993). Also ebbing is the assumption that families are immune to public regulation. Child abuse and wife battering have compelled public intervention into the formerly private sphere of family (French, 1992; Wood, 1998c).

Summing up, cultural values that affect relationships are embodied in a range of structures and practices. In addition to those we've discussed, other social values impinge on relationships. For instance, in the United States, living separate from a family of origin is a mark of maturity, and married couples are expected to establish independent families. In other cultures, several generations of a family live under one roof or close by and function as a single unit (Cowan, Field, Hansen, Skolnick, & Swanson, 1993).

As we participate in social life, we tend to internalize our culture's ideology and, with that, its views of what is normal, legitimate, and right for individuals and relationships. The presumptive power of cultural values, however, is not absolute. Although prevailing ideologies are highly influential, some individuals resist them and instigate change, which is why cultures are dynamic systems.

CURRENT SOCIAL TRENDS

The established order of a culture is continuously restructured not only by individual initiatives, but also by developments that transform personal and collective life. Technology and diversity are two of the most consequential trends that are profoundly reshaping the cultural context for intimacy in our era. We'll discuss the impact on personal relationships of these two major trends and a number of related trends to which they give rise.

Technology

The increasingly technological character of our society powerfully affects individuals and personal relationships. The United States began as a predominantly agrarian society in which most families settled in one place where they lived and worked together. With the Industrial Revolution, we moved into an era where machinery and mass production recontoured the rhythm of life, bifurcating home and work into separate spheres assigned respectively to women and men (Blumstein & Schwartz, 1983; Cancian, 1987). We have now entered a third era in which technology and information are reshaping the cultural landscape (Gergen, 1991; Naisbitt, 1982; Toffler, 1970). Catapulting us forward are technologies that revolutionize how we live and die, work and play, give birth and socialize, and communicate (The power of invention, 1997–1998). New and converging technologies are fundamentally altering how we live and work, expanding what we can do and making efficiency and information deities of our age.

Emblematic of technology's centrality to modern life are computers, which increasingly affect our work, recreation, and personal interaction. The Internet system allows instant global communication, and many people develop electronic mail buddies, with whom they "talk" daily and whom they consider close friends (Lea & Spears, 1995; Werman, 1992). In addition, millions of people regularly visit virtual communities and engage in ongoing conversations in chat rooms where they can talk about shared hobbies and interests such as politics and gardening (Springen, 1998).

K A R E N

I used to think online dating was for losers, but just for fun I tried it. I met a lot of guys I didn't find interesting, but one guy and I really hit it off, and we started talking several times a day online. It was weird getting to know someone so well without ever seeing him or being with him. Two months after we met online, we got together for real. It was love at first sight, and we're getting married this summer. I feel like our relationship developed more honestly than others I've had because we didn't start off with superficial things like whether we liked how each other looked.

Karen's not alone in finding that romance can flourish online. Each month 1 million America Online members visit the love@aol site, and others visit sites such as the "rendezvous room" (Springen, 1998). The leading online dating service is Match.Com, on which over 700,000 people have registered to search for compatible partners, and at least 600 of those people have married someone they met through the service. But Richard Booth, who wrote *Romancing the Net: A "Tell-All" Guide to Love Online* (1996), warns that general chat rooms often attract not just people who want to flirt but those who want to do bizarre things. The advent of online dating and mating challenges traditional criteria for choosing romantic partners. For instance, physical attraction and proximity have long been key determinants of selecting people to date. As Karen pointed out, when romance blossoms in cyberspace, partners may not know what each other looks like and may not live nearby.

NON SEQUITUR ©1998 Wiley Miller / dist. by The Washington Post Writers Group. Reprinted with permission.

Technology, of course, involves more than computers. The horse and buggy of our agrarian great-grandparents gave way to cars, then trains, planes, jets, and superjets. Letters are increasingly losing ground to faster alternatives such as Federal Express, electronic mail, and faxes. Phonographs were superseded by stereos, tape decks, and CD players. Conventional stoves have given way to microwave ovens in many homes.

Nowhere are technological advances more dramatic than in medicine. Once deadly diseases such as polio, diphtheria, and tuberculosis are now preventable. With dialysis, renal failure is no longer a death sentence. Sophisticated diagnostic techniques such as magnetic resonance imaging and sonograms allow life-saving early detection of many tumors. Neonatal medicine has progressed to the point that babies born as much as four months premature often survive. And medications and artificial support systems sustain people far beyond natural physiological limits. With modern medicine, we can alter virtually any part of our bodies, so women may augment or reduce their breasts and men may have pectoral implants and hair transplants. Early in pregnancy we can determine everything from a fetus's sex to whether it has physical or mental abnormalities. Children considered short can be given growth hormones, and ones labeled "hyperactive" can be chemically calmed. Today there is very little we cannot control or change.

We may lack the wisdom to make enlightened choices about how to use (or not use) the technologies available to us. Hiroshima was a dramatic testament to the danger of using new technology before fully understanding its implications, and many of the scientists involved in that project later regretted developing the A-bomb. Today we confront deeply unsettling issues arising from technological proficiency. Plastic surgery allows us to alter our bodies in minor and major ways to come closer to meeting cultural ideals of physical beauty. Yet, as many women have discovered, there can be painful and dangerous side effects to procedures such as breast implants. Should we reshape and remake our bodies to measure up to socially constructed ideals?

We have the capacity to control conception, alter fertility, end unwanted pregnancies, keep exceedingly premature infants alive, and detect genetic traits of fetuses. What do we do with such capabilities? Should couples be able to abort a fetus that is mentally deficient? Should they be able to abort one that isn't the sex or height they want? At the other side of the spectrum is death, and as a society we are as confused about the end of life as the start. We can keep people alive when their bodies no longer sustain them. Should we? Should we even if they prefer to die? What lines do we draw, where do we draw them, and who decides about drawing the lines?

Medicine is not the only area in which technology may be ahead of human wisdom regarding its use. Today we can generate nuclear power yet cannot ensure its safety, so accidents happen, taking dreadful tolls on humans and the environment. We have the ability to strip rain forests, ravage oceans, and destroy wildlife habitats for short-term economic gain. Should we? Children read less and use computers more; what's lost when reading declines? Mathematical skills wither as we depend on machines to perform operations we don't understand. Using computers, students produce well-written papers but often turn in exams plagued with misspellings and poor grammar.

Every dimension of our lives testifies to the technological character of our era (Gergen, 1991; Naisbitt, 1982; Toffler, 1980), but it's unclear whether this will enhance our individual and collective lives. Just as technology increases what we can do, it often reduces what we know how to do. It is true that we don't have to spend time learning rules of grammar and syntax as our parents did, yet it is also true that many of us don't know how to write on our own and may not learn as long as computers can do it for us. As we head toward a new century, an urgent question is whether we *should* do everything we *can* do.

Mobility

A direct outgrowth of technology is mobility, which affects how and with whom we create relationships. Historically, communities were relatively stable, so people often knew most of their neighbors and fellow citizens over a lifetime. By the 1970s, however, the average person reported moving 14 times (Wood, 1992), and more moves are predicted for people in the twenty-first century. Each move uproots us from an entire system of friends, colleagues, routines, and physical landscape. Even if we stay in one place, others move, so our social connections stay in flux. Mary Rohlfing (1995) reports that as many as 90 percent of North Americans currently have at least one long-distance friendship.

Technology makes mobility more feasible than in former times (Gergen, 1991). We don't need to organize a wagon train and sacrifice months to move from coast to coast. Instead, a moving company relocates us in days. We dart off to conferences in other countries, vacation around the globe, and book flights to visit friends and family. Mobility makes it likely you will know more people but have fewer lifelong friends than your parents (Toffler, 1970, 1980). Friendships that do endure over time will be conducted quite differently than in the past when physical proximity allowed frequent face-to-face contact.

Specialization also stokes mobility, because people often must relocate to advance in a chosen field. The family doctor of 1950 is as rare today as a general attorney or communication professor. Modern physicians specialize in pediatrics, urology, neurology, gynecology, podiatry, or allergies; attorneys restrict their practices to antitrust, property, estate management, or torts; communication professors focus on relational communication, gender and communication, environmental advocacy, or oral narratives. When a medical practice needs to cover a particular area, existing partners are seldom qualified because they specialize in other areas, so talent must be imported. The constant reshuffling of people erodes a traditional basis of personal and social stability. In its place we have adaptation and change as ways of life.

Acceleration

Imbricated with technology and mobility is the trend toward speed, which infuses modern life in Western society. Consider that most of the changes we've discussed transpired in the last two decades. It took thousands of years for humans to move from traveling on land or by water to air travel, but only 66 years after Wilbur and Orville Wright made their 1903 flight astronauts landed on the moon. In 1970, almost no one owned a personal computer, yet by the mid-1990s computers were a standard item in virtually all businesses and many homes and schools as well. The 386 model that topped the line in 1991 was obsolete by 1992, and each year since yet-faster models have supplanted their predecessors. Current development in networking and chips will quickly make present systems seem slow.

To grasp the increasing speed of technological developments, look at Table 5.2, which identifies major technological breakthroughs during the twentieth century that have changed our sense of time and the length and quality of our lives (The power of invention, 1997–1998).

The speed that is emblematic of our age radically alters our sense of time and identity (Bertman, 1998). Our ever-accelerated pace of living simultaneously condenses the amount of time we spend on any activity and expands what we accomplish in a given day, week, or year. One thoughtful commentator reflected, "There's more information than ever to absorb, more demands to meet, more roles to play, the technology to accomplish everything faster, and never enough time to get it all done" (Schwartz, 1989, p. 37). The pervasive pressure to do more may lead us to define personal value in terms of how much we do and how quickly we do it. Deborah Baldwin (1994) suggests, "In a quintessentially American way, being busy conveys self-worth, even status" (p. 56). Even leisure activities are often gauged by achieving results: pressing more weights, running longer distances, planting more flowers, and bird watching competitively (Baldwin, 1994; Creekmore, 1994).

Think about your average day. You arise and hop into the shower where hot water is immediately available. While you are dressing, your radio provides a 3-minute summary of key events. You microwave a muffin in 30 seconds and munch it while riding a bus into town. After dropping clothes at the cleaner for the 1-hour martinizing special, you zip into the copy shop to duplicate a paper—40 pages in as many seconds. Next, you take negatives to Fast Photo, and the clerk promises prints in 30 minutes. From there you go to the ATM and punch in your code whereupon $50 appears. You dash into a market to buy several microwave meals and instant coffee. Retracing your steps, you pick up the photos and clothes and catch the bus back to your place.

After a quick sandwich, you flip on your computer to finish writing a term paper. There you spend the afternoon, breaking only twice to place phone orders for merchandise. When you've drafted the paper, you run a spellcheck program, and within 90 seconds all errors are corrected in a 20-page manuscript. A keystroke saves the paper and a second stroke starts the printing while you switch into your

TABLE 5.2

Innovations in the Twentieth Century

TRANSPORTATION	MEDICINE AND HEALTH	COMMUNICATION TECHNOLOGIES	CONVENIENCE AND LIFESTYLE
Airplane (1903)	Novocain (1904)	Offset printing (1904)	Vacuum cleaner (1907)
Liquid-fuel rocket (1926)	Chemotherapy (1910)	Short-wave radio (1919)	Zipper (1914)
	TB vaccine (1923)		Frozen food (1924)
Jet engine (1930)	Penicillin (1928)	Talking movies (1926)	Beer can (1935)
V-1 and V-2 rockets (1944)	Heart-lung machine (1935)	Home television (1949)	Ballpoint pen (1938)
		Optic fiber (1955)	Microwave oven (1941)
Lunar landing (1966)	Kidney dialysis machine (1943)	Computer mouse (1968)	Bikini (1946)
Space station (1971)			
Space shuttle (1981)	Laser eye surgery (1962)	Personal computer (1975)	Nonstick cookware (1954)
Doppler radar (1988)			Astroturf (1965)
Stealth bomber (1989)	Test-tube baby (1978)	WWW (1990)	Post-its (1974)
Opening of Channel tunnel linking England and France (1994)	Fetal surgery (1984)	Pentium processor (1993)	Disposable contact lenses (1988)
	HIV protease inhibitor (1994)	JAVA (1995)	
First commercial electric car (1996)	Gene for obesity found (1996)		Microwave clothes dryer (1994)
	Cloning of adult mammal (1997)		

electronic mail program where you read notes from distant friends. Quickly you send responses, which will reach their destinations before you exit the program. To relax you order a pizza, which is delivered in 30 minutes. You eat it while listening to C-SPAN's news capsule.

Rarely do we question acceleration as a way of life. Instead, we regard rapidity as normal and ask only whether it's possible to do even more even faster. As a society we value speed and productivity (Gergen, 1991; Schwartz, 1989). We want what we want *right now*, whether it's instant credit, instant photos, or instant stimulation. Bored? Turn on the television or rent a film and voila! immediate entertainment. Hungry? Microwave a meal in minutes. Pushed to read a book assigned for class? Buy *Cliff's Notes*. Too busy to wash dishes? Use disposable plates. As expectations of speed permeate our lives, we become devotees of the Almighty Clock (Kelly, 1994; Keyes, 1992).

Transience as a Way of Life

Some social analysts see a dark side to the rapidity of modern life. They worry that it cultivates an expectation of transience that may jeopardize our capacity to savor experience and make long-term commitments. According to one social analyst, "by cramming each moment so full of events, we leave ourselves no time to actually experience these events in any meaningful way" (Rechtschaffen, 1994, p. 65). Acceleration as a basic orientation prompts us to expect instant gratification in each experience, then toss it aside as used up. We may, as Toffler (1970) warned years ago, develop a throwaway mentality to match our throwaway society (see Table 5.3). If a watch breaks, buy another; if a course takes too much time, drop it. We learn to throw away, not fix, and to replace, not repair.

Expectations of speed and impermanence permeate the cultural context in which we create our relationships. Tony Schwartz (1989) describes this as "life in a state of constant overdrive" (p. 37), indicating speed is an orientation to how we live, not just how we do specific activities. As expectations of transience saturate our lives, they may alter how we relate to others. Concerned about this, Toffler (1970) cautioned that we could come to regard not just things, but also people and relationships, as disposable or replaceable. The addiction to constant stimulation and productivity may spill over from our work lives to our relationships so that investing extended time and effort becomes alien (Kelly, 1994; Keyes, 1992).

MIRANDA

I never thought about this being a throwaway society, but I guess it really is. I don't think twice about throwing out clothes that need mending or just are out of style. I just junk them and buy new ones. Same thing goes for watches and radios and most anything that breaks. I never fix stuff or even go to the trouble of finding somebody who can fix it. I wouldn't say this attitude spreads to my relationships, but I do know I won't go to a whole lot of trouble to work out problems with friends or dates. Like, it's really just easier to find someone who isn't so hard to get along with.

With cultural trends encouraging us to push, rush, and do more, more, more, it's no wonder that burnout is epidemic in our era. According to one group of corporate consultants, the cultural obsession with speed encourages us to live in "high gear, making quick decisions, abrupt changes, and fast moves, always in an effort

JUMPSTART reprinted by permission of United Feature Syndicate, Inc.

TABLE 5.3

Throwaway Society

THEN	NOW
Refillable ink pens and ink wells	Disposable ink pens
Diapers	Disposable diapers
Glasses	Disposable contacts
Dishes	Paper plates
Handkerchiefs	Tissues
Darn socks with holes	Buy new socks
Milk bottles	Disposable cartons
Repair broken appliances	Replace broken appliances
Continue using old models of appliances until they break	Buy newest models when they're available

to reach their destination as quickly and efficiently as possible" (McGee-Cooper, Trammel, & Lau, 1992, p. 140). These consultants say many people today suffer from "hurrysickness" (p. 142). In his journal entry, Chuck seems to agree.

CHUCK

I have chronic hurrysickness. From the minute I wake up each day I rush to get everything done, usually doing two or more things at once. A lot of times I make lists or write letters while I'm in class, or I keep working at my computer while I talk on the phone. It's constant, and I really don't see how I can be any different. If I slow down, I'll get behind everybody who is going faster. What scares me is that if this is how I live in college, how much worse is it going to be when I have a career and family?

Chuck has imported the cultural obsession with speed into his own perspective. Chuck is right, of course—if he slows down, he may suffer consequences. However, there are also consequences of the choice not to slow down. Stephen Bertman (1998) warns that the accelerated pace of American culture contributes to a range of problems, including environmental dangers, political mismanagement, and social ills. Others (McGee-Cooper, Trammel, & Lau, 1992) point out that hurrysickness is associated with high blood pressure, depression, and susceptibility to infection and serious disease.

Acceleration, immediacy, and disposability are cultural trends that discourage focused, unrushed interaction with others. If high gear is our only speed, we tend to do several things at once or plan the next moment while in the present one. Pondering this, Tony Schwartz (1989) writes "more and more, what I find is that you don't really live in the present anymore. You're never fully engaged in what you're doing at any given moment, because what you really want to do is finish it, in order to get on to something else. You kind of skim along the surface of life" (pp. 41–42). What's lost by skimming? Some social critics (Keyes, 1992; Schwartz, 1989) suggest we sacrifice depth for breadth and genuine engagement for superficial contact.

Each of us chooses whether to live in a state of constant overdrive. We decide whether to internalize and act on current cultural trends that promote acceleration and transience into our personal lives. An alternative to accepting uncritically what the culture encourages is to ask when speed and transience are appropriate and when they are not. Skimming may work for reading adventure novels and watching situation comedies, but it cannot sustain intimacy. Less than full involvement will not allow partners to weave their lives together in a lasting way. Joanne Woodward and Paul Newman are that rarest of celebrity couples—they have an enduring marriage. An interviewer once asked Newman how they had remained together with their active careers and Hollywood's norm of divorce. His answer was, "We have a fix-it marriage."

Diversity

Diversity is a second major trend that is fundamentally reshaping our culture, individual identities, and personal relationships. Diversity means multiplicity or variation. Encompassing far more than race, class, sex, gender, and sexual orientation, diversity also refers to the range of values and lifestyles pulsating in cultural life. Diversity has fueled two tendencies that at first seem contradictory (Wood, 1993d, 1998b). One tendency is greater awareness of and respect for differences that allow us to forge a new collective identity reflecting a broad range of people and ways of living. As an outgrowth of this, we would have enlarged personal horizons resulting from learning about a wealth of different perspectives, experiences, values, and life circumstances.

A second tendency accents differences and invites what has been called "identity politics," which is relatively rigid and exclusive identification with a particular group and deliberate separation from other groups: Asians may identify with Asians, gays with gays, and women with women. Identity politics tends to enhance solidarity within groups and, at the same time, to harden divisions between groups. For Mela, the issue is whether to define herself as a woman or as an African American.

MELA

I'm proud of my African heritage, so I'm Black identified. But I am also a girl and identified with that. So what happens is this. My White feminist friends keep trying to convince me gender is the issue, and my Black friends say I'm betraying my race by spending so much time with Whites. And when I come down on Black guys for being sexist, they fuss that I have to be loyal to my race and tell me not to pit Black men and women against each other. It's like I can't be both a woman and an African American, and I just feel torn all of the time. It's like everybody is afraid of losing something to another group, so we bunch tighter and tighter in smaller and smaller groups.

As Mela's journal entry shows, there is a palpable tension between identity politics and commonality. We sometimes fear that greater understanding and acceptance of others might jeopardize our own rights and opportunities (What happens to my promotion if someone from that group is promoted?). As these tensions play out in social life, efforts to increase understanding between social groups go hand in hand with attempts to preserve distinctions and resist assimilation (Gitlin, 1995; Spelman, 1988).

Kenneth Boulding (1990) and Robert Coles (1990), among other social commentators (Campbell & Toms, 1990; Rothenburg, 1995), believe Western culture is confronting a social and moral crisis as it seeks to accommodate diversity without either oppressing some groups or ripping apart the common social fabric. In addressing the World Future Society in 1995, Harlan Cleveland urged people to learn how to be different together. Different and together—both. In "Human Family," poet laureate Maya Angelou (1990) wrote,

> I note the obvious differences
> Between each sort and type
> But we are more alike, my friends
> Than we are unalike.

Reflecting the increasing diversity in our society are the growing number of interracial and interethnic relationships. Most college students today have friends of races different than their own—something that was rare even 20 years ago. Similarly, today many people's friendship circles include gays, lesbians, bisexuals, and straights. Interethnic and interracial dating and marriage have also increased dramatically. Since the mid-1970s marriages between Blacks and Whites have tripled, and marriages between Hispanics and non-Hispanics have doubled (Crohn, 1995). When we consider all marriages in the United States between people of different races, the number has more than tripled since 1970 (Tucker & Mitchell-Kernan, 1995).

Relationships between people of different races and ethnicities offer unique challenges. The perspective of the generalized other may not be shared by, for instance, a German woman and an American man or an African American man and a Hispanic woman. Further, views of appropriate family closeness may differ as Dianne Dicks (1993) shows in her book of stories from people engaged in intercultural romance. The following excerpt from Dicks's book is the story of an American man married to an Italian woman:

> When you marry an Italian, you are, in reality marrying the family. . . . In the United States, children leave the nest early to lead their own lives and create their own families and homes. Italians, on the other hand, seek to roost at home until a late age, then, upon leaving, return on an almost daily basis. (Dicks, 1993, pp. 163–164)

Personal relationships between members of different cultures and races present opportunities as well as challenges. They offer us the chance to learn about unfamiliar traditions, ways of structuring relationships, and ways of relating to others. Perhaps intercultural relationships can also teach us that differences need not mean divisions. Differences need not obscure likenesses such as common goals and dreams and rights. If we follow the urgings of Harland Cleveland and Maya Angelou, we will find ways to respect our own and others' heritages, to be loyal to particular groups, and simultaneously to identify with a larger, shared social world.

Pluralistic Values

In 1992, Ben & Jerry's premiered chocolate peanut butter cookie dough as the newest palate pleaser in its lineup of gourmet ice cream. In 1991, 13,000 new products debuted, most of which were variations on existing ones (Keyes, 1992, p. 22). Futurist John Naisbitt (1982, p. 232) calls us a "multiple option society" with something for everyone. Even potato chips are multiple choice: regular, no salt, low salt, no cholesterol, extra crispy, light, ranch, deli-style, fat-free, barbecue, and so on. Campus bookstores stock dozens of brands of disposable ballpoint pens and nearly as many types of notebooks. In 1991, 553 new magazines hit the stands, and 679 debuted in 1992, each catering to a specialized market (Specialty magazines, 1993).

Once satisfied with chocolate, vanilla, or strawberry ice cream, a plain potato chip, and a Bic pen, we now expect a mind-boggling range of choices. Reflecting on this trend, psychologist Martin Seligman (1990) traces diversification directly to technology, which makes it possible to customize formerly standard products. According to Seligman, the plethora of options fosters a "maximal self" that demands choices to maximize gratification in all spheres of life. We've come to expect to have our varied and changing tastes honored whether they pertain to potato chips, ballpoints—or relationship styles.

Nowhere is diversification more clear and consequential than in the explosion of alternative values and lifestyles. In the United States today there are skinheads and yippies, Jesus freaks and neo-Nazis, Satan worshipers and hip-hop. In music we have hard rock, blues, Grrrl power, soul, crossover, new age, country, reggae, rap, and gangsta rap. Although some people are espousing the values of simplifying their lives by cutting down on expenses and possessions, others are happily caught up in acquiring as much as they can as fast as they can. Cable and satellite television have created extensive niche programming so that virtually anyone can find programs that speak to her or his values, lifestyle, and identity.

The diversification of values in today's Western culture is a departure from former times. Until the early 1960s, U.S. culture was defined by "Vision I," which consisted of relatively shared views of the good life and personal relationships (Prusank, Duran, & DeLillo, 1993). In the 1960s, a second vision ushered in a view of relationships as less traditional and more individualistic than in Vision I. Starting in the 1980s, a third vision emerged, which emphasized self-knowledge and equality of partners. You probably know people who embrace each of these visions. Whether we consider personal heritage, lifestyles, or relationships, the uniformity of earlier times has given way to a kaleidoscope of choices for identity and personal relationships.

Proliferating Family Forms

During the 1992 presidential campaign, a furor broke out when then-Vice President Dan Quayle castigated popular sitcom character Murphy Brown for becoming a single mother. Unmarried mothers, he said, mock family values. This launched a nationwide debate about what a family is. Quayle defined a family as married heterosexuals and children. But, objected many, that excludes *the majority*—yes, the majority—of Americans.

Whether by choice or circumstance, many parents are single, and women are not the only ones who are single parents. In 1997 there were 1.86 million single dads in the United States. Many of these fathers report that parenting is their most important role. Yet, they also note that society doesn't always respect men who place parenting ahead of career advancement. To combat negative social attitudes, some single dads belong to virtual support groups on the Internet. Others find support by belonging to Promise Keepers, a movement that emphasizes the importance of men's role in families (Milbank, 1997).

Another large group of people live in blended families in which children from two or more previous marriages live together with one of their parents and a stepparent. Other families consist of gay and lesbian couples without children. Add to this families that consist of gay or lesbian parents and their children. According to Charlotte Patterson, in 1992 between 1 and 5 million lesbians were mothers and between 1 and 3 million gay men were fathers. Other families are child-free couples, cohabiting partners, and people for whom blood and adoption do not define connections (Gaines, 1995). The 1992 political debate reflects a larger cultural conversation about families.

Interestingly, what is typically referred to as the traditional family—a father working outside the home, a homemaker-mother, and two to four children—was never standard except for upper- and middle-class White heterosexuals (Coontz, 1992, 1996; Footlick, 1990). Historically, most families in the United States have had at least two wage earners. Because medical advances have increased life spans, families increasingly include one or more parents of partners for an average of 18 years (The daughter track, 1990; Wood, 1994d; Zarit, Pearlin, & Schaie, 1993).

Diversity also characterizes how families operate. Although some contemporary couples adopt conventionally gendered arrangements, a growing number prefer equality (Prusank, Duran, & DeLillo, 1993; Wood, 1999) in both authority and responsibilities for home and family. Cultural conditions prompt other changes in how families function. For instance, unemployment and advocacy of active fathering combine to make fathers the primary caregivers for one in five preschoolers with working mothers (Belluck & Borowski, 1993; Milbank, 1997; More fathers, 1993). As computers make telecommuting viable, more homes will be work sites (Shellenbarger, 1993b). The "electronic cottage" that Toffler predicted in 1970 is now a reality as hot-wired homes allow people to interact with colleagues and massive databases without leaving their personal space (Lacy, 1993). Of course, this radically redefines what *personal* space is! Changes in how we live, work, and socialize alter how we view relationships and ourselves.

RECONFIGURING PERSONAL IDENTITY

In 1991, Kenneth Gergen wrote an important book, *The Saturated Self*, in which he explored transformations in personal identity and relationships that are wrought by the mushrooming variety of modern life. According to Gergen, diversification reconfigures identity and personal relations by fostering relational selves and saturated selves.

Relational Selves

Technology and diversity plunge us into multiple relationships, each of which evokes distinctive facets of our identities. Discovering and enacting diverse identities debilitates the idea of a stable, core self. Consider an example. On a morning before my partner and I flew to my sister's home, I was writing about a theory of intimacy and Robbie was analyzing the value of articulation theory for understanding the social justice movement within environmental politics. On our flight, Robbie proposed a romantic retreat for the two of us. When we arrived at my sister's home, her 3-year-old daughter Michelle graciously served us make-believe tea in imaginary teacups. Caught up in the spirit of the moment, I sang a chorus of "Little Bunny Foo Foo," Michelle's favorite song, which prompted Robbie to threaten, "Wait until I tell your colleagues about this!"

Which is the real Robbie? The scholar who writes eloquently about social justice, the man who remains romantic after 25 years together, or the rascal who threatens to tell colleagues I can be childlike? Which me is real? The scholar engrossed in theories of intimacy, the woman who relishes romantic retreats, or the aunt sipping imaginary tea and singing about Bunny Foo Foo? Gergen would say all of these are equally authentic Robbies and Julias. All are possibilities that may come forth in any moment.

Gergen says that the modern self is a **relational self**—a processual self that is constantly emerging and reforming as it moves in and out of various relationships. Gergen suggests that the self is not a fixed essence but emerges in relationships. I am a frivolous playmate with Michelle, a scholar in my work, and a romantic with Robbie. The multiple selves cause no problem as long as I don't sing "Bunny Foo Foo" to my students or bore Michelle with theories of intimacy. Yet, these multiple selves are not always compatible. When I am engrossed in my work, I am frustrated if Michelle wants to play. Sometimes we feel pressured to be selves that we don't like, and at other times one version of ourself seems at odds with another. These tensions are inherent in an era that situates each of us in multiple roles and contexts and that demands adaptation and versatility. Because each of us has the potential to be many selves, the ones that we realize depend on the relationships and contexts in which we situate ourselves.

Saturated Selves

The second sense in which cultural diversification reconfigures personal identity is through the saturation of our perspectives by the ever-increasing number of others we encounter. The idea of a **saturated self** (Gergen, 1991) extends symbolic interactionism's emphasis on internalizing others' perspectives to highlight the fact that individuals' identities are infused with the multiple and sometimes conflicting perspectives of others—ones that do not necessarily fit into the coherent whole that Mead described as the generalized other. We become saturated by widely diverse views, goals, and values that seep into our own perspectives. High-tech communications perforate our consciousness not only with people we know personally but also ones media bring us—famine victims, the rich and famous, terrorists, saints, politicians, and cult leaders. Through media we become aware of people and perspectives beyond those we experience directly. Our identities become *saturated*—tumescent with a deluge of others.

As the number and diversity of perspectives we encounter expands, a uniform sense of the social world and ourselves fractures. What makes sense from one viewpoint seems absurd from another, and no viewpoint is inherently superior. The multitude of others who saturate our consciousness provide points of comparison and views of who we are and what we do. Yet, because these other perspectives reflect diverse standpoints (Wood & Cox, 1993), they do not yield integrated, coherent images of our identities nor do they tell us how we should conduct our lives.

PAT

I just can't figure out how to do it all. Like today there's so much emphasis on eating healthy foods and exercising, but there's also a big push to party and drink. Well, you can't do both. Or I'm expected to land a job and bring in a good salary, so I have to be career focused. But I also want to be a good parent and spouse, which means I can't give everything to a career. And what

*about being involved with the community and social causes? That's important
too, and I know I'll feel bad about myself if I'm not contributing time. Got
any recipes for managing all of that in one lifetime?*

Like many of us, Pat is frustrated by the diverse options open to her and the
realization that each of them makes sense in its own terms, but they do not make
sense together. This kind of bewilderment is a natural by-product of an age in
which multiple, often incompatible perspectives suffuse our consciousness. When
we are saturated by a spectrum of views, values, identities, and lifestyles, an unvarying, consistent identity becomes untenable.

We struggle to make sense of the inconsistencies among the myriad perspectives we encounter and the diverse versions of ourselves we enact. As we do,
we come to realize they represent what Donna Haraway (1988) calls **situated
knowledges.** For Haraway this means, first, that we recognize all knowledge is situated or specifically located, so, second, there is no absolute, universal knowledge
or truth. Third, because no one perspective has inviolate claim to legitimacy, we
have to respect the distinctive knowledges cultivated in multiple, diverse locations.
Haraway speaks of truths and knowledges, rather than Truth or Knowledge, to
remind us that all perspectives make sense within their particular situations or
standpoints. Singing "Bunny Foo Foo" did make sense, and a (not the) real me did
do it at Michelle's tea party; immersion in abstract theory does make sense and a
(not the) real me enjoys that; and dewy-eyed romanticism is reasonable and a (not
the) real me relishes that in private moments with Robbie.

If all knowledge and action are situated, then any choice can seem both reasonable and unreasonable—depending on the perspective we use to assess it:
Michelle knows romantic interludes with Robbie don't hold a candle to a fine tea
party, and few theorists extol the merits of Bunny Foo Foo. Each activity makes
sense in its situation; none does outside of its context. All are situated truths about
me, none is The Truth of The Me. Diversity, then, begets relational selves and,
with them, situated knowledges and perspectives we may use to consider ourselves
from multiple standpoints.

Our awareness of multiple standpoints and varying versions of ourselves necessarily ousts the comfort of certainty. Every self, course of action, and value is per-
spectival; none is absolute. Understandably, lack of coherence is unsettling, yet it
is also liberating, because it heightens our awareness that the social world and ourselves are always in process, emerging, evolving. Deeply rooted in Western culture
is the idea of a constant, autonomous identity, and it is precisely this view of self
that crumbles in the face of varying, sometimes conflicting versions of ourselves
and social life. As belief in transcendent truth dissolves, individual identity and
relationship forms lose their resoluteness, becoming instead variable and emergent. Instead of losing the self, we may be exchanging a static identity for a flexible, multiple one suited to this era.

AFFIRMING PERSONAL AGENCY

Discussing cultural values and social trends could tempt us to believe that society *determines* who we are and how we create and engage in relationships. Yet that would be a misreading of the issues and the point of our discussion in the foregoing pages. The goal of this chapter is to enhance awareness of prevalent values and trends circulating in our culture so that you have a more informed basis for making choices and exercising agency in your life.

Influence, Not Determination

Individuals are not blank slates onto which culture inscribes values and lifestyles. Although society encourages, seduces, and prods us to conform, the I part of the self that Mead (1934) celebrated enables us to resist pressures for conformity and to create innovations. Thus, the I may overshadow the ME by saying, "ME, you don't have to remind me what society expects. I am fully aware of that, and I refuse to go along." Individuals who refuse to conform may instigate widespread change. As we've seen, social views have shifted over time, largely in response to dissident voices within the society: Current views include increased recognition of gay and lesbian partnerships, expanded views of family, and less pejorative attitudes toward divorce. In resisting prevailing views, individuals have impelled change. In other words, just as society creates individuals, so too do individuals create society.

The Agency of Relational Selves

Renouncing a view of self as singular and constant across time and space allows us to enlarge our understanding of personal identity. Precisely because we internalize pluralistic perspectives into our consciousness, we are continually emerging, forming, in process. This amplifies possibilities for who we might be beyond the narrow range available in prior eras. By observing others and experimenting with varied roles, we create a storehouse of possible selves. Diversity's capacity to expand the self balances the frustration of having overwhelming choices. By exploring options, we assume agency to create and re-create ourselves.

SHANNON

I love the choices available today! I like knowing there are different ways I can run my life and that I get to choose for myself. I really want a career and children too, and for a long time I thought I had to choose between those. But my older sister and her husband both work and they have two kids, and their kids are doing great in day care. Seeing them do it that way made it a real option for me. And another thing I like is the idea that I don't have to stick with a choice if it doesn't work out. My mom went back to work last year, but after six months she quit and said that wasn't right for her, and nobody thought she was wrong to try it or wrong to move on. Now she's going to

*school, and she says that is working out for her. If she can change like that at
48, then I can rethink choices I make, too.*

In addition to noting that others' choices expand our own, Shannon highlights the tentative character of human choice. Although some choices such as
becoming a parent cannot be forsaken, many can. We are largely free to experiment with alternative identities and lifestyles and to commit only to those we find
satisfying. This doesn't mean we should make or abandon choices cavalierly; it
does mean many need not be permanent. By extension, identities we try and discard are not failures but may be ways of clarifying who we want to be by experimenting with alternatives. Selves that are open and emergent are most able to
approach identity and relationships as ongoing processes.

Another important benefit of diversity and the relational selves it cultivates is
expanded perspectives we can bring to bear on ourselves and the world around us.
To understand this point we need only recall symbolic interactionism, which theo-
rizes that individuals develop minds and selves by communicating with others and
internalizing their perspectives. We have seen that technology and diversity saturate us with pluralistic voices and standpoints that open a world of possibilities to
each of us.

In tandem, technology and diversity cultivate an understanding of culture
and identity as processes and possibilities. When our own perspective includes
diverse viewpoints, then we have a rich variety of distinct MEs we can use to reflect
on the I in any moment. Multiple perspectives enlarge insight into ourselves and
expand the options we have for acting in any situation. Respecting multiple perspectives is not radical relativism, which proclaims all ways equally valid and denies
the possibility of preferring any single choice. Instead, it is honoring differences
and the standpoints from which they emanate and, simultaneously, reserving for
each of us the right to prefer some identities, lifestyles, and forms of relationship
over others.

FRED

*Last week I felt overcome by all I had to do—two papers plus an exam, and
I had to work 20 hours to boot. I thought about all my friends who have light
schedules or don't work, and I felt my situation was really unfair. But then I
caught myself and asked whether there were other ways to look at my situation, and so I thought about my friend Jim who has worked 20 or more
hours a week since high school, and he's in premed. Jim never complains; he
just does the best he can. And then I thought about several other friends who
also work and have tough loads. Considering their perspectives changed how
I felt about my situation.*

*I also had to catch myself with Ellen, my girlfriend. She was going on
about how little time I spend with her, and I was feeling put upon and*

remembering what my friends say about how they don't take any of that from their girlfriends. I was about to tell her to take me as I am or move on; then I asked myself how else I might look at what was happening. I remembered what my dad said once when I asked why he put up with Mom's nagging about how much time he spent at work, whether he was exercising, and so on. He told me that wasn't nagging; it was love. And then he asked me if I'd want a wife who didn't want me home and didn't care about my health. Things really look different, depending on what perspective you choose to apply.

Catching Ourselves

We could all learn from Fred's insight about choosing perspectives. He writes of "catching himself" in the common tendency of relying on a single perspective. Fred first saw himself as a martyr burdened by heavy responsibilities and Ellen's nagging, yet he sought alternative ways to interpret what was happening. Alternatives always exist if we look for them. To reap the benefit of multiple perspectives, we have to monitor tendencies to screen out views that aren't immediately comfortable.

SUMMARY

Trends toward increasing technology and diversity expand our freedom to craft personal identities and relationships in varied and unique ways. The constant companion of freedom, of course, is uncertainty. Because our culture no longer provides a single recipe for relationships or identities, we live with ambiguities. There is no societal consensus on which choices enrich relationships nor on when to transform or end them. Because issues such as these have no answers in the back of the book on cultural codes, each of us must invent our own answers as we go along. Freedom accompanied by uncertainty invite us to see ourselves as possibilities, rather than as fixed essences, and to regard ourselves in any moment as tentative and subject to revision and more revision. Like relationships and culture, we too are processes, always changing, always changeable.

Both the content and the tone of this chapter are deliberately reflective. I have not tried to resolve tensions between and within cultural trends, because they inhere in the times that we live. Thus, any resolutions I or you might attempt, however comforting, would be false. The technological sophistication of our era breathtakingly expands possibilities in work, relationships, even life itself; simultaneously, it generates profoundly troubling quandaries. Speed and efficiency increase our productivity and the experiences we have, yet they may also strain long-term commitment. Diversity holds promise of forging a new unity based on inclusiveness, and concurrently, it threatens to divide us into groups defined by race, gender, or other criteria. In the current cultural context, uncertainty is the only certainty, and ambiguity, tentativeness, and multiplicity are facts of modern life. Given this, communication between intimate partners becomes more critical than ever, because it is through communication that partners forge shared understandings and work out interpretations of the confusing and sometimes unsettling realities of life in this era. By embracing the tensions inherent in diversity and communicating with others to understand and respond to them, we maximize our options for defining identity, relationships, and society in creative, enriching ways. With its unique possibilities and puzzles, this era is, indeed, the best of times and the worst of times for personal relationships.

FOR FURTHER REFLECTION AND DISCUSSION

1. Have you ever or do you now experience overchoice? Describe what it feels like and how you respond to it.
2. Do you think we have the wisdom to make good choices about the technologies we do or soon will control? Are technological achievements outstripping our capacity to understand them and use them wisely?
3. Talk with grandparents or others at least two generations removed from you. Try to learn how they viewed relationships, the pace of life 30 years ago, and so forth. Share perceptions in a class dialogue.
4. Apply the concept of relational self to your own identity. What distinct versions of yourself can you identify? Do you feel they are complementary, in tension, or both?
5. Did the discussion of saturated self make sense in terms of your experiences? How does saturation affect your sense of yourself and your awareness of different standpoints?
6. What do you consider the most exciting implications of current Western culture for personal relationships? Which social trends, cultural values, or both do you consider to be the greatest threat to personal relationships?

RECOMMENDED READINGS

Andersen, M., & Collins, P. (Eds.). (1995). *Race, class and gender: An anthology* (2nd ed.). Belmont, CA: Wadsworth.

Coontz, S. (1992). *The way we never were: American families and the nostalgia trap.* New York: Basic Books.

Dicks, D. (Ed.). (1993). *Breaking convention with intercultural romances.* Weggis, Switzerland: Bergili Books.

Gergen, K. (1991). *The saturated self: Dilemmas of identity in contemporary life.* New York: Basic Books.

Marciano, T., & Sussman, M. B. (Eds.). (1991). *Wider families.* New York: Haworth.

Weston, K. (1991). *Families we choose.* New York: Columbia University Press.

PART
TWO

*The Evolution of
Personal Relationships*

Launching
Personal Relationships

ALTHOUGH WE SOMETIMES THINK of intimacy as an all-or-nothing matter, actually it grows and changes over the course of time. We meet a new person and interact for a while. Over time, we interweave our lives together until a sense of deep connection links us. If we stay together, that sense of connection grows deeper as we share and talk about important experiences in our lives. We may become dissatisfied with the relationship if communication between us ebbs, and we may eventually end the relationship. Although we may perceive intimacy only when we are aware of a profound union with another and declare it over only if we feel distant from someone, both coming together and growing apart are usually processes that develop over time. Through ongoing interaction and reflection, individuals weave understandings and connections that create, revise, and—sometimes—unravel personal relationships.

This chapter launches our examination of how individuals create, sustain, and dismantle personal relationships. We begin by considering what it means to think about personal relationships as developmental. Next, in Chapter 7, we will explore processes that partners typically associate with increasing closeness and commitment. Chapter 8 extends this discussion by examining how intimates sustain, refine, and transform relational cultures that are the crux of intimacy. We will focus on daily rhythms, communication patterns, rituals, managing disagreement, and rejuvenation as primary ways that partners sustain intimacy over time. In Chapter 8 we also examine the ways that partners attempt to repair ailing relationships. Transforming and ending relationships are the focus of Chapter 9. In tandem, these chapters explain how partners' perceptions of relationships change over time and describe some of the personal and interpersonal processes that influence intimate evolution. It is likely that some of what we discuss will already be familiar to you, because you have undoubtedly experienced the rise and fall of various relationships in your own life.

A DEVELOPMENTAL PERSPECTIVE ON INTIMACY

Because personal relationships develop and decay over time, a great deal of theory and research has concentrated on mapping the evolutionary course of intimacy.

Initial Developmental Thinking: Linear, External Models

The first generation of developmental thinking about personal relationships emerged in the 1970s and consisted of fairly simple models. For instance, Irwin Altman and Dallas Taylor (1973) proposed a social penetration model, which depicted relationships as advancing toward intimacy as a result of individuals' self-disclosures that penetrate deeper and deeper into each other's core selves (Figure 6.1). Similarly, George Levinger (1974) modeled relationships as becoming increasingly intimate as partners develop progressively personalized insights into each other.

FIGURE 6.1

Altman and Taylor's Social Penetration Model

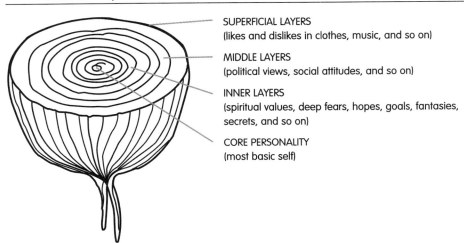

SUPERFICIAL LAYERS
(likes and dislikes in clothes, music, and so on)

MIDDLE LAYERS
(political views, social attitudes, and so on)

INNER LAYERS
(spiritual values, deep fears, hopes, goals, fantasies, secrets, and so on)

CORE PERSONALITY
(most basic self)

In the 1980s, more complex models of relationship development accounted for a greater number of influences on the development of intimacy, and they attended to relationship decline, which had been neglected in earlier models (Duck, 1982; Knapp, 1984; Phillips & Wood, 1983; Wood, 1982). Typically, models in the 1980s included multiple stages that were assumed to occur in a generally sequential fashion. Thus, intimacy was depicted as progressing through acquaintance, intensification, and intimate bonding; relationship decline was portrayed as moving through dissatisfaction, stagnation, and termination.

By the mid-1980s, relationship scholars began to raise questions about existing developmental models. One major criticism maintained that not all relationships progress in a linear manner but, instead, cycle back and forth among stages (Baxter, 1985, 1988; Van Lear, 1992). This criticism was supported by research findings that about one-third of couples who break up skip some of the early stages in models of decline but later engage in them (Lee, 1984). Two people may become acquainted and intensify their interactions but then back away from each other for a period before increasing intimacy further. Similarly, two friends may become dissatisfied with their interaction, drift apart for a period, and then rebuild closeness. Further, even in healthy, enduring personal relationships, feelings ebb and flow in response to ongoing negotiation of relational dialectics and changes in partners, relational cultures, and external systems with which personal relationships interact. Zigzag paths, which are not uncommon, were not well captured by linear models of relationship development.

Linear models also erred in implying an inevitability to relationship development. Most seemed to suggest both that there is a correct goal toward which personal relationships aspire and that each stage people go through propels them into the next (Wood, 1982). In Western culture, the apex stipulated for romantic intimacy is marriage, yet defining the height of intimacy by a formal marriage excludes gay, lesbian, and cohabiting couples. Defining marriage as the goal also implies that couples that do not choose to marry have somehow failed when, in fact, they may feel their relationship was wonderful yet they did not want to marry.

An even more troublesome criticism of early developmental models is that they focused almost exclusively on the relationships of White, middle-class, able-bodied, heterosexual college students. Other developmental courses might be followed by non-Anglos, members of the working class, gays and lesbians, persons with disabilities, and people older than 24.

FRANCES

As an older student, I have experience with forming relationships at different points in life. When I was in my twenties, intimacy happened faster. My pattern was to be attracted, rev up the relationship, and then lose interest. That happened a number of times before I met Jerry, my first husband. After ten years we divorced, and I was 36. Now I'm 41, and the relationships I've had with men in the last five years developed a lot more slowly. Part of that is because I am simply more cautious about commitments than I was at 20. Also, at 20 I could focus on a new relationship and let everything else go if I wanted to, so that stoked intimacy. But now I work full-time and have two young children. Relationships have to fit around other parts of my life.

Another criticism of developmental models is that they misrepresent intimacy as a state, rather than a process (Honeycutt, 1993). For instance, one model (Knapp, 1984; Knapp & Vangelisti, 1992) defines intimate bonding as a public ceremony. Yet, we might question whether intimate bonding is a single moment or event. Is it a static thing that, once achieved, is done forever? Or is bonding an ongoing process in which continuous conversation between partners weaves and reweaves their connection? Steve Duck (1990, 1991a) argues forcefully that the crux of personal relationships is motion, not an outcome or steady state. In previous chapters we've seen that intimacy is an ongoing process through which partners continuously recalibrate understandings of themselves and their relationship.

Finally, developmental models were criticized for implying a reality to relationship stages that exists apart from partners. Stages such as "intensifying" or "bonding" were reified and defined by objective events, activities, conditions, or factors. Altman and Taylor's (1973) social penetration model charts intimacy on the basis of increasingly personal disclosures. Mark Knapp and Anita Vangelisti (1992) define bonding as "a public ritual that announces to the world that commitments have been formally contracted" (p. 39). My own early developmental model (1982) classified stages in intimacy according to the presence and function of particular kinds of communication. In each case, points in a relationship's life cycle were designated by phenomena external to partners. It might be more reasonable, suggested critics, to rely on partners' views and feelings to define phases in personal relationships. Many couples, for instance, place greater weight on private pledges than public vows.

M E L Y A

Right now I'm planning my wedding and my mom is so excited. She keeps saying how my wedding day will be the most important day in my life, but I don't think so. The most important day was last October when Bart told me he loved me and always would and I told him the same thing. What we said to each other then, without any preacher or white dress and flowers, is what holds us together. The wedding is after the fact.

These criticisms convinced many scholars that the first generation of developmental models was too linear, static, and externally focused. Although the idea that relationships develop in patterned ways is intuitively appealing, early efforts to model that development proved unsatisfactory.

Individual Interpretations of Relationship Development

Despite disappointment with early developmental models, many researchers retained allegiance to the idea that personal relationships grow and deteriorate developmentally. In 1993, however, a conceptual breakthrough yielded a developmental perspective that represents relationships as progressing over time, but the idea is not encumbered by external, static, and linear assumptions.

In an exciting reconceptualization of relationship development, James Honeycutt (1993) proposed that the perception of progression of relationships happens as a result of individuals' cognitions, rather than as a result of external events or concrete activities between partners. In other words, the presence or absence of disclosures (an objective phenomenon) does not affect relationship development *unless and until* individuals ascribe meaning to disclosures. When we define revealing personal information as an intimate act, we perceive disclosure as escalating intimacy. It is the meaning we assign to acts, not the acts themselves, that leads us to sense a relationship has moved to a new phase. Honeycutt's perspective, in his words, "focuses specifically on the ways persons organize cognition about relational change" (1993, p. 60). Thus, individuals draw on their knowledge of relationships to define movement in intimacy. Similarly, even though partners may zigzag between closeness and distance, they typically have a sense of where they are in a relationship at any given moment.

Friends and romantic partners have what Honeycutt calls **imagined trajectories**, which consist of partners' understandings of the various tracks relationships follow and where each track leads. These trajectories function as scripts that define expected sequences of action and, thus, guide how we view behaviors that do and do not fit those sequences. For example, you may have an imagined trajectory for intensified romantic interest that consists of sharing personal information, having long conversations in person, and calling several times a day. If these things occur, you're likely to define a relationship as on an escalation trajectory, which you might label "infatuation," "falling in love," or "heating up." Notice that your interpretation of what transpires, not the events themselves, confers meaning on the interaction.

This view of relationship development suggests that we perceive relationships as moving along orderly paths based on our organized knowledge about relationships. As we interact with significant others and the generalized other, we gain information about how relationships work in our society. Rather than simply taking in and storing information, however, we organize it in our memories (Honeycutt, Cantrill, & Green, 1989; Schank, 1982); we put it together into a coherent framework that defines meaning and guides how we interpret new experiences.

Empirical evidence supports Honeycutt's view of how individuals experience relationship evolution. A series of investigations (Pryor & Merluzzi, 1985) showed that people are highly consistent in what they list as actions typical on a first date. In a similar study (Rose & Frieze, 1989), college students broadly agreed on how women and men should act on first dates. Beverly Fehr's (1993) research demonstrates that individuals in the United States share general understandings of what intimacy entails and how it progresses.

TABLE 6.1

Categories of Turning Points

TYPE OF TURNING POINT	EXAMPLES
Intrapersonal/normative	Occurs when an individual evaluates herself or himself, the partner, or the relationship against some ideal or normative standard.
	• He is not ambitious enough. • We are too young to be serious. • She's just what I always wanted.
Dyadic	Occurs directly in interaction between partners.
	• Saying "I love you." • Saying "We can't go on like this." • Walking out on an argument.
Social network	Occurs when people from either or both partners' social networks affect a relationship.
	• Parents approve of relationship. • Friends dislike partner. • Brother invites couple to visit.
Circumstantial	Occurs when events that are perceived as beyond partners' personal control affect the relationship.
	• Job relocation. • Need to work more hours each week. • Natural disaster.

Turning Points

Complementing Honeycutt's reconceptualization of relationship development are turning points, a concept we introduced in Chapter 2. We're now ready to discuss turning points in greater detail. The concept of turning point was conceived nearly four decades ago (Bolton, 1961) to refer to perceptions of events that transform relationships. Notice that events *per se* are not turning points; it is the perception of an event as transformative that makes it a turning point in the life of a relationship. Substantial research has identified four broad categories of turning points, which are summarized in Table 6.1 (Baxter & Bullis, 1986; Baxter & Pittman, 1996; Bullis, Clark, & Sline, 1993; Graham, 1997; Huston et al., 1981; Lloyd & Cate, 1985; Surra, 1985, 1987; Surra, Arizzi, & Asmussen, 1988).

In addition to categorizing types of turning points, scholars have found that turning points can be sequenced in different ways, resulting in distinct trajectories of relationship development. Researchers have identified four basic trajectories for the development of romantic relationships (Surra, 1985, 1987, 1990; Surra & Huston, 1987). These are summarized in Table 6.2. Relationship trajectories based on turning points reflect both greater variety and turbulence in the development of romantic relationships. Notice that in contrast to the first generation of develop-

TABLE 6.2

Trajectories of Courtship

Accelerated	Partners move quickly and smoothly to marriage
Accelerated-arrested	Relationship zooms to life quickly but loses momentum and commitment does not follow
Intermediate	Relationship develops gradually and includes some turbulence yet does achieve high commitment
Prolonged	Moderately stormy and slow development resulting in eventual commitment

mental models, viewing relationship development in terms of turning points places far greater attention on dynamism and less on static periods of stability.

Sources of Relationship Knowledge

From our discussion of symbolic interaction theory in Chapter 2, recall that individuals' perceptions and meanings for experience are strongly shaped by beliefs, ideals, and patterns learned from interaction with specific individuals and the culture as a whole. So how does interaction with others and the culture shape our understandings specifically of personal relationships? How does social interaction affect our perception of important turning points, as well as our overall sense of relationship development?

We've already suggested that one major source of knowledge about relationships is our culture. All societies have norms that define relationships and the roles of people in them. In Western culture, friendship is understood to include intimacy, respect, and assistance (Contarello & Volpato, 1991); in other cultures, friendship is assumed to entail more, less, and different forms of interdependence. Romantic relationships and marriage are also defined differently by various societies, with extended family being much more a part of a couple's life in countries other than the United States. The rigidity of traditional sex roles in marriage also varies across cultures.

There are other ways we learn about relationships. Some sources of relationship knowledge are indirect: media, third parties who instruct us formally or informally, and observation of others' relationships (Andersen, 1993; Honeycutt, Cantrill, & Greene, 1989). Movies, films, television, and literature offer models of relationships and intimate interaction. Admittedly, some of these models are unrealistic. Nonetheless, media contribute to our understanding of how relationships work. As we observe others in their relationships and as we talk to people about relationships, we also gain information (Andersen, 1993). Conversations with others provide perspective on our experiences and points of comparison we use to assess our own relationships (Harvey, Weber, & Orbuch, 1990; Planalp, Rutherford, & Honeycutt, 1988).

We also learn from direct experience in relationships and from reflecting on interactions (Andersen, 1993; Honeycutt, 1993). From empirical studies, we know that people who have been in serious relationships have more developed, detailed expectations for what will happen than people who have not been intimately involved (Honeycutt & Cantrill, 1991). Other research (Martin, 1991, 1992) supports this by demonstrating that greater relationship experience promotes more complex understandings of interaction. Thus, prior intimacies shape our expectations, perceptions, and interpretations of current relationships (Chelune, Robison, & Kammar, 1984; Planalp, 1985). Knowledge about relationships also arises from how we interpret, sort, resort, and edit experience. We do not just interact with others, but we interpret what occurs, assign significance to it, and ponder what happens and what it means. All of this affects our knowledge of how relationships work (Andersen, 1986, 1993; Metts, Sprecher, & Cupach, 1991; Reis & Shaver, 1988). Relying on both indirect and direct sources, individuals gather knowledge about relationships. Whether accurate or distorted, helpful or misleading, our beliefs and understandings about relationships shape our expectations, as well as our perceptions and actions.

INITIAL INTERACTION: THE GENESIS OF RELATIONSHIPS

Although people launch personal relationships in varied ways, there are some patterns that are common, albeit not universal. In this section we'll consider general tendencies in interpersonal attraction and in styles of communicating and interpreting interaction. Taken together, these affect initial interaction and, thus, the likelihood of forming deeper relationships. Many of the influences on interaction will be familiar, because they are formal descriptions of experiences you have had.

Attraction

We are not equally attracted to everyone, and we certainly don't try to start relationships with most people. Instead, our choices are sculpted by social systems that constrain whom we meet and by personal cognitive structures that guide how we communicate, as well as how we perceive others and their communication. Proximity and similarity are two of the most important influences on our feeling of being attracted to people with whom we might start relationships.

Proximity. Mundane as it may seem, **proximity,** or nearness, is a major influence on initial attraction. You can only interact with people whose paths cross yours (Phillips & Wood, 1983). If you reflect for a moment, chances are you'll realize that the majority of your friends and romantic interests are people who live near you and with whom you have regular contact. Had you attended another school, you would have different friends and romantic partners—and so would the people with whom you are now close! As Sharon Brehm (1992) notes, "To meet people is not necessarily to love them, but to love them, we must first meet them" (p. 61).

Social trends such as technology and mobility are affecting the nature and importance of proximity to attraction. Today, we can be in touch with people around the globe, and we can meet people and build relationships without physical proximity. Thus, being near another person physically is no longer a necessary criterion for attraction. Even in the virtual world of electronic communication, however, we can only meet and become attracted to those individuals who visit the web sites and chat rooms that we visit. So, proximity—whether virtual or real—continues to influence attraction. Further, it's good to keep in mind that the high profile accounts of people who fall in love in cyberspace are more the exception than the rule. In fact, college students today are more likely to date people in their residential areas than were college students in the 1950s (Whitbeck & Hoyt, 1994). Thus, even in our highly technological era, for most of us attraction is still strongly linked to physical proximity.

Early, classic studies by Leon Festinger and his associates (Festinger, 1951; Festinger, Schachter, & Back, 1950) confirmed the relationship between physical proximity and attraction. In mapping friendships among families living in student housing, the researchers found that friendships were most likely to form between people whose apartments were nearby. This suggests that where we locate directly influences our choices of relationship partners. A number of years ago, an entrepreneurial author exploited research on proximity and attraction by writing a book about how to marry a rich person. The gist of the book was that to marry rich, you had to put yourself in situations where rich people are. Thus, readers were advised to go to exclusive bars and restaurants, browse in expensive stores, and otherwise visit contexts populated by wealthy folks. Although most of us might eschew such calculation, the premise behind it is valid: You can only form relationships with people you meet.

Yet, proximity does not always lead to liking. This was demonstrated in a classic two-year study (Newcomb, 1961) of college students in an arranged living environment. During the first year there was no evidence that roommates were more likely to be friends than students not rooming together. In the second year of the experiment, however, roommates were markedly more likely to be friends than were non-roommates. What explains the difference between the two years? During the first year of his experiment, Theodore Newcomb had randomly assigned roommates, but during the second year, roommates were matched according to expressed values and attitudes. Thus, during the second year when proximity and attraction were strongly associated, roommates were people who had common values and viewpoints.

The connection between attraction and common values was confirmed by research (Ebbesen, Kjos, & Konecni, 1976) that showed proximity increases attraction only between people who share values and other qualities. If people differ or conflict in important ways, proximity may breed ill will. Coining the term **environmental spoiling,** the researchers reported that differences and conflicts between people are accented if they must live nearby. Environmental spoiling can also occur in electronic interaction. Perhaps you have had the experience of belonging to a listserve or frequenting a chat room and finding that you dislike one or two members of the virtual community. The more often they sent messages, the more your dislike of them grew.

JOEL

I understand environmental spoiling. During my freshman year, I was assigned a roommate whom I wound up despising. I come from a working-class family, and he was from a very well-to-do one, and it showed. He was sloppy in the extreme, because he'd always had maids to pick up after him. He was also used to having his own way and oblivious to how that affected anyone else. If he felt like listening to music, he would play it loud regardless of whether I was studying. He knew I was allergic to cigarette smoke, but he still smoked in the room. A lot of the things I dislike about him are ones that wouldn't have bothered me much if we hadn't been forced to live together.

Similarity. We've all been told that birds of a feather flock together, yet we've also heard that opposites attract. These two adages capture competing views of one of the bases of interpersonal attraction: Do we tend to like people who are like us or different from us? A great deal of research conducted to answer this question indicates that, for the most part, similarity is far more attractive than dissimilarity.

Similarity and difference, of course, exist on many levels. One of those most studied is demographic similarity, which involves likeness in background, class, ethnicity, age, and so forth. As we discussed previously, Newcomb (1961) matched students demographically in the second year, and he found that people with similar backgrounds and other characteristics liked each other more than people with dissimilar ones. This makes sense, because demographic factors such as background, age, race, and class shape our standpoints, making demographically similar people more alike in their experiences and understandings of social life. Although the relatively automatic comfort we feel with others like us is understandable, it may restrict our interpersonal experiences and perspectives.

The association between attitudinal similarity and interpersonal attraction has been the focus of extensive study, and results are somewhat mixed. In general, it seems people prefer others who have kindred attitudes or those whom they perceive as having attitudes similar to their own. Researchers studying this topic have found that attraction increases both when we perceive that others have attitudes consistent with our own (Bochner, Krueger, & Chmielewski, 1982; Byrne, 1971; Sachs, 1976) and when they actually do hold attitudes similar to ours (Byrne, Ervin, & Lamberth, 1970; Newcomb, 1961). Along the same line, between spouses the perception of similar attitudes about a relationship seems more important to satisfaction than actual similarity (Acitelli, Douvan, & Veroff, 1993). It may be that if we are initially attracted to someone, we assume his or her attitudes and values are similar to our own; once we assume the other person is similar to us, he or she becomes even more attractive (Marks & Miller, 1982). The perception of similarity may lead us to notice commonalities between us and the other person and to not perceive, or dismiss, areas of difference. Assumptions about similarity may also enhance attraction on the Internet. You might assume that someone in a chat room you visit has much in common with you, so you begin that relationship with a perception (one that hasn't been proved) of similarity, which inclines you to like the other person.

Other researchers (Rosenbaum, 1986), tackling this topic from a different angle, argue that attitudinal dissimilarity fosters dislike, or even repulsion. It seems that people generally like and seek out those with attitudes like their own and dislike and avoid those whose attitudes differ (Byrne, Clore, & Smeaton, 1986; Smeaton, Byrne, & Murnen, 1989). In a study of why couples break up, Diane Felmlee (1995) reported that some couples decided "we're just too different."

Yet there is some evidence to indicate attitude similarity alone may not always promote attraction. Two studies (Sunnafrank, 1991; Sunnafrank & Miller, 1981) found that people were no more attracted to individuals with similar values than ones with dissimilar values *if they had opportunities to interact*. This suggests that we may find it more gratifying to talk with others about what we believe than to simply match beliefs. Both Art Bochner (1991) and Steve Duck (1992) argue that communicating with others about attitudes influences initial attraction, perhaps more than similarity itself. This position does not necessarily refute findings that perceived and actual attitude similarity increase attractiveness; it does, however, qualify those findings by reminding us that only as people communicate can they discover similarities and use them to build further connections.

Another basis of similarity is personality, and here too the bulk of evidence indicates that likes attract more than opposites. In most respects, people gravitate toward others whose personalities are similar to their own. Researchers have demonstrated positive associations between attraction and similarity in how individuals organize perceptions (cognitive schema) (Neimeyer, 1984). Also, people tend to prefer others who have moods similar to their own; specifically, nondepressed people are more likely to form relationships with other nondepressed people and to avoid interacting with depressed individuals (Locke & Horowitz, 1990). Similarity in personality seems related to long-term satisfaction in marriage, with spouses who have similar personalities reporting greater satisfaction and happiness than couples whose personalities differ (Antill, 1983; Caspi & Herbener, 1990). Similarity in attachment styles also seems important, and people with similar attachment styles tend to pair up (Senchak & Leonard, 1992). It is important to note, however, that not all pairings lead to equally good marital adjustment and satisfaction. As you might predict, couples in which both partners have secure attachment styles are best adjusted. This suggests that although we may be attracted to people whose attachment styles are like our own, not all matches promote well-being.

ROTH

I was thinking about the guys I'm friends with, and most of them are pretty much like I am as far as personality goes. I'm very outgoing, and I guess I have more fun with friends who are the same. It's like we know how to play off of each other and how to egg each other on. Some of my fraternity brothers who are really nice guys are just too quiet for me. We're not on the same wavelength, so it's kind of awkward to do things together. I always feel like I have to keep the ball rolling and take charge, since they don't ever suggest things to do or talk about.

Many people assume that complementary personalities fit together well so that introverts and extroverts are well matched as are dominant and submissive individuals. Despite its intuitive appeal, there is little empirical support for the attractiveness of personality complementarity (Fishbein & Thelen, 1981; Nias, 1979). What may be the case is that complementarity of specific behaviors increases attraction (Strong et al., 1988). Thus, intimates may enact different roles in interaction but have similar personalities and overall status in a relationship.

Finally, similarity in physical attractiveness seems important to interpersonal attraction. You might think that people would naturally prefer to associate with physically attractive others, and this is true to an extent. What seems at least as important, however, is similarity of attractiveness between friends and romantic partners. In other words, we tend to form close relationships with people who are about as attractive as we are ourselves. This association holds for friendships (Cash & Derlega, 1978), casual and serious dating couples (White, 1980), and engaged or married couples (Hinsz, 1989). Further, continuing similarity in physical attraction may affect satisfaction in relationships. Spouses who perceived they had maintained their attractiveness but their spouse had not are less satisfied with their sexual life (Margolin & White, 1987). So, although we may fantasize about magnificent physical specimens, in reality most of us tend to seek and be most comfortable with friends and romantic partners who are about as physically attractive as we are and who stay that way.

Physiological influences. Although poets write about the heart in relation to love, our hearts may not be the most important part that matters when it comes to attraction. Helen Fisher, an anthropologist at Rutgers University, studies what she calls the mysteries of love. According to Fisher's research (1992) on nerve circuitry in human brains, lust, attraction, and attachment are distinct emotions that are linked to specific brain chemistry. She says attraction is dictated by the brain, not the heart. Further, Fisher says that attraction is a short-term phenomenon that must be supplanted by attachment if a relationship is to endure. Because attraction and attachment are distinct emotions, Fisher says it is entirely possible for a person to feel deep love for one person and infatuation or sexual desire for another.

TABLE 6.3

The Chemistry of Love

Acetylcholine	Produces a rush of excitement similar to that produced by amphetamines.
Dopamine	Generates a feeling of well-being similar to that induced by some anti-depressants
Endorphins	Leads to feelings of comfort and mellowness similar to those induced by heroin and morphine. This chemical is associated with enduring love relationships.
Norepinephrine	Produces feelings of pleasure, joy, and contentment.
Oxytocin	Induces feelings of wanting to hold, kiss, nuzzle, and caress another. Nicknamed the "cuddle chemical," oxytocin is released when babies nurse, making mothers cuddle them. It is also released during lovemaking.
Phenylethylamine	Causes a heightened sense of excitement. Nicknamed the "infatuation chemical," phenylethylamine causes us to tremble around a person we find attractive and induces feelings of euphoria and energy.
Serotonin	Sustains overall feeling of emotional serenity and well-being.

Consistent with Fisher's findings are those of other scientists who take a literal view of the phrase "the chemistry of love." They report studies showing a direct and strong relationship between certain emotional states and brain chemistry (Ackerman, 1994). Chemist John Bowers (That loving feeling, 1993) asserts that hormones determine romantic attraction, as well as infidelity and parent–child bonding. He describes "attraction junkies" as people who exit a relationship as soon as the first rush of passion fades and then look for a new relationship that will give them another dose of the ebullient feelings of infatuation (see Table 6.3).

Emerging research on physiological bases of attraction is yielding convincing evidence that feeling attracted to another person may be at least as much in our brains as our hearts. Clearly, attraction is a complex process that we are still working to understand fully. What we know at this time is that attraction tends to be enhanced by proximity—physical or virtual—and by perceived and actual similarities. It also seems that brain chemistry works with proximity and similarity to induce feelings of excitement and well-being and to make us want to touch and hold others.

Communicating Interest

Being attracted to another person is one matter; communicating that is another. When an individual finds another attractive, she or he must express that in some way. In initial encounters, we typically do this by following certain verbal and nonverbal codes generally understood in our culture or our more specific social communities. The scripts and rules that we discussed earlier shed light on the process of getting to know others. Scholars have shown that people follow widely shared scripts for getting acquainted (Contarello & Volpato, 1991; Ginsburg, 1988). Researchers have also identified friendship rules in Western culture, including providing emotional support, respecting privacy, and sharing confidences (Argyle & Henderson, 1984). Westerners also share schemata that distinguish between casual and close friendships by such criteria as trust, intimacy, and respect (Davis & Todd, 1985). We also have social rules for signaling interest, such as smiling, moving closer, or holding eye contact.

Verbal communication between strangers is usually launched by what are called **openers,** which are routinized ways of opening conversation: "Hi," "Have we met before?" "Weren't we in a class together last term?" "How do you like this band?" On the content level of meaning, openers are usually banal. However, on the relationship level of meaning, they communicate "I'm interested in you." Openers are invitations to conversation—and to a relationship. We initiate conversation with another person and get a response. Someone speaks to us, and we answer. This is Act I in relationship development, the initial interaction in which we indicate interest or lack of interest. If openers are met with positive responses that indicate reciprocal interest, then interaction moves into what we might call "auditioning," in which the two people present themselves and size up each other. This is a drama in which we choose how to present ourselves and how to interpret and respond to how others present themselves.

There are myriad ways to initiate conversation. Some people try for witty one-liners to start a conversation, whereas others prefer more straightforward openers. In a survey at my university (Students provide pointers, 1983), students said they used openers such as these: "This bartender is so slow," "Weren't you in my English 2 class?" and "Do you want to get lucky?"(p. 7). In the same survey, students indicated that they rejected attention from people by ducking out of the room, saying they were with someone else, passing a signal to a friend to rescue them, and claiming to have to need to get home because of an 8 A.M. class the next day. Openers reflect how individuals wish to be seen and their standpoints on appropriate ways to indicate interest or lack of interest. Thus, early communication may be thought of as scripted efforts to communicate identity and respond to others' communication about who they are.

Initial conversations tend to follow social scripts that prescribe how people are expected to become acquainted and engage in initial interaction. Regulative rules tell us how to sequence communication by taking turns talking and listening and asking and answering questions. Constitutive rules define topics of talk that are appropriate, kinds of responses that are legitimate, and what counts as interest and lack of interest on the relationship level of communication. For instance, we know that "Want to dance?" is more than its denotative meaning indicates, just as we know that "No, thank you" indicates lack of interest in the person, not just a desire not to dance. Likewise, a study of singles bars identified various "survival strategies" that women commonly use to chill out men whose advances they don't welcome (Snow, Robinson, & McCall, 1991). Because our society agrees on basic constitutive rules, we don't have to state bluntly "I like you" to show interest, and we need not shout "Go away" to indicate lack of interest. Instead, we rely on covert conversational bids in which the relationship level of meaning is what matters.

Social norms governing initial interaction vary over time and across groups and cultures. In an earlier era, it would have violated etiquette for a man to introduce himself to a woman who interested him, and it would have been *highly* inappropriate for a woman to do so! Rather, propriety demanded that they be introduced by a mutual acquaintance. Another change in sex roles involves initiation. Today many women phone men they want to date or are dating, but 20 years ago that would have been regarded as extremely forward. Chaperones, too, once accompanied dating couples, and they still do in some countries.

Interpreting Others

Much of what happens in early interaction occurs within individuals, rather than between them. We see actual interaction as people communicate verbally and nonverbally, yet equally pivotal is how individuals interpret each other and the desirability of advancing the relationship. To do so they rely on cognitive schemata, which we discussed in Chapter 2. We use prototypes to decide whether someone we've just met fits better in the category of friend, colleague, date, and so forth. Typically, we use some similar and some different personal constructs when perceiving people who are candidates for friendship and for romance. Although qualities such as attractiveness and trustworthiness seem important in how most people interpret others generally, we tend to have some specialized categories for assessing others as friends and dates. For example, being uncommitted may be important in someone you are considering as a potential romantic partner but less relevant in assessing someone as a potential friend.

Your schemata, like anyone's, are unique and reflect your experiences and the ways you've learned to think about others and interaction. Initial interaction allows individuals to discover whether their schemata are similar or compatible. For example, if intelligence and political activism are two important constructs in how you perceive others, then you're likely to be able to stir up a good conversation with someone who also makes sense of others in terms of their intelligence

JUMPSTART reprinted by permission of United Feature Syndicate, Inc.

and political activity. However, you would be likely to have less success instigating a gratifying conversation with a person who uses physical attractiveness and dancing skill as primary constructs for assessing others.

Communication between people provides the data for interpersonal perceptions (Bochner, 1991; Capella, 1988). We listen to what another says and notice how that person responds to what we say; we watch how the other moves, and we note whether eye contact is strong. The verbal and nonverbal behaviors that occur, however, become meaningful only as we rely on cognitive schemata to help us organize and attribute meaning to behaviors. As Joseph Capella (1988) observes, this is a dynamic process in which individuals interact, interpret, respond to each other, and continuously adjust both behaviors and the meanings they assign to them.

Relationship quota. Other relationships also influence decisions about initiating interaction with new people. Each individual has a preference for involvement with others in general. **Relationship quota** refers to an individual's standard for overall involvement. It specifies how many friendships and romances an individual is comfortable having at any one time (Phillips & Wood, 1983). Some individuals enjoy having many friends simultaneously, whereas others prefer to have only one or two close friends at a time. Similarly, people vary in whether they are comfortable having multiple, simultaneous romantic involvements. When the number of close connections in our lives exceeds our relationship quota, we may feel crowded and strained to maintain involvement with all of the people who matter to us. On the other hand, when we have fewer intimates than we'd like, we may feel lonely and understimulated.

NANCY

Penny and I had worked in the same building for about eight years and exchanged friendly small talk in the break room, but neither of us had ever moved beyond superficial chatting. Then one summer my two closest friends moved out of town at the same time, and I felt really lonely. One day when I was getting coffee, Penny came in the room, and we had our usual friendly exchange. But then I said to her, "Let's do lunch." She agreed and we went to lunch later that week, and we fit together amazingly from our first real conversation. We've been really close friends for 11 years now, but I doubt we ever would have gotten together if my other two friends hadn't moved away.

It's important to be aware of relationship quota when we consider possible new relationships. A person who is already over committed to friends might be unable to meet the responsibilities of a new relationship. Conversely, a person who is feeling adrift and alone might enter into a relationship that normally he or she would reject. We may make unwise choices when our relationship quota is unfulfilled. This explains many rebound romances—people accustomed to having a close romantic partner are likely to feel the need to fill the empty space in their lives when a romance breaks up.

Comparison levels. Social psychologists John Thibaut and Harold Kelley (1959) used social exchange theory to conduct pioneering work on how past and present relationships influence perceptions of current relationships and interest in new ones. They identified two standards that we use to assess relationships. The first of these, the **comparison level (CL),** is a subjective standard of what we expect in a relationship. Based on past and current relationships as well as ones we have observed or know about from others' reports and media, we form a general idea of what is average and acceptable for us in friendships and romantic relationships. Comparison levels vary among individuals, because what we consider normal relationships depends directly on our history of relationship experiences. People who have had rewarding relationships in which they felt valued will have higher comparison levels than individuals who have had troubled or disconfirming relationships. In early interaction, individuals gain first impressions that they measure against their CLs, asking whether the new person is sufficiently intelligent, interesting, considerate, and so forth to meet their basic expectations. The comparison level is a barometer for satisfaction in relationships, because we tend to be satisfied with relationships that meet or exceed our expectations and dissatisfied with those that don't.

A second way we assess relationships is by comparing them to real or perceived alternatives. **Comparison level of alternatives (CL_{alt})** is a relative standard for evaluating relationships that measures how good they are in comparison to other perceived relationships and the option of not being in a relationship at all (Thibaut & Kelley, 1959). The CL_{alt} is an assessment of how another relationship or being alone would be. If an option is perceived as more desirable than the current relationship, then the current one becomes unstable.

CRYSTAL

I know all about the comparison level of alternatives, even though I didn't know the term before now. I really made a big mistake last year. Eddy and I had been dating for nearly two years. We had a really good relationship, but we'd been having some problems. Right when we were trying to work them out, this new guy appeared on the scene and showed a lot of interest in me. I spent some time with him, and it was so nice to have fun again instead of dealing with hassles. He treated me really nice, and the more I saw him, the better he looked. Before long I left Eddy to start dating this guy, and as soon as I did, I started discovering his bad side—all the things he hadn't shown when he was trying to get me away from Eddy. That relationship was short—less than three months—but Eddy wasn't interested in getting back together when I tried later.

Research indicates that the Cl_{alt} relates to commitment to a relationship, because commitment tends to wane if we think a more gratifying relationship is available (Berg & McQuinn, 1986; Green & Sporakowski, 1983). The converse also occurs: When we are fully committed to a given relationship, we're less likely to notice, much less consider, alternatives to it. The Cl_{alt} is a gauge of stability and commitment in relationships, and these are not necessarily linked with satisfaction that is measured by CL. A person may leave a satisfying relationship if she or he perceives a more desirable option is available. On the other hand, somebody who is in an unsatisfying relationship may choose to remain if no better alternatives are perceived. Thus, one cognitive process that influences our decision of whether to launch a relationship is assessing whether the new option would be more desirable than a current one. We should keep in mind, however, that CL_{alt} isn't necessarily accurate: It is only an anticipation based on limited information about how rewarding an alternative relationship would be. It's easy to see what is good in a new relationship and to focus on problems in an established one, but it's likely a new relationship will develop its own warts in time!

In summary, initial interaction is a process in which proximity, similarity, and perhaps brain chemistry influence attraction between people. Once some attraction is felt, individuals present themselves and interpret each other's self-presentations. Relying on social scripts, individuals interact to discover whether they are available and interested. The impressions we form in initial interaction are influenced by our cognitive schemata, as well as by our relationship quotas, comparison levels, and comparison levels of alternatives. Throughout early interaction, communication tends to follow social norms that specify safe topics and widely held scripts for interacting. Because dual perspective is not well developed at this point, individuals cannot relate in highly individualized ways. For partners to gain dual perspective, they must engage in more communication and different kinds of communication.

EXPLORATIONAL COMMUNICATION: REDUCING UNCERTAINTY

Individuals engage in what may be called explorational communication if they are mutually attracted and interested in pursuing a relationship. Because initial interaction adheres closely to social norms and scripts, early exchanges seldom provide truly personal insights into individuals. Thus, a major purpose of explorational communication is to reduce uncertainty by allowing individuals to find out enough about each other to decide whether a closer relationship is desirable and possible. Communication is the primary means by which we reduce uncertainty about others. Through talking with others and observing them in interaction, we discover a lot about them, including how they might fit with us and how they respond to information we reveal. In addition, we learn about others by talking with third parties who sometimes know more about them than we yet do. Both breadth and depth of information reduce uncertainty, increase personal knowledge, and foster dual perspective.

Breadth of Information   — finding similarities (find connection)

In some ways, interaction between people who are exploring the possibilities of a relationship may be thought of as conversational fishing (Phillips & Wood, 1983). Individuals try out a range of topics to discover where they have common ground and interests. Each topic provides opportunities to clarify who the people are (Berger, 1988; Duck, 1991a). This phase of interaction tends to canvas an array of topics such as backgrounds, experiences, values, beliefs, attitudes, ambitions, hobbies, and interests in film, books, and music. As each topic is explored, individuals discover whether they have commonalities or complementarities on which they might build. It's important to discover whether you and another person share basic values, like the same kinds of food and restaurants, enjoy similar music and films, and find the same things funny, sad, and important.

Communication researchers Charles Berger and James Bradac (1982) claim that individuals focus on finding similarities because these reduce uncertainty—the more like you another person seems, the more you feel you know what she or he is like. This "filtering process" (Kerckhoff & Davis, 1962) is progressive as individuals move not just from one topic to another, but also to increasingly personal levels of talk. Early exchanges about musical tastes may allow later, more revealing discussions of what music means to us and what feelings certain pieces arouse in us. Initial conversations about career goals may be followed by more personal talk about basic philosophies that shape professional choices. As individuals advance through various filters on a range of topics, they construct progressively more detailed portraits of each other, thereby reducing uncertainty (Duck & Condra, 1989; Duck & Craig, 1978).

ANDY

The Internet is really great for getting to know someone without the expense and shallow stuff that is part of early dates. I met Lisa online, and we talked a long time before we ever met in person. It's easier to talk about yourself online—less embarrassing and awkward. By the time we met, we already knew so much about each other that it was easy to just start talking.

Depth of Information   — Self disclosure

Exploring the possibilities of a relationship involves more than gathering information about a breadth of topics. If individuals want to advance their relationship, they typically seek greater depth in their communication. Here the goal seems to be to gain insight into each other's unique, private self. We want to get beyond social roles and outward appearances to discover the personal, idiosyncratic character of another person.

To develop their relationship further, individuals engage in **self-disclosure,** which is disclosing personal or private information about oneself that others are unlikely to discover on their own. Individuals may reveal feelings, thoughts, disappointments, experiences, goals, dreams, fears, and so forth that they generally shroud from others. Self-disclosing tends to increase trust as well as knowledge between people. Because we reveal private information only to people we trust, doing so communicates that we feel safe with another. Likewise, we interpret others' disclosures as indicating they trust us. Studying both giving and receiving disclosures, Susan Sprecher (1987) found that the latter more keenly affected feelings about a partner. Hence, we tend to feel closer to people who entrust us with personal information.

Research indicates that we usually interpret self-disclosure as signaling escalation in intimacy (Jourard, 1971), probably because it heightens trust. Thus, choosing to disclose private information may communicate on the relationship level of meaning that we are willing to become closer (Berger & Bell, 1988; Duck & Miell, 1986; Miell, 1984). There is an exception to this generalization: Disclosures perceived as premature or manipulative do not increase intimacy but, in fact, seem to reduce it (Van Lear, 1987). This outcome probably reflects awareness of widely held social norms that excessive disclosures early in a relationship are inappropriate and evidence that the discloser lacks communication competence. Thus, only when suitable interpersonal foundations have been constructed and disclosures are perceived as spontaneous are they likely to promote greater intimacy.

In an embryonic relationship, reciprocity of self-disclosure is expected (Miell & Duck, 1986). When one person reveals something private to another, he or she invites an escalation in intimacy and becomes vulnerable. This vulnerability is reduced when self-disclosure is reciprocated (Duck, 1992; Jourard, 1971). Roughly equal amounts and degrees of disclosure keep individuals on the same plane. Further, mutual self-disclosures are necessary if two people are to get to know each other. If only one reveals personal information, the relationship will not be balanced and, most likely, will be unsatisfying. Thus, both frequency and depth of disclosures tend to be roughly equal between individuals who want to increase intimacy.

THERESA

When you're starting a relationship, I think it's really important for both people to disclose. Otherwise the one who does it feels exposed. When Bobby and I had been dating a while I told him something really private about my family. He was nice about it, but he didn't tell me anything similar. I wanted him to offer something back, like that would show he trusted me and was willing to risk exposure too. Later he did tell me some private things, and I felt a lot better about his trusting me and about our being on equal footing. But I really was uneasy until he shared something too.

Important as self-disclosure is to the development of relationships, it is not a primary dynamic of enduring intimacy. In other words, self-disclosing communication is more prevalent early in a relationship than later. Once a relationship is established, disclosures diminish for a number of reasons. First, partners may assume they know and trust each other and need not establish or prove that by further disclosures. Second, there's only so much personal information people have and choose to reveal, so there is a limit to how long this can be a focus of interaction. Finally, in ongoing intimacy, partners engage in a great deal of communication designed to maintain their bond and to coordinate their interaction in it, and these communicative goals do not require constant or major self-disclosures. Actually, the bulk of communication in established relationships is day to day and fairly routine—perhaps not very romantic but quite important in keeping partners connected (Duck et al., 1991; Wright, 1978). Of course, friends and romantic partners continue to disclose throughout the course of a relationship, and disclosures may dominate communication at perennial points of transition and crisis. Generally speaking, however, the importance and frequency of disclosure decrease, and other forms of communication assume primacy once partners have created intimacy.

DEVELOPMENTAL DIALOGUE

Intimacy develops over time as a result of communication between people. It grows directly out of verbal and nonverbal interactions that provide information, reduce uncertainty, and build feelings of knowledge, closeness, and trust. Also, intimacy grows indirectly out of communication, because partners interpret interactions as they transpire and reflect on them afterward. In other words, how we think about others and our communication with them are primary influences on how we view a relationship (Acitelli, 1988, 1993; Duck & Pond, 1989; Honeycutt, 1993; Honeycutt, Cantrill, & Greene, 1989). We ponder over particular exchanges, remember and relive others, and forget or downplay still others. Through this editing process, we create in our minds a selective, subjective sense of the relationship we are in.

> J U L I E
>
> *I sometimes wonder if two people are ever in the same relationship! A while back my fiancé and I were talking about our relationship, and I told him I had fallen for him because he brought me a flower on our first date. That was so special to me, and it convinced me that he was a really sensitive, thoughtful person. It turns out he didn't even remember that at all—it just wasn't part of his memory of our first date, but it was the key thing for me. What he remembered was the movie we saw, and how much we laughed at the same things in it. I didn't remember what the movie was. Strange.*

Accuracy isn't the only or necessarily the most important aspect of how we think about relationships. In fact, as Julie's journal entry illustrates, discrepancies routinely punctuate partners' views of their relationship and don't necessarily diminish intimacy (Acitelli, 1988; Acitelli, Douvan, & Veroff, 1993; Fitzpatrick & Best, 1979; McCarthy, 1983). The relationship—however we construct it—guides how we understand ourselves, our partners, and the connections between us. Our interpretations of past events guide our own present and future conduct in relation to others (Berger & Kellner, 1975; Miell, 1987). Thus, the relationships in which we believe ourselves to be are, in fact, the ones in which we are!

TENDENCIES IN EARLY RELATIONSHIP DEVELOPMENT

Just as certain issues and problems are more likely at specific stages in individuals' personal development, so too are certain issues and complications typical at particular points in relationship evolution. Although not every relationship will experience these, we want to identify features and problems that often arise in early phases of relationships.

Features of Early Interaction

One of the most important features of initial involvement is that individuals' investments are limited. Throughout initial and explorational communication, individuals have invested relatively little in each other and the relationship. As long as little has been put into a relationship, there's little to hold it together if problems develop. Individuals may lose interest if a better alternative appears, a minor disagreement occurs, or a health problem or family crisis arises. Such difficulties might not disrupt an established relationship, but they are sometimes sufficient to end an embryonic relationship. Commitment grows out of investments, and investments are made over time (Lund, 1985). Thus, a relationship with a short history may lack the foundation to weather tough times and significant conflict.

Flexibility in how a relationship is defined tends to be greatest at early stages in a relationship's life. As people interact, their views of a relationship become increasingly settled—it is a friendship or a romance or a marriage. All possibilities exist when people meet, but as they communicate and think about their interactions, they progressively define a particular trajectory for themselves. Once a relationship is established, it is more difficult to redefine it in new ways. From your own experience, you probably know how difficult it is to transform what has been a dating relationship into a friendship, because romantic expectations and roles exist and shape interaction. In essence, there are multiple options when two people start interacting, because no patterns have developed and nothing has been promised. As partners share experiences and communicate, however, the options may be progressively narrowed.

Finally, as we have noted, early interaction is more social than personal. In this chapter, we've seen that initial communication closely follows social norms and that individuals' expectations and interpretations are substantially guided by normative social scripts and understandings of relationships. As two people begin to self-disclose, they move toward more personal knowledge of each other and, thus, a more personal relationship. Yet until dual perspective develops and partners begin to form a relational culture, significant intimacy does not really exist.

Complications of Early Interaction

Several problems may plague the initial stages of relationships. One of the most common is misinterpretation. Because personal knowledge of each other is minimal, individuals lack the dual perspective necessary to interpret each other. Thus, it is not unusual for misunderstandings to occur. What one person means as casual flirting without serious intent another may interpret as an invitation for sexual engagement. When a woman says she cannot go out because she has to study, is this an honest statement or an indication of disinterest? Is a man who insults another person being hostile or inviting a game of verbal sparring? We cannot know what such communication means until we have enough information to interpret individuals personally.

Misrepresentation, and even outright deception, is easier to accomplish online than in person. Communicating electronically, individuals have deceived others about a range of issues, including their sex, profession, color, sexual orientation, and disability (Lea & Spears, 1995). Individuals may also post photos, allegedly of themselves but actually of other people. Thus, when we get to know someone via electronic communication, there is an increased chance of misrepresentation.

Another complication that may arise early in interaction is underestimating the influence of external factors (Werner et al., 1992, 1993). For example, someone whose relationship quota is unfulfilled may enter into a friendship or romance that would be avoided at other times. Similarly, family tragedy may incline people to advance toward intimacy more quickly than they otherwise would.

Likewise, when alternatives are limited, individuals may launch relationships that are unsatisfactory and that they will leave as soon as a better option comes along. This can be very unfair because one person may be genuinely interested and the other simply biding time until someone more attractive is available. The end of a serious romantic involvement may render individuals more receptive to a new relationship, as well as to escalating it quickly. Summer romances are so called because they typically span a summer and because people who happen to be in the same place for just the summer choose to have a fling.

Other external factors can influence our relationship choices. For instance, I've noticed that a great many students get engaged during their senior year, which suggests people are inclined toward commitment at that time. Similarly, breakups in student romances are most likely at the end of academic years, a timing that clearly reflects situational influences as well as interpersonal ones. The much remarked on midlife crisis typically occurs in the forties as people moving toward middle age confront issues of their own mortality. It's not uncommon for a 45-year-old married person to launch an affair with someone much younger. Although this choice is surely influenced by the spouse and the younger person, it is also shaped by the individual's life stage and by cultural recognition of midlife crisis as a real phenomenon that often has certain consequences.

SUMMARY

In this chapter, we have introduced the idea that relationships are developmental—they evolve over time as people interact with each other. Although original models of relationship development focused on external indicators of involvement, later ones concentrate on individuals' perceptions and turning points as the basis of the experience of movement in relationships. Thus, relationships escalate and deescalate as a result of how partners perceive and attribute meaning to behaviors and events. Because intimacy is a process, current interactions reflect past ones and influence what will happen in the future. Humans live simultaneously in all three dimensions of time. Hence, past experiences infuse what is happening in the moment, and reflections on what transpires now shape future feelings and actions.

In discussing early interaction, we've seen that a number of influences come into play. We've noted that individuals tend to be attracted to others who are nearby and who are like them in values and attitudes, as well as personality and physical attractiveness. Although some complementarity may be enticing, perceived and actual similarity are generally stronger predictors of attraction. In addition, interest in launching relationships is influenced by individuals' relationship quotas, by their comparison levels, and by their comparison levels of alternatives.

To signal availability and interest (or lack thereof), individuals rely on social scripts and rules, which are normative guidelines for relationships. As interaction continues, reducing uncertainty becomes a focus, so individuals exchange information both directly and indirectly. The majority of knowledge about others is gathered through routine talk about background and interests. By self-disclosing, individuals add depth and breadth to their knowledge of each other, and they begin to build a sense of trust and connection.

Communication is central to the development of personal relationships. As we have seen, interaction itself is the heart of relationships, because it is through the process of communicating that people learn about each other and discern what values, beliefs, and so forth they have in common. Communication is also pivotal in creating understandings of relationships. The language we use to label interactions and events reflects and shapes our perceptions of ourselves, others, and relationships. For instance, saying "She is a friend of mine" symbolizes something different from "We're acquainted," and "We go out together sometimes" means something different from "We're dating seriously."

The importance of communication between people is paralleled by the significance of individuals' communication with themselves—their intrapersonal symbolizing of what occurs. As we think over interactions, we may revise initial impressions, elaborate certain aspects, and minimize others. We constantly edit our personal and relationship histories to conform to how we currently see ourselves and our involvements. Our understanding of relationships changes over time as we gain additional information from interaction, reflect on what transpires, and begin to create a shared world with another person. The processes of committing and the ways in which they crystallize relational cultures are the focus of the next chapter.

FOR FURTHER REFLECTION AND DISCUSSION

1. What are primary sources of your own knowledge of relationships? What have you learned that you consider true from family, friends, television, books, and your own experiences?

2. Talk with people from other cultures to discover what they perceive as indications that a relationship is intensifying. How does this compare with perceptions in the United States?

3. Try going to several places that you don't usually frequent. What kinds of people do you see there? How are they similar to and different from people you find in the places to which you go more typically? What do your observations teach you about how choices affect the options for relationships?

4. Have you ever experienced the environmental spoiling effect of proximity? If so, describe what happened and how it affected your feelings about and interaction with the other person.

5. As a class, discuss your most and least favorite openers. Also, you might discuss your strategies for indicating interest and disinterest in others who make openers to you.

6. How have the three standards for evaluating relationships (relationship quota, comparison level, comparison level of alternatives) played roles in your friendships and romantic relationships? Have you ever misjudged CL_{alt}? What happened?

7. Do relationships initiated online follow the same patterns as those that are launched face to face? How is attraction displayed and assessed in initial online interaction? Has anyone ever misrepresented herself or himself to you in online interaction?

RECOMMENDED READINGS

Ackerman, D. (1994). A natural history of love. New York: Random House.

Duck, S. (1994). Meaningful relationships. Thousand Oaks, CA: Sage.

Felmlee, D. (1995). Fatal attractions: Affection and disaffection in intimate relationships. Journal of Social and Personal Relationships, 12, 295–311.

Honeycutt, J. (1993). Memory structures for the rise and fall of personal relationships. In S. Duck (Ed.), Understanding relationship processes, 1: Individuals in relationships (pp. 30–59). Newbury Park, CA: Sage.

Surra, C. A. (1985). Courtship types: Variations in interdependence between partners and social networks. Journal of Personality and Social Psychology, 49, 357–375.

Committing to Personal Relationships

COMMITTING IS AN EXTENDED PROCESS in which part-ners build a relational culture and choose to weave their lives together—not just in the present, but for the foreseeable future as well. Like other processes, committing doesn't happen in one fell swoop but evolves and changes over time as two people work out understandings about who they are and how their relationship does and will operate. As two individuals commit to each other and a shared future, the indi-viduals transform themselves from separate people into partners in a unit. Although each person retains an individual identity, they also create and commit to a joint identity. As committing transpires, partners increasingly perceive themselves in relation to each other. Simultaneously, partners compose a relational culture that reflects and shapes their unique relation-ship with its particular history and imagined future. To set a tone for thinking about committing, consider Robert Fulghum's reflections (1989).

ROBERT FULGHUM ON COMMITMENT

The real wedding and the real vows don't happen on the day of the formal social occasion. There comes a time, usually some days after the proposal and acceptance . . . when there is a conversation between two people in love, when they are in earnest about what they've agreed to do. The conversation happens over several days—even weeks. Partly in a car driving somewhere, partly at a kitchen table after supper, partly on the living room floor, or maybe on the way home after a movie. It's a conversation about promises, homes, family, children, possessions, jobs, dreams, rights, concessions, money, personal space, and all the problems that might arise from all of those things. And what is promised at that time, in a disorganized, higgledy-piggledy way, is the making of a covenant. A covenant—an invisible bond of commitment. Just two people working out what they want, what they believe, what they hope for each other. . . . And that's it. The wedding is done. All that's left to do is the public celebration, however they choose to do it.

That's why I always tell couples to pay more attention to what's going on in that talking time before the Big Day. They wouldn't want to miss their own wedding.

Source: Robert Fulghum (1989). *It Was on Fire When I Lay Down on It*. New York: Random House.

This chapter traces committing as a process that begins when initial and explorational communication fuel a desire to build a personal relationship that will endure. Initially, many partners experience an intense, even euphoric period in which they immerse themselves in each other and the joy they find in togetherness. Many relationships do not develop beyond a period of passionate engagement because intensity wanes or because one or both partners are not willing to make a long-term pledge. If interest continues, however, initial intensity may lead to a decision to create a common future. This happens as partners think and talk seriously about what they need from and want to give to a relationship meant to last. My awareness of these two phases in the commitment process was prompted by a student's observation that enduring intimacy requires that people fall out of love and into commitment. Hence, feeling love and deciding to stay together are distinct aspects of committing to personal relationships.

To understand lasting intimacy, we'll first distinguish between passion and commitment. Next we'll explore different styles of loving, which shed light on the varied ways people experience and express love. The third section of the chapter discusses communication processes through which partners develop dual perspective and an embryonic relational culture that they will refine and elaborate over the life of their relationship. To close the chapter, we define commitment as a decision to remain with a relationship for the foreseeable future.

PASSIONATE LOVE AND COMMITMENT: DIFFERENT ISSUES

When early interactions are gratifying, people may want to extend a relationship beyond the present and into the future. We may sense another could be a long-term friend or a romantic partner with whom we might share our lives. When individuals feel lasting intimacy is possible, involvement escalates, and they further test the viability of a shared future. As they do so, they may feel an array of feelings including excitement, love, passion, and warmth.

Efforts to define the feelings that are part of personal relationships are legion, as are attempts to distinguish among related concepts such as love, liking, intimacy, passion, and caring. One study (Fehr, 1988) identified 68 different features of love, and another (Luby & Aron, 1990) found 93 separate features. With so many attributes intertwined in the meaning of intimacy, it's no wonder that researchers have devoted considerable energy to clarifying intimacy, commitment, and love.

In an important investigation we first discussed in Chapter 1, Mary Lund (1985) reported that love and commitment are distinct, although they may be related. Commitment, you may recall, refers to the intention to continue a relationship. It is a decision, a pledge, an assumption about the future. Love, on the other hand, is a powerful feeling about another person. It is an emotion, an attraction, a feeling of closeness in the present. Two key findings from Lund's research are that commitment better predicts relationship continuity than does love and that commitment grows more closely out of investing in a relationship, whereas love is fueled by rewards. Thus, for relationships that endure, commitment enters the picture.

One of the more intriguing efforts to untangle the different dimensions of closeness is Robert Sternberg's triangular theory of love (1986, 1987). Assuming that what we call love is actually a combination of several factors, Sternberg advanced a model of love as having three separate, underlying dimensions. The

FIGURE 7.1

Sternberg's Triangle of Love

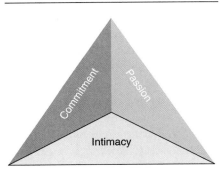

first, passion, involves intensity regarding not only sexuality, but also affiliation and emotional depth. The second dimension, commitment, refers to a deliberate choice to remain involved with another. Finally, intimacy is a dimension composed of feelings of closeness, connection, comfort, and tenderness between friends and lovers. Sternberg located intimacy at the base of his triangular model (Figure 7.1) because he believed that intimacy was the foundation of passion and love. Because Sternberg's theory is intuitively persuasive, it has been studied extensively, with mixed results.

Although the facets of closeness Sternberg identified have received empirical support, their independence of one another is questionable. One of the consistent problems to emerge from tests of Sternberg's theory is that intimacy, commitment, and passion appear to overlap considerably, suggesting they are not separate components. In an effort to validate his theory, Sternberg studied 84 adults whose mean age was 28 and who were in relationships with an average duration of $4\frac{1}{2}$ years. Of the 36 items used to assess the three dimensions, 22 either overlapped with others or were more strongly related to dimensions other than the ones they were designed to measure (for example, an item intended to measure commitment was more closely associated with intimacy). Similarly, in their study of 400 undergraduate students, Clyde Hendrick and Susan Hendrick (1989) reported very high overlap among items, which implies these three dimensions are interactive—not discrete aspects of personal relationships.

In another effort to test Sternberg's theory, Michele Acker and Mark Davis (1992) investigated 204 adults from 18 to 68 years old who were in relationships with an average length of $9\frac{1}{2}$ years. Consistent with prior research, this study found substantial overlap among dimensions hypothesized by Sternberg. However, Acker and Davis advanced the idea that two of Sternberg's dimensions, passion and commitment, are fairly distinct, whereas the third dimension, intimacy, is not separate but a part of both passion and commitment. This is particularly interesting, because earlier work (Sternberg & Barnes, 1985) suggests intimacy is strongly associated with satisfaction in personal relationships. Perhaps caring and warmth, which are the crux of intimacy, form a foundation for more specific dimensions such as passion and commitment.

Companionate Features

Additional insight into the complexities of closeness comes from a series of studies by Beverly Fehr and her colleagues (Fehr, 1988, 1993; Fehr & Russell, 1991), which sheds light on our prototype of love and the importance of different dimensions to that prototypical view. In a summary of six separate studies (Fehr & Russell, 1991), companionate features of closeness such as trust, caring, honesty, and friendship emerged as central to Western understandings of enduring love relationships. Passionate features such as euphoria, idealization, and butterflies in the stomach were more peripheral to how people defined lasting relationships. This echoes the work on brain chemistry that we discussed in Chapter 6 by suggesting that what initially attracts and excites us (passion) is different from what keeps us satisfied (intimacy and commitment) in a long-term personal relationship.

The centrality of companionate aspects of closeness has been repeatedly confirmed. In one study, Fehr (1988) asked participants to rate 68 features of love for their prototypicality (the extent to which they typify love) and found that compassionate features were rated most prototypical, and passionate features, although sometimes regarded as important, were perceived as less exemplary of love. To verify Fehr's findings a team of researchers (Button & Collier, 1991) asked university students, government employees, and citizens of Newfoundland to rate the typicality and importance of different features associated with close relationships. Using quite different participants than Fehr, this study supported Fehr's findings. Even in reference specifically to romantic love, companionate features eclipsed passionate ones in typicality and salience. Other scholars (Luby & Aron, 1990) reported similar results—the five features most highly rated as typical of love were companionate features: trust, caring, honesty, friendship, and respect. Again, this held true even for "being in love," a type of relationship most likely to involve intensity and passion. Further evidence comes from an investigation by Michael Hecht and his colleagues (Hecht, Marston, & Larkey, 1994). They found that the highest quality relationships were based on companionate and secure forms of closeness.

Sex Differences

Perhaps you are wondering whether men and women differ in the importance they accord to companionate and passionate features of closeness. If so, you're in good company. Several scholars have addressed this question. Efforts to test for sex differences have yielded mixed results (Fehr, 1988; Luby & Aron, 1990; Rousar & Aron, 1990). The majority of research has reported insignificant differences between women's and men's views of what typifies love. However, a sex difference does emerge when people describe their *personal* view of love instead of their perception of what is generally regarded as typical of love. Investigations pursuing this focus (Button & Collier, 1991; Fehr, 1993; Fehr & Broughton, 1991) indicate that companionate features (those having to do with intimacy and commitment) generally figure more prominently in women's than men's personal views of love. In general, women seem to assign greater importance to qualities such as patience, encouragement, friendship, companionship, and caring, whereas fantasy is the only feature to receive uniquely higher ratings by men (Button & Collier, 1991). A related study indicated no significant differences among heterosexuals, gay men, and lesbians (Rousar & Aron, 1990).

E L O I S E

I was married four years in my first marriage, and I've been married 22 years in my second, and I can confirm the research we've studied. Passion and ecstasy are nice, but believe me, they are the icing on the cake. The cake is the day-to-day business of living with another person who is pleasant, caring, and considerate. My first husband was a real romantic. He often brought me flowers or gifts, but those don't make a marriage. When he wanted to be loving he was, but he was not there for me and supportive of me and generally a good companion on a day-to-day basis. What makes a marriage work is constant companionship and acceptance. Without that, I don't think any couple can survive—at least not very happily.

What does all of this mean? Even though more research is needed, a clear and consistent picture emerges. Most people apparently perceive companionate features as necessary to enduring love relationships and regard passionate ones as less critical. This holds true across a broad range of people, ages, and relationship types, so it is a very robust finding. Perhaps, then, most of us enjoy the thrill and intensity of passion yet realize it is not the core of enduring intimacy. Perhaps passion is just the icing on the cake, as Eloise says in her journal entry.

Although ecstasy is pleasurable, it seems insufficient to sustain personal relationships through tough times and inevitable problems. The fragility of passion was noted by the eminent psychologist Harold Kelley (1983), who commented that "love based on unstable causes, for example, on transient passion, will not promote commitment" (p. 313).

Echoing this, psychiatrist Aaron Beck (1988) notes that "as passions subside after the initial infatuation, dedication to each other's welfare and happiness emerges as the major binding force in a relationship" (p. 171). It seems, then, that clinicians and researchers confirm the insight of my student: For a personal relationship to endure, partners must fall into commitment. Thus, initial intensity may provide an emotional basis and impetus to form a more abiding connection. Although passion may continue or resurge, it is not synonymous with commitment.

Passion happens; commitment is chosen. Love is a feeling; commitment is a decision. Love is in the present; commitment assumes a future. Love is fostered by

NON SEQUITUR ©1998, Washington Post Writers Group. Reprinted with permission.

rewards and gratifications; commitment is cultivated by investments, most particularly investments of oneself in a relationship (Kelley, 1983; Kelley & Thibaut, 1978). According to Sharon Brehm (1992, p. 171), "Commitment is the bottom line of relationship development" because it has the effect of crystallizing actions and thoughts about another person. As long as we have not said to ourselves or others that we intend to stay with a person and a relationship, we are free to leave. Empirical work indicates that once individuals decide to stay with another person, there is a decline in their interest in other candidates for relationships (Johnson & Rusbult, 1989) and an increased likelihood they will, in fact, remain committed (Hendrick & Hendrick, 1988; Hendrick, Hendrick, & Adler, 1988; Lund, 1985).

So far we've discussed one piece of the puzzle of intimacy: the distinction between love and commitment. Also affecting intimacy are different styles of loving that contour thought and action in personal relationships. We turn now to that topic.

STYLES OF LOVE

Elizabeth Browning's well-known poem begins with these lines: "How do I love thee? Let me count the ways." The nature of love and how it enriches and complicates human life is a favorite topic of poets. Yet they hold no monopoly on this subject, which has been vigorously explored by relationship researchers as well. A substantial body of scholarship indicates there are differences in the ways individuals express and experience closeness. Although we accept diversity in everything from food to religion, we seem less willing to acknowledge the legitimacy of differences when it comes to love. Each of us knows what *real love* is, and we may believe that anything else doesn't really count. We may even derogate what others call love by labeling it "infatuation," "a sexual fling," or "merely affection." Despite personal beliefs about what love is, research indicates there are actually many ways of loving, and different people have distinct preferences for specific styles.

In the 1970s, Canadian sociologist John A. Lee published a book called *The Colours of Love* (1973). In it, he reported the results of his analysis of literature on love and his interviews with individuals about what love meant to them. Using the color wheel as an analogy, Lee defined three primary styles of love parallel to the three primary colors of blue, red, and yellow. He also defined secondary styles of love that are combinations of the primary styles: Just as green is a mixture of blue and yellow, so secondary love styles are blends of primary styles. Although Lee originally reported six secondary styles, researchers have narrowed the number to three. Thus, there are a total of six styles of love—three primary and three secondary (Figure 7.2).

Since Lee's original book, other research has extended his ideas. To test the validity of Lee's ideas and to apply them in practical ways, two scholars (Lasswell & Lasswell, 1976) developed a scale for measuring love styles. Later, other researchers refined that instrument and used it in a number of empirical studies (Hendrick & Hendrick, 1988; Hendrick, Hendrick, & Dicke, 1998; Hendrick, Hendrick, Foote, & Slapion-Foote, 1984). These investigations and others (Hatkoff & Lasswell, 1979; Lasswell & Lobsenz, 1980; Lee, 1973, 1988) have provided convincing evidence that there are indeed distinct ways of loving, each with its own particular features and modes of communication.

Primary Styles of Love

There are three primary styles of love, and each has its own distinctive character and modes of expression.

Storge. **Storge** (pronounced "store-gay") is a comfortable, best-friends type of love (Lee, 1973). It is peaceful affection that tends to grow gradually and to be stable and constant. Typically, storgic love is based on common interests, values, attitudes, and life goals (Lasswell & Lobsenz, 1980). It grows out of friendship; in fact, friendship and comfortable companionship are the crux of this style. Storgic lovers create even-keeled relationships, ones with few great highs or deep lows. If they lack dewy-eyed romanticism, they also experience few flashes of fiery conflict and anger (Lasswell & Lobsenz, 1980). Storgic people resent and resist being rushed, preferring to let personal relationships grow gradually. This kind of love develops slowly, and once established it tends to be highly stable and enduring. These characteristics of storgic love suggest certain tendencies in managing dialectics. For instance, predictability would probably be emphasized more than novelty, and connection would be more pronounced than autonomy.

FIGURE 7.2

Styles of Love

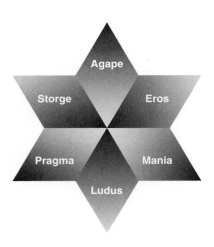

My boyfriend is my best friend. We were friends for two years, and dating was a natural extension of the friendship. The romantic feelings we have are like extra dimensions maybe but the friendship is the basis. Some of my friends say I'm not really in love because I don't get all ga-ga about Roy and we don't have the kind of storms and furies they do, but I say we are in love. Also, I wouldn't want all of that frenzy that my friends think is "true love." Give me the steady caring and the friendship, because they can last.

Eros. Eros is the second primary style of love. Based on Freud's view of eros as the life force, this is powerful, passionate, intense love that tends to flame suddenly and to be full of drama and fireworks (Lee, 1973). It would be a mistake to equate erotic love exclusively with sexual passion. It is more than that. It is an intense love based on an ideal that may focus on sexuality, spirituality, intellectual commitments, or other aspects of a loved one. More than other styles, erotic love is intuitive, spontaneous, and rapid (Lasswell & Lobsenz, 1980). Unlike slow, steady storge, erotic lovers move quickly to share their innermost selves, so disclosures may be early, numerous, and deep. Because erotic love is powerful, it is difficult to sustain at its initial intensity, yet it may smolder for periods and then reignite (Grote & Frieze, 1998; Lasswell & Lobsenz, 1980; Lee, 1988). Partners who have erotic love styles have among the most satisfying and rewarding relationships, and they tend to make higher investments than people with most other love styles (Morrow, Clark, & Brock, 1995). Erotic lovers might manage relational dialectics so that novelty, openness, and connection are more pronounced than predictability, closedness, and autonomy.

When I fall, I fall hard and fast, and there are no holds barred. I just throw myself into a relationship completely. Sure, I've been hurt more than once, but I really wouldn't want anything less intense. To me that would be like settling for humdrum instead of the height of human feeling. Just two weeks ago I met this fabulous new girl, and I knew the minute I saw her, it was love. I mean that—love at first sight. It was like she was the living embodiment of my fantasies of the woman in my life. Right now we're really moving fast, and the relationship is on high.

Styles of love apply just as much to friends as to boyfriends and girlfriends. My style is erotic, and it shows up both with my women friends and with the men I date. The first time I met Josina, it was like I had found my other half. I mean we bonded from the word go. I fell for her with the same kind of intensity that I have fallen in love with men. For the first few weeks when we were becoming friends, I was as obsessed with her as I ever have been with a guy. I just thought about her all the time and couldn't wait until we would get together again. I couldn't share enough with her or learn enough about her life. Our friendship grew out of my erotic love style.

Ludus. The final primary style of love is **ludus,** named after what the Roman poet Ovid called *amour ludens,* or playful love (Lee, 1973, 1974). For ludic lovers, love is a game—a series of challenges, puzzles, and lighthearted adventures. The game of love, not an outcome of commitment, is the goal. In fact, commitment is anathema to ludics, who eschew serious involvements. "Playing the field," ludic lovers enjoy variety and like to experiment with different kinds of people. Ludic love, like other games, has rules, and true ludics play by the rules (Lee, 1974). For instance, a key rule might be to not date a person too frequently, because that would encourage the other to assume a commitment. Similarly, ludics often tell others they are not seeking involvements, a warning that is discounted at risk.

Ludics cherish novelty and, conversely, loathe routine. More than other styles of love, ludic relationships would tend to be marked by greater autonomy than connection, because ludic lovers are not seeking interdependence. Also, openness and disclosures might be limited, because revealing the self would interfere with the mystery and uncertainty that keep the game of love challenging. Because ludics are playful, they regard relationships as fun and enjoyable but not the serious stuff of life. A number of my students report ludic periods, but they are not enduring ludics. After a serious relationship, a person may play the field and avoid serious involvements for a time. Likewise, many see the college years as a time for experimenting with a range of people before committing seriously, which may involve moving to a different love style.

Secondary Styles of Love

There are three secondary styles, each of which is made up of two of the primary styles. Thus, these may be thought of as blends of two distinctive modes of loving. Secondary styles are not inferior to primary ones, just as purple is no less beautiful than the blue and red primary colors that create it.

Mania. Deriving its name from the Greek term *theia mania* (Lee, 1974), which means "madness from the gods," **mania** is a blend of eros and ludus. Manic lovers feel the passion and commitment of eros but play by the rules of ludus (Lasswell & Lobsenz, 1980), which can make this style unsettling for both manic lovers and those they love. Thus, a manic lover might be consumed by thoughts of another and be intensely devoted to that person but feel the need to play ludic games to test the other's commitment. Unconvinced of his or her own self-worth, the manic lover constantly needs reassurance of the other's love, yet no matter what tests the other passes, he or she will remain unconvinced. Manics may experience emotional extremes, alternately euphoric over a relationship and despairing because of some real or imagined sign the other's love is waning (Lee, 1988).

Last year I was dating a girl who had to be a manic. At first our relationship was great, but pretty soon it got very weird. She would come up with all of these tests like being late to meet me to see what I'd do or calling me when I was with friends to make sure I wasn't dating behind her back. Once she even put one of her girlfriends up to trying to get me to go out with her just to see if I would take the opportunity. What was really bad was that no matter what I did, it wasn't enough. Each test was just the prologue for the next one. I couldn't go on like that—feeling I was always having to prove myself and no proof was good enough. I don't see why anyone would put up with that.

Agape. Another secondary style of love is **agape,** which is a blend of storge and eros. The word *agape* comes from St. Paul's letter to the Corinthians, in which he wrote of the duty to love all others without expectation of personal return (Lee, 1974). Thus, agapic lovers have the passion of eros and the constancy of storge. They tend to be generous, unselfish, and willing to put their beloved's happiness ahead of their own. In fact, for agapic lovers, others' happiness *is* their own. They do not need or expect reciprocity for their investments, because loving another is its own reward. If this sounds more like a description of saintly than mortal love, it won't surprise you to learn that few people are totally agapic. In fact, Lee's original studies (1973, 1974) identified no pure agapic lovers. However, agapic inclinations inflect many people's styles of love, and they tend to foster strong, committed relationships in which satisfaction is high (Morrow, Clark, & Brock, 1995).

Pragma. Finally, there is **pragma,** or pragmatic love. As the name implies, pragma is a practical love that blends ludic and storgic styles. Pragmas use conscious, even manipulative means (the ludic influence) to find a partner with whom they can develop a stable, enduring love (the storgic focus). Pragmas are goal oriented and have definite criteria for love relationships. Typically, these include religious affiliation, socioeconomic status, desirable career goals, and so forth (Lasswell & Lobsenz, 1980). Pragmas also tend to be conscious of their own assets and liabilities, so they are realistic in the matches they seek. It would be easy to disparage pragma as coldly practical, yet that distorts its character. The pragmatic lover is not necessarily unfeeling at all. It's simply that reason and practical considerations predominate over feeling until a sensible choice is made (Lasswell & Lobsenz, 1980; Lee, 1973). Deep and enduring emotional connections may develop once pragmas feel it is safe to let themselves care and invest in relationships.

BANYA

My perspective is different from most students because I am from India, and we still have arranged marriages there. In fact, the person I am expected to marry was picked out for me years ago, and we've not even met yet. I don't know whether I will go through with the arranged marriage or not, since my thinking has changed a lot in the years I've been here studying. What I do know, though, is that arranged marriages work—actually, they probably work better than the free-choice ones in this country. Marriages are arranged by matching people who have similar family status, backgrounds, and experiences, so the couple starts off with a lot of common ground. Most of the couples I know in India have come to love each other over the years. It has grown gradually and gotten deeper, whereas in this country it seems relationships usually start off with a lot of passion but cool off over time. Arranged marriages actually make pretty good sense.

Understanding Your Love Style

You may have diagnosed your own style of love from the foregoing descriptions. If you want to assess your style formally, you might take tests with established validity and reliability (Hendrick et al., 1984; Lasswell & Lobsenz, 1980). Table 7.1 provides sample items from one of those tests.

As you think about styles of love, you should keep a few caveats in mind. First, most people have blended styles that combine two or more of the six (Hendrick et al., 1984). Thus, a person might be primarily storgic with agapic and erotic tendencies or basically erotic with streaks of ludic mischief. Further, particular partners may evoke different styles from an individual. Because most of us have degrees of several styles, partners' ways of loving may influence our own.

Second, your current love style is not necessarily fixed for all time. There is no evidence that love styles are permanent. In fact, research shows that love styles change as we have more experiences in loving and as we continue to evolve personally (Grote & Frieze, 1998; Morrow, Clark, & Brock, 1995). Someone who is ludic at the moment might well settle into a different love style later in life. A recent or dramatic love experience may also strongly affect current feelings and, thus, responses on the test. One of my students took the test in the wake of a very destructive relationship with a man who exploited her, lied to her, and otherwise gave her reasons to be anxious and untrusting. Not surprisingly, her test scores indicated her style was manic. I encouraged her to take the test again in several months, and when she did, her predominant style was storgic, which was consistent with her sense of herself. In an early discussion of love styles, Lee (1974) cautioned that a single manic episode doesn't confirm a person as an obsessive lover, nor does one affair make somebody ludic. Rather, a basic love style reflects overall, enduring patterns of relating.

Our styles of love may change over time even within the same relationship. In 1998 Nancy Grote and Irene Frieze published a study of 594 people who had

TABLE 7.1

Sample Items Measuring Love Styles

Eros	My partner and I have the right physical chemistry between us. I feel that my partner and I were meant for each other. My partner fits my ideal standards of physical beauty/handsomeness.
Ludus	I have sometimes had to keep my partner from finding out about other lovers. I believe that what my partner doesn't know about me won't hurt him/her. My partner would get upset if he/she knew of some of the things I've done with other people.
Storge	Our love is the best kind because it grew out of a long friendship. Our friendship merged gradually into love over time. Our love relationship is the most satisfying because it developed from a good friendship.
Pragma	A main consideration in choosing my partner was how he/she would reflect on my family. An important factor in choosing my partner was whether or not he/she would be a good parent. One consideration in choosing my partner was how he/she would reflect on my career.
Mania	When my partner doesn't pay attention to me, I feel sick all over. I cannot relax if I suspect my partner is with someone else. If my partner ignores me for a while, I sometimes do stupid things to try to get his/her attention back.
Agape	I would rather suffer myself than let my partner suffer. I cannot be happy unless I place my partner's happiness before my own. I am usually willing to sacrifice my own wishes to let my partner achieve his/hers.

Source: Clyde Hendrick, Susan Hendrick, & Amy Dicke. (1998). The love attitudes scale: Short form. *Journal of Social and Personal Relationships, 15,* 147–159.

been married to each other for 25 years. Among other findings, they found that participants in their study reported experiencing and expressing love differently during the life of the relationship. Over the years, erotic love diminished but was still moderately strong for many people. Storgic love remained stable over time, and ludic love declined markedly. Grote and Frieze also found that husbands in long-lasting marriages became more agapic over time. In a related study Gregory Morrow, Eddy Clark, and Karla Brock (1995) found that erotic and manic love styles declined for both women and men as they aged.

In developing instruments to measure various individual inclinations, researchers systematically establish validity (a test measures what it is supposed to measure) and reliability (an individual receives similar scores when taking the test at different times). Thus, once an instrument has been developed and tested, it has earned credibility. Yet even validated, reliable instruments occasionally mismeasure a particular individual. Just as SATs misdiagnose some students' aptitude for college, social scientific tests sometimes provide results that do not accurately reflect specific individuals. If the love styles test or others you take yield results that seem erroneous to you, it is prudent to seek additional evidence and expertise before drawing firm conclusions about yourself.

Before moving on, we should also note that our discussion has focused on individuals' styles of love. Yet relationships involve two people, so the relevant issue is how styles fit or fail to fit together. Research shows that couples tend to match on love styles, with the exception of mania and ludus (Morrow, Clark, & Brock, 1995). Yet, we don't always select partners who have our own love styles. An agapic lover might fit well with most other styles but could easily be exploited by a ludic. A storgic person might bore an erotic person, and a manic or ludic would be very unsettling to a storgic individual. How partners' styles combine and how each person's style shapes that of the other are the pertinent issues. No style is intrinsically good or bad, healthy or unhealthy. What really matters is whether partners have compatible love styles and each understands the other's.

Finally, it's important to place styles of love in a larger perspective on personal relationships. As we've seen in preceding chapters, many factors influence intimacy. It would be inappropriate to assume people's love styles explain whether they can be intimates and, if so, what kind of relationship they will have. The possibilities for relationships are also contoured by systemic influences such as financial circumstances, employment and the stresses it produces, and the presence or absence of children and others. In addition, intimacy is shaped by individual factors, including attachment styles, health, and cognitive schemata. Love styles, then, are only one of many influences on personal relationships.

So far we have examined differences between love and commitment and considered how styles of loving shape individuals' expectations and experiences of personal relationships. With that foundation, we're now ready to discuss communication processes that usually accompany a relationship's move into commitment.

COMMUNICATION PROCESSES DURING COMMITTING

As you know from your own experiences, every relationship develops uniquely. Even so, five communication processes generally seem to promote the dual perspective and initial relational culture that are key developments of committing.

Private Intensifying

Often a first clue that committing is underway is **private intensifying** in which partners' talk and reflections immerse them in each other and the relationship. For most of us, the dawning sense that another person can be a really special friend or romantic partner ignites a desire to be with that other and to get to know him or her more deeply. To satisfy that desire, people who are launching intimacy typically increase their time and involvement with each other and temporarily reduce time and involvement with other people and events (Milardo, Johnson, & Huston, 1983). The rate of intensifying varies in response to contextual influences and individuals' qualities. For instance, rapid escalation into private intensifying would be more typical of erotic than storgic partners. A slower and less complete move into private intensifying would be predictable for individuals who have major family responsibilities that prevent them from blocking out everyone but the partner.

Private intensifying is characterized by more interaction between partners and decreasing need for external events to structure their time together. Partners may spend whole days together and then call to say good night. Their time together is likely to be relatively unregulated by external stimuli. Whereas initial interactions tend to occur in public places and to be structured by activities such as movies, during private intensifying, partners typically spend more unstructured time in private settings (Davis, 1973). Talk meanders naturally from one topic to the next in an easy, stream-of-consciousness style that bespeaks partners' increasing comfortableness with each other. Also, as intensifying progresses, partners find they enjoy being together without talking; shared silence, as Murray Davis (1973) notes, is comfortable only between people who are intimate. Punctuating private intensifying are progressively personal exchanges that allow partners to develop the increasingly individualized understanding of each other that fosters dual perspective.

Disclosures are made and risks are taken in order for partners to know and be known by each other. The I part of the self that is not revealed to most people is increasingly unveiled as partners share private thoughts, fears, hopes, and secrets. In addition, partners begin to fill in their personal histories. Exchanging autobiographies allows partners to weave together their pasts as well as their present (Berger & Kellner, 1975; Davis, 1973). Understanding each other's historical identity enables partners to feel that they were connected even before they met. This is sometimes humorously evident when one partner corrects the other's memory of personal history—as if the partner had been involved in it! Davis (1973) observes that "a shared past is supposed to be one of the strongest factors leading to a shared present" (p. 178). Sketching life histories enables partners to deepen intimacy by extending their sense of connectedness backward in time. Thus, communication about histories allows partners to feel intertwined beyond the here and now.

Dual perspective develops as partners intensify privately. Removing each other from broad social roles and categories, partners increasingly gain highly personalized knowledge of each other, which allows them to understand and predict each other's feelings, thoughts, and responses. As each person understands and internalizes the other's perspective, partners are able to imagine how the other would see or act in a situation and thus to "be" together even when physically separated. We come to understand not just what our intimates think, but *how* they think, which allows us to generalize our knowledge of their perspectives beyond situations we have actually shared. The result is what we commonly call "getting inside the head" of another (Davis, 1973, p. 180). Given what is happening between partners during private intensifying, they may hurt long-time friends by being temporarily unavailable and disinterested (Milardo, Johnson, & Huston,

1983). Friends who have themselves been through private intensifying should understand that the distance is likely to be short-lived.

Personalized Communication

Private intensifying typically leads to forms of communication that are unique to partners and not understood, much less used, by others. **Personalized communication** enhances feelings of connection by highlighting shared private understandings and by excluding others, which tends to solidify the boundaries of intimacy (Knapp & Vangelisti, 1992). In other words, language that reflects the pair's existence and uniqueness makes the relationship more real to partners.

Personalized communication takes several forms. One of the most common is nicknames that express private identities partners negotiate (Bell & Healy, 1992; Public pillow talk, 1987). My nicknames for Robbie include "Ollie" and "Sherpa," both of which designate private ways I know him that others do not. Another form of personalized communication is using ordinary words in special ways that have a private meaning for partners. Private codes allow partners to signal each other it's time to leave a party or to convey their impressions of others (Hopper, Knapp, & Scott, 1981). Perhaps even more important, the private codes remind the partners of a shared world that others cannot enter (Bell, Buerkel-Rothfuss, & Gore, 1987). Partners also develop teasing routines and insults that are understood not to be taken literally (Hopper, Knapp & Scott, 1981; Public pillow talk, 1987). Thus, one friend might call the other "dumbo" or "noodle brain," and each would understand this is a term of affection, not an insult.

FIGURE 7.3

Personalized Communication Between Intimates

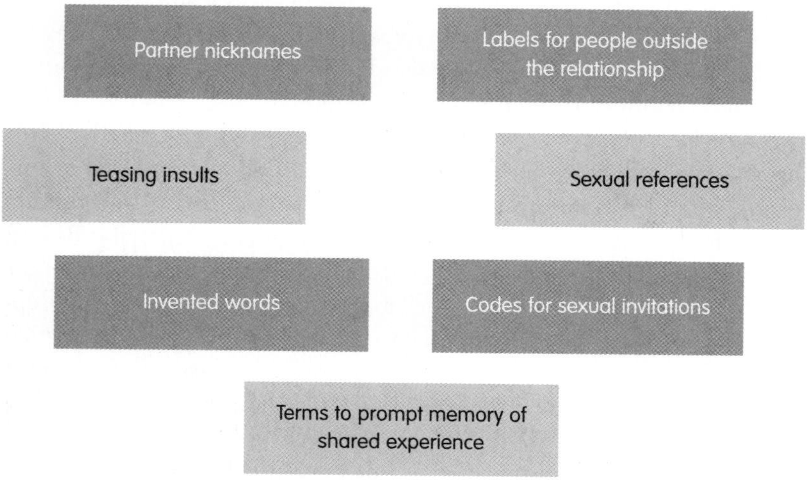

Partner nicknames

Labels for people outside the relationship

Teasing insults

Sexual references

Invented words

Codes for sexual invitations

Terms to prompt memory of shared experience

Yet another kind of personalized communication is invented language (Davis, 1973). Sometimes new words are born by accident as when a close friend of mine once ordered a "burgler" instead of a "burger." That amused us both, and "burglers" became part of our private vocabulary. My father once coined the term "duffer rebuffer" for a wooden sculpture he claimed should be used to rebuff any duffers who found their way into our home. In conversations with people he found dull, he would wink at me and ask if I had seen the duffer rebuffer, a joke we enjoyed without offending the duffer at hand! At the same time, our use of private language that others didn't understand solidified the closeness between us.

Finally, partners may develop a vocabulary to prompt recall of shared experiences and, by implication, of a shared life (Baxter, 1987). For instance, when Robbie and I traveled to Nepal, our guide, Concha, taught us the words *namaste*, which is a friendly greeting, and *bistari*, which means "gradually." Now we often say *namaste* to greet each other, and we say *bistari* to encourage each other to slow down. Using these words evokes memories of a treasured experience we shared. Researchers report that "the greater the number and diversity of couples' idioms . . . the stronger their feelings of love, commitment, and closeness" (Public pillow talk, 1987, p. 18), suggesting that personalized communication both reflects and furthers feelings of intimacy. Figure 7.3 describes types of personalized communication identified by researchers.

Idealizing

A third intensifying process is **idealizing,** in which partners perceive and describe each other and their relationship in idealistic ways. Sometimes idealizing involves minimizing or recasting problems or undesirable qualities of individuals. Thus, two partners with strong personalities may regard dogmatic arguments as amusing or unimportant. Similarly, qualities we would normally consider undesirable may be dismissed or reinterpreted if a partner has them (Davis, 1973). When Robbie and I were committing to each other, I found his absentmindedness funny and endearing. That, my mother said, convinced her I was in love, because I am highly organized and typically have little tolerance for absentmindedness. If I could laugh at Robbie's chronic forgetfulness, she concluded I was "a goner."

Idealization also occurs when partners emphasize and exaggerate good features of each other and a relationship. It isn't just a good relationship—it is the best ever; she isn't just intelligent—she's the brightest woman I've ever known; he isn't simply fun to be with—he's the most engaging person around. In conversation and private reflection, partners' idealism tends to further fuel commitment and closeness. By emphasizing positives and downplaying or recasting negatives, partners convince themselves and each other that they and the relationship are really special and worthy of continuing investment. "Idealization in Action" shows some communication typical of idealizing.

IDEALIZATION IN ACTION

A number of years ago, that chronicler of romance, *Cosmopolitan*, published a collection of ways people exaggerate good qualities and reinterpret undesirable ones. Following is a sample:

"I think bald men are cute."

"What weak jaw? Yours is Napoleonic."

"I've never cared how much money a man earns."

"Of course it doesn't bother me that I like to read in bed and you don't. I'll just turn off the light whenever you're ready to go to sleep."

"You've enriched my life so much. . . . Camping, fishing, going to the fights and races."

"Flowers die so soon. The toaster oven is much more practical."

"You have the *liveliest* group of friends."

"Of course I don't mind browsing in the hardware store — it's fascinating.

"I never celebrate Valentine's Day anyway."

> Source: "Lies Told While Courting." (1981, November). *Cosmopolitan*, p. 330)

Some interesting research has focused on idealizing, which seems most prominent when couples are "in love." From a series of studies, Clyde and Susan Hendrick deduced that people who are in love are more erotic and agapic, being more passionate and selfless (1986, 1988). As you might predict, ludic tendencies are not common when people are in love, because game playing is not the point. In addition, the Hendricks (1988) report that being in love heightens self-esteem and lowers tendencies to monitor the self, which suggests people feel less need to control how they appear.

There are also sex differences in the process of idealizing that often accompanies committing. Susan Sprecher and Sandra Metts (1989) reported that American college-age males are more romantic than their female counterparts, but this was not confirmed in a study of Australians (Cunningham & Antill, 1981). In studies of American couples, males generally say they fell in love first (Huston et al., 1981), but it seems that males' romanticism, as well as females', levels off with age (Hieger & Troll, 1973; Morrow, Clark, & Brock, 1995), suggesting that in enduring love relationships romanticism may be supplanted by more companionate feelings. Women, on the other hand, typically report more intense feelings (Dion & Dion, 1973; Kanin, Davidson, & Scheck, 1970), more detailed and stronger memories of partners (Harvey, Flanary, & Morgan, 1986), and a greater tendency to idealize those they love (Dion & Dion, 1975). It's important to realize that idealization is a process that accompanies creating intimacy, and partners and the relationship may appear considerably less rosy when idealization wanes—as it invariably does!

Building Relational Culture

Relational cultures tend to be largely unconscious creations that grow out of partners' interaction. They evolve directly out of communication, reflection, and interweaving of routines. As partners spend more and more unstructured time together, they develop their own rhythms and patterns to define themselves as a pair. Many of these patterns reflect initial resolutions of primary relationship dialectics. Thus, James and Kareena read or work in separate rooms part of the time they spend together, and Betty and Dave are continuously in each other's presence: The two couples manage the autonomy/connection dialectic differently. Similarly, friends develop different norms for privacy and openness on various topics, and for routine and spontaneity.

Equally important to the emergence of a relational culture is partners' growing sense of fitting together (Aron, Aron, Tudor, & Nelson, 1991; Reis & Shaver, 1988). This tends to be cultivated, in large measure, simply by being together a great deal and by sharing experiences and discussion of them (Davis, 1973). As partners interact, they discover some common ground and create other similarities, both of which enlarge their sense that they have a shared world. After a while, write Peter Berger and Hansfried Kellner (1975), no experience is truly real until and unless it is talked through with one's partner. The capacity to see the world through a partner's eyes and to count on a partner to understand your ways of experiencing is what George Herbert Mead (1934) described as importing others' perspectives into our own. Once relational culture begins to form, partners' perspectives are no longer totally distinct. To a substantial extent, they merge their ways of understanding and experiencing life, and this provides a strong sense of we-ness.

Rules of communication, which we discussed previously, also tend to be crafted during the process of committing. Interaction generates rules for how to communicate and what various things mean. According to Maggie Scarf (1987), every couple creates "unspoken rules that regulate their existence together" (p. 189). For example, couples develop different patterns of talking—some enjoy longer and more frequent periods of silence than others. They also establish norms—usually without awareness—for a range of relationship issues: When and where do they eat? Do they share expenses? Is conflict to be aired or squelched? Who prevails when partners differ? How are anger, affection, and sexual interest expressed? Who initiates talk about the relationship? Without conscious intent, partners develop rules to regulate how they interact and interpret each other.

Relational culture is also shaped by direct communication between partners. Most obviously, saying "I love you" may transform a relationship from serious dating to a connection with an implied future. As Murray Davis (1973) notes, "To the extent that two individuals define or conceive of their relationship as being intimate, it becomes intimate. . . . [I]t is intensified by being so defined" (p. 184). For the same reason, intimacy is amplified when partners explicitly label feelings such as trust, security, comfort, and pleasure. Naming feelings confers a reality on them. Communication also operates in more subtle ways to create a sense of unity as partners speak of "we" and "us," terms that denote their common identity (Davis, 1973).

As relational culture arises, communication often links partners in the past and future as well as the present. They may assume each other's presence as, for example, when one friend says to another, "What do you want to do this weekend?"—a question that presumes they will spend time together. References to shared history also reflect and sustain the sense of connection (Baxter, 1987): "Remember when we went to the Outer Banks last spring?" "Didn't you think this concert was better than the last one we went to?" "Remember the first time we ate here?" The import of these remarks is not at the content level of meaning. More important is the relationship level at which partners are enriching intimacy by infusing the present with shared history.

Publicizing the Relationship

The final step in the process of committing is publicizing the relationship. The processes we've discussed so far occur privately between partners as they interact and within each individual as she or he reflects on the relationship. Unlike these private processes, publicizing the relationship directly involves others. Once two people have woven an intimate relationship, they may want to announce it to oth-

BIZARRO © by Dan Piraro. Reprinted with permission of UNIVERSAL PRESS SYNDICATE. All rights reserved.

ers. It's only natural to want to proclaim an important connection so that others acknowledge and, ideally, support it.

Relationships may be publicized in several ways. Partners may consistently appear together by merging their routines and social circles (Davis, 1973). A variation on this is to refer to partners in conversations with others, which symbolizes the connection even when partners are physically separated. For example, Ellen may allude to "Reed's opinion" when talking with her friends, and in so doing, she indicates to them that Reed is an important part of her life. While shopping with one person, Navita may note that her friend Coyna would like this outfit, would not like that one, and so forth, a clear signal that Coyna's perspective is part of Navita's own.

Publicizing is also accomplished through symbols that are publicly recognized as indicating pairedness (Baxter, 1987; Davis, 1973). What those symbols are changes with the times, but there are always socially understood symbols of relatedness. Childhood friends often exchange friendship rings. In the 1960s, couples in high school went steady and symbolized this by the woman's wearing of the man's high school class ring, usually well wrapped with tape to make it fit her typically smaller finger. In the 1970s, fraternity men gave their partners lavaliers with their fraternity letters, and if intimacy escalated, fraternity pins were given. Engagement rings and wedding bands are also culturally recognized symbols of serious commitment. One of the current indicators of pairing is the promise ring, which both women and men may wear to symbolize they are in a serious relationship. Another indicator of pairing is a woman's wearing of her partner's shirt or jacket. Exchanging clothes has long indicated friendship, especially among women. Intimates may also acquire common property, to symbolize to themselves and others they have "joined their lot" (Davis, 1973, p. 188).

REED

I guess Diane and I sort of realized we were committed when we adopted Buckey. We hadn't planned to get him, but he was in a box of puppies a little girl was trying to find homes for one day when we were out. Well, we both fell for Buckey, and it just seemed natural to take him home with us. As I think back, it was getting him that first made me really aware that I assume Diane and I are permanent. Now we joke about having to stay together because we cannot divide our "joint property"—Buckey!

Perhaps the classic way to announce a relationship is to take a romantic partner home to meet the family. Parents and siblings typically recognize this as a proclamation that a relationship is serious. When we introduce friends and romantic partners to other significant people in our lives, we publicly declare their importance to us. How we introduce intimates to others is a further way we publicly define a relationship—friend, special friend, roommate, lover, and fiancé suggest varying degrees of commitment. Others may affirm a relationship by responding to one partner as part of a couple. Davis (1973) notes that others enhance intimates' "common identity actively by treating them together as a package" (p. 185). Someone may say to Navita, "When you see Coyna, tell her I said hello" or to Mike, "Where's Ellen tonight?" Sending messages to one partner through another signals others' recognition that they are linked.

Not all friends and romantic partners choose to publicize their relationships. Sometimes there are good reasons to keep intimacy secret. We may anticipate others would disapprove of a particular partner or, more generally, of any serious involvement because they might think us too young or not yet established. When partners think third parties would interfere with a relationship, they may hide or deny involvement (Baxter, 1993; Klein & Milardo, 1993). People are also likely to conceal relationships that are socially taboo. For instance, extramarital affairs are often shielded from public scrutiny (Weis, 1995). Privacy may also be maintained by partners in interracial and interethnic romances, polygamous arrangements, and gay and lesbian bonds because they anticipate disapproval from others. For any of these reasons, partners may choose to hide their relationship in the hope of avoiding disapproval, interference, or discrimination. However, concealing also precludes social acknowledgment and support. Those who do publicize their intimacy may gain public recognition for their pair identity. This adds another layer to intimacy by making the reality of the bond that much more concrete.

The five communication processes we have discussed are often part of committing, yet they are not universal in presence or sequence. Some partners may not engage in certain processes. For instance, publicizing is seldom done for affairs, and two pragmatic people may experience little or no idealization. Further, there is no prescribed or empirically established order to the processes we've considered. Idealization may signal the onset of committing for one couple, whereas private intensifying launches it for another. Friends and romantic partners may engage simultaneously or repeatedly in all five processes.

INTIMATE COMMITMENT

We turn now to the final focus of this chapter: the decision to commit to a future of intimacy. At the outset of our discussion, it's important to realize that commitment is not necessarily something to aim for in every personal relationship. Not all people who care about each other do or should commit to a shared future. It is entirely possible to love someone with whom we don't want to share our lives and to care deeply for people when circumstances and issues in our lives do not allow us to commit to the future. In other words, we can love without commitment and can be intimate without long-term intentions.

Preparing to Commit

Committing yourself and your future to another person is a major decision. For this reason, many couples who are considering marriage attend workshops or counseling that is designed to help them build strong, enduring relationships. About 80 percent of religious organizations now require some form of premarital counseling for couples who want their religion's blessing (Hamilton & Wingert, 1998). Many state and local governments are considering requiring couples who want to marry to attend counseling. In June 1998 Florida enacted a law reducing the cost of marriage licenses for couples who prove they've attended at least four hours of marriage counseling. Meanwhile, Louisiana is considering offering couples two forms of marriage: One is the standard form; the other, the "high test marriage," makes it more difficult for a couple to divorce. The goal, say supporters of this plan, is to discourage abandoning marital commitments.

Young adults today are unsure that marriage can work, perhaps because so many of them saw their parents divorce. "If my parents couldn't make it work, how can I?" they ask. Yet, this generation of people is not antimarriage at all. According to Judith Wallerstein (1995), they want commitment, but are afraid of being abandoned. They're willing to make a strong, serious commitment, but they often lack good models of healthy marriage. As a whole, this generation longs for a return to more traditional family values. A recent survey by the Yankelovich firm found that 73 percent of Gen-Xers favor traditional standards for family life. When the same question was asked in a survey 20 years ago, only 56 percent of those polled favored a return to more traditional family values (Hamilton & Wingert, 1998). A national study conducted by researchers at the University of Chicago reports that members of Gen-X were least likely of all age groups to think divorce is the best option for troubled marriages (Hamilton & Wingert, 1998).

The profile that emerges shows a group of young adults who know how difficult it is to sustain a marriage and who, nonetheless, want to do so. They understand what commitment is, and they want the stability of a lifelong relationship. But they don't know how to make commitment work—in large part because so many of them witnessed their own parents divorce. For them, some form of premarital counseling is a welcome way to learn what perhaps they didn't learn in their own families: how to not just make a commitment, but to live it in daily life.

The Meaning of Commitment

In those instances where intimates do commit to a shared future, additional dimensions are added to a relationship. According to Aaron Beck (1988), the crux of commitment is "the determination to maintain the relationship even after difficulties, disappointments, and disillusionment" (p. 177). This suggests commitment involves a decision, investments, responsibility, and a focus on the future. With regard to the first of these aspects, commitment is a decision, a conscious choice made by an individual agent. It is not something that happens to us, nor is it the result of biological ties. Instead, commitment is a deliberate act to join with another person. Rather than just a hope that a relationship will continue to be gratifying, commitment is a resolution to stay with a relationship, even if it is not always fulfilling. In a broad study of Americans' values, Robert Bellah and his colleagues (1985) noted that most people recognize that something more than transient feelings of love and goodwill is necessary for relationships to endure. Inevitably there will be bad times, hurts, and losses. Partners who have not made a decision to stick together often cannot weather trials and troubles.

Because commitment is a choice, it involves *responsibility*, which Beck (1988) calls the hallmark of commitment. Partners assume responsibility for continuing to invest in their relationship and for persisting through bad times as well as good. The responsibilities of commitment include investing energy to work out problems, managing the normal conflict inherent in closeness, supporting each other, nourishing the relational culture, and, in general, continuously making the relationship a high priority. Without responsibility, a relationship becomes an ad hoc matter more subject to the whims of feeling than the direction of a personal choice that is honored in daily life.

Because commitment depends on investments more than rewards (Lund, 1985), it need not wane during the unrewarding times that inevitably punctuate long-term relationships (Rusbult & Buunk, 1993). An **investment** is something an individual puts into a relationship that could not be recovered if the relationship were to end (Brehm, 1992). The most profound investment we make in intimacy is, of course, ourselves (Kelley, 1983). In addition, we invest time, feeling, thought, hopes, and dreams, as well as material things such as money and assistance (Reis & Shaver, 1988). We also develop shared memories that link us to partners and that are sustained by collaboratively recollecting (Wegner, Erber, & Raymond, 1991). Individuals may also be invested in moral values such as fidelity or not divorcing (Johnson, 1991).

Should a relationship end, we cannot get back the period of our lives spent with a partner, nor can we recoup feelings, hopes, and personal identity carved in relation to a partner. Because we cannot recover what we invest, irretrievability is inherent in investments (Rusbult, 1980a, 1980b, 1983) and explains why they strengthen commitment: Leaving means suffering a loss of irretrievable investments. Even if a relationship is unsatisfying, we sometimes feel we cannot forsake it because of what we have invested (Brockner & Rubin, 1985).

Central to the idea of commitment is future. Writing of this, Davis (1973) comments with equal parts humor and insight that "intimates, like college professors, want tenure. And in order to guarantee that their relationship will continue, they must make a commitment to each other" (p. 192). Unlike attraction or passion, commitment reaches beyond the present to link partners in the future by setting the presumption for continuation. The relationship becomes a given, an anchor around which other choices are made. No longer is a relationship contingent on good moments and positive feelings; no longer is its status iffy. The assumption of future radically transforms a personal relationship, making it an assumed, continuing part of who one is and how one's life will be arranged. As Davis sagely notes (1973, p. 395), "One's future, in Western society at least, is one's most prized possession. To commit it to another is the most important gift we can give." It is a gift to be made only after serious reflection and only if both partners are ready to live up to the responsibilities that accompany the choice to commit.

SUMMARY

In this chapter, we've discussed general patterns that typify committing, which often commences with partners' intense, even euphoric focus on each other and the new relationship. In some relationships, initial passion leads to a decision to stay together for the long term. As my student observed, lasting intimacy becomes possible if people fall into commitment.

The process of building a personal relationship involves expressing intimacy and engaging in communication processes that interweave partners' lives and identities. We have seen that individuals have different styles of love, which shape how they experience and express intimacy, as well as what it means to them. To build a viable relational culture, partners develop dual perspective and create common understandings and patterns that accommodate their distinctive needs and perspectives.

Five communication processes tend to be present when partners are committing. As partners intensify privately, personalize communication, idealize, begin creating relational culture, and publicize their intimacy, they develop dual perspective and an embryonic private world that has increasing reality and salience in their individual and joint lives. Over the course of time, partners whose relationships endure refine and elaborate their relational culture to keep it vibrant and responsive to changes in them and their circumstances. Whether committing is gradual, rapid, or intermittent, it is not a solitary event but a process that occurs over time.

Although intimacy may involve both love and commitment, the two are distinct. Love involves feelings and rewards, which, however enjoyable, seem not to be an adequate foundation for enduring intimacy. Commitment, on the other hand, is a determination to continue a relationship. Involving a decision, responsibility, investments, and a focus on the future, commitment transforms how partners perceive a relationship so that they see it as a personal anchor and a bond whose continuing existence is assumed. In later chapters, we'll explore how partners sustain and modify their commitment over the life of their relationship.

FOR FURTHER REFLECTION AND DISCUSSION

1. Reflect on your personal prototype of enduring love. How consistent is it with Fehr's findings about the general prototype of love in Western society?

2. Based on the discussion in this chapter, can you identify your style of love and that of a past or current romantic partner? Discuss how your two styles fit or clash. How do you experience different love styles in different relationships?

3. What do you see as likely associations between attachment styles and love styles? For instance, do you think people with preoccupied attachment styles would tend to be more manic lovers? Would secure attachment styles most likely yield storgic or erotic love styles?

4. Think about times when you've felt really understood by an intimate. Describe how that felt and how that relates to the importance of dual perspective in intimacy.

5. Think about private language in your personal relationships. What nicknames, code words, and so forth are part of relationships with members of your family, your closest friend, and with a current or past romantic partner? Are these important? Why or why not?

6. Have you had experiences in loving someone to whom you didn't want to commit? Can you identify the array of personal and contextual influences that affect decisions to commit?

RECOMMENDED READINGS

Davis, M. (1973). *Intimate relations*. New York: Free Press.

Hendrick, C., & Hendrick, S. (1986). Lovers wear rose-colored glasses. *Journal of Social and Personal Relationships, 5*, 161–184.

Lee, J. A. (1973). *The colours of love: An exploration of the ways of loving*. Don Mills, Ontario: New Press.

Lund, M. (1985). The development of investment and commitment scales for predicting continuity of personal relationships. *Journal of Social and Personal Relationships, 2*, 3–23.

May, R. (1969). *Love and will*. New York: Norton.

Maintaining and Repairing
Personal Relationships

THROUGHOUT THIS BOOK, WE'VE emphasized the processual nature of personal relationships. Always changing, moving, evolving, personal relationships are ongoing creations. Because personal relationships are dynamic, they require ongoing effort and investment to remain vital and viable. Thus, as long as intimacy endures, partners continuously refine, revise, and reform their private world so that it continues to reflect and nurture the personal and relationship identities they have crafted. A personal relationship that continues requires active efforts to maintain and sometimes repair the relational culture that is the heart of intimacy. Dan Canary and Laura Stafford make the point well when they write that "relationships fall apart unless people invest the energy to keep them together" (1994, p. 7).

Relationship maintenance is communication and other actions that partners use to sustain a personal relationship at a standard and desirable level of functioning and satisfaction. Relationship maintenance may be thought of as what partners do to keep their relationship healthy. Borrowing a medical analogy, we can think of relationship maintenance as efforts to maintain the wellness of a relationship. **Relationship repair,** on the other hand, is communication and other actions designed to *restore* a relationship to a standard and desirable level of functioning and satisfaction. Unlike maintenance, repair occurs *after* one or both partners perceive a relationship has become unsatisfactory in some respect; the repair aims to treat the sickness or problems that are undermining the relationship's wellness.

This chapter explores how partners sustain and repair personal relationships over time. Our goal is to understand how partners keep intimacy alive, despite changes, threats, and a variety of internal and external circumstances that could jeopardize the relationship. We will begin by discussing and evaluating alternative ways of thinking about relationship maintenance and repair. Next we consider everyday processes intimates use to weave their lives and identities into the relational culture that is the nucleus of their relationship. Unremarkable routines and communication are, in fact, a cornerstone of committed relationships. To complement our focus on daily rhythms of intimacy, we'll explore why and how personal relationships change over time in ways that call for maintenance and repair if the relationships are to remain vital and viable. Examining how partners maintain and repair intimacy, we'll identify ways to manage changes and renew relationships that have become stale or otherwise unsatisfactory. Finally, to close the chapter, we'll discuss how gendered standpoints distinctively sculpt how many women and men, in general, experience and express satisfaction, as well as how they maintain and repair personal relationships.

ALTERNATIVE APPROACHES TO RELATIONSHIP CONTINUITY

Researchers have developed a number of approaches to relationship continuity. We'll discuss early approaches briefly and then turn our attention to more recent developments.

Early Approaches to Relationship Continuity

Efforts to explain how and why relationships continue have historically focused either on qualities present in individuals or on outcomes of interaction. The former explanations claim that individual variables such as attitudes and values provide the basis for relationships. Thus, goes the reasoning, if two people share common values, beliefs, and so forth, a relationship is tenable. When we examined research on similarities in Chapter 6, we discovered that both perceived and actual similarities between people influence attraction and relationship stability. Yet explanatory schemes that concentrate on individual variables tell us little about interpersonal dynamics. They cannot account for processes by which partners realize and act on similarities in ways that influence how they think and feel about themselves, each other, and their relationship.

A second focus of explanatory efforts has been outcomes of interaction, which some researchers regard as the reasons relationships arise and continue. For instance, the development and stability of relationships might be attributed to satisfaction, rewards from association, or partners' comparison levels of alternatives (Rusbult & Buunk, 1993; Rusbult, Drigotas, & Verette, 1994). Clearly variables like these affect decisions to enter and remain in personal relationships. Yet, like research that emphasizes individual variables, the focus on outcomes neglects the interaction processes that yield outcomes such as satisfaction. Thus, outcome-oriented accounts shed little light on how interaction between people affects the character and continuity of intimacy.

Taken together, these two explanatory emphases highlight what exists before (individual variables) and after (outcomes) intimacy, but tell us little about what happens between individuals and relationship outcomes—the actual dynamics of intimacy. Further, both explanations assume personal relationships are relatively static entities that achieve homeostasis (Argyle & Dean, 1965; Patterson, 1976, 1984). Yet as we've seen, intimacy is an evolutionary process in which moments of stability are only transitions between changes (Montgomery, 1993). Because these explanations of relationship continuity are static and obscure processes that create and maintain intimacy, they tell us little about how partners' interaction sustains—or fails to sustain—commitment over time.

Existing research indicates that satisfaction with personal relationships is linked to perceived equity in the relationship, trust, affirmation of personal worth, enjoyment of joint activities and each other's company, and love (Canary & Stafford, 1994; Gottman, 1994a; Guerrero, Eloy, & Wabnik, 1993; Wilmot, 1994). Thus, scholars seek to identify the kinds of actions and interactions that foster equity, trust, personal affirmation, enjoyment of shared activities, and feelings of love.

Social Exchange

Some scholars who are interested in how and why relationships continue or end endorse social exchange theory or particular variants such as interdependence theory. Social exchange explains relationship continuity in terms of partners' satisfaction with the balance of rewards and costs and the overall sense of equity in a relationship (Blau, 1967; Rusbult & Buunk, 1993; Thibaut & Kelley, 1959). Satisfaction may be based on whether rewards exceed costs, the net outcome (rewards minus costs) of a relationship surpasses individual comparison levels, or the net outcome is greater than those anticipated from alternatives (Kelley, 1983; Rusbult & Buunk, 1993). The social exchange perspective views maintenance as keeping a relationship well by maintaining partners' benefits at satisfying levels (Benin & Agnostinelli, 1988; Thibaut & Kelley, 1959; Yougev & Brett, 1985).

Exchange theorists claim that individuals are in relationships for what they can get out of them and that they will leave if profits fall below an acceptable level or if more profitable alternatives are available. Critics of this perspective point out that personal relationships are not capitalistic endeavors in which personal gain is the primary goal. Art Bochner (1984), for instance, argues that social and intimate interactions are notably different from marketplace transactions, and exchange applies only to the latter. Although all of us enjoy rewards and assume they will be part of intimacy, they are not the sole or primary reason we form or remain in relationships.

Another criticism of exchange theories is that they focus more on individuals than relationships. Social exchange assumes each person is a rational actor who calculates rewards and costs of involvement. This implies that individuals continuously compute and compare costs and rewards (Wood, 1993b, c). Yet, when we're in a relationship, the lines between self and other tend to blur—how do we demarcate our own satisfaction from the satisfaction of those we love? To the extent that intimates care about each other's needs and feelings, they no longer think in strictly individual terms (Aron et al., 1991; Wood, 1993b).

In considering exchange theory critically, we should also note several empirical studies that suggest limits to this view of how relationships operate. More than a decade ago, one scholar (McDonald, 1981) reported that exchange principles are suspended in relationships where trust and commitment are present. Confirming this, another study (O'Connell, 1984) found that in long-term committed relationships, partners routinely accept imbalances in rewards and outcomes without feeling resentful. Mary Lund's (1985) work, too, indicates that rewards are less important than investments in sustaining intimacy. Finally, a study of different types of relationships (Clark, Quellette, Powell, & Milberg, 1987) revealed that although reciprocity of exchange is expected in marketplace interactions, it is actually disliked and unsatisfying in communal relationships such as close friendship and romance.

Perhaps the most accurate and balanced evaluation of exchange theory is that it has some value and some limits for understanding how relationships operate over time. It is useful in providing an orderly way of assessing what a relationship takes from us and gives to us and in deciding whether what we get is equal to what our partners get. It is a practical framework for explaining whether our net outcomes are good enough to keep us committed.

The social exchange approach is also valuable because it focuses attention on equity and inequity. Over many decades, research quite consistently shows that inequity is a major cause of dissatisfaction in relationships (Hatfield, Traupmann, Sprecher, Utne, & Hay, 1985; Rusbult, Drigotas, & Verette, 1994; Sprecher, 1986; VanYperen & Buunk, 1990). In zeroing in on equity, social exchange theories highlight a key influence on satisfaction with personal relationships. Yet, as research we have discussed shows, social exchange theories do not adequately address some of the dimensions and processes of personal relationships that may be as important as perceptions of equity.

A Dialogical Approach

In recent years, many relationship scholars have devoted substantial energy to developing an approach to relationship continuity that emphasizes the processes by which partners maintain and repair intimacy. These scholars are also sensitive to the impact of culture and social groups on personal relationships, so they are concerned with explaining continuity for personal relationships as those relationships exist within multiple systems. One of the most important systemic influences on personal relationships is the change in the cultural view that marriage is an obligation or duty. Whereas that view was widely held prior to the 1950s, it no longer dominates cultural thinking about personal relationships. As Robert Sternberg and Mahzad Hojjat (1997) point out, in Western society today, the continuance of personal relationships depends much more on satisfaction than on duty. Thus, to explain how and why relationships endure, we must ask what affects the satisfaction of relationships in our era.

A particularly impressive effort to illuminate relationship processes comes from scholars who adopt a dialectical perspective (Baxter, 1988, 1993, 1994; Baxter & Montgomery, 1996). As we have seen in previous chapters, this point of view holds that inherent in relationships are contradictory and interacting forces. Writing in 1994, Leslie Baxter claimed that "relational maintenance, conceived dialogically, is the process of coping with the ceaseless change that results from the struggle of contradictory tendencies inherent in relating" (p. 233). Friends and romantic partners have to work out ways to satisfy needs for autonomy and connection, openness and privacy, and novelty and predictability. Yet no resolution is permanent, because tensions between contradictory forces are always present, even if not pronounced in particular dialectical moments.

From a dialogical perspective, maintaining a relationship is not occasional preventive maintenance but rather an ongoing and unending process inherent in relating. To sustain a relationship, partners must continuously address dialectical tensions that arise in the course of intimacy and affect the character of the relationship and partners' satisfaction. The dialogical perspective is the most dynamic of all the approaches to relationship maintenance and repair that we have considered. Change and process are the foundation of a dialogical view of relationship continuity. Says Barbara Montgomery (1993), "relationships cannot be maintained in a stable state because they are constantly changing" (p. 168). Tensions between contradictory forces generate relationship change and even transformations, and, because tensions are continuous, change is a constant feature of enduring intimacy.

Temporary periods of equilibrium between contradictory forces are what Baxter (1993) refers to as "dialectical moments," that are only intermissions in the ongoing flux of relationship life. Viewing intimacy as a continuous process in which the only constant is change, scholars have studied how intimates manage tensions that arise from dynamics internal and external to a bond. Sometimes intimates adjust in response to tensions between dialectics. For instance, after a period of intense togetherness and openness, partners may seek distance and may temporarily be more closed in conversation. At other times, partners respond to external pressures as when, for example, a partner loses a job or suffers medical injury and the partners become temporarily more connected than they were before.

In her study of couples who remained happily married for 25 or more years, Judith Wallerstein (1995) began by asking long-lasting couples to explain the secret of their success. What Wallerstein discovered, however, is that there is no single secret to a good marriage because marriages differ dramatically, as do the issues and problems that arise within them. Wallerstein's key finding was that happy couples consistently regarded their marriages as "works in progress" that required continuous attention and adjustment. Because the dialogical perspective highlights change as inherent in intimacy (Dindia & Canary, 1993), it offers an especially dynamic and processual explanation of how partners sustain personal relationships as they simultaneously and continuously redefine what it means and how to live together.

Drawing on a dialogical approach to relationship maintenance, Dan Canary and his colleagues (1993) discovered a number of strategies people use to maintain their relationships at satisfactory levels. The strategies cover a range of personal relationships, including romance, friendship, and family ties. The strategies were inductively derived from students' descriptions of what they do to maintain their relationships. Table 8.1 summarizes the strategies students said they used most frequently.

TABLE 8.1
Strategies for Maintaining Personal Relationships

Positivity	Efforts to make interaction pleasant by being cheerful, doing favors for each other, deferring to the other, showing affection.
Openness	Efforts to keep the lines of communication open by making disclosures and listening to a partner's disclosures, discussing problems, giving and seeking advice, talking directly about the relationship, metacommunicating, and showing empathy.
Assurances	Efforts to assure a partner that she or he is loved, respected, and valued by communicating support and encouragement, comforting and standing up for a partner, and expressing unconditional love.
Joint Activities	Spending time with each other in unstructured ways (hanging out), routine ways (attending church or games), spontaneous ways, and by reserving time for couple talk.
Cards, Letters, and Calls	Relying on various kinds of communication to sustain contact.
Avoidance	Evading a partner or issues that foster unconstructive conflict; also, planning separate activities and respecting each other's privacy.

The maintenance strategies identified by Canary and his colleagues reveal that intimates rely on a broad array of means to maintain their personal relationships. The findings from this study give us some very useful insights into the actual process of relationship maintenance. We see how partners use particular kinds of interaction and engage in specific actions to keep their relationships satisfying.

Building on the work of Canary and other scholars who take a processual approach to relationship maintenance and repair, we'll now explore the everyday activities that partners rely on to maintain intimacy. As we do so, we'll gain insight into the processes that partners use to intertwine their lives and continuously compose their relational cultures.

EVERYDAY RHYTHMS IN PERSONAL RELATIONSHIPS

When you think about it, relationships are pretty amazing. How do two individuals who are strangers transform themselves into an intimate pair? How do we move from attraction to investments to a relationship that keeps working over time? To understand these transformations we need to scrutinize the everyday processes by which partners actually continuously create and live out their relationships. This focus reflects recent thinking among relationship scholars, who argue that day-to-day patterns and processes are the heart of long-term commitment (Baxter, 1994; Bolger & Kelleher, 1993; Duck, 1992, 1994a, b; Duck & Pond, 1989; Shea & Pearson, 1986). We will discuss five processes that link partners' lives on a day-to-day basis. If you have been involved in long-term intimacy, then much of what we discuss may be familiar and even obvious. Nonetheless, it's important not to let dramatic topics such as love styles or relationship crises overshadow awareness of more routine, everyday activities that are probably considerably more important in influencing relationship life.

Routines for Contact

One way partners keep their lives aligned is through behavioral routines that bring them together on a frequent basis. Recall that the study by Canary and his colleagues (see Table 8.1) found that one maintenance strategy people use is reserving time for couple talk. One of my friends and I have a standing date for brunch every Sunday. By setting up regular meetings, partners guarantee their lives will intersect. Similarly, romantic couples settle into routines that relieve them of the need to set up each specific get-together. Many couples have established times for reconnecting at the end of each day.

People engaged in long-distance relationships also work to keep their lives connected. Many long-distance partners designate times for phone calls and arrange their lives to accommodate scheduled contacts. E-mail is another increasingly popular strategy that long-distance partners rely on to maintain contact. Despite these ways of communicating, what long-distance couples say they miss most by living apart is ordinary routines and exchanges (Rohlfing, 1995; Routine of marriage, 1985). They long for the in-person exchanges about the large and small things that make up the texture of each day.

ELAINE

Habits are funny things. You think they're pretty trivial, but really relation-ships depend on habits. Betsy and I met when we shared a class. Since the class ended at noon, we started going to lunch together after it each day. One fall we had lunch three times a week, and we got to know each other really well and got involved in each other's lives. Sometimes we called or got togeth-er at other times, but our friendship mainly took place in those after-class lunches. The next term we didn't have a class together, and whenever one of us called to suggest getting together, the other had a conflict. It was like we hadn't reserved a space for each other in our lives.

Cohabitation or marriage multiplies joint routines by locating partners in a common environment within which activities such as eating, sleeping, and talking are coordinated. According to Murray Davis (1973, pp. 192–193), "Living together maximizes the number of occasions intimates can conjoin themselves and thick-ens the glue that cements their psychological joints together." From sleepy-eyed "good mornings" to daily checks on each other's plans, to cozy "good nights," part-ners who live together participate in joint routines that weave their lives together day by day.

Yet even partners who live together may have to invest effort to sustain regu-lar contact. Elaine's journal entry offers us an important insight. Unless partners in a relationship make regular contact a priority, it's likely to wane. Couples often find their standard contact routines are disrupted when one person's schedule changes. Routine contact may ebb if Carmen and Tony have shared their days from 5 to 6 each day after work and Carmen takes a new job that requires her to work until 7. Similarly, when a couple has a baby, the baby's schedule may wreak havoc on the couple's established routines of contact.

Common Involvements

Another process that joins intimates is involving themselves in mutual concerns and activities. These might be shared hobbies, recreation, religious involvements, or community commitments, all of which provide common points of reference for intimates and which prompt mutual engagement and enjoyment (Berscheid, 1983). Long recommended by counselors, joint activities can be beneficial to inti-macy. Research, however, indicates that not all activities have the same impact on personal relationships. Exciting or stimulating ones seem to enhance marital close-ness and satisfy needs for predictability (Reissman, Aron, & Bergen, 1993), whereas less dramatic activities may contribute to familiarity and comfort. Perhaps this explains why friends, particularly males, often arrange get-togethers around athletic matches (Swain, 1989). Intimates may also create joint property—including a home, furniture, pets, and joint checking and savings accounts. Things owned in common provide tangible evidence that a relationship exists and presumably will continue.

Particularly enriching of intimacy is creating something that concretely reflects the joining of partners' lives. The exemplar of this is, of course, children, who are literally created from a sexual and genetic intermingling of their parents. Children and, more broadly, family represent a profound joining of individuals' lives. Children and other family members also provide an ongoing focus for collaboration and mutual activity between partners.

JERRY

Anne and I had been married four years when our first baby arrived. I thought I loved Anne as much as anybody can love another person, but when Roseanne was born a whole new kind of love grew between us. Every time we look at our daughter, we see living proof that we love each other and that something that is both of us now exists. It's like Roseanne expresses our love but also extends it somehow—makes it bigger and different.

In addition to children, there are other common creations through which intimates embody their union. One of these is a home, which couples decorate and inhabit together. Representing their unique tastes and functional preferences and layered with symbols of their experiences and values, homes are physical symbols of joined lives. In Chapter 4 we discussed this process of placemaking through which partners create and continuously reform their common environment. This is a primary way intimates realize and express their commonness and shape their interactions (Bateson, 1990; Werner et al., 1992, 1993). It is also one of the ways intimates express changes in their relationship, as when creating a nursery for a baby or transforming a child's room into a den when she or he leaves home. Friends, too, use common objects to symbolize their connection. Collaborating on a book, starting a homeless shelter, or team-teaching workshops on self-defense are examples of shared interests that promote interaction and enlarge relational culture.

JACKSON

Jed and I got to be friends when we put our heads together to create a campus newsletter for African Americans. It started when there was a rally for African American students and we happened to stand beside each other. At one point, Jed said to me, "If we had a regular newsletter, that would keep Blacks on campus better informed about issues affecting us than rallies over each new thing." That hit a chord in me because I'm a journalism major, so I said, "Well, why don't we start one?" He took the bait, and we agreed to meet that night. For three months after that we were together almost every night and weekend—planning, working on stories, and getting advertising and start-up funds. It was like this was our baby. When we put out our first issue, we celebrated over a big steak dinner. For over a year now we've worked shoulder to shoulder on that project, and we've talked about just about everything in our lives.

Patterns of Interaction

Intimates also coordinate themselves by working out rules and roles to organize interaction. As we have seen, regulative rules specify how various interactions are to take place. The content of regulative rules is less important than that partners share them. For instance, some friends constantly interrupt and talk over each other, whereas others take turns in conversation. Some spouses have regulative rules that call for avoiding conflict, whereas others have ones that encourage confrontation (Fitzpatrick, 1988). Female friends, more than males, endorse rules for disclosing personal information, openly showing affection, providing emotional support, and respecting privacy (Argyle & Henderson, 1985). Among male friends, regulative rules typically call for covert displays of affection and limited verbal disclosure (Inman, 1996; Swain, 1989; Wood & Inman, 1993) and for engaging in one-upmanship in conversation (Gaines, 1994).

Constitutive rules define how things count. In the course of interaction, friends and romantic partners work out agreements about what conveys support, affection, and commitment. Equally important, they generate understandings of what counts as betrayal or violation. When one partner violates a rule by being unfaithful or breaching a confidence, intimacy suffers, and a relationship may be disrupted (Argyle & Henderson, 1985; Roloff & Cloven, 1994). Because rules regulate and define behaviors, they organize a relationship and provide a sense of continuity and predictability.

Interaction is also patterned by roles partners assume in relation to each other. Intimates count on each other to do certain things, respond in particular ways, and initiate in specific areas. In this sense, intimates collaboratively define each person's identity within the relationship (Berger & Kellner, 1975; Kelley, 1983). Partners' expectations of each other are born out of their history of interaction, realized in current moments, and projected into the future. Like other relationship matters, roles are not fixed permanently. Instead, they are open to renegotiation as changes in partners and relationships make transformations desirable. Within relationships, partners often specialize so that each one provides something the other does not (Lederer & Jackson, 1968; Scarf, 1987). One of my friends approaches issues emotionally and concretely, whereas I am inclined to be analytical and conceptual. When we talk, I count on her to illuminate affective dimensions of issues, and she relies on me to analyze them. Our complementary roles are part of who we are in relation to each other.

The best evidence that intimates develop roles and count on each other to enact them is what happens when one partner fails to fulfill a role. Because relationships are systems, what each person does affects the other and the relationship as a whole. Thus, when one person doesn't perform her or his role, either the system will be disrupted or the partner will take over the role abandoned by the other. If the partner who typically minds the emotional pulse of a relationship and initiates discussion of potential problems ceases to do so, tensions may arise and go unaddressed. Eventually, the unmet needs of the relationship will erupt unless either the partner who normally attends to them resumes the role or the other partner takes it on. The point is that the role itself is part of how the relationship works, and either it must be filled by someone or the relationship must be reconfigured to operate without it.

SHUPHORA

Our marriage really changed when I came back to finish my degree. It had to change or it would have come apart. Before I returned to school, I did all of the cleaning and cooking even though both Barry and I worked. But I couldn't keep up with all of that once I was studying. My first semester back was pretty rough because Barry wasn't used to doing housework. Laundry piled up and so did dust balls. Finally, he figured out I wasn't going to do it all any more, and we talked and we split the chores.

Like Shuphora and Barry, many couples renegotiate homemaking chores when one of the partners begins work or school. Sue Shellenbarger, reporter for the *Wall Street Journal*, notes that dual-worker couples are gradually shifting toward shared responsibility for housework. Although most men do not yet assume a full 50 percent of homemaking and child-care chores, they are becoming more equal partners in home life. Men are also assuming more responsibility for taking care of children. According to Shellenbarger's research (1996), many fathers today spend 66 percent as much time with children as mothers. Younger couples seem most committed to an egalitarian approach to household chores and family responsibilities.

Everyday Talk

Particularly important to sustaining intimacy is everyday talk. The basic fabric of a relationship is interaction between partners. In day-to-day conversations, people live out their relationships. We realize intimacy, or make it real, by engaging in routine dialogues that over and over again confirm the existence and importance of our connections (Beck, 1988; Berger & Kellner, 1975). Research demonstrates that the majority of communication between intimates is about common experiences and everyday issues (Duck, 1994a, b; Duck & Rutt, 1988; Duck et al., 1991; Shea & Pearson, 1986; Spencer, 1994). A study of commuter marriages (Gerstel & Gross, 1985) revealed that what these couples miss most is trivial sharing, comfortable silence, and routine conversation rituals. More than the occasional grand moment and major talks, the day-in, day-out rhythm of interaction sustains a shared world. Steve Duck brings the point home when he writes that "talk is the essence of relational maintenance" (1994b, p. 52).

In a series of four studies Deanna Goldsmith and Leslie Baxter (1996) investigated what kinds of everyday talk are most common between friends and partners in romantic relationships. Their research identified 29 types of talk that people report occurs in personal relationships. Of these, six types of talk appear to dominate everyday interaction:

- Gossip: "You'll never guess who I saw Amy with."

- Making plans: "What do you want to do this weekend?"

- Joking around: "I'm burned out. Let's run away and never come back."

- Catching up: "I wanted to tell you about my conversation with mom last weekend."

- Small talk: "I wonder if this winter's going to be cold."

- Recapping the day's events: "There was a wreck on the main road into campus when I drove in today."

The fact that most talk in personal relationships is relatively unremarkable shouldn't mislead us into thinking it is unimportant. Daily, mundane contact and connection between partners provides confirmation of their importance to each other, and it concretizes the reality of the relationship over and over again. Hence, the significance of everyday talk lies in its relationship level of meaning. As Duck notes, "The apparently idle chatter of partners serves to demonstrate a 'symbolic union' between their two independent ways of looking at life" (1994b, p. 53).

The importance of small talk was crystallized for me in a conversation with my mother. Two years after my father had died, she called one day to report that her car had refused to start when she tried to drive home from the supermarket and she returned two hours late. I asked if she and the car were okay now, to which she responded, "That's not the point. I felt so alone, because there was nobody who knew I was out and nobody who cared I was late getting home. I missed your father more in that moment than on anniversaries or holidays." For my mother, as for most of us, the crux of intimacy was ordinary, not extraordinary moments. She missed having someone to whom she could say, "Sorry I'm late," "This is a heavy rain, isn't it?" and "What do you want for lunch today?" On the relationship level of meaning, commonplace conversation says "I acknowledge you exist. I know you are there. You matter to me." Table 8.2 illustrates some of the relationship level meanings of everyday talk between partners.

Alan Sillars and his colleagues (1992) examined themes in the conversations of 52 married couples. They found that couples who were more interdependent and satisfied with their relationships relied more on communal themes than individual ones. Communal themes are topics that concern togetherness, cooperation,

TABLE 8.2

Relationship Level Meanings of Everyday Talk

EVERYDAY TALK	RELATIONSHIP LEVEL MEANING
"It's raining today."	I'm here. Do you want to talk?
"I'm starting a new project at work."	I want you to be aware of what's happening in my career.
"I bought some of those berries you love when I went shopping today."	I care about you. I keep your preferences in mind.
"I heard a funny joke today. . . ."	Confirm that I am interesting. Let's enjoy a laugh together.
"Could you believe the way Ed and Janet bickered at the party last night?"	We're not the kind of people who quarrel in public.
"Do you want to rent a movie this weekend?"	Let's spend some fun time together.
"I'm thinking about cutting my hair."	Do you think my hair is attractive like it is? Will you be upset if I cut my hair?
"You really should get back to your aerobics."	I care about your health.

and communication with each other. Individual themes focus on individual differences, personalities, and separate activities. Sillars and his colleagues concluded their research report by noting that conversational themes express and uphold definitions of personal relationships by emphasizing degrees of autonomy and connection.

Reflection

A final process that sustains committed relationships is reflection, or thinking about the relationship. How we think about relationships decisively affects what they mean to us as well as how we feel and act in them (Beck, 1988; Duck, 1992, 1994a; Shotter, 1993). We play back conversations we have had, savor special moments of intimacy, consider various ways to resolve tensions, and plan for future interactions. Reflections about partners and relationships lace our everyday lives, keeping

SALLY FORTH reprinted with permission of King Features Syndicate.

us aware of and anchored in intimacy, even when our partners are not physically with us.

Research (Miell, 1987) shows that how people recall and recast prior interactions shapes their future actions. Extending this, Linda Acitelli's research (1986, 1988, 1992) centers on relationship awareness, which is "a person's thinking about interaction patterns, comparisons, or contrasts between himself or herself and the other partner" (1993, p. 151). Among other things, thinking about relationships seems to increase individuals' confidence that they understand a partner and how a relationship operates (Berger & Calabrese, 1975; Parks & Adelman, 1983; Surra & Bohman, 1991). Because feeling we understand our relationships is comforting, reflection is related to satisfaction. After reviewing research on how thinking about relationships affects individuals and interaction, Acitelli (1993) suggested that individuals' thinking and perceptions are "the threads from which the fabric of the shared reality is constructed" (p. 145).

Managing Disagreements

Disagreements are an inevitable part of all personal relationships. Having disagreements is not a measure of relationship health, but how they are managed definitely affects relationship quality and partners' satisfaction.

Researchers have repeatedly found that satisfied couples disagree as much as dissatisfied couples and they tend to disagree about the same things: money, sex, jealousy, children, housework, in-laws, and how to spend time. What differs between satisfied and dissatisfied couples is *how* they express and deal with disagreements (Marriage builders, 1998).

John Gottman, a distinguished clinician and scholar, has spent years studying marriage and divorce. In his 1994 book *What Predicts Divorce?* Gottman identifies four communication patterns during disagreements that undermine satisfaction and corrode marriages. First, he identifies recurrent complaining and criticism as a pattern that sets a negative tone for a relationship. Second, he points out that many people express critical and contemptuous attitudes toward partners who disagree with them. Consistent with Gottman's findings, Alan Sillars and his colleagues (1992) reported that dissatisfied couples engage in more personalized complaints when disagreeing. These personalized complaints often feel like attacks on personal worth, so they disconfirm a partner. Personalized complaints and disdainful attitudes toward a partner foster a third pattern, which is defensiveness on the part of the partner being treated contemptuously.

The final pattern Gottman identifies is **stonewalling,** which is withdrawing from interaction and refusing to talk about problems and issues of disagreement. In his research, Gottman has found that husbands are more likely than wives to stonewall and slam the door shut on conversation. Stonewalling is poisonous for personal relationships because it eviscerates the possibility of resolving differences. Other research supports Gottman's finding that stonewalling is toxic to intimacy.

Sandra Metts and William Cupach (1990) reported that refusing to discuss issues or minimizing a partner's concerns is linked to dissatisfaction with relationships.

The research we've discussed informs us about destructive ways of managing disagreements, but what are more productive and loving ways to deal with the inevitable disagreements in personal relationships? Fortunately, we have some answers to that question. Three general strategies of engaging in disagreement seem to allow couples to discuss differences without harming their relationship.

Express criticism gently and respectfully. Partners should express disagreement and make criticisms in ways that do not negate love for the other partner or undermine the other partner's self-worth. In *Why Marriages Succeed or Fail* (1994), written with Nan Silver, John Gottman reports that one of the clearest qualities of unhappy marriages is belligerence during disagreements or when criticizing a partner. Gottman advises people to express complaints gently and in ways that do not cause partners to doubt that they are loved. Humor, too, goes a long way to take the sting out of criticism. Fran's description of how she expressed criticism about her boyfriend's messiness illustrates the use of humor.

FRAN

Ever since Chad and I moved in together, his sloppiness has driven me crazy. At first I asked him to pick up after himself. When he didn't, I told him I didn't like living with a slob. That really angered him and he was even messier than ever. One day I took three coffee cups he'd left around the apartment and balanced one on top of the other two. Then I balanced a stack of papers he'd left in the bathroom on the top cup. Finally I picked his socks off the bedroom floor and stuffed one into each of the bottom cups. When he saw my "sculpture," he cracked up. And he also put the things where they belong.

Engage disagreement with positive expectations. A second productive approach to disagreement is for partners to engage each other. We have seen that stonewalling is poison to personal relationships. Couples have to agree to engage their differences respectfully and lovingly. According to Sandra Metts and William Cupach (1990), many couples avoid disagreements because they have dysfunctional beliefs about conflict. They think it must be destructive, so they avoid it as much as possible. In reality, conflict is inevitable and not necessarily destructive for individuals or relationships. When partners express love and respect for each other during disagreements, they are unlikely to damage their relationship or each other.

The same principle applies to dealing with criticisms. When two people are in an intimate relationship, it is inevitable that they will do things that irritate each other. When this happens, partners need to tell each other honestly and gently that they resent or dislike certain behaviors or attitudes. In response, partners need to listen to criticisms thoughtfully and consider how they might alter their behaviors. In an interview with Thomas Maugh (1998), Gottman said that husbands are generally more likely to ignore criticisms than wives: "The autocrats who failed to listen to their wives' complaints were doomed" (p. 11A). Relationships cannot thrive if partners don't listen to each other's criticisms and aren't willing to consider modifying personal behaviors.

Keep disagreements in proportion. The third strategy for managing disagreements and criticisms productively is to outweigh them with pleasant interactions. Both his counseling of couples and his research have led Gottman (1994a, b; Gottman with Silver, 1994) to emphasize that it isn't whether couples disagree or have bad moments that determine the happiness of relationships. Instead, he says, satisfaction with relationships is closely linked to whether good moments predominate. Gottman (1994b) suggests the ideal is a ratio of five positive moments for each negative moment.

Disagreements need not jeopardize loving relationships. Partners can disagree honestly and productively if they communicate in ways that give assurances of love and respect, engage disagreement and criticism, and keep an overall positive balance of interaction in relationships.

Revitalizing Relationships

A final way to maintain intimacy in personal relationships is to engage in occasional revitalizing activities. To revitalize is to make vital again. Thus, partners who engage in revitalizing activities are working to renew the vitality of their love. Several ways of revitalizing were reported by participants in the study by Canary and his colleagues that we discussed at the beginning of this chapter. Occasional trips together are a way partners revitalize their relationship. A trip can interject novelty by moving the couple out of familiar routines and into new places, events, and activities. Another strategy mentioned by participants is surprising partners every so often—a gift for no special occasion, proposing an evening out, cleaning

BABY BLUES reprinted with permission of King Features Syndicate.

TABLE 8.3
Couples' Reasons for Renewing Marriage Vows

"The kids have been real concerned about divorce for a long time now, and it might give them more of a sense of security."

"I think by going through this process we're strengthening our marriage a great deal—then it strengthens the family unit."

"We wanted to honor our families. And so it was kind of a tribute to everybody [that] had such an impact on our lives."

"Celebrating the whole family, the whole experience."

"The first time through you say those vows, they are just words. When you say them after 25 years' experience, you have flashbacks, and you say, 'Yeah, that's right.'"

"We've just come to a different place in our relationship, and so we thought our vows need to reflect that."

"It was important for our children to see that. I think they saw concretely what commitment can lead to. They heard our own witness to marriage."

Source: Adapted from Braithwaite & Baxter, pp. 184–191.

the whole apartment, or cooking a special meal are ways to surprise partners pleasantly and to communicate affection.

Many couples in established relationships also engage in more formal revitalizing activities. Dawn Braithwaite and Leslie Baxter (1995) noted one formal way of invigorating intimacy—renewal of marriage vows. Table 8.3 presents some of the reasons couples cited for renewing their marriage vows.

Another way of revitalizing is to participate in relationship enhancement workshops. Often these are long weekends in which one or more facilitators help partners rediscover the depth of their love and relearn how to be with and appreciate each other. In 1998 more than 1,000 advocates of building a better marriage through good communication gathered in Washington, DC, to attend a conference (Marriage builders, 1998). And those who believe in enriching marriages aren't restricted to people who do that for a living. One physician at Duke University has begun teaching marital communication skills as part of his rehabilitation program for heart-attack survivors (Marriage builders, 1998).

In the course of a long-term relationship, it's easy for partners to drift apart and to let intimacy slide. Careers, family needs, and other demands on partners can make quality time together a low priority. Marriage enrichment courses and workshops are designed to help couples put intimacy back in the center of their relationships by helping them remember how to enjoy each other and to communicate in personal and caring ways.

We have discussed seven processes that partners engage in to maintain personal relationships by keeping their lives intertwined and their relationship satisfying. In ongoing routines and practices, partners continually coordinate and embody the relational culture that is the hallmark of intimacy. More than momentous pledges of love or big events, it is everyday processes that transform individuals into intimate partners and that allow them to maintain a common world, despite the gamut of small and large changes punctuating their lives. With this foundation, we're ready to consider how researchers have thought about and studied relationship maintenance.

NATALIE

When I broke up with a guy I'd lived with for three years, all my friends tried to support me. But they didn't understand that I didn't need heavy-duty emotional support nearly as much as I needed some everyday stuff. What I missed was being able to ask someone, "Is it cold out today?" or having someone to watch a stupid sitcom with or somebody to say hello to when I got in each evening. Once I called one of my friends who had told me she wanted to help me get through the breakup. It was 6:30, and I'd just gotten in from my job. I called Sue and said, "You know my boss said today I was getting a lot better at handling complaints from customers." There was this long pause, and then Sue said, "Yeah, so what about it?" That was it. It wasn't a major event or anything, but there was nobody to share the ordinary parts of a day with. I didn't know how to explain that I just wanted a response, any response.

DYNAMIC EQUILIBRIUM: CHANGE AS CONSTANT

Personal relationships can be thought of as being in **dynamic equilibrium,** a term that captures both the continuous movement and change of relationships and the tendency of relationships to settle into routines. Thus, maintenance is change, because a relationship that doesn't change and adapt is dying.

Relationships change for many reasons. Some changes are small, incremental shifts that go largely unnoticed as partners deal with normal tension and conflicts and as they adapt to variations in work schedules, health, the coming and going of children, and other factors. Larger changes may be either deliberately sought or responsive to circumstances. Deliberate changes come about when partners want to alter the nature of their relationship. Responsive changes occur when partners adjust their relationship to some event or circumstance they did not consciously choose. Maintaining intimacy requires managing factors within and outside of a relationship that might affect its quality. Our systemic perspective tells us that personal relationships exist in larger contexts of other families, friendships, work, and society. Each of these contexts, as well as interaction among them, affects what happens within private relationships.

Sources of Relationship Change

Relationships change in response to external events and people and in response to internal dynamics and tensions.

External sources of change. In Chapter 5, we saw that current trends are prompting reconfigurations in how people form and sustain intimacy. Medical technology's capacity to extend the life span means that many people will face the decision of whether to invite one or more parents into their homes and daily lives. Adding another person to a family, whether it be a child or a parent, affects the entire relationship and all of the processes and dynamics that are part of it.

Societies also make particular relationship options more or less available and attractive (Gergen, 1991). Currently, a number of romantic couples cohabit, an option that was strongly sanctioned just a few decades ago. Economic conditions may also have a serious impact on personal relationships. When two salaries are needed, the time and energy for family life are jeopardized, and, at the same time, the partners have greater financial resources and identities outside the relationship. Additional friction may arise if one partner receives a good job offer in an area that offers little career opportunity for the other. If one person loses a job, fiscal strains and wounded self-esteem may provoke tension and discord between intimates. Such tensions are normal in healthy, committed relationships and, if handled well, they can lead to constructive new directions for individuals and partners.

WALTER

At first Dad was just mad that he'd been let go when the plant, as they say, downsized. But when he applied for jobs for six weeks and still hadn't gotten anything, not even a nibble, he started to change. He got quieter and moodier. At first, he still went out looking for jobs, but after a while he didn't even try. Then he started drinking. And that's when Mom drew a line in the dirt. She told him to get off his rear and off the bottle. She told him to take some kind of work, even work not up to his status, or apply for unemployment. When he didn't, she really laid it on the line and told him to shake his self-pity. He did quit drinking and did get unemployment and kept looking for new work. Finally, after about five months, he got a good job, and he got to be his old self again. Later I told Mom I had been afraid they were headed for divorce, and she laughed and said, "No way." She said that wasn't the first rough spot or fight they'd had and probably wouldn't be the last.

Other relationships in which individuals participate also affect intimacy. As we noted earlier in this book, families and friends can affect what happens between two people. Families especially have a historical impact, because early interactions in them shape individuals' basic working models and attachment styles, both of which contour adult intimacies (Bartholomew, 1993; Miller, 1993). Elaine Scharfe and Kim Bartholomew (1995) reported that individuals with secure attachment styles tend to respond to conflict with constructive accommodation styles (addressing problems, remaining committed to a partner), whereas individuals with fearful attachment styles are more likely to rely on destructive accommodation strategies (stonewalling or downplaying problems).

Close friends also influence our basic orientations toward and expectations of personal relationships. In addition, close friends provide us with perspectives on current feelings, thoughts, actions, and lifestyles (Buunk, Collins, Taylor, VanYperen, & Dakof, 1990; Surra & Milardo, 1991). We see how our friends act toward their intimates and how their intimates treat them, and this becomes one criterion for how we assess our own partners and relationships. We talk with friends to sort out feelings of attraction, confusion, anger, hope, and fear: Are our feelings normal, or realistic? How should we deal with them? What do they mean? Friends also serve as reference points by which couples assess how well they are doing. "Keeping up with the Joneses" is no myth, as we all want to keep pace with others (Buunk et al., 1990). Because there are no objective measures of what it means to be "doing well enough," we figure it out by observing, comparing, and talking with others in our social circles (Buunk & VanYperen, 1991). Thus, friends and social circles may influence how intimates judge each other and the success of their relationship.

Sometimes others in our social systems directly affect intimacy through various forms of interference or support. A young couple in financial straits might survive if parents or others provide a loan, whereas another couple falls apart because there is no economic support from its social network. Others may also tempt individuals to stray from a primary commitment, drive a wedge between partners, or derogate and criticize a relationship or partner.

Internal sources of change. Change also comes from within relationships. An obvious and continuous internal impetus for change is dialectical tensions, which continuously reverberate through personal relationships. In the process of falling in love, people typically relish intense connection, while needs for autonomy are temporarily somewhat dormant. After initial intensity fades, however, impulses for autonomy tend to reassert themselves, and couples may experience confusion and tension as they try to work out previously unfelt needs for separate space and time and for individuation. Similarly, the high self-disclosure that often characterizes intensifying may leave individuals feeling vulnerable, thereby ushering in a period of more closeness. Friends and romantic partners whose relationships become too predictable may inject novelty to alleviate staleness, and this change may produce discomfort at least initially. The way a couple manages dialectics at any one moment may be unsatisfactory, even destructive, in the next, so partners should be ready to rework, re-rework, and re-re-rework dialectics to keep the relationship healthy and adaptive. For this reason, a degree of tension and conflict is normal and often constructive in fueling changes that allow a relationship to remain vital and to continue.

Systemic Change

Because relationships are systems, dialectics, as well as other factors, are interrelated so that any alteration affects all aspects of a relationship. Sometimes intimates choose to make a specific change and only later discover its repercussions elsewhere in their relationship. An example from my life may clarify the systemic nature of change. During the first 15 years of my marriage, spontaneity was far more pronounced than was routine. Often Robbie and I decided on the spur of the moment to go somewhere for a weekend or to invite friends over for dinner. When my widowed mother's health made it impossible for her to live alone, we invited her into our family. Soon after she moved in with us, routines began to dominate our lives. Mother's medication schedule demanded that we be there at specific hours each day, her needs for privacy and calmness made inviting friends over a strain on her, and her physical fragility precluded us from darting off for a weekend without making detailed arrangements in advance.

The shift toward greater routine was not an isolated change. Our long-standing preference for talking openly was constrained, because we didn't want to exclude my mother from conversation nor did we want to share all of our personal topics with her. The autonomy/connection dialectic was also affected by mother's presence in our home. Before, we had operated independently as a general rule and had met our needs for connection in particular moments. When my mother joined us, we had to coordinate our lives continuously: If one of us wanted to go out when an aide was not available, the other had to stay home in case Mother needed assistance; if Mother had a doctor's appointment, one of us had to leave campus to drive her, and the other covered the campus responsibilities of the one who accompanied her. Our emotional interdependence grew as we tried to help each other cope with the sadness of watching Mother weaken and die. Although these changes inconvenienced us in some ways, they also enriched our relationship by uniting us in a commitment to make Mother's final passage comfortable and loving. The changes we made also taught both of us that we liked being more interdependent than we had been before my mother joined us, and we have remained more interdependent since her death. This example illustrates both the systemic character of relationship change and the ways in which dialectical tensions cultivate growth between partners.

Our experience is not atypical. People seldom realize in advance all the implications of a particular change in their relationship. Although Robbie and I deliberately chose to invite Mother into our home, we did not anticipate all of the ways in which her presence would affect our relationship with each other. In fact, it's impossible to predict how one change will reverberate throughout a

relationship. The best we can do is to realize adjustments are ongoing, change is systemic, tension naturally accompanies change, and relationships are always in process. Understanding the inevitability of change allows us to have realistic expectations for our relationships.

IRENE

How do you spell change? I spell it b-a-b-y! About 15 changes every day, in fact. Until you've had a baby, you can't realize how much it changes every single aspect of a relationship. After our son was born, sleep was disrupted for both of us for about seven months, so we were more tired and irritable with each other. It was impossible to have a conversation without interruption, or at least the possibility of interruption, if Joey needed to nurse or to have his diaper changed or just wanted company. My husband and I were used to having each other's undivided attention, but that isn't possible anymore. Go out for dinner? Forget it. By the time we stock the diaper bag and pick some toys to keep the baby amused and pack some food he can eat and get the car seat for driving and the portable high chair for the restaurant table, we're out of energy for going out. And yet, for all of the hassles, neither of us would trade Joey for the world. He's brought us close in whole new ways and made us feel more solid as a family.

As Irene's journal entry illustrates, most changes are desirable in some ways and undesirable in others. Partners who concentrate only on the negatives are likely to resist and resent change. A more constructive alternative is to recognize that changes are usually a mixed blessing and to look for how the changes we did not seek may enhance a relationship. Within limits, we can choose how to perceive changes that arise in our lives.

STRATEGIES TO MAINTAIN AND REPAIR RELATIONSHIPS

Like individuals, relationships require both standard care to stay satisfying and corrective action to address acute problems or deterioration that hasn't been managed through maintenance. The relational dialectics perspective highlights how intimates manage both routine maintenance and repair to sustain relationships. The distinction is important, because different processes and strategies may be effective in keeping a relationship satisfactory and in restoring satisfaction once it has lapsed. In the next few pages we'll pull together some of the strategies we have discussed earlier in this chapter.

Maintaining Relationships

Intimacy is not automatically self-perpetuating. Without a good deal of basic effort and attention, personal relationships deteriorate. The tendency of all living systems is toward decline—bodies wear down, civilizations die out, relationships become stale. Constantly we strive to forestall, reverse, or repair decline in our personal, interpersonal, and social worlds. As with everything from automobiles to personal health, preventive maintenance is advisable. One way to do this is to monitor interpersonal rhythms and feelings so that even minor slips in relationship health are noted and dealt with before they escalate. Changes in how, how often, and where partners interact bear noticing, as do declines in satisfaction, shared concerns, and investments.

It's important for partners to engage in the everyday processes we discussed earlier in this chapter, because those weave the basic fabric of intimacy. For the most part, routine maintenance is a matter of continuing to engage in daily interaction that sustains the perception of a common world and nurtures feelings of loving and being loved. Marianne Dainton and Laura Stafford (1993) found that for both dating and married couples, the most frequently reported form of routine maintenance was sharing everyday tasks such as cooking and keeping house. Other research (Huston, McHale, & Crouter, 1986; Zietlow & Sillars, 1988) confirms that sharing household tasks tends to positively affect partners' satisfaction and relationship health. Sharing time—both companionable silence and conversation or activities—is also a way couples report they routinely maintain connection (Dainton & Stafford, 1993; Dindia & Baxter, 1987; Stafford & Canary, 1991). In addition, Kathryn Dindia and Leslie Baxter (1987) found that introducing variety into a relationship is a prevalent strategy for preventing boredom.

Routine maintenance is also accomplished by accepting as normal the tension inherent in contradictory needs. A partner who wants time alone may be expressing normal autonomy needs, not a decline in commitment. Nothing is necessarily wrong just because a person prefers not to share some aspects of her or his life. A spurt of spontaneous activities is followed by immersion in routines; a period of predictability precipitates impulsive interactions, often romantic ones (Dindia & Baxter, 1987). Understanding that fluctuations in ways of relating are normal alleviates some of the discomfort they may occasion.

To respond to contradictory dialectical needs, partners rely on a variety of maintenance strategies (Baxter, 1988; Baxter & Simon, 1993) that we discussed in Chapter 2 and will review here. You should keep in mind that partners do not always respond to dialectical tensions in identical or even congruent ways. One method, called selection, is to accord priority to one dialectical need and neglect the companion need. For instance, a couple might agree to be totally open about everything and have no areas of secrecy (Montgomery, 1993). A second strategy, separation, allows partners to oscillate between domination by one impulse, then the other (Baxter, 1988, 1993; Montgomery, 1993). By zigzagging between dialectical poles, partners alternately satisfy each companion need constituting dialectics (Ayres, 1983; Baxter, 1988; Stafford & Canary, 1991; Wilmot, 1987). Another form of the separation strategy is to segment interaction into areas, some of which stress each dialectical polarity (Baxter, 1990; Baxter & Simon, 1993). For example, couples may designate certain topics as ones about which they will be open and other areas as private, or they may assign routine and spontaneity to distinct domains. Women and men who are friends report that avoiding flirting and romantic or sexual expressiveness is an important strategy for maintaining friendship (Canary, Hause, & Messman, 1993).

The strategy of neutralization aims for the middle ground between two dialectical poles. Friends embracing this strategy might have some, but not total, openness; a degree of both autonomy and connectedness; and a continuous balance of spontaneity and routine. Arguably less effective is the strategy of disqualification, because it tends to involve deliberate ambiguity (Montgomery, 1993) and perhaps some duplicity. Relying on disqualification, a person might agree to totally open communication but privately decide to disqualify certain topics from that rule. Finally, reframing is a strategy by which partners redefine dialectical needs as complementary, not oppositional. Relying on reframing, a couple might agree that the autonomy they enjoy professionally enhances their connectedness by making them more interesting companions.

Repairing Relationships

Relationships, like individuals, sometimes need more than routine or preventive care. Partners sometimes need to repair a relationship that has seriously deteriorated or is in crisis (Davis, 1973; Duck, 1988). Although less research has focused on efforts to rescue faltering relationships than on normal maintenance activities, we know something about causes of grave problems and some strategies partners use to repair seriously impaired relationships.

Personal relationships may be jeopardized by overt action or by chronic neglect. In either case, the relational culture is wounded, and partners may no longer believe in their bond. Perhaps the majority of relationships that erode do so gradually and without conscious intent, rather than as a consequence of a crisis or dramatic action. Called "benign neglect" (Phillips & Wood, 1983, p. 175), unintentional decline occurs when partners simply stop making an effort without even realizing that they have done so. They don't consciously decide to invest less in intimacy, and they may even be unaware that they are giving less. Often, benign neglect arises because one or both partners are preoccupied with other matters — demands of a job, caring for children, family crises, or personal health. Attention and energy once channeled into the relationship are diverted in other directions. The consequence may be an emotionally numbed relationship in which partners feel bored or unconnected to each other (Byrne & Murnen, 1988; Zimmer, 1986).

Benign neglect is often fostered by the dysfunctional belief that relationships are self-supporting. Many people believe that a good relationship doesn't require a lot of energy or continuous investment. That can be a fatal misperception, because it encourages partners to continue to neglect each other and the relational culture that unifies them in a common world (Lederer & Jackson, 1968).

A book aptly titled *When Love Dies* (Kayser, 1993) reports both qualitative and survey research on marriages in which benign neglect occurs and feelings of love and closeness gradually wane. Tracing this process, the author offers a hopeful conclusion: Both maintenance and repair strategies may resuscitate relationships in which love has eroded. Just as relationships can decline from satisfactory to unsatisfactory states, so can they ascend from unsatisfactory to satisfactory functioning.

Benign neglect may progress for some time before one or both partners realize something is wrong. At that point, there are several options. If no ill will has been generated and both partners want to revive the relationship, they may recommit to intimacy and recommence investing in it. Sometimes all it takes to revive commitment is for partners to realize a relationship they value is in trouble. If intimacy has become boring, then introducing surprise and novelty may be a good prescription (Baxter & Simon, 1993; Dindia & Baxter, 1987). Some couples find it valuable to work with a counselor who can help them understand how they drifted apart and assist them in developing patterns of thought and interaction that promote closeness. William Lederer (1981), for instance, teaches couples how to cherish and listen to each other. Aaron Beck's (1988) cognitive therapy focuses on changing negative patterns of thinking about relationships.

Personal relationships may also shatter abruptly, sometimes in a single encounter. Such dramatic ruptures typically involve a momentous confession or a shocking discovery. Particularly damaging to intimacy are violations of values and rules that are central to the relational culture. Infidelity is an example of breaking rules in many marriages (Argyle & Henderson, 1985; Scarf, 1987). Physical violence also desecrates many couples' agreements about who they are and how they treat each other, although, sadly, there are other couples in which violence is an accepted part of the actual relational culture (Jacobson & Gottman, 1998). Among friends, serious infractions include breaking confidences (Argyle & Henderson, 1985), not providing emotional support, disrespecting each other, or criticizing the other in public (Argyle & Henderson, 1984).

A M Y

When I found out my husband was having an affair, I was devastated. I went through all of the typical things—blaming myself, asking what I did wrong, trying to figure out how I had failed to satisfy him. He didn't want a divorce. He claimed that he didn't know why he'd had the affair and that she didn't mean anything to him. I didn't want a divorce either, but I didn't have any idea how to get our marriage back on track. So we went to a counselor, and she saved our marriage. The main thing she taught us was that the affair was not the real problem but only a symptom of a more basic one. We found out that my husband was really afraid of getting too close to me, like he would be swallowed up in the marriage. For him the affair was a way to affirm that he was still a separate person. Since we figured this out, we've been working on our problem in two ways. I am giving him more distance and freedom, and he is trying to understand better his fear of intimacy by continuing with individual therapy. It's funny—I surely wouldn't prescribe affairs for intimacy, but his has actually made us closer than we were because we understand our needs more clearly than we ever did before.

Violating a rule of relational culture is meaningful on two levels. First, the content of a violation may harm a partner (Beck, 1988), as when a violated confidence results in embarrassment or other negative consequences. Second, disregarding relational culture—regardless of the content of a violation—is significant at the relationship level of meaning. Individuals who disdain core rules of their relational cultures may be interpreted as communicating that they no longer believe in or care about the relationship itself (Beck, 1988; Scarf, 1987).

When a relationship is in serious disrepair, partners have to decide whether to revive it and, if so, how. Kathryn Dindia and Leslie Baxter (1987) report that to repair badly damaged relationships, couples tend to favor the strategy of talking directly about the relationship and its problems. This concurs with Linda Acitelli's (1988) finding that both women and men see talking about a relationship as important when there are problems. To repair intimacy following a violation, partners must make sense of why the infraction occurred and must create a belief that it will not recur. When talk between them cannot achieve this, counseling may be valuable. Professionals can often help couples see beyond a violation per se to discern its relational import, what it symbolizes, and how to prevent future violations (Scarf, 1987).

In sum, change is constant in intimate relationships. In small and large ways partners, their contexts, and their relationships change over time. Every change induces others, because relationship systems are embedded in other systems, all of which interact. Partners constantly refine the everyday processes that join their lives amid the flux of large and small changes in and around relationships. By understanding that tensions between dialectics and ones generated by changes are natural, and by engaging in appropriate maintenance and repair work, partners can keep intimacy in working order. In addition, we've seen that partners rely on strategies to maintain intimacy and to repair it when problems arise. In the final section of this chapter we consider one other factor that affects how individuals understand intimacy and how they work to maintain it: gendered understandings of intimacy and patterns in it.

GENDERED STANDPOINTS ON PERSONAL RELATIONSHIPS

Writing in 1992, Sharon Brehm observed that "probably the most powerful individual difference that affects how we experience love is that of gender. . . . [M]ales and females construct their realities of love in very different terms" (p. 110). Research studies on topics ranging from emotional expressiveness (Christensen & Heavey, 1990), to love styles (Hendrick & Hendrick, 1988), to conflict styles (Gottman, 1994a; Jones & Gallois, 1989) report general differences between women and men. So significant are differences between the sexes' approaches to intimacy that a 1993 popular magazine (*Utne*, January) carried this cover headline: "Men and Women: Can We Get Along? Should We Even Try?" Although most of us seem to think it's worth the effort to get along, doing so is sometimes very frustrating and confusing. Much of the misunderstanding that plagues communication between women and men results from the fact that they are typically socialized in discrete speech communities. Recalling the discussion of standpoint theory in Chapter 2, you may remember that social structures and processes in Western society foster gender-distinctive perspectives on relationships and equally distinctive communication and perceptions within relationships.

Gendered speech communities teach most men and women to understand, interpret, and communicate in ways consistent with society's views of femininity and masculinity. Through gender-differentiated contexts, activities, and instruction, a majority of boys and girls internalize views of relationships and how to interact that reflect their respective genders. Pragmatically, this implies that women and men, in general, may have somewhat different views of what closeness is and how to create, express, and sustain it (Inman, 1996; Wood & Inman, 1993). Numerous studies and reviews of research demonstrate that distinct gender cultures exist and that they differ systematically in some important respects (Aries, 1987; Beck, 1988; Coates & Cameron, 1989; Gottman & Carrère, 1994; Johnson, 1989; Kramarae, 1981; Maltz & Borker, 1982; Wood, 1993b, 1994a, b, c, 1995, 1996, 1999). Although not all women operate from feminine standpoints and not all men act from masculine ones, research indicates that many women and men do adopt the standpoints of their respective speech communities.

Feminine Standpoints on Personal Relationships

Perhaps the two most basic principles of a feminine standpoint on relationships are that intimacy is understood as a continuous process and that personal communication is regarded as the primary dynamic that sustains connections with others (Riessman, 1990; Wood, 1986, 1993c, 1996, 1999). Because women are generally taught to build and nurture relationships, they typically understand close connections as fluid processes. Thus, even when commitment is secure, women tend to see partners and relationships as continuously evolving in large and small ways (Gilligan, 1982; Schaef, 1981; Wood, 1986, 1993c). From this standpoint, intimacy is never finished, never resolved in a final form. There is always more to be learned about each other, new layers of understanding and experience to be added to a relationship. Because women, more than men, are socialized to prioritize relationships, intimacy is a central and continuing focus of thought, interest, and investment (Acitelli, 1988, 1993; Gilligan, 1982; Wood, 1986, 1993b, 1999). A formal commitment such as marriage does not settle intimacy but is only one moment in an ongoing process.

Perhaps because feminine socialization emphasizes building and refining connections with others, women generally regard communication as a primary way to create, express, enlarge, and celebrate closeness with others. From her study of troubled marriages, Catherine Riessman (1990) concluded that women see talking deeply and closely as "the centerpiece of relationships" (p. 24). In general, women's communication is more emotionally expressive than men's (Christensen & Heavey, 1990; Roberts & Krokoff, 1990); it is also more verbally responsive to others than men's (Beck, 1988; Burleson, 1982; Miller, Berg, & Archer, 1983).

Expressive communication is especially prominent in some lesbian relationships. Lesbian partners, more than heterosexuals or gay men, rely on communication to provide emotional support and responsiveness (Eldridge & Gilbert, 1990; Kurdek & Schmitt, 1986; Wood, 1994b). Women are also more likely than men to find talking about a relationship rewarding, even when there are no major issues or problems (Acitelli, 1988; Wood, 1998b). Thus, spending an evening discussing a relationship may enrich a woman's sense of connection to a partner more than doing something together.

But what is meant by communicating? Substantial research indicates that women tend to place high priority on daily talk and the process of engaging others, whether or not the topics of discussion are important (Riessman, 1990; Wood, 1993c, 1998b, 1999). Thus, most women find pleasure and significance in talking about unremarkable, daily issues with partners and see this as important to continually enriching personal relationships and keeping lives interwoven (Aries, 1987; Tannen, 1990). To capture how women typically create closeness, women's friendships are described as "an evolving dialogue" (Becker, 1987). Within a feminine perspective on relationships, talk is not just a means to other objectives such as resolving problems or coordinating activities. In addition, talk is a primary goal in its own right—the process of engaging is the *raison d'être* of communicating.

Masculine Standpoints on Personal Relationships

Two linchpins of a masculine orientation toward close relationships are a view of intimacy as an event that is resolved at some point and a focus on activities as the heart of closeness. Unlike women in general, many men tend to see intimacy as something that is established at one time and then stays more or less in place (Rubin, 1985; Schaef, 1981). Thus, when a commitment is made, some men regard it as a given that does not need ongoing comment or attention. This diverges from a feminine view of relationships as ongoing processes that call for and are enriched by continuous attention and talk.

Because masculine socialization emphasizes accomplishments, an instrumental view of communication tends to be endorsed by most men (Block, 1973; Brehm, 1992). Thus, more than women, men tend to use communication as a way to achieve particular objectives—to settle a problem, express an idea, arrange a plan, and so forth. In other words, it should serve some purpose, should accomplish something (Maltz & Borker, 1982; Riessman, 1990; Wood, 1993c). From this perspective, small talk may seem pointless, and conversation about a relationship itself may seem unnecessary unless there are specific problems that need attention (Acitelli, 1988; Wood, 1993c, 1998b). Masculine communication, both verbal and nonverbal, also tends to be relatively unexpressive verbally, because its focus is not feelings, but content, and because men, more than women, are socialized to control emotions (Christensen & Heavey, 1990; Fletcher & Fitness, 1990; Roberts & Krokoff, 1990). Gay partners, both of whom usually are socialized in masculine speech communities, tend to be the least emotionally attentive and expressive of all types of couples (Blumstein & Schwartz, 1983; Eldridge & Gilbert, 1990; Kurdek & Schmitt, 1986; Wood, 1994d).

In place of communication, activities tend to occupy center stage in how men generally create and express closeness. Dubbing this "closeness in the doing," Scott Swain (1989) found that men's friendships typically grow out of shared activities. Swain interpreted the focus on doing not as a substitute for intimacy but as an alternate path to closeness, as well as an alternative form. Research by other scholars (Paul & White, 1990; Sherrod, 1989; Tavris, 1992; Wood & Inman, 1993; Wright, 1988) supports Swain's findings and his interpretations that activities are a means to closeness, one that differs from but is just as legitimate as closeness through dialogue. Doing things with and for partners also seems to characterize many men's orientations toward heterosexual romantic relationships (Cancian, 1987, 1989; Inman, 1996; Riessman, 1990; Wood, 1993b, 1998b). Thus, a man might wash his partner's car to express affection and might consider going out to a ball game a good way to celebrate an anniversary.

Tensions Between Gendered Views of Relationships

Differences between masculine and feminine standpoints suggest why misunderstandings can — and often do — occur. For example, a woman may perceive a man's lack of interest in talking about a relationship as evidence he cares less about it than she does. Yet from his perspective, as long as the relationship is solid there's no need to focus on it. Similarly, men sometimes feel women's talk about small issues is trivial, and they regard women's interest in discussing a relationship that is in good shape as pointless. This interpretation, however, is based on only the content level of meaning, and it ignores the relationship level at which the point of talking is to connect with each other.

Another frequent frustration is what linguist Deborah Tannen (1990) calls "troubles talk." For example, a woman might tell her partner about a problem with a co-worker in the hope that he will sympathize with her and support her feelings. Instead, he may offer advice on how to solve the problem. To her, this may seem cold, because advice fails to acknowledge her feelings. Yet his intention was to support her by fixing the problem. He is communicating at the content level of meaning, she is communicating at the relationship level, and neither understands the other. Similarly, when men want to do things instead of talking, women some-times feel the men are rejecting intimacy. Conversely, men generally experience closeness through activities, so they may not experience closeness in dialogue (Riessman, 1990; Wood & Inman, 1993). Problems arise not because either style of relating is bad but because partners don't understand each other's ways of expressing and creating closeness.

LENNY

Ever since I started having relationships with girls, it seems I've had prob-lems. I did not understand why they obsessed on talking about a relationship when nothing was wrong, or why they would get bent out of shape if I sug-gested we watch a game or go to a movie instead of talking. Now I under-stand a lot more about what things mean to girls. Also, I'm now able to explain to my girlfriend what I mean. Like the last time I suggested we go out to a game, I explained to her that I felt close to her when we did things together. She mulled that one over a bit and agreed to go. We've been having some pretty interesting conversations about different ways we see things in our relationship.

In sum, gendered standpoints are one of many influences on how partners view a relationship and how they interpret each other's actions. As we've seen, socialization is generally sex segregated to a large degree, so many women and men learn different ways of communicating and develop distinctive understand-ings of how intimacy operates. The differences themselves are not necessarily trou-blesome, but how we interpret or misinterpret each other can be toxic. Perhaps the soundest course of action is to avoid interpreting others through our own perspec-tives and to try, instead, to understand them on their own terms. Learning to do this requires partners to communicate openness to each other's ways of experienc-ing and expressing closeness.

SUMMARY

This chapter has been longer than others, which is appropriate because we hope that maintaining intimacy will be the longest part of our personal relationships. The theme of this chapter is that change is constant in intimacy. Because of dialec-tical contradictions inherent in close relationships, change is normal, inevitable, and productive. Sustaining a commitment over time requires that partners under-stand change and tension as natural and healthy and that they develop everyday processes and strategies for maintenance and repair that keep their relationships in good working order. Over the course of enduring intimacy, the relational culture originally created will be refined and transformed over and over again as partners adapt to changes in themselves, circumstances, and the relationship itself. Relational cultures, like the people who create them, are vibrant and dynamic. Thus, only by changing can they sustain gratifying, healthy intimacy.

At the heart of ongoing intimacy are everyday processes that link partners' lives and identities together. Everyday routines, shared concerns, ways of patterning interaction, conversation, and reflection are five processes that intertwine intimates. These unremarkable daily routines are the lifeblood of personal relationships because they, more than occasional dramatic moments, ensure that a shared private world continues.

Complementing our focus on daily rhythms of intimacy was attention to changes in relationships. We identified types and sources of common changes in relationships, and we considered diverse ways partners maintain and repair intimacy. The final section of this chapter focused on the gendered standpoints women and men, in general, bring to relationships, and we traced how these distinctively sculpt how women and men may create, experience, and express intimacy.

Commitment is most likely to be sustained when partners view changes as normal and potentially generative and when they work out ways to keep intimacy healthy on a routine basis and to intercede to rescue it if serious problems threaten continuity. When partners do not know how to manage changes or when they let benign neglect erode intimacy, relationships decline. In the next chapter we'll consider how personal relationships unravel and how partners transform them or cope with the endings.

FOR FURTHER REFLECTION AND DISCUSSION

1. Describe common involvements that you have with friends. How do these sustain or enhance your sense of closeness?

2. Think about everyday routines that are part of your intimate friendships and romantic relationships. Do they matter to you? Would anything be lost if small talk, interaction routines, and so forth were to disappear?

3. Discuss how the maintenance and repair strategies identified by researchers have figured into your own relationships. Have you found some strategies more effective in managing particular dialectics? Why?

4. Have you experienced gendered standpoints in your friendships and romantic relationships? As a class, discuss closeness in dialogue and closeness in action to enrich understandings of these two distinct paths to intimacy.

5. How do you maintain and repair your friendships and your romantic relationships? Do you find different kinds of dialectical tensions more prevalent in these different types of relationships? Do you find different maintenance and repair strategies more useful in the two kinds of relationships?

6. Review a relationship that has lasted a long time and that is very important to you. Can you identify differences in it over time? How have you and your partner negotiated dialectics at various points in the relationship?

7. Review the different theoretical approaches to relationship maintenance and repair that we discussed in this chapter. What do you see as the values and limits of each approach? Do you think they work together in a complementary fashion?

RECOMMENDED READINGS

Braithwaite, D., & Baxter, L. (1995). "I do" again: The relational dialectics of renewing marriage vows. *Journal of Social and Personal Relationships, 12,* 177–198.

Canary, D., & Stafford, L. (Eds.). (1994). *Communication and relational maintenance.* New York: Academic Press.

Gottman, J. (1994). *Predicting divorce: The relationship between marital processes and marital outcomes.* Hillsdale, NJ: Erlbaum.

Gottman, J., with Silver, N. (1994). *Why marriages succeed or fail.* New York: Simon & Schuster.

Wallerstein, J. (1995). *The good marriage: How and why love lasts.* Boston: Houghton Mifflin.

Transforming and Ending
Personal Relationships

TROUBLED RELATIONSHIPS DO NOT FIT into a single, cut-and-dried pattern. There is no universal path of decay, no one set of causes for decline, and no single outcome of relationship distress. Just as each personal relationship develops in its own way, so does each experience unique difficulties and responses to them.

This chapter describes the typical course of deterioration in personal relationships and explores some of the reasons for relationship decline and some of the options partners have in responding to it. To launch our discussion, we will trace intrapersonal and interpersonal phases that are often part of the process of relationship deterioration. Next, we'll consider factors that simultaneously reflect and contribute to weakening the relational culture that embodies intimacy. Finally, we will survey a range of ways partners end or redefine personal relationships that have become unsatisfying.

Dissolving and reforming personal relationships might seem like an odd topic for a book on intimacy. Yet relationship decline is a very real part of human experience. A comprehensive understanding of personal relationships includes knowing how they come apart or are transformed, just as we explored how they are created in the first place. Further, studying the process of relationship deterioration enhances our capacity to make wise choices in our own circumstances. Knowledge about trajectories and causes of decline enables us to diagnose early symptoms of erosion and to intervene if we wish to preserve a relationship. Insight into how and why relationships unravel should also assist you in coping with endings you cannot or do not wish to prevent.

PROCESSES OF RELATIONSHIP DETERIORATION

At the outset of this section, we should note that not all relationships deteriorate. Many remain gratifying throughout a lifetime. When partners continue to invest and maintain loyalty, when relationships change to stay viable, and when external systems do not undermine commitment, intimacy can endure and thrive. But if either personal effort or good fortune is absent, intimacy is jeopardized and may wither, end, or be transformed.

DEENA

The hardest part about breaking up with Paul was that I didn't understand what was happening. I didn't know what the changes between us meant. As it got more clear that we were splitting up, I didn't know if the feelings I was having were normal or weird or what. I just felt like I was floundering. Breaking up was bad enough, but doing it without a clue about what was happening and what that meant made it a lot worse.

In 1982, Steve Duck proposed a four-phase model of relationship dissolution, which he later (1984) revised to include five phases, each centered on particular processes and concerns. Duck's model departs in important respects from other accounts of relationship demise (Altman & Taylor, 1973; Knapp, 1978; Phillips & Wood, 1983; Wood, 1982). Alternative models tend to portray deterioration as simply the reverse of the growth processes that establish intimacy. In contrast, Duck portrays relationship dissolution as a series of processes that do not precisely mirror those of escalation. Duck's formulation also varies from others in decisively emphasizing *processes* of decline. Rather than focusing on events or stages in relationships, Duck stresses the intrapersonal and interpersonal dynamics at work during deterioration.

According to this formulation, deterioration may include dyadic breakdown, an intrapsychic phase in which one or both partners think about their dissatisfaction, a dyadic phase when partners may talk about problems and options, a social phase in which members of partners' social networks are informed of the breakup and asked for support, and "grave dressing" in which partners develop a coherent account of a relationship's life and ending or transformation. Although we discuss the phases in a particular sequence, actually their order may vary, partners may cycle through some phases several times, and not all intimates will go through every phase. Specific turning points may reroute a relationship, pushing it further onto or off of the deterioration trajectory. Thus, the model is a prototypical, but not a universal, description of the dissolution process.

Dyadic Breakdown

During **dyadic breakdown,** the first phase of relationship decay, degeneration of dyadic processes propels dissatisfaction, although partners may not be consciously aware that something is amiss. Everyday routines and patterns of interacting may lapse, thereby disrupting the relational culture that weaves partners' lives together. As the relational culture atrophies and its rules cease to be observed, dissatisfaction emerges.

Sources of dissatisfaction. Dissatisfaction may arise for many reasons. In an insightful study, Catherine Riessman (1990) found that reasons for divorce were generally different for the sexes. The women in her study linked diminishing intimacy to communication problems (Schaef, 1981; Wood, 1986, 1994d). Women became disheartened if they felt communication no longer kept them connected to partners. Expressing the source of dissatisfaction with a faltering relationship, women are likely to say, "We don't really communicate with each other."

The men in Riessman's study said they became dissatisfied when there were behavioral lapses in their marriages. They mentioned lapses such as not engaging in joint activities anymore or wives who ceased to do special things for them. One repeated complaint of men was that their ex-wives had not demonstrated love by greeting them at the door when they came home each day (Riessman, 1990). Focusing on events and activities, men more typically complain that "we don't enjoy doing things together" (Swain, 1989). Other research supports Riessman's findings by reporting that men's dissatisfaction with relationships tends to revolve around infrequent interaction, lack of shared interests and activities, and a decline in good sex (Bergner & Bergner, 1990; Buss, 1989; Schneider & Gould, 1987). It seems, then, that there are some general differences in how women and men define intimacy and, thus, breakdowns in relationships. Whether a decline in joint activities or communication precipitates dissatisfaction, its emergence signals a threat to partners' happiness and joint future.

Noticing breakdown. The sexes also seem to differ in tendencies to notice relationship problems. According to existing research, women are more likely than men to perceive and be disturbed by problems in personal relationships (Macklin, 1978; Rubin, Peplau, & Hill, 1981). Because relationships are generally central in feminine standpoints (Gilligan, 1982; Rubin, 1985; Ruddick, 1989; Schaef, 1981; Wood, 1995, 1998b), and because women, more often than men, assume primary responsibility for monitoring relationship health (Cancian, 1989; Miller, 1986;

Okin, 1989; Tavris, 1992; Thompson & Walker, 1989), they may be more sensitive to tensions and early indicators of waning closeness. According to one research team, "Women, as relationship specialists, appear more finely attuned to the subtleties of communication within intimate relationships" (Wamboldt & Reiss, 1989, p. 321).

THE MEANING OF SEX

According to clinician Catherine Riessman (1990), sexual activities generally mean different things to women and men, and the sexes may misunderstand each other's motives and feelings: "Instead of viewing sex as women tend to—as a way to express intimacy already established by talking and sharing—men expected to become intimate with their wives through sex" (p. 46). This difference in how the sexes, in general, tend to define the meaning of sex reflects gendered socialization. Within a masculine perspective, the primary path to closeness is usually through doing things with or for partners, whereas women more typically assume that talking is the primary way to become and remain close to another person.

Regardless of whether breakdowns center on activities or communication, degeneration in feelings of closeness stokes dissatisfaction. If intimates do not address and repair problems, dissatisfaction is likely to fester, providing a fertile breeding ground for further decline.

Intrapsychic Phase

Once dyadic processes begin to break down, one or both partners may engage in the **intrapsychic phase,** a second step in the process of relationship dissolution. Steve Duck describes this phase as involving "a brooding focus on the relationship and on the partner" (1992, p. 95). Several studies indicate that what people brood about may be linked to whether women or men are doing the brooding. Not surprisingly, problems in communication and closeness are salient in many women's reflections on unsatisfying relationships, whereas men's thinking often centers more on what partners do and don't do for and with each other (Riessman, 1990; Wood, 1986). In addition, women tend to see problems in a relationship as interlinked, whereas men are more likely to view each problem individually and as unconnected to other issues and overall interaction patterns (Schaef, 1981; Wood, 1986, 1993b, c, 1994a, b).

During this phase individuals often adopt a negative outlook that highlights problems and obscures positive aspects of relationships and partners. As pessimistic thoughts magnify and positive ones dwindle, individuals may create a self-fulfilling prophecy in which defining a relationship as failing brings about failure (Bradbury & Fincham, 1990). Individuals are also likely to begin contemplating alternatives to the relationship and the likely fallout of ending it. Finally, individuals may think about whether to talk with the partner and, if so, how to discuss the problems and the options for dealing with them. Toward the end of this phase, partners may begin to complain to close friends, perhaps to test the idea of terminating the relationship (Duck, 1992).

Dyadic Phase

In his original model, Duck (1982) indicated that a dissatisfied person would confront her or his partner, but he later amended this to acknowledge that people don't always talk with partners about problems or intentions to leave (Duck, 1984, 1992). The more formal and complex a relationship, the more likely some form of dyadic negotiation will occur. This negotiation, if it occurs, is the **dyadic phase.** Because marriages are highly structured, spouses must talk to reach decisions about custody if there are children, division of joint property, and legal dissolution of their ties. Friends and cohabiting couples may or may not talk with each other. Because discussing relationship tensions is difficult, many people just exit, do not return calls, or otherwise circumvent confronting a partner (Baxter, 1984; Lee; 1984; Metts, Cupach, & Bejlovec, 1989).

Responses to distress. An impressive program of research by Caryl Rusbult and her colleagues (Rusbult, 1987; Rusbult, Johnson, & Morrow, 1986; Rusbult & Zembrodt, 1983; Rusbult, Zembrodt, & Gunn, 1982; Rusbult, Zembrodt, & Iwaniszek, 1986) clarifies ways people respond to relationship distress (Figure 9.1). The model defines responses in terms of whether they are active or passive and whether they are constructive or destructive in their impact on the relationship's viability. The **exit** response, as the name implies, involves leaving a relationship, either physically or psychologically. Stonewalling, which we discussed in Chapter

FIGURE 9.1
Responses to Relationship Distress

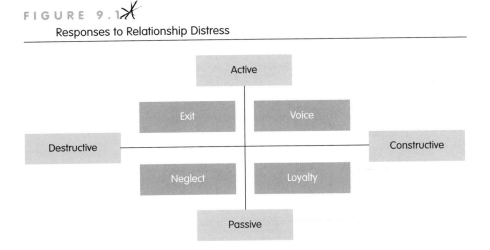

8, is a form of exit because it precludes interaction. Because exiting doesn't address problems, it is destructive; because it is emphatic, it is active. **Neglect** also fails to address relationship tensions, but it operates passively by denying or minimizing problems or refusing to discuss them when a partner initiates dialogue.

The two more constructive responses to relationship problems are loyalty and voice. The **loyalty** response involves sticking with a relationship despite distress. A person who enacts loyalty doesn't do anything to address problems but also doesn't give up on the relationship. Because loyalty is silent allegiance, it is passive; it is constructive in preserving commitment and the possibility of repair. Finally, **voice** directly intervenes with efforts to talk about and fix problems. Of all the responses to relationship distress, voice holds the greatest potential for mending intimacy. It allows partners to discuss problems and to collaborate to resolve them.

Rusbult's research team reports sex differences in response tendencies, with women employing loyalty and voice more often and men relying more on exit and

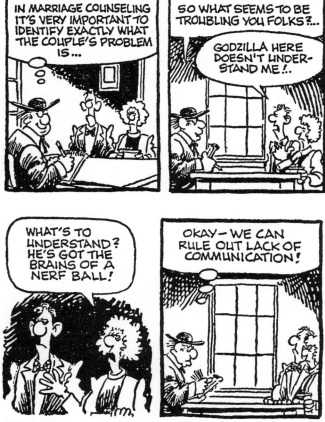

KUDZU © 1998 Doug Marlette. Reprinted with permission.

neglect responses. Consistent with this, my own work (Wood, 1986, 1994b) indicates women try to talk with partners when they perceive a relationship crisis, whereas men often exit or resist requests to talk about problems. However, it would be a mistake to assume that men who resist addressing relationship problems are irresponsible or obstinate. John Gottman's (1994a) research shows a very clear physiological basis for many men's reluctance to deal with emotionally charged issues. As husbands and wives engaged in conflict about issues in their relationships, Gottman took steady measures of spouses' blood pressure. He discovered that when discussing troubling relationship issues men's blood pressure rose more quickly and to higher levels than women's. Further, Gottman found that it took men longer to return to normal blood pressure levels after tense discussions ended. This suggests that men and women may experience emotionally difficult interaction differently. For many men the costs of talking about problems may be higher than those women incur.

Although Gottman's research helps us understand why some men may resist addressing relationship problems, it shouldn't lead us to conclude that partners can or should avoid painful discussions about relationship issues. Gottman certainly did not draw that conclusion. Instead, he strongly encourages men to learn to deal with conflict, even if it is upsetting. The reason is simple: If partners don't discuss problems, they cannot solve them.

Another investigation (Snell, Hawkins, & Belk, 1988) found that men, more than women, use unilateral power strategies both to avoid discussing problems and to address them (for example, insist on their resolution). Sexual orientation seems to exert less influence than sex on how individuals respond to relationship distress (Huston & Schwartz, 1996; Rusbult, Zembrodt, & Iwaniszek, 1986; Wood, 1994b).

MITCH

When something is wrong in a relationship I'm in, my impulse is to avoid talking about it. It's not that I don't want to make things better, but I really don't know how to talk about interpersonal stuff. I just freeze up and feel inadequate to do anything, and that makes me angry and frustrated. So I try to avoid dealing with the stuff. Maybe that's not very constructive, but it's all I know how to do.

What happens during this phase depends on many things: the problems themselves, partners' levels of commitment, whether attractive alternatives to the relationship are perceived, and—especially important—how partners respond to problems and each other. If they are strongly committed, and if they have worked out ways to deal openly and constructively with problems, they may be able to resolve their problems, revitalize their relational culture, and continue. Whether partners have the communication skills and the inclination to engage in productive discussion of problems depends in large part on the patterns and rules they have established for their relationship. Especially important is whether the relational culture they created encourages openly addressing conflict in ways that are gentle, respectful, and productive. If interaction patterns do not encourage partners to discuss difficulties, dissolution is likely to progress and social networks are likely to become actively involved.

Social Phase

During the **social phase,** partners experience tensions between wanting to conceal problems and wanting to reveal issues to others who might support them (the openness/closedness dialectic). If partners are sure they are ending a relationship, their thoughts will turn to how to introduce the breakup to their social networks and how to contend with any resistance from friends and family (Levinger, 1979; Macklin, 1978, 1980). In addition, intimates who have decided to separate face the problem of what to tell joint friends. Some couples cooperatively work out explanations so that neither partner loses face. When partners don't cooperate, friends may choose one partner's side, then gossip and publicly downgrade the other partner (La Gaipa, 1982).

Dissolution is inherently stressful, even if both partners believe a relationship should end. Thus, when parting is imminent, people look to others to provide understanding, sympathy, help, and acceptance. Friends provide substantial support by being available and willing to listen. In addition, separating intimates may need assistance with logistical matters such as finances and a new place to live.

During this phase, partners may begin to circulate a public explanation of the separation. The account told to others is not necessarily the truth, the whole truth, and nothing but the truth. Instead, it aims to secure others' support for the breakup and one or both partners and, in some cases, to ward off pressure to stay in the relationship (Levinger, 1979). Frequently partners tell others stories that fault the ex-partner for the breakup or that show the breakup is unavoidable. To preserve their reputation and social standing, partners may assert how hard they tried or how dreadful a partner was (La Gaipa, 1982). Many individuals want friends and family to support them by saying they are right to end the relationship and perhaps even that the ex-intimate was no good and doesn't deserve them (Harvey, Weber, Galvin, Huszti, & Garnick, 1986). Sometimes individuals criticize ex-partners in conversations with others (Duck, 1992; Weber, 1983), and they may count on confidantes to take their side and even to join them in derogating and spreading disparaging views of the partner (McCall, 1982). Although such responses to breaking up are common, they aren't usually constructive for those involved. During breakups, it is wise to monitor responses and communication and to resist destructive impulses that would later be regretted (Wood, 1986).

Grave Dressing

In our culture, funerals provide a sense of finality and allow us to bid a last good-bye to someone we loved. Relationships, like individuals, need a proper burial (Duck, 1992), and this is the focus of the **grave dressing phase.** So that they may get on with their lives, individuals develop a coherent story of the relationship and why it passed away. Thus, in one sense, grave dressing extends the account-making process launched earlier. In addition, grave dressing entails important intrapersonal processes.

When an important relationship ends, each person must make sense of it individually. That is, in addition to creating a public account, each partner privately reflects on a relationship to define what it meant, why it ended, and who she or he is now. In short, we mourn the end of intimacy and try to make sense of the relationship's life and death. During this process, individuals may grieve for a promise that was not fulfilled or didn't endure. They may lament lost futures, because what they anticipated with the ex-partner is no longer tenable. They may also contemplate what they learned and how that affects their identity and future commitments. It is normal for the grave dressing phase to foster temporary feelings of loneliness and depression. If such feelings persist or intensify, however, individuals should seek professional help in getting over a relationship that has ended. By defining a relationship's meaning in their lives and the causes of its demise, a postmortem helps individuals put a relationship to rest and get on with their separate lives. Grave dressing completes the process of relationship dissolution.

H O L L Y

You don't have to tell me how hard it is to get on with your life when you can't put a relationship to rest. I am the wife—or widow—of a Vietnam soldier who was listed as MIA. At first, I was sure he was alive and in prison and would eventually be back. So I felt still married. After two years and no further word, I wasn't so sure. If he was dead, then we couldn't be married. My friends encouraged me to start dating, but I didn't know if I was wife or widow. Four years after the war ended, I finally decided he must be dead, and I started dating and eventually remarried. But I'm still not absolutely sure. Sometimes I have dreams, and I wake up knowing Joe is alive and trying to get back. It's pure hell when you can't ever end a relationship completely.

In sum, deterioration in personal relationships typically involves a breakdown in dyadic processes and closeness, feelings of dissatisfaction by one or both partners, a dyadic phase in which partners may negotiate about their problems and options, interaction with social networks, and mourning and putting the relationship to rest. As with other relationship phenomena, decline is a process that varies among couples. Sequences other than the one we considered occur as a result of particular individuals' needs, options, cognitive styles, social networks, and circumstances. For instance, two partners might first discuss problems, enter the intrapsychic phase, and then return to the dyadic phase for more discussion. Other partners might involve social networks before talking to each other, and interaction with social networks might fuel dissatisfaction and dyadic breakdown.

Whatever the course of deterioration in personal relationships, there are a number of factors that tend to lead to dissatisfaction and consideration of ending or transforming a relationship. We'll now consider some of the factors that contribute to and reflect declines in intimacy.

SYMPTOMS AND SOURCES OF DECLINE IN PERSONAL RELATIONSHIPS

What propels intimacy into a downward spiral? What does a troubled relationship look and feel like? Learning to recognize sources and symptoms of relationship decline, especially early ones, enables us to diagnose problems and to intervene if we choose. Even if we do not wish to repair a faltering intimacy or if efforts at restoration fail, understanding helps us cope with endings.

We'll consider six factors that both contribute to and reflect distress in intimacy: deterioration in communication, destructive conflict, changes in standards for evaluating relationships, major transgressions, inequity, and partners' reflections. As you may already have surmised, these factors often interact systemically. Thus, declining investment may fuel perceptions of inequity, which, in turn, change how partners interact and think about a relationship.

Deterioration in Communication

As we've seen in earlier chapters, everyday interaction is the lifeblood of personal relationships. Intimates' presence and responsiveness in each other's daily lives sustain the relational culture (Berger & Kellner, 1975). For this reason, often the first and most important symptom of fading intimacy is lessening quantity and quality in partners' communication.

Reduced quantity of communication. Declines in the amount of talk typically indicate and further fuel dyadic breakdown. In a survey of 730 marriage counselors, the single most common reason given for waning intimacy was "breakdown in communication" (Safran, 1979). Other counselors agree that good communication is critical to intimacy and that lack of it often augurs trouble (Beck, 1988; Gottman with Silver, 1994; Lederer, 1981; Scarf, 1987; Walsh, 1993). One of the primary benefits of intimacy is having another person with whom to share the comings and goings of ordinary days, as well as momentous thoughts, feelings, and events. In ongoing conversation, partners update each other and keep their lives interwoven. When communication dwindles, so does knowledge of each other. Without talk, dual perspective suffers, as do feelings of connectedness. Thus, decreased communication tends to weaken the relational culture that ties partners together.

Reduced quality of communication. Along with lessened quantity, floundering relationships also experience declines in the quality of communication. Interaction may devolve into news bulletins and logistical planning. Although we've seen that routine communication is valuable, alone it cannot sustain intimacy. Deeper engagement is also needed. In her study of reasons people divorce, Catherine Riessman (1990) found that the lack of intimate communication was primary, especially for women. My own research (Wood, 1986, 1994b) underlines the centrality of communication in enduring relationships and also confirms the finding that women in general place greater priority on it than men. Thus, intimacy suffers when partners don't talk about their personal lives and feelings and the relationship itself, including plans for the future. As meaningful communication between partners diminishes, dual perspective withers and the relational culture atrophies.

S A M

I think I knew our relationship was over when I realized that we just never talked anymore. It wasn't that I felt hostile or negative exactly. It was just that I didn't feel Sue and I had anything to talk about. I found I was talking a lot more with other friends about big and small stuff than with Sue. If you don't have anything to say to each other, the relationship is dead in the water.

Sam's journal entry is a good reminder that we shouldn't overgeneralize research findings that women place greater priority than men on communication. Most men also value communication, and some, like Sam, may see it as central to their personal relationships.

Negative tone of communication. As interaction becomes less frequent and less satisfying, positive feelings about the relationship may weaken. Negativity in thinking may surface in partners' communication about the relationship and each other, leading them to make statements such as these:

"You don't care how I feel."

"We never do anything interesting anymore."

"You always want time for yourself."

"Problems seem to be all we have anymore."

"It's no use."

"We never talk anymore."

"Why even bother trying?"

What these statements have in common are negative tone and sweeping generalization. Words such as *never* and *always* ignore any exceptions to what is perceived as a general pattern. This is important, because language shapes our views of reality, including the reality of intimacy (Beck, 1988; Duck, 1994a; Shotter, 1993). Thus, how we talk about relationships pivotally affects our experience of them. Reflecting on the causes of divorce, one counselor observed that "whatever the apparent reason for the collapse of a marriage . . . the ultimate decision to separate is usually preceded by conversation that subverts hope, quenches love and undermines efforts at reconciliation" (Lobsenz, 1970, p. 18). In other words, intimates can talk themselves into believing a relationship is hopeless, in which case it may become so—an example of self-fulfilling prophecy.

Negative communication may also be nonverbal. Studies of spouses reveal that discordant couples employ more negative nonverbal behaviors than do harmonious couples—scowls, disdainful glances, rolling eyes (Gottman, 1979, 1993; Gottman, Markman, & Notarius, 1977; Noller, 1982, 1985). In addition, compared to contented couples, unhappy ones sit farther from each other, look less frequently at each other, adopt more closed postures, and are less likely to turn toward each other in conversation (Beir & Sternberg, 1977). Partners who are dissatisfied with each other may also avoid contact—perhaps the strongest nonverbal expression of distance and dislike. Thus, partners in a distressed relationship may nonverbally communicate the distance and lack of openness that is debilitating to their relationship.

DIVORCE TALK

Family counselors have long pointed out that open and loving communication between a husband and wife can work wonders for a marriage. Now some experts in this field have identified a different pattern of communications—"conversation of divorce"—that may well be a key factor in marital breakup.

Words of love, they say, produce and strengthen feelings of love. By the same token, the conversation of divorce intensifies the climate of discord.

The time between the "first mention" of a possible divorce and the "final decision" to end the marriage averaged a mere four and a half months.

A vast borderland is littered with broken marriages that just might have lasted if the conversation of divorce had been avoided.

Be constantly aware that "talking divorce" has the power to pull apart a marriage that might otherwise endure.

Source: Norman Lobsenz (1970, April). Marriage talk. Woman's Day, pp. 18, 88–90.

Clifford Notarius (1996) believes that personal relationships are shaped by three elements that interact in a cyclic pattern, each affecting the others. The three elements are words, thoughts, and emotions. Words between partners, as well as nonverbal behaviors, shape how they feel about themselves, each other, and their relationship. The words we use shape our thoughts and emotions. Notarius says that how partners talk to and about each other shapes how they think about each other and their relationship. In turn, our emotions are shaped by our words and thoughts. How we feel about ourselves, our partners, and our relationships is intimately linked to the language and thoughts we use about them. Figure 9.2 illustrates the interaction between words, thoughts, and emotions.

Marriage counselors Aaron Beck (1988) and Howard Markman (1990) agree that communication between partners profoundly affects the quality of, and satisfaction with, personal relationships. They identify reciprocal negativity as one of the communication patterns most likely to poison intimacy. In this pattern, one partner makes a negative comment and the other partner responds with negativity, then the first partner responds with more negativity, and so on. Communication scholars Cynthia Burggraf and Alan Sillars (1987) reported similar findings in their study of marital conflict. When Burggraf and Sillars designed their study, they intended to investigate how sex and relationship structure influence communication patterns when conflict is experienced. What they found, however, is that neither sex nor relationship structure is nearly as important in predicting conflict communication as reciprocal mutual influence. In summing up their findings, Burggraf and Sillars wrote, "there was an exceptionally strong tendency for each type of act to be reciprocated by one's spouse" (p. 290). They reported that if one partner responded to the other partner's negative or criticizing comments with conciliatory communication, the first partner was unlikely to express more negativity. On the other hand, if negative communication is responded to with negative communication, partners are likely to become caught in spiraling negativity. Figure 9.3 illustrates the spiral of negative reciprocity.

Declining quality and quantity of communication can be progressive once launched. Because partners are not talking about feelings and events in their lives, they feel distant; because they feel distant, they find it increasingly awkward to talk intimately; because they don't talk intimately, they feel more distant, and on and on. If negativity also punctuates conversations, it further undermines dual perspective and relational culture. As these erode, so do commitment and belief in a shared future.

FIGURE 9.2
The Circle of Words, Thoughts, and Emotions

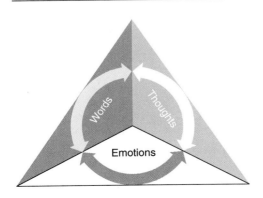

Destructive Conflict

Conflict and tension, as we've seen, are normal parts of healthy relationships. Even in the best intimacies, some discord is natural and often productive in instigating positive change. You'll recall that we first discussed conflict and disagreement in Chapter 8, which focused on sustaining personal relationships over time. Thus, conflict itself is not a barometer of deterioration in intimacy.

What distinguishes conflict in a relationship that is healthy from conflict that reflects or fuels serious distress is the extent to which it dominates interaction and the degree to which it is or is not balanced by more positive communication. It's easy to understand why conflict may be prominent during deterioration, because it is painful to realize an important relationship is in danger or over. Even if partners agree they should part, they often feel uncertain and unanchored. Shared history and anticipated future are disrupted as partners confront the twilight of intimacy. Thus, feelings of confusion, anger, sadness, frustration, failure, and loss may escalate conflict.

Consistent with gendered socialization, in conflict situations women tend to defer and compromise, whereas men more often resort to bullying and unilateral fiats (Belk & Snell, 1988; Howard, Blumstein, & Schwartz, 1986; Vuchinich, 1987). Relatedly, men are more likely to adopt coercive stances during conflicts, whereas women are inclined to be affiliative (White, 1989; Wood, 1993b). Coercion may be enacted either by intimidating a partner in conversation or by stonewalling a partner's efforts to address problems. Long-term studies (Bass, 1993) of marriages indicate that husbands are more likely than wives to withdraw from arguments and to resist wives' requests for problem solving. Anne Campbell (1993) found that one of the greatest frustrations wives report is husbands "who evade, deny, or downright ignore their attempts to resolve conflict" (p. 41). Similarly, as

FIGURE 9.3

The Spiral of Negative Reciprocity

If I did that, there would be NO communication between us. You're such a total imbecile when it comes to communicating.

Forget it. I'm tired of your constant carping and chattering. We'd work a lot better if you would shut up.

You're sick of my griping? Well then why don't you do something that doesn't cause me to gripe?

Oh, no. Not again. Are you gonna start your griping again? I'm so sick of that from you.

I'm unhappy with our relationship.

we noted in Chapter 8, John Gottman reports that stonewalling by husbands is strongly predictive of divorce (Bass, 1993; Gottman, 1993).

When conflict escalates into violence. Intense tension and dissatisfaction sometimes explode in violence. Contrary to our ideals of close relationships, violence between intimates is unfortunately common. Between 1985 and 1991, the estimated number of children who were abused rose 40 percent (Adler, 1994). Current estimates are that over 50 percent of college students have been abusers or victims of abuse in their relationships (Willis, 1994). In the United States, a woman is battered every 12 seconds, and four women are battered to death each day by "intimates" (Wood, 1999). Violence seems to be increasing in heterosexual marriages (French, 1992; Goldner et al., 1990; Stets, 1990), dating relationships (Muehlenhardt & Linton, 1987; Thompson, 1991), and especially cohabiting couples (Stets & Straus, 1989).

Violence between intimates is linked to gender. To understand the connection, we need to review the distinction between sex and gender. *Gender* refers to cultural meanings and expectations for women and men, which are instilled through socialization. Sex, on the other hand, is a biological identity resulting from chromosomes and hormones. As we've seen, masculine socialization emphasizes assertion, independence, and a focus on outcomes. In contrast, feminine socialization promotes affiliation, interdependence, and a sensitivity to processes. Because women are generally socialized to be feminine and men to be masculine, sex and gender often overlap. Yet, because not all of us conform to standard social patterns, some women are masculine and some men are feminine.

The connection between violence and gender emerged clearly in Edwin Thompson's (1991) study of violence in the dating relationships of 336 undergraduates. Initially, Thompson was surprised to find that women and men did not differ in tendencies to be violent toward an intimate. Close analysis of data revealed that both women and men with masculine orientations were more likely to use violence than either women or men with feminine values and identities. A number of other researchers have confirmed the link between gender and both responses to distress and tendencies toward violence (Dobash & Dobash, 1979; Gordon, 1988; Ptacek, 1988; Thompson & Walker, 1989; White & Bondurant, 1996). Although both sexes can be violent, all evidence shows that men are far more likely to impose violence, and more serious violence, on women than women are on men.

In 1998 Neil Jacobson and John Gottman published their findings from a decade's study of over 200 marriages in which violence occurred. In addition to confirming links between gender and violence, Jacobson and Gottman's book added new knowledge. They concluded that not all batterers are alike, and they identified two distinct types of batterers. The first they call Pit Bulls, because with these batterers, emotions rise to the boiling point quickly and erupt in violence. Pit Bulls are driven by profound insecurity, making them both uneasy with dependency on a partner and fearful that the partner may leave. Pit Bulls commonly turn to stalking if a partner leaves, because they are unwilling to let go of the relationship. The U.S. Department of Justice estimates that 1 in 12 American women has been the object of at least one stalker (Monaghan, 1998). The Justice Department's figures may be conservative because it defines stalking as occurring only if victims are fearful. When the definition of stalking includes people who are alarmed, at least 1 million women a year are stalked. Researchers who have studied stalking state that about one-half of female victims are stalked by ex-partners and another 25 percent by men they dated at least once (Meloy, 1998; Orion, 1997; Spitzberg, Nicastro, & Cousins, 1998). The effects of stalking can be powerful and damaging. As of 1996, all 50 states had passed laws against stalking (Murphy-Milano, 1996).

PAULA

I think the worst thing I ever went through was being stalked by my ex-boyfriend. We'd dated for about a year when I broke up with him. He was so jealous—wouldn't let me go out with friends or anything, so I finally decided to end the relationship. But he didn't want it to end. He followed me around campus, showed up at movies when I was out with other guys, and called at all hours of the night. Sometimes he would tell me he loved me and beg to get back together; other times he would threaten me. I finally called the police and that put an end to his terrorism.

The second type of batterer identified by Jacobson and Gottman is the Cobra. Cobras are cool and methodical as they commit violence. Unlike Pit Bulls, Cobras do not feel overcome by emotions that have come to a boil. Instead, they are calm and calculating as they plan and enact violence. The distinction between Pit Bulls and Cobras has important practical implications. Jacobson and Gottman believe that Pit Bulls can sometimes change if they commit to serious therapy, but Cobras are highly unlikely to change. Figure 9.4 on page 229 shows profiles of Pit Bulls and Cobras.

Changes in Standards for Evaluating Relationships

Another factor that may affect satisfaction and commitment is how individuals evaluate relationships. You'll recall that people rely on two standards to evaluate relationships (Thibaut & Kelley, 1959). Comparison level (CL) assesses whether a particular relationship meets (or exceeds) an individual's overall standard for relationships. Comparison level of alternatives (CL_{alt}) measures a given relationship in comparison to alternatives perceived as available, including other relationships and being alone. What constitutes CL depends on individuals' cognitive schema, gender, attachment styles, love styles, and the values and trends currently aswirl in cultural life.

FIGURE 9.4

How to Tell a Pit Bull from a Cobra

	Cobras	Pit Bulls
Typical Backgound	Antisocial since adolescence Chaotic family life, often with abuse History of drug, alcohol abuse May have criminal record	Witnessed father abusing mother May have been abused in family Less likely to have criminal record
Personality Traits	Hedonistic Impulsive High sense of entitlement Seek instant gratification	Highly insecure Crave approval Nearly insatiable need for contact Jealous, clingy
Personal Relationships	Incapable of forming truly intimate relationships Often withdrawn Will not tolerate being controlled Know they are dangerous and don't care	Emotionally dependent on partners Deeply fear abandonment Resist change Demand change in others (partners) Do not believe they are dangerous
Violence	Can be violent toward anyone Strongly inclined toward emotional abuse Violence is often severe, brutal Strike swiftly and brutally but quickly get distracted and move on Feel in control when violent	Violence usually confined to family members Less inclined to be emotionally abusive Usually, but not always, less violent than cobras More likely to persist in pursuing target through stalking and other tactics Feel out of control when violent

The CL is fairly persistent over time, and it measures satisfaction with a relationship. On the other hand, the CL_{alt} fluctuates as options appear and disappear, and it measures a relationship's stability. Thus, a person might leave a satisfactory relationship if a better option emerges. Conversely, a person might remain in an unsatisfying relationship because nothing better is available. And, of course, sometimes people are both satisfied and committed.

At the time of commitment, relationships presumably meet or exceed partners' CLs and CL_{alts}. Yet these standards are not static, so either or both may vary in ways that affect satisfaction and commitment (Bolger et al., 1989). Because relationships change over time, a once-satisfying relationship may cease to meet one or both partners' CLs, which will impair satisfaction, perhaps to a breaking point. For a person who regards good communication as a key criterion for satisfaction, unfulfilling communication may generate serious dissatisfaction. If companionship is critical to an individual's satisfaction and a partner begins to travel frequently, satisfaction may likewise plummet.

Changes in individuals may also occasion revisions in CLs, so that qualities once considered vital become less important or even undesirable (Dickins & Perlman, 1981; Werner et al., 1992). Her experience counseling couples led Maggie Scarf (1987) to deduce that "it is a fact of marital reality, well known to experts in the field, that those qualities cited by intimate partners as having first attracted them to each other are usually the same ones that are identified as sources of conflict later on in the relationship" (p. 27). One reason this happens is that during the intensity of initial attraction, we may view the loved one's qualities through "rose-colored glasses" (Hendrick & Hendrick, 1988). Dianne Felmlee's (1995) study of why couples succeed or fail in sustaining affection revealed that 29.2 percent of her respondents listed the same qualities as ones that initially attracted them to a partner and later repelled them. One respondent had been attracted to a partner because he was fun and easygoing; later she lost interest in him because "he didn't take life seriously." Another person was attracted to a person because she was the opposite of him; later he left her because "we were too different."

When we recover from the enjoyable irrationality of euphoria, we may find the very qualities that we originally liked considerably less attractive. The absent-mindedness I found so endearing when Robbie and I first fell in love later came to frustrate me (giving my mother the last laugh, after all!), just as the efficiency he initially admired in me ceased to charm him. Also, we're most likely to notice particularly strong aspects of another's personality. Precisely because they are pronounced, they may become tiresome or worse when experienced on a constant basis. Hence, what an individual perceives as a virtue in limited doses may be regarded as a vice in large measure.

How individuals evaluate relationships also changes as a result of experiences, observations, reflections, and interactions with others and their perspectives (Surra & Milardo, 1991; Titus, 1980). Thus, although CLs are relatively stable, they are not rigidly fixed. Changes in values, needs, and circumstances affect what individuals seek in relationships and partners and how they manage relational dialectics (Baxter, 1993; Werner et al., 1993). In the early phases of committing, partners typically prioritize connectedness over autonomy. Later, if one partner wants more autonomy (Eidelson, 1983), that may displease a mate whose CL assumes continuing high connectedness. Similarly, novelty and unpredictability tend to predominate early in a relationship when partners are discovering each other and creating an initial relational culture. Normal rises in predictability later in a relationship's life may provoke dissatisfaction.

NELL

Remember the fairy tale where the frog turns into a prince? Well, sometimes it works the other way around, and the prince turns into a frog. When I started dating Ron, what I liked best about him was how he took charge of things and took care of me. He decided what we'd do and where we'd go and made all the plans. I never had to do anything except enjoy being together, and I loved that about him. But that is driving me crazy now. Sometimes I don't want to do what he has arranged, sometimes I want to make plans, and sometimes I just want to be consulted. But Ron is so dominating. He just won't let anybody, me included, help run the show.

From research discussed in previous chapters, we know that commitment is fueled by investments. This gives us a clue about another source of declining commitment to personal relationships. Caryl Rusbult and her colleagues (1994) claim that partners who reduce their investments in a relationship are also likely to reduce their feelings of commitment. This claim has been well supported by a series of studies (Duffy & Rusbult, 1986; Felmlee, Sprecher, & Bassin, 1990; Lin & Rusbult, 1993; Simpson, 1987). In other words, as long as partners are investing in relationships, they have a strong interest in maintaining them. Inversely, if they are investing little or nothing, they tend to have less commitment to maintaining relationships.

Relationship structures may also change, and this, too, sometimes affects satisfaction. The relative symmetry many modern couples initially esteem may become untenable if a baby joins the family, one partner is disabled, or a parent requires care and housing. Because circumstances and the needs of individuals and couples vary, enduring relationships must be flexible enough to redefine satisfaction to accommodate structural change.

DREW

I feel like a real heel, because Jannie and I agreed we wanted a baby and we wanted her to be a stay-at-home mother, but I really don't like what it's done to our marriage. We used to talk about what happened in our days, but now she doesn't have interesting business stories to share. I care what happens with Danny, our son, but it just isn't interesting to talk about progress in potty training. Then, too, we used to go places and do things without having to plan every movement. We sure can't do that anymore. Even when we do go somewhere, either Danny is with us, and that means Jannie is focused on him, or she's worried about how he's doing. Like I said, I feel like a heel, but I really miss Jannie and our relationship.

Drew's feelings are not uncommon. Research recurrently finds that marital satisfaction tends to decline once children arrive (Belsky, 1990; Steinberg & Silverberg, 1987) and continues to be less than that of child-free couples until children leave home, at which point satisfaction rises again (Skolnick, 1981). However, satisfaction with marriage also tends to decline after the first few years of marriage for couples who don't have children. Howard Markman and his colleagues (1991) began studying 135 couples who were planning marriage and then did follow-up study with those couples annually since 1980. What they discovered is that marital satisfaction tends to decline after a few years, regardless of whether the couple has children. Markman and his colleagues suggest that the dip in satisfaction may arise because the novelty of marriage wears off, reality sets in, or both. Many people have heard jokes about the seven-year itch in which people who have been married for seven years start itching to be free of each other. The work by Markman and his colleagues suggests there may be a factual basis to the jokes. If partners realize that marital satisfaction typically dips after a few years, they are less likely to interpret temporarily diminished happiness as necessarily meaning something is wrong with their relationship.

Major Transgressions

As we saw in Chapter 8, deterioration may be gradual and unintentional, as with benign neglect, or a single incident may sound the death knell of a relationship. Yet, these two reasons for deterioration may not be entirely distinct: Gradual processes of decline often underlie and fuel a pivotal event that ostensibly causes a fatal rupture in intimacy. For instance, distance between partners often precedes affairs, which may be symptoms of deeper problems (Scarf, 1987).

In cases of a fatal rupture, the precipitating event usually violates the relational culture. Infidelity, abuse, drinking, financial irresponsibility, and lying are frequently regarded as unpardonable acts that preclude a future together. One couple I knew broke up because one partner became a born-again Christian; yet another couple came apart when one partner renounced Christianity. This highlights the point that events themselves do not cause relationships to end. Rather, the meanings partners assign to events and the ways they manage the events shape how the problems will affect a relationship and the possibility of repair.

A serious betrayal or offense does not necessarily end a relationship. Some partners work through major transgressions and repair their relationship, sometimes making it stronger than it had been. When partners do overcome a serious violation of the relational culture, asking for and granting forgiveness is usually part of the process by which partners reconcile and repair their relationship (Baxter & Bullis, 1986; Wilmot & Stevens, 1994).

Douglas Kelley has studied forgiveness as a turning point in personal relationships. In 1997 he reported on a study involving 187 individuals who ranged in age from 15 to 83. He asked each person to describe the nature of the offending event, what the person who had committed the offense did, what the person who suffered offense did, and how the relationship changed as a result.

Kelley's findings are very interesting. He discovered that the nature or severity of the offense did not predict whether a relationship survived or ended. Instead, how partners handled offenses was the primary influence on what happened to the relationship. Of all the ways that both those who committed and suffered offense responded, the most effective in repairing relationships were explicit apologies for offenses and direct expressions of forgiveness. Kelley also found that forgiveness was a major turning point in the personal relationships of the people he studied. Following a transgression, Kelley's respondents reported significant drops in intimacy, satisfaction, relationship stability, and relationship quality. After forgiveness was given, however,the levels of all these dimensions of relationships gradually rose, often surpassing the original ones. Table 9.1 summarizes the ways partners handled transgressions.

Forgiveness involves both intrapersonal and interpersonal aspects. Obviously, when one person forgives another, there are interpersonal benefits, including increasing partners' understanding of each other and clearing the air so partners can reconcile and rebuild their relationship. Intrapersonally, forgiveness facilitates healing in the person who was harmed. When we let go of anger, blame, and resentment, we free both ourselves and others from the consequences of these toxic feelings.

It is only recently that forgiveness has emerged as an area of scholarly study (Enright & North, 1997; Flanigan, 1992). In 1994 Robert Enright, a professor of educational psychology at the University of Wisconsin at Madison, founded the International Forgiveness Institute. The institute organizes conferences and brings together scholars who study the healing effects of forgiveness in couples and families, as well as in nations plagued by ethnic and religious divisions. Enright firmly believes that forgiveness can be good for both the forgiver and the one forgiven. He cautions, however, that forgiving is not a quick fix for problems. It is a moral choice that is difficult and complex (Heller, 1998). Involved in forgiving are cognitive, emotional, and behavioral actions that go beyond mere reconciliation and enlarge the possibility that relationships can continue after serious wrongdoing.

If partners cannot forgive serious transgressions, their relationship is unlikely to return to satisfying levels of trust, closeness, and commitment. Partners may remain together, but their relationship may be disabled by simmering resentment, hostility, and ill will. The other option is to part ways, and we'll discuss that later in this chapter.

TABLE 9.1

Strategies for Seeking and Granting Forgiveness

Strategies for Seeking Forgiveness

Verbal apology	"I am sorry"; "I feel bad about what I did"; "Please forgive me."
Nonverbal apology	Look partner straight in the eye; hug partner; behave differently, nicer.
Progressive/gifts	Ask repeatedly for forgiveness; say they would do whatever the partner wanted; give gifts, did favors.
Explanation	Offer reasons for committing offense; explain circumstances surrounding the offense.
Humor	Try to get partner to see the humor in what had happened; joke about the situation.

Strategies for Granting Forgiveness

Nonverbal	Touch or look at partner in a way that signals forgiveness.
Conditional	Agree to forgive partner but only if the offense never happens again; agree to forgive partner but only if things change.
Downplaying	Tell partner it was no big deal; tell partner not to worry about it; joke about the offense.
Discussion	Initiate discussion about the offense; discuss the offense with partner.

Inequity

Although many issues influence satisfaction and commitment, perceptions of equity seem particularly important. Relationship distress is likely to arise if a partner feels she or he is not getting a fair deal in the relationship. Few people apply rigid exchange criteria to calculate immediate costs and benefits in long-term personal relationships. However, most partners seem to think that over the long haul a relationship should be basically fair to both. When inequity is perceived as chronic, satisfaction may decline.

Of the many influences on perceptions of equity, one of the most pronounced is the division of responsibilities for housework and caregiving. Since the Industrial Revolution, marital roles have been strongly defined in the United States: Men are expected to earn income and make decisions for the family, and women are charged to take care of the home and family members. These roles were once practical, although they may have constrained specific individuals (Wood, 1994d, 1999). On the edge of the twenty-first century, however, these roles are no longer sensible, fair, or functional. Even so, they continue largely unmodified (Riessman, 1990), and they generate substantial stress for many couples.

Today the majority of women, with or without children, work in the paid labor force. In 1991, only 17 percent of North American marriages had a single male wage earner (Wilkie, 1991). In 1993, 54 percent of women who had given birth in the past year were employed (Shellenbarger, 1993a). The number of mothers who work outside the home increased from 10.2 million to 16.8 million — 65 percent between 1970 and 1990 (Adler, 1994). Not only are a majority of women working, but many married women workers make salaries that are equal to or greater than those of their husbands. A 1995 poll conducted by the Families and Work Institute found that 48 percent of married working women provide at least half of their family's income (Shellenbarger, 1996). The breadwinner role is shared equally in many families.

What is not as frequently shared equally is responsibility for keeping a home and taking care of children. Like men, women who work in the paid labor force put in long hours, endure job stress, and return home tired. However, at the end of salaried work each day, the majority of women face another job. Dubbing this the "second shift," Arlie Hochschild reported that in 1989 husbands in only 20 percent of dual-worker families met their half of responsibilities for homemaking and child care. More recent polls indicate that more men are assuming a greater, though still not equal, share of responsibilities for homemaking and child care (Shellenbarger, 1996).

JOCELYN

I'm an older student, married with two kids. Two days a week I come to campus and take classes, and three days a week I work at my job. I have reading and papers and studying for exams to do nights and weekends, but do my husband and kids pitch in around the house? No way. In fact, the only thing they do is sometimes raise a ruckus if a meal is late or I don't get their laundry done. Sometimes I watch my husband glued to the television at night or the kids playing computer games, and I wonder how they can be so blind to the fact that one of the four of us is working double time and never has a free moment, while the other three have lots of leisure time.

Often, caregiving responsibilities include not only children but also elderly parents and in-laws. Taking care of parents and in-laws also tends to fall disproportionately on women. According to *Newsweek* (The daughter track, 1990), the average woman in the United States will spend 17 years raising children and 18 years caring for elderly parents and in-laws. If she is heterosexual, she is likely to do so without substantial assistance from her partner (Pleck, 1987; Wood, 1994d). The sexual division of domestic life that most heterosexual couples continue to adopt tends to have harmful relationship repercussions. Hochschild (1989) found that women who worked a second shift had higher levels of stress, fatigue, and vulnerability to illness than women whose partners shared fairly in home responsibilities. In addition, unfairness generates intrapsychic resentment, which can erode satisfaction. In fact, marital stability—its very survival—is linked more closely to equity in home responsibilities than to income or other factors (Fowers, 1991; Suitor, 1991).

Partners' Reflections

How we think about relationships, partners, and specific interactions profoundly affects our experience of intimacy. As we have seen, events and behaviors are not meaningful in themselves; rather, individuals interpret them and assign meanings. Thus, how we think about and label relationship phenomena establishes what they mean to us (Duck, 1994a; Shotter, 1993). Throughout the process of deterioration, individuals' thinking actively shapes how they understand and feel about relationships and partners.

Attributional processes. Research on attributions provides insight into how individuals' thoughts influence feelings and actions. **Attributions** are causal accounts— explanations of why things happen and why people behave as they do (Heider, 1958; Kelly, 1969; Orvis, Kelley, & Butler, 1976). To see how attributions influence feelings, consider how Myra might account for her friend Anne's not calling after promising she would. Myra could attribute the lapse to Anne's not liking her, forgetfulness, the current stress in Anne's life, thoughtlessness, and so on. These different reasons will distinctively contour Myra's experience of Anne and their friendship. Thus, how Myra feels depends less on Anne's failure to call than on how Myra explains the lack of a call.

Attributions have four dimensions, which we can illustrate by showing different ways we might explain a woman's being critical of a friend. The first dimension is internal/external, which defines a behavior as caused by internal factors (she's upset, she's irresponsible) or external factors (her boss fired her, traffic was terrible). The second dimension, stable/unstable, refers to whether the cause of a behavior is continuing (she's a mean person) or temporary (she was in a bad mood today). Third, the global/specific dimension defines a behavior either as an isolated case (she can be nasty on that particular issue) or as a general characteristic (she's always nasty about everything). We'll get to the fourth dimension of attributions in a moment.

Causal attributions of happy and unhappy couples. Substantial research suggests that happy and unhappy intimates employ distinctive attributional styles (Bradbury & Fincham, 1990; Fletcher & Fincham, 1991; Holtzworth-Munroe & Jacobson, 1987). It seems that happy couples predominantly make attributions that enhance their relationships (Brehm, 1992). Thus, positive actions by a partner are explained as internal, stable, and global: "She gave me the present because she's a thoughtful person who consistently lets me know she cares." Happy couples attribute negative actions to external, unstable, and specific causes: "He didn't call to say he'd be late because he couldn't leave that particular meeting to phone." Contented partners make attributions that assume the best about each other's motives for both good and bad actions.

In contrast, the attributional patterns of unhappy couples tend to maintain or even increase distress. Unhappy partners invert the patterns of happy couples to assume the worst motives for both good and bad actions (Brehm & Kassin, 1990). Thus, a nice action might be explained as "She only gave me the gift because she got a raise today" (external, unstable, and specific). A negative action might be accounted for this way: "He didn't call because he never considers my feelings" (internal, stable, and global).

The fourth dimension of attributions is responsible/not responsible. Attributions not only explain the causes of behavior, but also fix responsibility by defining whether a person is accountable for an action. Although attributions that assume an internal cause seem to pinpoint responsibility, there is an important distinction. We may believe a behavior results from something internal to a person, yet feel they aren't responsible because of attenuating circumstances: Insomnia, drinking, grief, and sickness are conditions that may affect how fully we hold others responsible for what they do (Shaver, 1985). As with attributions of cause, attributions of responsibility are distinct for happy and unhappy couples. Again, happy couples make the most generous attributions of responsibility, assuming there are external, unstable, and specific reasons for negative conduct. Unhappy couples make the least charitable attributions, assuming the worst motives and the most personal responsibility.

The dissimilar attributional patterns in happy and unhappy couples suggest that partners' interpretations and labels have a great deal to do with how they think and feel about their relationships. We still need to ask whether unhappiness generates distress-maintaining attributions and happiness promotes relationship-enhancing ones or whether the quality of a relationship fosters attributional styles. Several studies suggest some individuals have enduringly pessimistic attributional styles that incline them to see the glass as always half empty and to focus selectively on what they dislike about relationships and partners (Baucom, Sayers, & Duhe, 1989; Doherty, 1982; Fincham & Bradbury, 1987; Fincham, Bradbury, & Scott, 1990).

Even if there are serious problems in a relationship, negative attributions are seldom constructive. Instead, they tend to squelch hope and undermine motivation to repair problems. Among counselors there is general consensus that how partners think about relationships is a crucial influence on commitment, as well as their efforts to improve matters (Beck, 1988; Eidelson & Epstein, 1982; Lederer, 1981; Rusk & Rusk, 1988). Common to many ailing relationships are partners' "terminal hypotheses" that define problems as unchangeable (Hurvitz, 1970). This invites a self-fulfilling prophecy that can send a relationship careening to its death.

We've seen that intimacy falters for many reasons and exhibits a variety of symptoms. Among the most common factors that both reflect and precipitate relationship deterioration are diminished communication, destructive conflict, changes in standards for evaluating relationships, transgressions, perceived inequity, and partners' reflections. These interacting factors affect the relational culture that holds intimates together—or tears them apart. We'll now consider options for partners respond to relationship distress.

ENDING AND REDEFINING PERSONAL RELATIONSHIPS

In the 1970s, Paul Simon had a hit song titled "Fifty Ways to Leave Your Lover." In it, he catalogued ways people end romances. Both research and experience confirm Simon's insight that we have many ways to deal with relationship decline. In Chapter 8, we noted strategies partners use to maintain and repair intimacy. Now we'll explore ways people end or redefine relationships.

Parting Ways

Perhaps the most obvious response to dissatisfaction is for intimates to part ways, and many people elect this course of action (Macklin, 1978, 1980). *How* people end relationships, however, varies widely. Some partners talk with each other about dissatisfactions and reasons for wanting to end a relationship (Duck, 1982). A number of people, however, do not face each other directly but instead just leave, an option that is most likely for couples who are not married (Baxter, 1984; Lee, 1984; Wood, 1986, 1994b). Alternatively, some people evade explicitly declaring that a relationship is over and instead suggest future contact although they intend none. "I'll be in touch" and "Let's still see each other as friends" are (in)famous last lines from people who then vanish. When one person ends a relationship unilaterally and without discussion, the partner has no chance to participate in closing the relationship or, alternatively, to argue for repair.

The tendency to collaborate with a partner about ending a relationship seems to be linked to sex. Two studies that I conducted (1986, 1994b) indicate that men, both heterosexual and gay, are more likely than either heterosexual or lesbian women to decide on their own that a relationship is over and to exit without discussion. Confirming this is Caryl Rusbult's (1987) finding that women, more than men, try to discuss and resolve problems with partners. This makes sense in light of feminine inclinations to see relationships as processes and to value talking about

LUANN reprinted by permission of United Feature Syndicate, Inc.

interpersonal issues and feelings. These general differences between women and men suggest that heterosexual partners may not agree on how to close a relationship, even if they do agree it should be ended. If not resolved, disparate preferences for terminating intimacy may increase strain. A clear-cut ending, whether mutual or not, provides resolution so that partners can get on with their lives. At the same time, a firm end leaves no hope for reviving or transforming intimacy.

Divorce is commonly thought of as an ending, but Mircea Eliade (1960) reminds us that the word *divorce* does not mean ending. He writes that the ending of a relationship is a passage to a new level of experience. *Divorce* comes from the Latin word *diverte*, which means to turn in different directions, as two people often do when they end a marriage. Even when partners do choose to end a relationship, that doesn't necessarily mean the time together was in vain. According to Eliade, "Every relationship that touches the soul leads us into a dialogue with eternity" (1960, p. 257).

Living with Languished Intimacy

If we reverse the advantages and disadvantages of straightforward endings, we grasp what's involved in allowing a relationship to languish. In this scenario, one or both partners are dissatisfied, but neither moves to end or improve it. Thus, the relationship languishes in a twilight zone. If neither partner perceives a better alternative to the current relationship (either starting another relationship or being alone), staying put may be perceived as the best of nonideal options (Rusbult, Drigotas, & Verette, 1994). Partners may also choose this path to defer ending until a better time. Parents often delay divorce until children reach a certain age. In other cases, an exit may be delayed because a partner is undergoing extreme stress. Maxine's reflection illustrates this:

> MAXINE
>
> *I knew it was over, and I knew there was nothing Josh and I could do to make our relationship right again. But I waited nearly a year after I'd decided to divorce him to actually tell Josh and leave. It was the year that his father was diagnosed with cancer and was undergoing radical treatments. Josh was very close to his father, so he was devastated. After all he and I had shared, I really didn't want to walk out on him right then, so I stayed and supported him through his father's dying and death. Then a few months later I initiated the divorce. I felt a lot better about handling it that way than just leaving when it suited me.*

Another reason people sometimes stay in a languishing relationship is that they cannot convince themselves it is really over or that they would be better off leaving. Yet neither can they summon the commitment to work on improving the relationship. Describing this ambivalence, Murray Davis (1973) writes:

The relationship is likely to modulate into a particularly unsatisfying and unstable state, which may be called "perpetual check." . . . As soon as they begin to cut themselves apart, they become aware of how much they need each other and how little they can stand solitude; as soon as they begin to paste themselves together again, they become aware of how little they can stand each other and how much they dislike their relationship. They have neither the strength to break it off nor the strength to make it work. They can neither live without each other nor live with each other. (pp. 272–273)

"Perpetual check," to use Davis's chess metaphor, may be transient or prolonged. Temporary delay may allow partners to reconcile themselves to separating, adjust psychologically, make arrangements for living apart, and find alternatives — either other relationships or living alone. In other cases, partners may live for years in bonds from which intimacy has faded.

Trial Separations (Recess)

A third way to deal with unsatisfying relationships is to agree to a trial period of living apart. Friends may follow this path informally, perhaps by not calling or getting together for a period and assessing whether they miss each other's presence in their lives. A probationary separation may also be useful if partners are genuinely uncertain whether they want to end or repair their ailing intimacy. Sometimes we are truly confused, because we realize there is much good as well as much that's not desirable in a relationship. If partners don't know if problems can be corrected or accepted, they may gain perspective by living apart on a trial basis. Professional counselors may also increase partners' insight into relationship problems and help them think through options for repair and ending. Trial separations preserve the option of later repair by allowing partners to avoid the conflict, resentment, and brooding that often accompany staying in an unsatisfying relationship.

An experience from my own life illustrates when this option may be constructive. In 1986, Robbie and I chose a trial separation after 11 years of marriage. For the prior four years I'd cared for my dying father, which had left me physically and emotionally drained, and Robbie had become deeply involved in working for environmental justice. Both of us had been immersed in experiences that did not include each other, so we felt and were unconnected. Further, at that time both of us lacked energy that we would need to repair our relationship. Yet, neither were we convinced our many years of loving closeness were bygone history. Knowing that our dissatisfaction and discomfort would be likely to harden and lead to damage if we stayed together, we decided to separate for a time.

During the time we lived apart, each of us dated others and took the time to recenter ourselves. When we saw each other a year later, we were attracted with even greater intensity than when we first met. We decided in that first moment of reunion to recommit to our relationship, and we invested the time and energy and effort needed to repair it and go forward with even greater love and strength than we'd ever had. For us, trial separation prevented harming the relationship irrevocably and preserved the option of repairing it. For others, trial separations may persuade one or both partners that ending is the preferred course of action. In either case, a probationary separation allows time for reflection.

In a case study of relationship transitions, Richard Conville (1988) identified a pattern of relationship repair that involved a temporary separation. The couple he studied, Howard and Judy, became unsatisfied as they were getting ready to move from the place they had lived and that Judy considered her home. As Judy anticipated moving, she became less and less willing to go with Howard; in turn, he began to anticipate moving without her. Next, they separated and each engaged in reflection and spiritual contemplation. The third part of their process was rediscovering that they were committed to each other and that their love was steadfast. Finally, they reconciled. The temporary separation gave Howard and Judy the time and space to reflect on their priorities, and they were able to choose a sound course of action.

Suspending Interaction

Another choice when a relationship is not working well is to affirm commitment but put a relationship temporarily on hold. This differs from staying in a relationship drained of closeness, because intimacy has not subsided. It also differs from a trial separation because a shared future is not questioned. Suspending interaction may be a reasonable choice when partners are sure a connection is enduring, but one or both cannot currently invest in it.

For varied reasons, people who are abidingly committed to each other may be unable to invest in intimacy for a time. During graduate or professional studies, individuals may lack the time and emotional energy to nourish intimacy. Similarly, friendships may be interrupted when circumstances consume one person's energies (Dickins & Perlman, 1981; Werner, Peterson-Lewis, & Brown, 1989). Lack of investment, of course, decreases commitment, so friends and romantic couples are likely to be frustrated if they try to sustain a relationship when one or both cannot give much to it. Thus, it may make sense to suspend the relationship until circumstances once again allow investing. There is, of course, the risk that one or both individuals will have a change of heart and not be interested in resuming intimate interaction later.

I followed this path with a very close friendship that had lasted 16 years. After my friend had two children, we both found getting together difficult and generally unsatisfying. Her attention was riveted on her babies, whose needs and activities were rightly her priorities. At the same time, her preoccupation with the children constantly interrupted our conversations. Although we stayed in touch, we suspended intimate involvement during her children's early years. This choice enabled her to focus on them during their infancy and allowed us to avoid the frustration of trying to sustain closeness when circumstances made that impossible.

Transforming Personal Relationships

The final choice we will consider is transforming personal relationships. Sometimes we feel a relationship cannot continue as it has been, yet we want to retain a connection. Thus, it is necessary to reform the relationship by reconfiguring how it is defined and who partners are to each other. Examples of this strategy are friends who decide to become romantic partners or romantic partners who metamorphose into friends. Transformation also occurs in families when parents and children work out friendships as adults and when older and younger siblings transcend their roles to become peers and friends.

Perhaps the most common example of redefining a personal relationship is when divorcing spouses reconfigure their relationship so that they can continue being parents who work closely together in raising and nurturing their children (Coleman & Ganong, 1995; Graham, 1997; Stewart, Copeland, Chester, Malley, & Barenbaum, 1997). Formal custody arrangements made by a court are insufficient to ensure a good parental relationship, so partners must negotiate that themselves. Transforming a relationship is challenging, because it requires letting go of old scripts, rules, and roles that wove partners together and forging new connections consistent with the redefined relationship.

We've seen that partners have multiple options when a relationship is unsatisfying in its current state. A first choice is to repair intimacy by investing the time and effort to resolve problems and establish patterns and understandings that will return the relational culture to a strong and satisfying state. If partners do not wish to repair an ailing bond or if their efforts are ineffective, they may choose to end intimacy, stay in a relationship that is no longer gratifying, separate on a trial basis, suspend involvement for a time, or transform the bond into a new kind of relationship that is viable. Of course, these are not mutually exclusive options, because one may blend into another and because partners may experiment with several alternatives before finding a course of action that works for them.

SUMMARY

Relationships, like the individuals who create them, are complex and inherently challenging to keep healthy and vital. Sometimes we or our relationships change in ways that make them no longer satisfying. In this chapter, we've traced a prototypical process of decline and identified key factors that both reflect and propel relationship dissolution. When a relationship we care about is endangered, we have many options for responding. Often friends and romantic couples choose to revive intimacy by investing time and effort working with each other or in conjunction with a professional counselor.

When partners aren't mutually willing to repair a relationship, or when efforts to revive it fail, there are several courses of action. As we have seen, partners in distressed relationships may choose to end them, separate on a trial basis, suspend intimacy for a time, linger in a less than intimate state, or reform relationships in alternative ways that are viable.

Because personal relationships are so important to us, good ones uniquely enrich our lives, and harmful ones can devastate us. If we nurture and maintain healthy relationships, and if we are not undermined by external events and circumstances, intimacy may last a lifetime. But if we find ourselves in relationships that are not healthy or that represent threats to our safety, and if we cannot restore their quality, then we need to know how to leave, ideally with grace and kindness to our partners. This chapter and those that preceded it clarify the difference between loving, rich relationships that enhance partners' lives and those that do not. In addition, this book should heighten your understanding of the choices open to you and others in defining and responding to a range of relationship issues that will surface in your life.

FOR FURTHER REFLECTION AND DISCUSSION

1. Is your own experience consistent with the general finding that perceived communication problems are often a primary source of women's dissatisfaction with relationships and lapses in joint activities are more frequently a source of men's dissatisfaction? Discuss the implications of this difference.

2. Plan a class discussion in which members of the class talk openly with one another about relationships and what ways of managing endings are most helpful and hurtful.

3. Think about your CL. What is generally important to you in evaluating relationships? Have the salient constructs of your CL changed over time? Are they different for friendships and romantic relationships?

4. Discuss the imbalance typical of women's and men's contributions to domestic work and child care. To what extent does this pattern result from individual choice and to what extent from social norms and institutional practices? What does your answer imply about the possibilities and means of change?

5. Have members of your class conduct an informal survey of friends to find out how they end friendships and romantic relationships. Then, work together as a class to identify trends in responses from all of the surveys. Are there patterns linked to sex, age, or other factors?

6. If your parents divorced, how did they work out their relationship as parents? How were you affected by the changes in their relationship?

RECOMMENDED READINGS

Ahrons, C. (1994). *The good divorce*. New York: HarperCollins.

Coleman, M., & Ganong, L. (1995). Family reconfiguring following divorce. In S. Duck & J. T. Wood (Eds.), *Understanding relationship processes, 5: Confronting relationship challenges* (pp. 73–108). Thousand Oaks, CA: Sage.

Stewart, A., Copeland, A., Chester, N., Malley, J., & Barenbaum, N. (1997). *Separating together*. New York: Guilford.

Wallerstein, J., & Blakeslee, S. (1990). *Second chances: Men, women and children a decade after divorce*. New York: Ticknor & Fields.

Summing Up: Communication, Choice, Commitment, and Change in Personal Relationships

IN A BOOK TITLED *LOVE AND WILL,* Rollo May wrote that "life comes from physical survival, but the good life comes from what we care about" (1969, pp. 289–290). The quality, or meaning, of our lives arises out of our capacity to care for others, and caring is an exercise of will as well as a feeling. Humans are uniquely endowed with agency, which allows us to choose to care about others and to sustain commitments we make. This book has focused on the ways we choose to create and express caring as we begin and sustain personal relationships. In closing, I want to pull together what we have learned by highlighting four themes that have woven through our discussions in preceding chapters. The themes are communication, choice, commitment, and change.

COMMUNICATION

Infusing this book is the theme that we and our relationships arise in and are sustained by communication. Distinguished by the ability to use and interact with symbols, humans transcend the concrete, present world to enter a realm where meaning and significance are continuously created. We rely on words and nonverbal communication to interpret ourselves and our relationships and to share and create meanings with others. Symbols not only represent things, but, more important, they present meanings and persuade us to particular understandings of ourselves, others, and experiences.

Communication Creates Identity

As children, we first learn who we are in communication with family members and others who are significant in our lives. As George Herbert Mead (1934) said, we are literally talked into humanity, because both mind and self are acquired in the process of interaction. In interaction with others we also form initial working models of relationships, which we refine, revise, and rely on throughout our lives. Continually, we adjust, enlarge, and transform our identities as we engage in conversations with others and as we communicate with ourselves, using symbols to define and make sense of our experiences, to reflect on who we are, and to direct how we act in relationships with others. We also depend on symbols to interpret and edit past interactions and to imagine and plan for future ones and the selves we wish to be in them. Through interpersonal communication we reveal ourselves to others, discover who they are, and elaborate our identities in the context of personal relationships.

Communication Creates Personal Relationships

We also rely on communication as the primary means by which we create and enact relational cultures, which are the vital nuclei of intimacy. In interaction with partners, we make real the existence of a relationship. We negotiate rules and roles; develop dual perspective; define, initiate, and respond to changes in intimacy; manage relational dialectics; and keep our lives and perspectives interwoven. Communication, especially on the relationship level of meaning, allows us to express how we feel about others and relationships with them. Through participation in different social groups, each of us develops a unique standpoint, which sculpts how we communicate and how we interpret the communication of others. In the process of interacting, intimate partners are guided by their standpoints, learn to interpret their partners' standpoints, and work out common perspectives that coordinate their activities and the meanings they assign to them. Because communication enables us to live in a world of meanings we ourselves create, it is the lifeblood of personal relationships and identity.

CHOICE

Writing in 1994, bell hooks noted that love is a choice and an action. Echoing hooks, this book has emphasized the choices we make in forming, sustaining, and transforming personal relationships. We choose the people with whom we interact, decide how to present ourselves and respond to others, choose whether and when to escalate intimacy, select ways to express closeness and sculpt relational cultures, and choose how much and in what ways to invest in relationships. We also choose to maintain and enrich intimacy or let it languish, to accommodate or resist changes, and how to act when a relationship is in jeopardy. In making choices such as these, we shape not only our relationships but also our personal identities. Within the limits of genetics and environment, we choose who we will be, constantly remaking ourselves and our relationships in the process of interacting with others.

Choices have consequences. We choose particular identities, styles of interacting, ways of patterning relationships, and responses to problems, and we must then live with the results of our choices. The choices we make, of course, are not wholly free. Instead, they are constrained by our personal histories, as well as by cultural, social, and interpersonal systems in which we and our relationships are embedded. As we participate in these systems, we import into ourselves the perspective of the generalized other (Mead, 1934), which is society's definitions, values, and codes of conduct. In other words, social practices and structures influence the alternatives open to us and the value we assign to them (Epstein, 1988; Giddens, 1973). Thus, the time and place in which we live contour the choices we recognize and what they mean to us. Currently our culture approves some relationships more than others, recognizes only some family forms as legitimate, and prescribes gendered roles for intimates.

Yet cultural structures and practices and the values they reflect are not static nor absolutely binding on individuals. Instead, they are dynamic, changing over time and in response to individuals' actions. In the last 20 years, we've seen increasing acceptance of gay and lesbian commitments, child-free marriages, and single-parent families. These changes reflect choices made by a number of individuals who refused to accept prevailing social values and the limits they impose. Individuals, then, are neither passive nor powerless in the face of social values. They constrain us but do not and cannot determine who we are and the kinds of relationships we form. Individuals and society participate in an ongoing dialectic in which each influences the other. Thus, we have the capacity to shape the very structures and practices that shape us.

Responsibility

Because we are able to make choices, we assume responsibility for the courses of feeling, action, and thought that we adopt. Choices and the responsibilities they entail are inevitable. To disclaim responsibility is what the philosopher Jean Paul Sartre called "bad faith." We engage in bad faith when we think or say, "He makes me unhappy," "I was forced to do it," "You make me feel sad," "I have to be critical because you are so irresponsible," or "The circumstances left me no option." In disavowing will, such statements imply that what happens and how we act, feel, think, and communicate are unrelated to choices we make.

Within relationships there are three primary kinds of responsibility. First, we are responsible to the integrity of our own selfhood. Intimacy profoundly influences who we are and can be, so we should be careful in our choices of friends and romantic partners, and we should monitor how our identities evolve as a result of involvements. Because we import intimate partners' perspectives, participation in personal relationships deeply influences how we see ourselves, our worth, and our possibilities. If we come to like or respect ourselves less in a relationship than before it, then changing or ending the relationship may be required to meet our responsibilities to ourselves.

Second, in relationships we have a responsibility to our intimates. Just as others affect who we are and can be, so do we influence their identities. Although we are not responsible *for* others, we are responsible *to* them when we make a commitment. We are responsible for the impact of our choices on our partners' development and well-being. Intimates elevate each other to central significance in their lives. Thus, they have unparalleled power to affect each other—to enhance or harm each other's self-esteem, to enlarge or constrain each other's potential (Davis, 1973). Our partners' happiness and sense of self-worth are nourished or impeded by how we choose to respond to them, support their growth, and protect their vulnerabilities.

Finally, we have a responsibility to build relationships carefully and to keep them in good repair. The relational cultures that we craft may enrich and enlarge us and our partners or diminish our lives and self-esteem. In designing and maintaining relational cultures, partners establish a primary context for individual and joint development. Because personal relationships are largely what we make them, we have a responsibility to choose carefully how we invest energy, time, thought, and ourselves. In writing *Relational Communication*, I have not prescribed "right" choices, but rather tried to enlarge your awareness of your capacity to make choices and to inform you of probable consequences that accompany some of the alternatives open to you in creating and sustaining personal relationships.

"Small" Choices

Too often it seems we focus on major choices and clear junctures in relationships: whether or not to commit, how to commemorate an anniversary, how to respond to a serious crisis. Yet, not all choices are so defined nor so obvious. The less dramatic, less obvious everyday choices are what create the basic fabric of intimacy.

In your own relationships you will confront a series of daily choices—ones that seem minor but that profoundly affect the quality of your bonds. Will you make time during a frenetic day with a deadline closing in on you to listen to a friend who is troubled? Will you take on so many professional and civic responsibilities that you have little energy left to devote to intimacy? Will you continue to support your partner's growth and listen to each other's dreams after the initial euphoria wanes? Will you care enough about a relationship to confront and work through problems, even when doing so is painful? As the years go by, will you invest in quality conversations or settle for ritualistic exchanges? Will you care enough to explore the issues that punctuate your intimates' days, or will you turn on the stereo or television to relieve you of the effort required for meaningful interaction? If you have a bad day, will you take it out on intimates by being short, critical, or unresponsive? Will you find the time when busy and the energy when tired to share a moment with your partner, to soften a pain, or to celebrate a victory? These are the seemingly small choices that define and sustain intimacy. They appear so insignificant that they may easily escape our attention, yet these unremarkable daily acts of creativity and commitment weave the fabric of personal relationships.

COMMITMENT

In titling a recent book *Love Is Never Enough*, Aaron Beck (1988) emphasized that enduring intimacy requires more than love alone. It also requires commitment—a decision to remain in a relationship even when it does not feel loving, gratifying, or affirming. Commitment is actually a process in which we continuously enact a decision to stay with another person. Relationships that last are not free of problems but are ones in which partners solve, ride out, or accept problems and remain dedicated in spite of them (Bellah et al., 1985). Commitment is possible for humans because, unlike other creatures, we do not live only in the here and now. We also live in the past and the future, so we are able to draw on history and to look forward to the future to weather the inevitable rough and unrewarding periods that punctuate all relationships.

Ours is also a moral world in which personal codes of ethics allow us to curb immediate urgings and biological impulses and to resist courses of conduct we feel are dishonorable. In our private relationships, making and living out commitments depend on individuals' conscience, values, and will. Personal integrity, not public law, governs intimate relationships. There are no external regulators of intimate conduct, no outside agencies to enforce commitment. We can give less than our best effort with little fear of being fired. We can be petty, vindictive, violent, or unresponsive without worrying about quality control by an outside institution. We can be less than kind, less than supportive, less than caring, and no public court will convict us. We can renege on agreements made to partners and violate trust, and no honor court will punish us. Only we, as moral beings, can choose to value and abide by the commitments we make.

It is not always easy to care, and it is certainly not always easy to summon the energy required to sustain a healthy, vibrant relational culture. Public responsibilities, professional obligations, and individual involvements compete for the energy and time we have. Necessarily, we make choices about where to invest energy, time, and effort. Choices, however, may be informed or uninformed, wise or imprudent. What we've discussed in this book and what you've learned in the course it accompanies should inform you about probable consequences of choosing to invest continuously in personal relationships or to let them coast. Broken marriages and friendships are grim testimonies to choices uninformed by knowledge that to endure intimacy requires abiding commitment that is expressed through ongoing investments. In committed relationships there is simply no substitute for a personal resolution to remain constant.

CHANGE

A final theme of this book is that change is a natural, continuous part of human life and human relationships. People and the relationships they form are dynamic, developmental, ever evolving. Further, we and our relationships exist within other systems that are also changing in ways that affect us, the relationships we create, and how we interpret the meaning of our experiences. The changes we encounter may challenge, charm, or concern us; they may frustrate, delight, or surprise us; they may be welcome or unwanted, ones we seek or ones imposed on us. But always, always changes will punctuate our lives.

Personal Changes

In the years to come, you, your relationships, and the contexts in which you and they exist will change. Your personal identity will evolve in ways shaped by choices you make about relationships, professional engagements, personal growth, and involvements in political and social causes. Your identity as a single person may be transformed into that of a partner, a mother or father, a caregiver for parents. Tests as gauges of your ability and success will be eclipsed by criteria such as family quality, income, promotions, and prestige. Worries about how to pay tuition will give way to concerns about funding your retirement and children's college education. You constantly revise your personal identity by choices you make about whom to let into your life and what contexts to enter. The challenges you take on and resist, the people you listen to, the work that you do, the commitments that you make all reverberate back into who you are and who you are becoming.

Relationship Changes

So too will your relationships change in the future. What you value in a relationship at 40 will not be identical to what you seek at 21. What you find satisfying in midlife will differ from what gratifies you today. What you consider a good

SALLY FORTH reprinted with permission of King Features Syndicate.

relationship will evolve in the course of being in various relationships and observing and talking with others. Many marriages and committed romantic partnerships begin with relatively symmetrical structures but adopt more complementary ones if children arrive, and structural change reconfigures other aspects of intimacy including roles, rules, and patterns of interaction and decision making. How you and your partners manage dialectics will vary over the course of relationships as needs for autonomy and connection, privacy and sharing, novelty and predictability rise and fall in salience. The everyday patterns, rituals, and communication routines in which you and partners engage will be redefined many times in the life span of intimacy. Those friendships and romances that endure in your life will be seasoned by the challenges, crises, disappointments, victories, and experiences that occur and by how you and your partners define, discuss, and respond to them. Relationships that last will also most certainly be ones that are flexible enough to adapt to changes and creative enough to make them workable.

Cultural Changes

In the years ahead, the culture will also change in many ways that affect us and the possibilities in personal relationships. A cure for AIDS may be found, more effective treatments for infertility may be developed, life spans may be extended further, and currently unaccepted family forms may gain social recognition. Our increasingly diverse society is honeycombed with various ethnicities, spiritual paths, lifestyles, values, and types of relationships, allowing us to know ever more people and participate in an astounding array of relationships. Our era provides us with virtually boundless possibilities for creating relationships that suit us and for recasting them over time so that they continue to be satisfying as we ourselves change. It's also safe to assume that options for relationships will expand further in the years ahead.

Current social trends that emphasize speed, instant gratification, and a throwaway mentality do not encourage the patience, investment, and long-term vision that nurture intimacy. Yet, social trends are not written in stone; they can be changed by generating alternative ways of building lasting connections with others. In the meantime, we can resist being seduced by fashions that we deem unworthy, and, within limits, we can craft our own paths and values in personal relationships.

We cannot predict how society, we, and our relationships will change, but we can be sure they will. We cannot foretell how our faith in a relationship will be tested, but for each of us there will be tests. We cannot anticipate choices that will confront us or how we will respond to them, but all of us will make choices that transform our personal identities and our relations with others. Amid this sea of inconstancy, perhaps we can be sure of only two things about personal relationships: Change will be constant, thereby impelling us to transform ourselves and our relationships over and over again. And communication will remain the primary process we rely on to define and manage change and to continually re-create ourselves and our relationships.

Glossary

abstract Removed from concrete reality. Symbols are abstract because they represent concrete reality but are not the reality they represent.

agape One of three secondary styles of love, agape combines the passion of eros with the constancy of storge to yield a selfless love that demands no reciprocity.

agency A person's recognition that she or he is a choice-making agent, rather than a passive object governed by external people and circumstances. Assuming agency implies accepting responsibility for personal choices and their consequences on self, others, and relationships.

ambiguous Unclear meaning. Symbols are ambiguous because their meanings vary from person to person, context to context, and so forth.

anxious-avoidant attachment model Develops when a caregiver responds in consistently negative, unloving, unsupportive ways to a child; cultivates distrust of others and relationships. This model fosters either a belief that the self is not loveable or that the self is okay but others are not trustworthy.

anxious-resistant attachment model Develops when a caregiver behaves in inconsistent and unpredictable ways toward a child. This model fosters positive views of others, negative views of self, and preoccupation with personal relationships.

arbitrary Random or unnecessary. Symbols are arbitrary because there is no necessary reason for any particular symbol to stand for any particular referent.

attachment theory Description and explanation that links patterns of interaction between caregivers and children in the early years of life to the ways that individuals learn to perceive themselves, others, and personal relationships.

attribution Causal accounts that explain why something happened or why a person behaved as she or he did.

autonomy and connection One of three relational dialectics that generate change in personal relationships. Involving tension between needs for independence and togetherness, this dialectic is both an individual and a couple issue.

behavioral interdependence Interaction in which each partner relies on the other to act in certain ways.

buffer zone An allowance for not meeting the usual homemaking and child care responsibilities. A buffer zone is more often provided to men than women.

commitment A determination to maintain an intimate relationship, despite disappointments, difficulties, and disillusionments. Commitment is a conscious, deliberate action taken by an individual agent.

communication A dynamic, ongoing process through which humans interact with symbols to create meanings.

comparison level (CL) A subjective standard based on current and prior relationships, as well as relationships we have observed and ones we know about. The comparison level defines what an individual considers average and acceptable in a relationship.

comparison level of alternatives (CL_{alt}) A relative standard for evaluating relationships that indicates how good they are in comparison to other relationships considered possible.

complementary structure A relationship organization in which partners have unequal power, or authority, and are highly interdependent on each other.

constitutive rule Assigns meaning to symbolic activities by specifying what counts as what. For example, a person might define love as doing things for others.

constructivism Also known as social cognition theory, explains how knowledge schemata create meaning. It identifies mental-psychological structures and processes through which individuals structure understandings. It examines how individuals' mental-psychological processes guide the ways they structure, evaluate, explain, and recall information, events, and knowledge about self, others, and relationships.

content level of meaning The literal or denotative meaning of communication—what the actual words mean in a dictionary sense.

culture Structures and practices that uphold a given social organization by producing and reproducing particular values, expectations, meanings, and patterns of thought, feeling, and action.

dialectical theory Explains personal relationships in terms of ongoing processes and contradictions that produce changes over time. Tension between the three dialectics of autonomy and connection, novelty and predictability, and openness and closedness appears to generate changes in personal relationships.

dual perspective Recognizing both your own and another's point of view on an issue, topic, experience, and so on. To understand another's perspective is not necessarily to agree with it.

dyadic breakdown The first phase in the process of relationship dissolution. During dyadic breakdown, patterns, rules, routines, and understandings constituting the relational culture break down or cease to be observed by partners.

dyadic phase The third phase in the process of relationship dissolution. During the dyadic phase, partners discuss problems and dissatisfactions and consider how to repair them or, alternatively, how to end the relationship. Not all intimate partners engage in this phase because not all seek to collaborate on issues.

dynamic equilibrium A double-sided quality of human relationships. On one hand, relationships strive for balance or a steady state of functioning. Yet, at the same time they are constantly, inevitably changing. Thus, their equilibrium is dynamic or in motion.

emotional interdependence Results from an interaction pattern in which relationship partners rely on each other to fulfill similar or complementary emotional needs.

empathy Feeling another person's feelings as your own; feeling what he or she feels. Some scholars consider empathy an impossible ideal between people and prefer to focus on dual perspective, which refers to having a cognitive understanding of another's perspective and how it fits with your own.

environmental spoiling Ill will that is fostered by proximity between people whose values differ or conflict.

eros One of three primary styles of loving, eros is intense, passionate, and typically rapid in its development. Erotic love is not restricted to sexuality.

exchange theory Explains personal relationships in terms of economic principles of cost, benefit, and equity of exchanges between partners.

exit One of four possible responses to relationship distress. The exit response involves leaving a relationship, either physically or psychologically. It is destructive in that it curtails the potential to repair and continue intimacy, and it is active in that it makes an assertive move.

gender A social, symbolic construction that expresses the meanings a society confers on biological sex. *Feminine* and *masculine* are gender terms that refer to socially expected and prescribed qualities in women and men, respectively. Sex and gender are not absolutely correlated so women and men may be masculine or feminine or degrees of both.

generalized other The viewpoint of the society as a whole; an organized understanding of attitudes and perspectives common to members of a social community. (See also *perspective of the generalized other.*)

grave dressing The fifth and final phase in the process of relationship dissolution. Grave dressing may include both personal and interpersonal activities. On the personal level, individuals make sense of a relationship's life and death and mourn its passing. Interpersonally, grave dressing may entail talk between partners and partners' talk with friends and family, all of which is designed to provide resolution of the relationship so that individuals may get on with their lives.

I One of two complementary aspects of the self. The I is the agent, the actor, the part of the self that performs or behaves in ways the self and others can observe. I is sometimes impulsive and is the source of individuality and creativity.

idealizing The process in which partners perceive and describe each other and their relationship in idealistic ways. Idealizing tends to be most pronounced when a personal relationship is escalating in intensity but has not yet become committed.

imagined trajectory Understanding of a particular track in relationship development. Imagined trajectories function as scripts that guide how individuals behave and judge the behaviors of others.

interpretation An active process whereby individuals perceive and assign meaning to phenomena, relying on cognitive schemata to do so.

intrapsychic phase The second of five phases in the process of relationship dissolution. This phase occurs within individuals as they think about a relationship, partner, and problems. Attributions for relationship problems figure prominently in shaping individuals' thoughts and feelings about the relationship and its future.

investment Something an individual puts into a relationship that could not be recovered if the relationship ended. Investments are more closely linked to commitment, whereas rewards are more closely associated with love.

listening A complex process of attending to, receiving, perceiving selectively, organizing, interpreting, responding to, and remembering messages. Listening is not the same as hearing.

love Strongly positive feeling about another person.

loyalty One of four possible responses to relationship distress. Loyalty is a response that maintains commitment to intimacy but does so quietly. For example, a loyalty response to problems would be to hope things get better. The response is constructive in that it supports commitment and passive in that it does not actively intervene to address problems.

ludus One of three primary styles of love, ludus is playful love or love as a game. Ludic lovers enjoy the game of love but do not want commitment.

mania One of three secondary styles of love, mania combines the intensity of eros with the manipulation or game orientation of ludus. If constant, mania may be obsessive and unsatisfying for both manics and those they love.

ME One of two complementary aspects of self. The ME is the socially conscious thinker who reflects on I's activities from the perspective of others in a society. The ME is critical, socially aware, and analytical.

meaning A human construction arising out of interpreting and negotiating interpretations with others.

metacommunication Communication about communication. Metacommunication allows partners in a relationship to discuss patterns of interaction between them.

mind Within symbolic interaction theory, mind is the ability to use significant symbols, that is, symbols that have a common significance among members of a society. Like self, mind is not present at birth but is acquired through interacting with others.

monitor Process of observing ourselves and our actions. Monitoring is possible because humans are self-reflective.

neglect One of four possible responses to relationship distress. Neglect involves minimizing or denying problems in intimacy. The neglect response is destructive in that it does not support improvement of the relationship, and it is passive in that it

avoids straightforward and open responses.

neutralization One of four identified responses to the tension of relationship dialectics. Neutralization involves compromising so that both needs in a dialectic are met to a degree, but neither need is fully satisfied.

novelty and predictability One of three relational dialectics that generate change in personal relationships. This dialectic is the tension between partners' needs for what is new, stimulating, or novel and what is familiar, routine, and predictable.

openers Routinized forms for opening conversation between strangers. In openers, the relationship level of meaning tends to be more important than the content level.

openness and closedness One of three relational dialectics that generate change in personal relationships. This dialectic entails the tension between the need to be open in sharing information and feelings about ourselves and the need to preserve our privacy.

overchoice Feeling overwhelmed by an abundance of choices and a lack of rules for choosing among them.

parallel structure A relationship organization in which partners have equal overall power (authority)—yet each partner has primary say-so in specific areas—and in which partners are moderately interdependent.

personal constructs Mental yardsticks that individuals use to ask how people measure up on specific qualities. We use personal constructs to interpret people and social situations by assessing similarities and differences between the phenomenon we are interpreting and others in the class.

personalized communication Using nicknames, coded terms, and special vocabulary to enhance partners' feelings of being connected and to exclude others by demarcating the boundaries of an intimate relationship.

personal relationship Voluntary commitments that are marked by continuing and significant interdependence between particular individuals and that are constantly in process.

perspective of the generalized other The viewpoint of society as a whole or of specific social communities. (See also *generalized other*.)

pragma One of three secondary styles of love, pragma combines the conscious planning of ludus and the constancy of storge. Pragmatic lovers are not necessarily unfeeling but do prefer to restrain feeling until the practicality of a match is established.

private intensifying A process in which partners immerse themselves in each other and the relationship by intensely interacting and thinking about the relationship and each other. Typically private intensifying involves spending more time together and using less external structure on that time.

prototype An organized understanding of what the defining qualities are of some category of people, events, objects, or situations. An exemplar.

proximity Nearness or presence of others in surroundings. Proximity (physical or virtual) is a fundamental condition for the development of relationships.

punctuation The process by which individuals define beginnings and endings of communication episodes.

reframing One of four identified ways of responding to the tension of relational dialectics. Reframing involves reinterpreting polar needs in a dialectic so that they are not in contradiction.

regulative rule Specifies how to communicate by indicating the kinds of communication appropriate in particular contexts. For instance, asking questions is appropriate in a college classroom but not when listening to a public address in an audience of 5,000 people.

relational culture Intimate partners' shared understandings of their identities and relationship. Relational culture is an ongoing process through which partners create common understandings of who they are, how they operate, and what rules, values, beliefs, and so forth are appropriate in their private world.

relational dialectics Opposing forces in relationships that rise from the presence of conflicting needs, or impulses, that are never resolved in a final sense. Three dialectics are autonomy/connection, novelty/predictability, and openness/closedness.

relational self An identity that departs from traditional views of a core individual essence and, instead, is continually emerging and reforming as we move in and out of various relationships.

relationship level of meaning Defines the identities of communicators and expresses the relationship between them. Responsiveness, affection, and power are dimensions of the relationship level of meaning.

relationship maintenance Communication and actions that partners use to sustain a personal relationship at a standard and desirable level of functioning and satisfaction.

relationship quota An individual standard for overall involvement that specifies how many relationships or relationships of particular sorts an individual is comfortable having at any one time.

relationship repair Communication and actions designed to restore a relationship to a standard and desirable level of functioning and satisfaction.

rules Shared understandings about what is appropriate and inappropriate in various situations.

saturated self Identity that is populated by the perspectives of others—multiple viewpoints that are different and sometimes conflicting. We become saturated because frequent and often intense contacts with widely diverse others allow us to import their views, goals, values, and identities into our own perspective and identity.

scripts Guides to action. Scripts delineate an appropriate or typical sequence of events for some particular situation.

secure attachment model Develops when a caregiver responds in consistently loving, reassuring, and attentive ways to a child; cultivates confidence in self, trust of others, and comfort in personal relationships.

selection One of four identified responses to the tension of relational dialectics. Selection involves satisfying one of the two needs in a dialectic and neglecting the other.

self Within symbolic interaction theory, self refers to the ability to take one's self as an object of reflection—to self-reflect. Like mind, self is not present at birth but is acquired in interaction with others.

self-disclosure Disclosing personal or private information about oneself to another.

separation One of four identified ways of responding to the tension of relational dialectics. Separation involves assigning each need in a dialectic to separate spheres, times, or issues.

sex A biologically and genetically determined quality. *Male* and *female*, *man* and *woman* are sex terms.

situated knowledge A term that highlights the situated, or context bound, nature of all knowledge, truth, and identity. The term implies (1) all knowledges and identities are situated; so (2) there is no absolute truth, knowledge, or real self; and (3) all knowledges and identities make sense within their standpoints and not outside of them.

social comparison Process of gauging ourselves in relation to others to see how we measure up.

social exchange theory A group of theories that describe and explain human behavior in terms of rewards, costs, and efforts to achieve and maintain equity in personal relationships.

social phase Third phase in the process of relationship dissolution. During this phase, individuals who have decided to end a personal relationship look to friends and family for support and may begin circulating an account of the breakup in social circles.

social relationships Relationships in which participants interact with social roles but do not significantly depend on each other as individuals.

speech community A social group defined by sex, race, sexual orientation, or other factors that understands and uses communication in ways not shared by people outside of the group.

standpoint theory Useful in understanding personal and social systems that influence relationships, standpoint theory concentrates on the ways in which a social group's placement in a culture shapes what its members experience as well as how they interpret experiences, others, themselves, and relationships.

stereotypes Predictive knowledge based on understandings of how members of some category can be expected to act.

stonewalling Withdrawing from interaction and refusing to talk about problems and issues of disagreement. Stonewalling is one of four patterns that undermine couples' ability to resolve differences and to maintain satisfaction in a relationship.

storge One of three primary styles of love, storge is a calm, abiding love that tends to grow out of friendship and commonalities between people. Peaceful and abiding, storgic love tends to be very stable.

symbol An arbitrary, ambiguous, and abstract representation of something. All language is symbolic, although not all symbols are linguistic.

symbolic interaction theory (symbolic interactionism) Describes and explains human development and social life as a result of interaction with and through significant symbols.

symmetrical structure A relationship organization in which partners have equal power in most or all areas and in which they are highly independent, rather than interdependent.

systems theory A theory especially influential in shaping research on the personal and social contexts of personal relationships. Systems theory holds that individuals and relationships exist within contexts that affect them, and that relationships are systems in which all parts interrelate and interact.

theory A theory identifies and describes features of a phenomenon, explains relationships and interactions among features, and predicts outcomes from interaction among variable features.

turning points Events that are perceived to transform, or fundamentally change, a personal relationship.

voice One of four possible responses to relationship distress, voice makes an effort to address and resolve problems through open discussion between partners. The response is constructive in that its intent is to improve the relationship, and it is active in that it is assertive.

working model A model of how things work based on prior experience. This term is especially useful in thinking about working models of relationships, which are individuals' beliefs about how they and others relate to one another.

References

Acitelli, L. (1986). The influence of relationship awareness on perceived marital satisfaction and stability. *Dissertation Abstracts International, 47* (10-B), 4340. (University Microfilms, Inc.)

Acitelli, L. (1988). When spouses talk to each other about their relationship. *Journal of Social and Personal Relationships, 5,* 185–199.

Acitelli, L. (1992). Gender differences in relationship awareness and marital satisfaction among young married couples. *Personality and Social Psychology, 18,* 102–110.

Acitelli, L. (1993). You, me, and us: Perspectives on relationship awareness. In S. W. Duck (Ed.), *Understanding relationship processes, 1: Individuals in relationships* (pp. 144–174). Newbury Park, CA: Sage.

Acitelli, L., Douvan, E., & Veroff, J. (1993). Perceptions of conflict in the first year of marriage: How important are similarity and understanding? *Journal of Social and Personal Relationships, 5,* 5–20.

Acker, M., & Davis, M. H. (1992). Intimacy, passion and commitment in adult romantic relationships: A test of the triangular theory of love. *Journal of Social and Personal Relationships, 9,* 21–51.

Ackerman, D. (1994). *A natural history of love.* New York: Random House.

Adler, J. (1994, January 10). Kids growing up scared. *Newsweek,* pp. 43–49.

Adler, J. (1996, June 17). Building a better dad. *Newsweek,* pp. 58–64.

Ainsworth, M. D. S., Blehar, M. C., Waters, E., & Wall, S. (1978). *Patterns of attachment. A psychological study of the strange situation.* Hillsdale, NJ: Erlbaum.

Allan, G. (1993). Social structure and relationships. In S. Duck (Ed.), *Understanding relationship processes, 3: Social context and relationships* (pp. 1–25). Newbury Park, CA: Sage.

Allan, G. (1989). *Friendship.* Boulder, CO: Westview.

Altman, I., & Taylor, D. A. (1973). *Social penetration: The development of interpersonal relationships.* New York: Holt, Rinehart & Winston.

Altman, I., Vinsel, A., & Brown, B. B. (1981). Dialectic conceptions in social psychology: An application to social penetration and privacy regulation. In L. Berkowitz (Ed.), *Advances in experimental social psychology* (vol. 14, pp. 107–160). New York: Academic Press.

Andersen, P. (1986). Consciousness, cognition, and communication. *Western Journal of Speech Communication, 50,* 87–101.

Andersen, P. (1993). Cognitive schemata in personal relationships. In S. Duck (Ed.), *Understanding relationship processes, 1: Individuals in relationships* (pp. 1–29). Newbury Park, CA: Sage.

Angelou, M. (1990). Human family. *I shall not be moved.* New York: Random House.

Antill, J. K. (1983). Sex role complementarity versus similarity in married couples. *Journal of Personality and Social Psychology, 45,* 145–155.

Argyle, M., & Dean, J. (1965). Eye contact, distance and affiliation. *Sociometry, 28,* 289–304.

Argyle, M., & Henderson, M. (1984). The rules of friendship. *Journal of Social and Personal Relationships, 1,* 211–237.

Argyle, M., & Henderson, M. (1985). The rules of relationships. In S. W. Duck & D. Perlman (Eds.), *Understanding personal relationships: An interdisciplinary approach* (pp. 63–84). Beverly Hills, CA: Sage.

Argyle, M., Henderson, M., Bond, M., Iizuka, Y., & Contarello, A. (1986). Cross cultural variations in relationship rules. *International Journal of Psychology, 21,* 287–315.

Aries, E. (1977). Male-female interpersonal styles in all male, all female, and mixed groups. In A. Sargent (Ed.), *Beyond sex roles* (pp. 292–299). St. Paul, MN: West.

Aries, E. (1987). Gender and communication. In P. Shaver (Ed.), *Sex and gender* (pp. 149–176). Newbury Park, CA: Sage.

Aron, A., Aron, E. N., Tudor, M., & Nelson, G. (1991). Close relationships as including other in the self. *Journal of Personality and Social Psychology, 60,* 241–253.

Askham, J. (1976). Identity and stability within the marriage relationship. *Journal of Marriage and the Family, 38,* 535–547.

Askham, J. (1984). *Identity and stability in marriage.* Cambridge, England: Cambridge University Press.

Ayres, J. (1983). Strategies to maintain relationships: Their identification and perceived usage. *Communication Quarterly, 31,* 62–67.

Baldwin, D. (1994, January–February). As busy as we wanna be. *Utne Reader,* pp. 52–58.

Barge, J. K., & Musambira, G. W. (1992). Turning points in chair-faculty relationships. *Journal of Applied Communication Research, 20,* 54–77.

Barnett, O., & LaViolette, A. (1993). *It could happen to anyone: Why battered women stay.* Newbury Park, CA: Sage.

Bartholomew, K. (1993). From childhood to adult relationships: Attachment theory and research. In S. W. Duck (Ed.), *Understanding relationship processes, 2: Learning about relationships* (pp. 30–62). Newbury Park, CA: Sage.

Bartholomew, K., & Horowitz, L. M. (1991). Attachment styles among young adults: A test of a four-category model. *Journal of Personality and Social Psychology, 61,* 226–244.

Basow, S. L. (1992). *Gender: Stereotypes and roles* (3rd ed.). Belmont, CA: Brooks-Cole/Wadsworth.

Bass, A. (1993, December 5). Behavior that can wreck a marriage. *Raleigh News and Observer*, p. 8E.

Bateson, M. C. (1990). *Composing a life*. New York: Penguin/Plume.

Baucom, D. H., Sayers, S. L., & Duhe, A. (1989). Attributional style and attributional patterns among married couples. *Journal of Personality and Social Psychology, 56*, 596–607.

Baxter, L. A. (1984). Trajectories of relationship disengagement. *Journal of Social and Personal Relationships, 7*, 141–178.

Baxter, L. A. (1985). Accomplishing relationship disengagement. In S. W. Duck & D. Perlman (Eds.), *Understanding personal relationships: An interdisciplinary approach* (pp. 243–265). Beverly Hills, CA: Sage.

Baxter, L. A. (1987). Symbols of relationship identity in relationship cultures. *Journal of Social and Personal Relationships, 4*, 261–279.

Baxter, L. A. (1988). A dialectical perspective on communication strategies in relationship development. In S. W. Duck, D. F. Hay, S. E. Hobfoll, W. Ickes, & B. Montgomery (Eds.), *Handbook of personal relationships* (pp. 257–273). London: Wiley.

Baxter, L. A. (1990). Dialectical contradictions in relationship development. *Journal of Social and Personal Relationships, 7*, 69–88.

Baxter, L. A. (1992). Forms and functions of intimate play in personal relationships. *Human Communication Research, 18*, 336–363.

Baxter, L. A. (1993). The social side of personal relationships: A dialectical perspective. In S. Duck (Ed.), *Understanding relationship processes, 3: Social context and relationships* (pp. 139–165). Newbury Park, CA: Sage.

Baxter, L. A. (1994). A dialogic approach to relationship maintenance. In D. Canary & L. Stafford (Eds.), *Communication and relational maintenance* (pp. 233–254). New York: Academic Press.

Baxter, L. A., & Bullis, C. (1986). Turning points in developing romantic relationships. *Human Communication Research, 12*, 469–493.

Baxter, L. A., & Dindia, K. (1987). Strategies for maintaining and repairing marital relationships. *Journal of Social and Personal Relationships, 4*, 143–158.

Baxter, L. A., & Montgomery, B. (1996). *Relating: Dialogues and dialectics*. New York: Guilford.

Baxter, L. A., & Pittman, G. (1996, November). *Remembering turning points of relational development: Communicative forms of continuity in romantic relationships*. Paper presented at the Speech Communication Association Convention, San Diego.

Baxter, L. A., & Simon, E. P. (1993). Relationship maintenance strategies and dialectical contradictions in personal relationships. *Journal of Social and Personal Relationships, 10*, 225–242.

Beck, A. (1988). *Love is never enough*. New York: Harper & Row.

Becker, C. S. (1987). Friendship between women: A phenomenological study of best friends. *Journal of Phenomenological Psychology, 18*, 59–72.

Beir, E. G., & Sternberg, D. P. (1977). Marital communication. *Journal of Communication, 27*, 92–103.

Belk, S. S., & Snell, W. E., Jr. (1988). Avoidance strategy use in intimate relationships. *Journal of Social and Clinical Psychology, 7*, 80–96.

Bell, R. A., Buerkel-Rothfuss, N. L., & Gore, K. E. (1987). Did you bring the yarmulke for the cabbage patch kids? The idiomatic communication of young lovers.

Human Communication Research, 14, 47–67.

Bell, R. A., & Healy, J. G. (1992). Idiomatic communication and interpersonal solidarity in friends' relational cultures. *Human Communication Research, 18*, 307–335.

Bellah, R., Madsen, R., Sullivan, W., Swindler, A., & Tipton, S. (1985). *Habits of the heart: Individualism and commitment in American life.* Berkeley: University of California Press.

Bellah, R., Madsen, R., Sullivan, W., Swindler, A., & Tipton, S. (1991). *The good society.* New York: Knopf.

Belluck, P., & Borowski, N. (1993, October 3). The daddy track: More men stay home to care for children. *Raleigh News and Observer,* p. 20A.

Belsky, J. (1990). Children and marriage. In F. D. Fincham & T. N. Bradbury (Eds.), *The psychology of marriage: Basic issues and applications* (pp. 172–200). New York: Guilford.

Belsky, J., Lang, M., & Huston, T. L. (1986). Sex typing and division of labor as determinants of marital change across transition to parenthood. *Journal of Personality and Social Psychology, 50*, 517–522.

Belsky, J., & Pensky, E. (1988). Developmental history, personality, and family relationships: Toward an emergent family system. In R. A. Hinde & J. Stevenson-Hinde (Eds.), *Relationships within families: Mutual influences* (pp. 193–217). Oxford, England: Clarendon.

Bem, S. (1993). *The lenses of gender.* New Haven, CT: Yale University Press.

Benin, M. H., & Agnostinelli, J. (1988). Husbands' and wives' satisfaction with the division of labor. *Journal of Marriage and the Family, 50*, 349–361.

Berg, J. H., & McQuinn, R. D. (1986). Attraction and exchange in developing relationships. In S. Duck (Ed.), *Hand-book of personal relationships* (pp. 239–255). New York: Wiley.

Berger, C. R. (1988). Uncertainty and information exchange in developing relationships. In S. W. Duck, D. F. Hay, S. E. Hobfoll, W. Ickes, & B. Montgomery (Eds.), *Handbook of personal relationships* (pp. 239–256). Chichester, England: Wiley.

Berger, C. R., & Bell, R. A. (1988). Plans and the initiation of social relationships. *Human Communication Research, 15*, 217–235.

Berger, C. R., & Bradac, J. (1982). *Language and social knowledge.* London: Arnold.

Berger, C. R., & Calabrese, R. J. (1975). Some explorations in initial interaction and beyond: Toward a developmental theory of interpersonal communication. *Human Communication Research, 1*, 99–112.

Berger, P., & Kellner, H. (1975). Marriage and the construction of reality. In D. Brissett & C. Edgely (Eds.), *Life as theatre* (pp. 219–233). Chicago: Aldine.

Bergner, R. M., & Bergner, L. L. (1990). Sexual misunderstanding: A descriptive and pragmatic formulation. *Psychotherapy, 27*, 464–467.

Berscheid, E. (1983). Emotions. In H. H. Kelley, E. Berscheid, A. Christensen, J. Harvey, T. L. Huston, G. Levingher, E. McClintock, L. A. Peplau, & D. R. Peterson (Eds.), *Close relationships* (pp. 110–168). New York: Freeman.

Berscheid, E., & Peplau, L. A. (1983). The emerging science of relationships. In H. H. Kelley, E. Berscheid, A. Christensen, J. Harvey, T. L. Huton, G. Levingher, E. McClintock, L. A. Peplau, & D. R. Peterson (Eds.), *Close relationships* (pp. 1–19). New York: Freeman.

Bertman, S. (1998). *Hyperculture: The human cost of speed.* Westport, CT: Praeger.

Binswanger, L. (1963). *Being-in-the-world*. New York: Basic Books.

Bishop, J. (1993, October 12). Word processing. *Wall Street Journal*, pp. A1, A14.

Blau, P. M. (1967). *Exchange and power in social life*. New York: Wiley.

Block, J. H. (1973). Conceptions of sex role: Some cross-cultural and longitudinal perspectives. *American Psychologist, 28*, 512–526.

Blumer, H. (1969). *Symbolic interactionism: Perspective and method*. Englewood Cliffs, NJ: Prentice-Hall.

Blumstein, P., & Schwartz, P. (1983). *American couples: Money, work, and sex*. New York: Morrow.

Bochner, A. (1984). The functions of human communication in interpersonal bonding. In C. Arnold & J. Bowers (Eds.), *Handbook of rhetorical and communication theory* (pp. 544–621). Boston: Allyn & Bacon.

Bochner, A. (1991). The paradigm that would not die. In J. Anderson (Ed.), *Communication yearbook 14*. Newbury Park, CA: Sage.

Bochner, A. P., Krueger, D. L., & Chmielewski, T. L. (1982). Interpersonal perceptions and marital adjustment. *Journal of Communication, 32*, 135–147.

Bolger, N., DeLongis, A., Kessler, R. C., & Wethington, E. (1989). Effects of daily stress on negative mood. *Journal of Personality and Social Psychology, 57*, 808–818.

Bolger, N., & Eckenrode, J. (1991). Social relationships, personality, and anxiety during a major stressful event. *Journal of Personality and Social Psychology, 61*, 440–449.

Bolger, N., & Kelleher, S. (1993). Daily life in relationships. In S. Duck (Ed.), *Understanding relationship processes, 3. Social context and relationships* (pp. 100–108). Newbury Park, CA: Sage.

Bolton, C. D. (1961). Mate selection as the development of a relationship. *Marriage and Family Living, 23*, 234–240.

Booth, R. (1996). *Romancing the net: A "tell-all" guide to love online*. Rocklin, CA: Prima.

Boulding, K. (1990). *Building a global civic culture*. Syracuse, NY: Syracuse University Press.

Bowlby, J. (1973). *Separation (Attachment and loss)*, vol. 2. New York: Basic Books.

Bowlby, J. (1977). The making and breaking of affectional bonds: 1. Aetiology and psychopathology in light of attachment theory. *British Journal of Psychiatry, 130*, 201–210.

Bowlby, J. (1988). *A secure base: Parent–child attachment and healthy human development*. New York: Basic Books.

Bradbury, T. N., & Fincham, F. D. (1990). Attributions in marriage: Review and critique. *Psychological Bulletin, 107*, 3–33.

Braithwaite, D., & Baxter, L. (1995). "I do" again: The relational dialectics of renewing marriage vows. *Journal of Social and Personal Relationships, 12*, 177–198.

Brehm, S. (1992). *Intimate relationships*. New York: McGraw-Hill.

Brehm, S. S., & Kassin, S. M. (1990). *Social psychology*. Boston: Houghton Mifflin.

Brockner, J., & Rubin, J. Z. (1985). *Entrapment in escalating conflicts: A social psychological analysis*. New York: Springer-Verlag.

Brock-Utne, B. (1989). *Feminist perspectives on peace and peace education*. New York: Pergamon.

Bruess, C., & Pearson, J. (1996). Gendered patterns in family communication. In J. T. Wood (Ed.), *Gendered relationships*. Mountain View, CA: Mayfield.

Bullis, C., Clark, C., & Sline, R. (1993). From passion to commitment: Turning points in romantic relationships. In P. Kalbfleisch (Ed.), *Interpersonal communication: Evolving interpersonal relationships* (pp. 213–236). Hillsdale, NJ: Erlbaum.

Bumpass, L., & Sweet, J. (1989). National estimates of cohabitation. *Demographics, 26,* 615–625.

Burgess, R. L. (1981). Relationships in marriage and the family. In S. W. Duck & R. Gilmour (Eds.), *Personal relationships, 1: Studying personal relationships.* London: Sage.

Burgoon, J., Buller, D., Hale, J., & deTurck, M. (1988). Relational messages associated with nonverbal behaviors. *Human Communication Research, 10,* 351–378.

Burggraf, C., & Sillars, A. (1987). A critical examination of sex differences in marital communication. *Communication Monographs, 54,* 276–294.

Burke, K. (1968). *Language as symbolic action.* Berkeley: University of California Press.

Burleson, B. R. (1982). The development of comforting communication skills in childhood and adolescence. *Child Development, 53,* 1578–1588.

Burns, A., & Homel, R. (1989). Gender division of tasks by parents and their children. *Psychology of Women Quarterly, 13,* 113–125.

Burns, A., & Scott, C. (1994). *Mother-headed families and why they have increased.* Hillsdale, NJ: Erlbaum.

Buss, D. M. (1989). Sex differences in human mate preferences: Evolutionary hypotheses tested in 37 cultures. *Behavioral and Brain Sciences, 12,* 1–14.

Button, C. M., & Collier, D. R. (1991, June). *A comparison of people's concepts of love and romantic love.* Paper presented at the Canadian Psychological Association Conference, Calgary, Alberta.

Buunk, B. P., Collins, R. L., Taylor, S. E., VanYperen, N. W., & Dakof, G. A. (1990). The affective consequences of social comparisons: Either direction has its ups and downs. *Journal of Personality and Social Psychology, 59,* 1238–1249.

Buunk, B. P., & VanYperen, N. W. (1991). Referential comparisons, relational comparisons, and exchange orientation: Their relation to marital satisfaction. *Personality and Social Psychology Bulletin, 17,* 709–717.

Byrne, D. (1971). *The attraction paradigm.* New York: Academic Press.

Byrne, D., Clore, G. L., & Smeaton, G. (1986). The attraction hypothesis: Do similar attitudes affect anything? *Journal of Personality and Social Psychology, 51,* 1167–1170.

Byrne, D., Ervin, C. E., & Lamberth, J. (1970). Continuity between the experimental study of attraction and real-life computer dating. *Journal of Personality and Social Psychology, 16,* 157–165.

Byrne, D., London, O., & Reeves, K. (1968). The effects of physical attractiveness, sex and attitude similarity on interpersonal attraction. *Journal of Personality, 36,* 259–271.

Byrne, D., & Murnen, S. (1988). Maintaining loving relationships. In R. Sternberg & M. Barnes (Eds.), *The psychology of love.* New Haven, CT: Yale University Press.

Campbell, A. (1993). *Men, women, and aggression.* New York: Basic Books.

Campbell, J., & Toms, M. (1990). *An open life.* New York: Harper & Row.

Canary, D., & Dindia, K. (Eds.). (1998). *Sex differences and similarities in communication.* Mahwah, NJ: Erlbaum.

Canary, D. J., & Hause, K. S. (1993). Is there any reason to research sex differences in communication? *Communication Quarterly, 41,* 129–144.

Canary, D., Hause, K., & Messman, S. (1993). *Motives, strategies, and equity in the maintenance of cross-sex friendships.* Paper presented to the Speech Communication Association, Miami.

Canary, D., & Stafford, L. (1992). A new look at similarity and attraction in marriage: Similarities in social-cognitive and communication skills as predictors of attraction and satisfaction. *Communication Monographs, 59,* 243–267.

Canary, D., & Stafford, L. (Eds.). (1994). *Communication and relational maintenance.* New York: Academic Press.

Canary, D., Stafford, L., Hause, K., & Wallace, L. (1993). An inductive analysis of relational maintenance strategies: A comparison among young lovers, relatives, friends, and others. *Communication Research Reports, 10,* 5–14.

Cancian, F. (1987). *Love in America.* Cambridge, England: Cambridge University Press.

Cancian, F. (1989). Love and the rise of capitalism. In B. Risman & P. Schwartz (Eds.), *Gender in intimate relationships* (pp. 12–25). Belmont, CA: Wadsworth.

Capella, J. N. (1988). Personal relationships, social relationships and patterns of interaction. In S. W. Duck, D. F. Hay, S. E. Hobfoll, W. Ickes, & B. Montgomery (Eds.), *Handbook of personal relationships* (pp. 325–342). Chichester, England: Wiley.

Carlozo, L. (1995, March 3). Couples today aren't rushing down the aisle. *Raleigh News and Observer,* p. 7D.

Carter, B. (1991, May 1). Children's TV, where boys are king. *New York Times,* pp. Al, C18.

Cash, T. F., & Derlega, V. J. (1978). The matching hypothesis: Physical attractiveness among same-sex friends. *Personality and Social Psychology Bulletin, 4,* 240–243.

Caspi, A., & Elder, G. H. (1988). Emergent family patterns: The intergenerational construction of problem behavior and relationships. In R. A. Hinde & J. Stevenson-Hinde (Eds.), *Relationships within families: Mutual influences* (pp. 218–240). Oxford, England: Clarendon.

Caspi, A., & Harbener, E. S. (1990). Continuity and change: Assortive marriage and the consistency of personality in adulthood. *Journal of Personality and Social Psychology, 58,* 250–258.

Cassirer, E. (1944). *An essay on man.* New York: Bantam.

Cathcart, D., & Cathcart, R. (1997). The group: A Japanese context. In L. Samovar & R. Porter (Eds.), *Intercultural communication: A reader* (8th ed., pp. 329–339). Belmont, CA: Wadsworth.

Chelune, G. J., Robison, J. T., & Kammar, M. J. (1984). A cognitive interactional model of intimate relationships. In V. Derlega (Ed.), *Communication, intimacy, and close relationships* (pp. 11–40). New York: Academic Press.

Cherlin, A. (1992). *Marriage, divorce, and remarriage.* Cambridge, MA: Harvard University Press.

Chodorow, N. J. (1978). *The reproduction of mothering. Psychoanalysis and the sociology of gender.* Berkeley: University of California Press.

Chodorow, N. J. (1989). *Feminism and psychoanalytic theory.* New Haven, CT: Yale University Press.

Christensen, A., & Heavey, C. (1990). Gender and social structure in the demand/withdraw pattern in marital conflict. *Journal of Personality and Social Psychology, 59,* 73–81.

Clark, M. S., Quellette, R., Powell, M. C., & Milberg, S. (1987). Recipient's mood, relationship type, and helping. *Journal of*

Personality and Social Psychology, 53, 93–103.

Cleveland, H. (1995, March–April). The limits to cultural diversity. *The Futurist,* pp. 23–26.

Coates, J., & Cameron, D. (Eds.). (1989). *Women and their speech communities.* New York: Longman.

Cohen, S. (1988). Psychosocial models of the role of social support in the etiology of physical disease. *Health Psychology, 7,* 269–297.

Coleman, M., & Ganong, L. (1995). Family reconfiguring following divorce. In S. W. Duck & J. T. Wood (Eds.), *Understanding relationship processes, 5: Confronting relationship challenges* (pp. 73–108). Newbury Park, CA: Sage.

Coles, R. (1990). *The spiritual life of children.* Boston: Houghton Mifflin.

Collins, N. L. (1991). *Adult attachment styles and explanations for relationship events: A knowledge structure approach to explanation in close relationships.* Unpublished doctoral dissertation, University of Southern California, Los Angeles.

Collins, N. L., & Read, S. J. (1990). Adult attachment, working models, and relationship quality in dating couples. *Journal of Personality and Social Psychology, 58,* 644–663.

Collins, P. H. (1986). Learning from the outsider within. *Social Problems, 23,* 514–532.

Contarello, A., & Volpato, C. (1991). Images of friendship: Literary depictions through the ages. *Journal of Social and Personal Relationships, 8,* 49–75.

Conville, R. (1988). Relational transitions: An inquiry into their structure and function. *Journal of Social and Personal Relationships, 5,* 423–437.

Coontz, S. (1992). *The way we never were: American families and the nostalgia trap.* New York: Basic Books.

Coontz, S. (1996, May–June). Where are the good old days? *Modern Maturity,* pp. 36–43.

Cornforth, M. (1968). *Materialism and the dialectical method.* New York: International Publishers.

Cowan, P., Field, D., Hansen, D., Skolnick, A., & Swanson, G. (Eds.). (1993). *Family, self, and society: Toward a new agenda for family research.* Hillsdale, NJ: Erlbaum.

Coyne, J. C., Burchill, S. A., & Stiles, W. B., (1990). An interactional perspective on depression. In C. R. Snyder & D. R. Forsyth (Eds.), *Handbook of social and clinical psychology.* New York: Pergamon.

Creekmore, C. (1994, January–February). Theory of the leisure trap. *Utne Reader,* p. 61.

Crohn, J. (1995). *Mixed matches.* New York: Fawcett Columbine.

Crouter, A., & Helms-Erickson, H. (1997). Work and family from a dyadic perspective: Variations in inequality. In S. Duck (Ed.), *Handbook of personal relationships* (2nd ed., pp. 487–503). West Sussex, England: Wiley.

Crowley, G. (1995, March 6). Dialing the stress-meter down. *Newsweek,* p. 62.

Cunningham, J., & Antill, J. (1981). Love in developing romantic relationships. In S. Duck & R. Gilmour (Eds.), *Personal relationships, 2: Developing personal relationships* (pp. 27–51). New York: Academic Press.

Cunningham, J., & Antill, J. (1995). Current trends in nonmarital cohabitation: In search of the POSSLQ. In J. Wood & S. Duck (Eds.), *Understanding relationship processes, 6: Understudied relationships: Off the beaten track,* (pp. 148–172), Newbury Park, CA: Sage.

Cunningham, L. (1996, February 15). Valentine's Day: A short history. *Bottom Line*, p. 12.

Dainton, M., & Stafford, L. (1993). Routine maintenance behaviors: A comparison of relationship type, partner similarity, and sex differences. *Journal of Social and Personal Relationships, 10,* 255–271.

Database. (1993, September 6). *U.S. News & World Report*, p. 14.

The daughter track/trading places. (1990, July 16). *Newsweek*, pp. 48–54.

Davis, K. E., & Todd, M. J. (1985). Assessing friendship: Prototypes, paradigm cases, and relationship description. In S. W. Duck & D. Perlman (Eds.), *Understanding personal relationships* (pp. 17–38). London: Sage.

Davis, M. (1973). *Intimate relations*. New York: Free Press.

Davis, V. T., & Singh, R. (1989). Attitudes of university students from India toward marriage and family life. *International Journal of Sociology of the Family, 19,* 43–57.

DeFrancisco, V. (1991). The sounds of silence: How men silence women in marital relations. *Discourse and Society, 2,* 413–423.

Denzin, N. K. (1970). Rules of conduct in the study of deviant behavior: Some notes on the social relationship. In G. J. McCall, M. M. McCall, N. K. Denzin, G. D. Suttles, & S. B. Kurth (Eds.), *Social relationships* (pp. 62–94). Chicago: Aldine.

Dermer, M., & Thiel, D. L. (1975). When beauty may fail. *Journal of Personality and Social Psychology, 31,* 1168–1176.

Dickins, W. J., & Perlman, D. (1981). Friendship over the life cycle. In S. W. Duck & R. Gilmour (Eds.), *Personal relationships, 2. Developing personal relationships*. London: Academic Press.

Dicks, D. (1993). *Breaking convention with intercultural romances*. Weggis, Switzerland: Bergili Books.

Dickson, F. (1995). The best is yet to be: Research on long-lasting marriages. In J. T. Wood & S. Duck (Eds.), *Understanding relationship processes, 6: Understudied relationships: Off the beaten track* (pp. 22–50). Thousand Oaks, CA: Sage.

Dillard, J. P., & Miller, K. I. (1988). Intimate relationships in task environments. In S. W. Duck, D. F. Hay, S. E. Hobfoll, W. Ickes, & B. Montgomery (Eds.), *Handbook of personal relationships*. Chichester, England: Wiley.

Dindia, K. (1987). The effects of sex of subject and sex of partner on interruptions. *Human Communication Research, 13,* 345–371.

Dindia, K., & Allen, M. (1992). Sex differences in self-disclosure: A meta analysis. *Psychological Bulletin, 12,* 106–124.

Dindia, K., & Baxter, L. A. (1987). Strategies for maintaining and repairing marital relationships. *Journal of Social and Personal Relationships, 4,* 143–158.

Dindia, K., & Canary, D. (1993). Definitions and theoretical perspectives on maintaining relationships. *Journal of Social and Personal Relationships, 10,* 163–174.

Dion, K. K., Berscheid, E., & Walster, E. (1972). What is beautiful is good. *Journal of Personality and Social Psychology, 24,* 285–290.

Dion, K. L., & Dion, K. K. (1973). Correlates of romantic love. *Journal of Consulting and Clinical Psychology, 41,* 51–56.

Dion, K. L., & Dion, K. K. (1975). Self-esteem and romantic love. *Journal of Personality, 43,* 39–57.

Dixson, M., & Duck, S. W. (1993). Understanding relationship processes: Uncovering the human search for meaning. In S. W. Duck (Ed.), *Understanding rela-*

tionship processes, 1: Individuals in relationships (pp. 175–206). Newbury Park, CA: Sage.

Dobash, R. E., & Dobash, R. P. (1979). Violence against wives: A case against the patriarchy. New York: Free Press.

Doherty, W. J. (1982). Attributional style and negative problem solving in marriage. Family Relations, 31, 201–205.

Dow, B. (1996). Primetime feminism. Philadelphia: University of Pennsylvania Press.

Duck, S. W. (1980). Personal relationships research in the 1980s: Towards an understanding of complex human sociality. Western Journal of Speech Communication, 44, 114–119.

Duck, S. W. (1982). A topography of relationship disengagement and dissolution. In S. W. Duck (Ed.), Personal relationships, 4: Dissolving personal relationships (pp. 1–30). New York: Academic Press.

Duck, S. W. (1984). A perspective on the repair of personal relationships: Repair of what? when? In S. W. Duck (Ed.), Personal relationships, 5: Repairing personal relationships. London: Academic Press.

Duck, S. W. (1988). Relating to others. London: Dorsey; Monterey, CA: Brooks/Cole.

Duck, S. W. (1990). Relationships as unfinished business: Out of the frying pan and into the 1990s. Journal of Social and Personal Relationships, 7, 5–24.

Duck, S. W. (1991). Friends for life. Hemel Hemstead, England: Harvester-Wheatsheaf.

Duck, S. W. (1992). Human relationships (2nd ed.). Newbury Park, CA: Sage.

Duck, S. W. (Ed.). (1993a). Understanding relationship processes, 1: Individuals in relationships. Newbury Park, CA: Sage.

Duck, S. W. (Ed.). (1993b). Understanding relationship processes, 2: Learning about relationships. Newbury Park, CA: Sage.

Duck, S. W. (1994a). Meaningful relationships. Thousand Oaks, CA: Sage.

Duck, S. W. (1994b). Steady as (s)he goes: Relational maintenance as a shared meaning system. In D. Canary & L. Stafford (Eds.), Communication and relational maintenance (pp. 45–60). New York: Academic Press.

Duck, S. W., & Condra, M. B. (1989). To be or not to be: Anticipation, persuasion, and retrospection in personal relationships. In R. Neimeyer & G. Neimeyer (Eds.), Review of personal construct theory (pp. 187–202). Greenwich, CT: JAI Press.

Duck, S. W., & Craig, G. (1978). Personality similarity and the development of friendship. British Journal of Sociology and Clinical Psychology, 17, 237–242.

Duck, S. W., & Miell, D. E. (1986). Towards an understanding of relationship development and breakdown. In H. Tajfel, C. Fraser, & J. Jaspars (Eds.), The social dimension: European perspectives on social psychology. Cambridge, England: Cambridge University Press.

Duck, S. W., & Pond, K. (1989). Friends, Romans, countrymen, lend me your retrospections: Rhetoric and reality in personal relationships. In C. Hendrick (Ed.), Close relationships (pp. 17–38). Newbury Park, CA: Sage.

Duck, S. W., & Rutt, D. J. (1988). The experience of everyday relational conversations: Are all communications created equal? Paper presented at the Speech Communication Association Convention, New Orleans.

Duck, S. W., Rutt, D. J., Hurst, M. H., & Strejc, H. (1991). Some evident truths about conversations in everyday relationships: All communications are not created equal. Human Communication Research, 18, 228–267.

Duck, S., & Wright, P. (1993). Reexamining gender differences in same-gender friendships: A close look at two kinds of data. *Sex Roles, 28*, 709–727.

Duffy, S., & Rusbult, C. (1986). Satisfaction and commitment in homosexual and heterosexual relationships. *Journal of Homosexuality, 12*, 1–23.

Eagly, A. H., & Crowley, M. (1986). Gender and helping behavior: A meta-analytic review of the social psychological literature. *Psychological Bulletin, 108*, 283–308.

Eagly, A. H., & Johnson, B. T. (1990). Gender and leadership style: A meta-analysis. *Psychological Bulletin, 108*, 233–256.

Eagly, A. H., & Karau, S. J. (1991). Gender and the emergence of leadership: A meta-analysis. *Journal of Personality and Social Psychology, 60*, 685–710.

Early bonding seen as key to healthy emotional life. (1993, August 19). *Raleigh News and Observer*, p. 7E.

Ebbesen, E. B., Kjos, G. L., & Konecni, V. J. (1976). Spatial ecology: Its effects on the choice of friends and enemies. *Journal of Experimental Social Psychology, 12*, 505–518.

Eckenrode, J., & Gore, S. (1989). *Stress between work and family*. New York: Plenum.

Eidelson, R. J. (1983). Affiliation and independence issues in marriage. *Journal of Marriage and the Family, 45*, 683–688.

Eidelson, R. J., & Epstein, N. (1982). Cognition and relationship maladjustment: Development of a measure of dysfunctional relationship beliefs. *Journal of Consulting and Clinical Psychology, 50*, 715–720.

Eiduson, B. T., & Zimmerman, I. L. (1985). Nontraditional families. In L. L'Abate (Ed.), *The handbook of family psychology and therapy* (vol. 2, pp. 811–844). Homewood, IL: Dorsey.

Eldridge, N. S., & Gilbert, L. A. (1990). Correlates of relationship satisfaction in lesbian couples. *Psychology of Women Quarterly, 14*, 43–62.

Eliade, M. (1960). *Myths, dreams, mysteries* (Trans. P. Mairet). New York: Harper & Row.

Enright, R., & North, J. (1997). (Eds.). *Exploring forgiveness*. Madison: University of Wisconsin Press.

Epstein, C. F. (1968, November). Women in professional life. *Psychiatric Spectator*, n.p.

Epstein, C. F. (1981). *Women in law*. New York: Basic Books.

Epstein, C. F. (1982). *Changing perspectives and opportunities and their impact on careers and aspirations: The case of women lawyers*. Paper presented at the Annual Scientific Meeting of the Gerontological Society of America, Boston.

Epstein, C. F. (1988). *Deceptive distinctions*. Hillsdale, NJ: Erlbaum.

Erickson, M. F., Stroufe, L. A., & Egeland, B. (1985). The relationship between quality of attachment and behavior problems in preschool in a high-risk sample. In I. Bretherton & E. Waters (Eds.), *Growing points of attachment theory and research* (Monographs of the Society for Research in Child Development, vol. 50, serial no. 209, pp. 147–166). Chicago: University of Chicago Press.

Faludi, S. (1991). *Backlash: The undeclared war against American women*. New York: Crown.

Fehr, B. (1988). Prototype analysis of the concepts of love and commitment. *Journal of Personality and Social Psychology, 55*, 557–579.

Fehr, B. (1993). How do I love thee? Let me consult my prototype. In S. W. Duck (Ed.), *Understanding relationship processes, 1: Individuals in relationships* (pp. 87–122). Newbury Park, CA: Sage.

Fehr, B., & Broughton, R. (1991). *Individual differences in views of love.* Unpublished manuscript, University of Winnipeg, Manitoba, Canada (cited in Fehr, 1993).

Fehr, B., & Russell, J. A. (1991). Concept of love viewed from a prototype perspective. *Journal of Personality and Social Psychology, 60,* 425–438.

Felmlee, D. (1995). Fatal attractions: Affection and disaffection in intimate relationships. *Journal of Social and Personal Relationships, 12,* 295–311.

Felmlee, D., Sprecher, S., & Bassin, E. (1990). The dissolution of intimate relationships: A hazard model. *Social Psychology Quarterly, 53,* 13–30.

Festinger, L. (1951). Architecture and group membership. *Journal of Social Issues, 7,* 152–163.

Festinger, L. (1954). A theory of social comparison processes. *Human Relations, 2,* 117–140.

Festinger, L., Schachter, S., & Back, K. W. (1950). *Social pressures in informal groups: A study of human factors in housing.* New York: Harper and Brothers.

Fincham, F. D., & Bradbury, T. N. (1987). The impact of attributions in marriage: A longitudinal analysis. *Journal of Personality and Social Psychology, 53,* 510–517.

Fincham, F. D., Bradbury, T. N., & Scott, C. K. (1990). Cognition in marriage. In F. D. Fincham & T. N. Bradbury (Eds.), *The psychology of marriage: Basic issues and applications* (pp. 118–149). New York: Guilford.

Fishbein, M. D., & Thelen, M. H. (1981). Psychological factors in mate selection and marital satisfaction: A review. *JSAS: Catalog of Selected Documents in Psychology, 11,* 84 (MS 2374).

Fisher, A. (1987). *Interpersonal communication: Pragmatics of human relationships.* New York: Random House.

Fisher, H. (1992). *The anatomy of love: The mysteries of mating, marriage and why we stray.* New York: Fawcett/Columbine.

Fishman, P. (1983). Interaction: The work women do. In B. Thorne, C. Kramarae, & N. Henley (Eds.), *Language, gender, and society* (pp. 89–102). Rowley, MA: Newbury House.

Fitzpatrick, M. A. (1988). *Between husbands and wives: Communication in marriage.* Newbury Park, CA: Sage.

Fitzpatrick, M. A., & Best, P. (1979). Dyadic adjustment in relational types: Consensus, cohesion, affectional expression and satisfaction in enduring relationships. *Communication Monographs, 46,* 167–178.

Flanigan, B. (1992). *Forgiving the unforgivable and forgiving yourself.* New York: Macmillan.

Fletcher, G. J., & Fincham, F. D. (1991). Attribution in close relationships. In G. J. Fletcher & F. D. Fincham (Eds.), *Cognition in close relationships* (pp. 7–35). Hillsdale, NJ: Erlbaum.

Fletcher, G. J., Fincham, F. D., Cramer, L., & Heron, N. (1987). The role of attributions in the development of dating relationships. *Journal of Personality and Social Psychology, 59,* 464–474.

Fletcher, G. J., & Fitness, J. (1990). Occurrent social cognition in close relationship interaction: The role of proximal and distal variables. *Journal of Personality and Social Psychology, 59,* 464–474.

Fletcher, G. J. O., Rosanowski, J., & Fitness, J. (1992). *Automatic processing in intimate settings: The role of relationship beliefs.* Manuscript.

Footlick, J. K. (1990, Winter/Spring). What happened to the family? *Newsweek Special Edition,* pp. 14–20.

Foreit, K. G., Agor, T., Byers, J., Larue, J., Lokey, H., Palazzini, M., Patterson, M., & Smith, L. (1980). Sex bias in the newspaper treatment of male-centered and female-centered news stories. *Sex Roles*, 6, 475–480.

Fowers, B. J. (1991). His and her marriage: A multivariate study of gender and marital satisfaction. *Sex Roles*, 24, 209–221.

Franz, C. E., McClelland, D. C., & Weinberger, J. (1991). Childhood antecedents of conventional social accomplishment in mid-life adults: A 36-year prospective study. *Journal of Personality and Social Psychology*, 60, 586–595.

French, M. (1992). *The war against women*. New York: Summit.

Fulghum, R. (1989). *It was on fire when I lay down on it*. New York: Random House.

Gaines, S., Jr. (1994). Exchange of respect-denying behaviors among male-female friendships. *Journal of Social and Personal Relationships*, 11, 5–24.

Gaines, S., Jr. (1995). Relationships among members of cultural minorities. In J. T. Wood & S. Duck (Eds.), *Understanding relationship processes, 6: Understudied relationships: Off the beaten track* (pp. 51–88). Newbury Park, CA: Sage.

Gelles, R., & Loeseke, D. (Eds.). (1993). *Current controversies on family violence*. Newbury Park, CA: Sage.

Gergen, K. (1991). *The saturated self: Dilemmas of identity in contemporary life*. New York: Basic Books.

Gerstel, N., & Gross, H. (1985). *Commuter marriage*. New York: Guilford.

Giddens, A. (1973). *The class structure of advanced societies*. London: Hutchinson University Library.

Gilligan, C. (1982). *In a different voice: Psychological theory and women's development*. Cambridge, MA: Harvard University Press.

Ginsburg, G. P. (1988). Rules, scripts and prototypes in personal relationships. In

S. W. Duck, D. F. Hay, S. E. Hobfoll, W. Ickes, & B. Montgomery (Eds.), *Handbook of personal relationships*. Chichester, England: Wiley.

Gitlin, T. (1995). *The twilight of common dreams*. New York: Metropolitan.

Goldner, V., Penn, P., Scheinberg, M., & Walker, G. (1990). Love and violence: Gender paradoxes in volatile attachments. *Family Process*, 19, 343–364.

Goldsmith, D. (1990). A dialectic perspective on the expression of autonomy and connection in romantic relationships. *Western Journal of Speech Communication*, 54, 537–556.

Goldsmith, D., & Baxter, L. (1997). Constituting relationships in talk: A taxonomy of speech events in social and personal relationships. *Human Communication Research*, 23, 87–114.

Gordon, L. (1988). *Heroes of their own lives*. New York: Viking.

Gordon, S. (1991). *Prisoners of men's dreams: Striking out for a new feminine future*. Boston: Little, Brown.

Gottman, J. (1979). *Marital interaction*. New York: Academic Press.

Gottman, J. (1993). The roles of conflict engagement, escalation, or avoidance in marital interaction: A longitudinal view of five types of couples. *Journal of Consulting and Clinical Psychology*, 61, 6–15.

Gottman, J. (1994a). *What predicts divorce? The relationship between marital processes and marital outcomes*. Hillsdale, NJ: Erlbaum.

Gottman, J. (1994b). Why marriages fail. *The Family Therapy Newsletter*, pp. 41–48.

Gottman, J., & Carrère, S. (1994). Why can't men and women get along? Developmental roots and marital inequities. In D. Canary & L. Stafford (Eds.), *Communication and relational maintenance* (pp. 203–229). New York: Academic Press.

Gottman, J., & Levenson, R. (1988). The social psychophysiology of marriage. In P. Noller & M. A. Fitzpatrick (Eds.), *Perspectives on marital interaction* (pp. 182–200). Clevedon, England: Multilingual Matters.

Gottman, J., Markman, H., & Notarius, C. (1977). The topography of marital conflict: A sequential analysis of verbal and nonverbal behavior. *Journal of Marriage and the Family, 39,* 461–477.

Gottman, J., with Silver, N. (1994). *Why marriages succeed or fail.* New York: Simon & Schuster.

Graham, E. (1997). Turning points and commitment in post-divorce relationships. *Communication Monographs, 64,* 350–368.

Gray, J. (1992). *Men are from Mars, women are from Venus.* New York: HarperCollins.

Green, R. G., & Sporakowski, M. J. (1983). The dynamics of divorce: Marital quality, alternative attraction, and external pressure. *Journal of Divorce, 7,* 77–88.

Grote, N., & Frieze, I. (1998). "Remembrance of things past: Perceptions of marital love from its beginning to the present. *Journal of Social and Personal Relationships, 15,* 91–109.

Guerrero, L., Eloy, S., & Wabnik, A. (1993). Linking maintenance strategies to relationship development and disengagement: A reconceptualization. *Journal of Social and Personal Relationships, 10,* 273–283.

Guttman, J. (1993). *Divorce in psychosocial perspective: Theory and research.* Hillsdale, NJ: Erlbaum.

Halford, W., Hahlweg, K., & Dunne, M. (1990). The cross-cultural consistency of marital communication associated with marital distress. *Journal of Marriage and the Family, 52,* 487–500.

Hall, D., & Langellier, K. (1988). Storytelling strategies in mother–daughter communication. In B. Bate & A. Taylor (Eds.), *Women communicating. Studies of women's talk* (pp. 197–226). Norwood, NJ: Ablex.

Hall, J. (1987). On explaining gender differences: The case of nonverbal communication. In P. Shaver & C. Hendrick (Eds.), *Sex and gender* (pp. 177–200). Newbury Park, CA: Sage.

Hamilton, K., & Wingert, P. (1998, July 20). Down the aisle. *Newsweek,* pp. 54–57.

Hamlet, J. (1994). Understanding traditional African American preaching. In A. Gonzalez, M. Houston, & V. Chen (Eds.), *Our voices: Essays in culture, ethnicity, and communication* (pp. 100–103). Los Angeles: Roxbury.

Haraway, D. (1988). Situated knowledges: The science question in feminism and the privilege of partial perspective. *Signs, 14,* 575–599.

Harding, S. (1991). *Whose science? Whose knowledge: Thinking from women's lives.* Ithaca, NY: Cornell University Press.

Harrell, S. (1982). *Ploughshare Village: Culture and context in Taiwan.* Seattle: University of Washington Press.

Harrison-Greer, L. L. (1991). *Styles of attachment in marital relationships.* Unpublished master's thesis, York University, Toronto, Canada.

Hartsock, N. C. M. (1983). The feminist standpoint: Developing the ground for a specifically feminist historical materialism. In S. Harding & M. B. Hintikka (Eds.), *Discovering reality* (pp. 283–310). Boston: Ridel.

Harvey, J. H., Flanary, R., & Morgan, M. (1986). Vivid memories of vivid loves gone by. *Journal of Social and Personal Relationships, 3,* 359–373.

Harvey, J. H., Weber, A. L., Galvin, K. S., Huszti, H. C., & Garnick, N. N. (1986).

Attribution and the termination of close relationships: A special focus on the account. In R. Gilmour & S. W. Duck (Eds.), *The emerging field of personal relationships.* Hillsdale, NJ: Erlbaum.

Harvey, J. H., Weber, A. L., & Orbuch, T. L. (1990). *Interpersonal accounts: A social psychological perspective.* Oxford, England: Basil Blackwell.

Hatcher, M. A. (1991). The corporate woman of the 1990s: Maverick or innovator? *Psychology of Women Quarterly, 15,* 251–259.

Hatfield, E., Traupmann, J., Sprecher, S., Utne, M., & Hay, J. (1985). Equity and intimate relationships: Recent research. In I. Ickes (Ed.), *Compatible and incompatible relationships* (pp. 91–117). New York: Springer-Verlag.

Hatkoff, S., & Lasswell, T. E. (1979). Male–female similarities and differences in conceptualizing love. In M. Cook & G. Wilson (Eds.), *Love and attraction: An international conference.* Oxford, England: Pergamon.

Hazen, C., & Shaver, P. R. (1987). Conceptualizing romantic love as an attachment process. *Journal of Personality and Social Psychology, 52,* 511–524.

Hecht, M. L., Marston, P. J., & Larkey, L. K. (1994). Love ways and relationship quality in heterosexual relationships. *Journal of Social and Personal Relationships, 11,* 25–44.

Hegel, G. W. F. (Trans. J. B. Braillie). (1807). *The phenomenology of mind.* Germany: Wurtzburg and Bamberg.

Heidegger, M. (Trans. J. Macquarrie & E. S. Robinson, 1962). (1927). *Being and time.* New York: Harper & Row.

Heider, F. (1958). *The psychology of interpersonal relations.* New York: Wiley.

Heller, S. (1998, July 17). Emerging field of forgiveness studies explores how we let go

of grudges. *Chronicle of Higher Education,* pp. A18–A20.

Hendrick, C., & Hendrick, S. S. (1986). A theory and method of love. *Journal of Personality and Social Psychology, 50,* 392–402.

Hendrick, C., & Hendrick, S. S. (1988). Lovers wear rose-colored glasses. *Journal of Social and Personal Relationships, 5,* 161–184.

Hendrick, C., & Hendrick, S. S. (1989). Research on love: Does it measure up? *Journal of Personality and Social Psychology, 56,* 784–794.

Hendrick, C., Hendrick, S., & Dicke, A. (1998). The love attitudes scale: Short form. *Journal of Social and Personal Relationships, 15,* 147–159.

Hendrick, C., Hendrick, S., Foote, F. H., & Slapion-Foote, M. J. (1984). Do men and women love differently? *Journal of Social and Personal Relationships, 2,* 177–196.

Hendrick, S. S., Hendrick, C., & Adler, N. L. (1988). Romantic relationships: Love, satisfaction, and staying together. *Journal of Personality and Social Psychology, 54,* 980–988.

Hess, R. D., & Handel, G. (1959). *Family worlds: A psychosocial approach to family life.* Chicago: University of Chicago Press.

Hewlett, S. A. (1986). *A lesser life: The myth of female liberation in America.* New York: Morrow.

Hewlett, S. A. (1991). *When the bough breaks: The cost of neglecting our children.* New York: Basic Books.

Hieger, L. J., & Troll, L. A. (1973). A three-generation study of attitudes concerning the importance of romantic love in mate selection. *Gerontologist, 13* (3, Part 2), 86.

Hiller, D. V., & Philliber, W. W. (1986). The division of labor in contemporary marriage: Expectations, perceptions, and performance. *Social Problems, 33,* 191–201.

Hinsz, V. B. (1989). Facial resemblance in engaged and married couples. *Journal of Social and Personal Relationships, 6,* 223–229.

Hochschild, A. (1975). The sociology of feeling and emotion: Selected possibilities. In M. Millman & R. M. Kanter (Eds.), *Another voice* (pp. 180–207). New York: Doubleday/Anchor.

Hochschild, A., with Machung, A. (1989). *The second shift.* New York: Viking.

Holtzworth-Munroe, A., & Jacobson, N. S. (1987). An attributional approach to marital dysfunction and therapy. In J. E. Maddux, C. D. Stoltenberg, & R. Rosenwein (Eds.), *Social processes in clinical and counseling psychology* (pp. 153–170). New York: Springer-Verlag.

Honeycutt, J. M. (1989). A functional analysis of imagined interaction activity in everyday life. In J. E. Shorr, P. Robin, J. A. Connelia, & M. Wolpin (Eds.), *Imagery: Current perspectives* (pp. 13–25). New York: Plenum.

Honeycutt, J. M. (1993). Memory structures for the rise and fall of personal relationships. In S. W. Duck (Ed.), *Understanding relationship processes, 1: Individuals in relationships* (pp. 30–59). Newbury Park, CA: Sage.

Honeycutt, J. M., & Cantrill, J. G. (1991). Using expectations of relational actions to predict number of intimate relationships: Don Juan and Romeo unmasked, *Communication Reports, 4,* 14–21.

Honeycutt, J. M., Cantrill, J. G., & Greene, R. W. (1989). Memory structures for relational escalation: A cognitive test of the sequencing of relational actions and stages. *Human Communication Research, 16,* 62–90.

Honeycutt, J. M., Woods, B., & Fontenot, K. (1993). The endorsement of communica-

tion conflict rules as a function of engagement, marriage and marital ideology. *Journal of Social and Personal Relationships, 10,* 285–304.

hooks, b. (1994). *Outlaw culture.* New York: Routledge.

Hopper, R., Knapp, M., & Scott, L. (1981). Couples' personal idioms: Exploring intimate talk. *Journal of Communication, 31,* 23–33.

House, J. S., Umberson, D., & Landis, K. (1988). Structures and processes of social support. *Annual Review of Sociology, 14,* 293–318.

Howard, J. A., Blumstein, P., & Schwartz, P. (1986). Sex, power, and influence factors in intimate relationships. *Journal of Personality and Social Psychology, 51,* 102–109.

Hurvitz, N. (1970). Interaction hypotheses in marriage counseling. *Family Coordinator, 19,* 64–75.

Huston, M., & Schwartz, P. (1995). Relationships of lesbians and gay men. In J. T. Wood & S. W. Duck (Eds.), *Understanding relationship processes, 6: Understudied relationships: Off the beaten track* (pp. 89–121). Newbury Park, CA: Sage.

Huston, M., & Schwartz, P. (1996). Gendered dynamics in the romantic relationships of lesbians and gay men. In J. Wood (Ed.), *Gendered relationships* (pp. 163–176). Mountain View, CA: Mayfield.

Huston, T. L., McHale, S. M., & Crouter, A. C. (1986). When the honeymoon's over: Changes in the marriage relationship over the first year. In R. Gilmour & S. W. Duck (Eds.), *The emerging field of personal relationships.* Hillsdale, NJ: Erlbaum.

Huston, T. L., Surra, C. A., Fitzgerald, N. M., & Cate, R. M. (1981). From courtship to marriage: Mate selection as an interpersonal process. In S. Duck & R. Gilmour (Eds.), *Personal relationships,*

2: *Developing personal relationships* (pp. 53–88). New York: Academic Press.

Indulgent "boomers" bring an unraveling of society. (1993, October 17). *Raleigh News and Observer*, p. 6E.

Ingrassia, M. (1993, August 30). Endangered family. *Newsweek*, pp. 16–26.

Inman, C. C. (1996). Friendships among men: Closeness in the doing. In J. T. Wood (Ed.), *Gendered relationships* (pp. 95–110). Mountain View, CA: Mayfield.

Issacson, W. (1989, November 20). Should gays have marriage rights? *Time*, pp. 101–102.

Jacobson, N. & Gottman, J. (1998). *When men batter women*. New York: Simon & Schuster.

James, K. (1989). When twos are really threes: The triangular dance in couple conflict. *Australian and New Zealand Journal of Family Therapy, 10*, 179–186.

Janeway, E. (1971). *Man's world, woman's place*. New York: Dell.

Johnson, D. J., & Rusbult, G. E. (1989). Resisting temptation: Devaluation of alternative partners as a means of maintaining commitment in close relationships. *Journal of Personality and Social Psychology, 57*, 967–980.

Johnson, F. (1989). Women's culture and communication: An analytic perspective. In C. M. Lont & S. A. Friedley (Eds.), *Beyond boundaries: Sex and gender diversity in communication*. Fairfax, VA: George Mason University Press.

Johnson, F. (1996). Friendships among women: Closeness in dialogue. In J. Wood (Ed.), *Gendered relationships* (pp. 79–94). Mountain View, CA: Mayfield.

Johnson, M. P. (1991). Commitment to personal relationships. In W. H. Jones & D. W. Perlman (Eds.), *Advances in personal relationships* (vol. 3, pp. 117–143). London: Jessica Kingsley.

Johnson, M., Huston, T., Gaines, S., Jr., & Levinger, G. (1992). Patterns of married life among young couples. *Journal of Social and Personal Relationships, 9*, 343–364.

Jones, E., & Gallois, C. (1989). Spouses' impressions of rules for communication in public and private marital conflicts. *Journal of Marriage and the Family, 51*, 957–967.

Jourard, S. M. (1971). *The transparent self*. New York: Van Nostrand.

Kanin, E. J., Davidson, K. D., & Scheck, S. R. (1970). A research note on male–female differentials in the experience of heterosexual love. *Journal of Sex Research, 6*, 64–72.

Kaplan, N., & Main, M. (1985, April). Internal representations of attachment at six years as indicated by family drawings and verbal responses to imagined separations. In M. Main (Chair), *Attachment: A move to the level of representation*. Symposium conducted at the meeting of the Society for Research in Child Development, Toronto, Canada.

Karpel, M. (1976). Individuation: From fusion to dialogue. *Family Process, 15*, 65–82.

Kayser, K. (1 993). *When love dies: The process of marital disaffection*. New York: Guilford.

Kelley, D. (1997). *Forgiveness as a turning point in intimate relationships*. Paper presented at the annual convention of the National Communication Association, Chicago.

Kelley, H. H. (1983). Love and commitment. In H. H. Kelley, E. Berscheid, A. Christensen, J. H. Harvey, T. L. Huston, G. Levinger, E. McClintock, I. A. Peplau, & D. R. Peterson (Eds.), *Close relationships* (pp. 265–314). San Francisco: Freeman.

Kelley, H. H., & Thibaut, J. W. (1978). *Interpersonal relations: A theory of interdependence.* New York: Wiley.

Kelly, G. A. (1955). *The psychology of personal constructs.* New York: Norton.

Kelly, G. A. (1969). Attribution theory in social psychology. In D. Levine (Ed.), *Nebraska symposium on motivation* (vol. 15, pp. 192–238). Lincoln: University of Nebraska Press.

Kelly, M. (1994, January–February). You can't always get done what you want. *Utne Reader,* pp. 62–66.

Kerckhoff, A. C., & Davis, K. E. (1962). Value consensus and need complementarity in mate selection. *American Sociological Review, 27,* 295–303.

Keyes, R. (1992, February 22). Do you have the time? *Parade,* pp. 22–25.

Klein, R., & Milardo, R. M. (1993). Third-party influence on the management of personal relationships. In S. W. Duck (Ed.), *Understanding relationship processes, 3: Social context and relationships* (pp. 55–77). Newbury Park, CA: Sage.

Knapp, M. L. (1978). *Social intercourse: From greeting to goodbye.* Boston: Allyn & Bacon.

Knapp, M. L. (1984). *Interpersonal communication and human relationships.* Boston: Allyn & Bacon.

Knapp, M. L., & Vangelisti, A. (1992). *Interpersonal communication and human relationships* (2nd ed.). Boston: Allyn & Bacon.

Kobak, R. R., & Sceery, A. (1988). Attachment in late adolescence: Working models, affect regulation, and representations of self and others. *Child Development, 59,* 135–146.

Kramarae, C. (1981). *Women and men speaking: Frameworks for analysis.* Rowley, MA: Newbury House.

Krupnick, C. G. (1985, May). Women and men in the classroom: Inequality and its remedies. *On Teaching and Learning. Journal of the Harvard-Danforth Center for Teaching and Learning,* pp. 18–25.

Kurdek, L. A., & Schmitt, J. P. (1986). Relationship quality of partners in heterosexual married, heterosexual cohabiting, and gay and lesbian relationships. *Journal of Personality and Social Psychology, 51,* 711–720.

Labov, W. (1972). *Sociolinguistic patterns.* Philadelphia: University of Pennsylvania Press.

Lacy, B. (1993, September 30). Nurturing their assets. *Raleigh News and Observer,* pp. 1E, 8E.

La Gaipa, J. J. (1982). Rituals of disengagement. In S. W. Duck (Ed.), *Personal relationships, 4: Dissolving personal relationships.* London: Academic Press.

La Gaipa, J. J. (1990). The negative effects of informal support systems. In S. W. Duck with R. C. Silver (Eds.), *Personal relationships and social support.* London: Sage.

Lakoff, R. (1990). *Talking power. The politics of language.* New York: Basic Books.

Landale, N., & Fennelly, K. (1992). Informal unions among mainland Puerto Ricans: Cohabitation or an alternative to legal marriage? *Journal of Marriage and the Family, 54,* 269–280.

Langer, S. K. (1953). *Feeling and form: A theory of art.* New York: Scribner's.

Langer, S. K. (1979). *Philosophy in a new key. A study in the symbolism of reason, rite and art* (3rd ed.). Cambridge, MA: Harvard University Press.

Lannaman, J. W. (1991). Interpersonal communication research as ideological practice. *Communication Theory, 1,* 179–203.

Lasswell, M., & Lobsenz, N. M. (1980). *Styles of loving.* New York: Doubleday.

Lasswell, T. E., & Lasswell, M. E. (1976). I love you but I'm not in love with you. *Journal of Marriage and Family Counseling, 38,* 211–224.

Lea, M., & Spears, R. (1995). Love at first byte: Relationships conducted over computer networks. In J. Wood & S. W. Duck (Eds.), *Understanding relationship processes, 6: Understudied relationships: Off the beaten track* (pp. 197–233). Newbury Park, CA: Sage.

Lederer, W. (1981). *Marital choices.* New York: Norton.

Lederer, W., & Jackson, D. (1968). *Mirages of marriage.* New York: Norton.

Lee, J. A. (1973). *The colours of love: An exploration of the ways of loving.* Don Mills, Ontario: New Press.

Lee, J. A. (1974, October). The styles of loving. *Psychology Today,* pp. 44–50.

Lee, J. A. (1988). Love-styles. In R. J. Sternberg & M. L. Barnes (Eds.), *The psychology of love* (pp. 38–67). New Haven, CT: Yale University Press.

Lee, L. (1984). Sequences in separation: A framework for investigating endings of the personal (romantic) relationship. *Journal of Social and Personal Relationships, 1,* 49–73.

Levinger, G. (1974). A three-level approach to attraction: Toward an understanding of pair relatedness. In T. L. Huyston (Ed.), *Foundations of interpersonal attraction* (pp. 100–120). New York: Academic Press.

Levinger, G. (1979). A social exchange view of the dissolution of pair relationships. In R. L. Burgess & T. L. Huston (Eds.), *Social exchange: Advances in theory and research.* New York: Academic Press.

Lewis, R. A. (1972). A developmental framework for the analysis of premarital dyadic formation. *Family Process, 1,* 17–48.

Lidz, T. (1976). *The person: His and her development throughout the life cycle* (rev. ed.). New York: Basic Books.

Lies told while courting. (1981, November). *Cosmopolitan,* p. 330.

Lin, Y., & Rusbult, C. (1993). *Commitment to dating relationships and cross-sex friendships in America and China: The impact of centrality of relationship, normative support, and investment model variables.* Unpublished manuscript, University of North Carolina at Chapel Hill.

Lloyd, S. A., & Cate, R. M. (1985). The developmental course of conflict in dissolution of premarital relationships. *Journal of Social and Personal Relationships, 2,* 179–194.

Lobsenz, N. M. (1970, April). Marriage talk. *Woman's Day,* pp. 18, 88–90.

Locke, K. D., & Horowitz, L. M. (1990). Satisfaction in interpersonal interactions as a function of similarity in level of dysphoria. *Journal of Personality and Social Psychology, 58,* 823–831.

Lott, B. (1989). Sexist discrimination as distancing behavior: II. Prime-time television. *Psychology of Women Quarterly, 13,* 341–355.

Luby, V., & Aron, A. (1990, July). A *prototype structuring of love, like, and being in love.* Paper presented at the Fifth International Conference on Personal Relationships, Oxford, England.

Lund, M. (1985). The development of investment and commitment scales for predicting continuity of personal relationships. *Journal of Social and Personal Relationships, 2,* 3–23.

Lyons, R., & Meade, D. (1995). Painting a new face on relationships: Relationship remodeling in response to chronic illness. In S. Duck & J. Wood (Eds.), *Understanding relationship processes, 5: Confronting relationship challenges* (pp. 150–180). Thousand Oaks, CA: Sage.

Macklin, E. D. (1978). Review of research on nonmarital cohabitation in the United States. In B. I. Murstein (Ed.), *Exploring intimate lifestyles* (pp. 197–243). New York: Springer-Verlag.

Macklin, E. D. (1980). Nontraditional family forms: A decade of research. *Journal of Marriage and the Family, 42,* 905–922.

Mahlstedt, D. (1992). *Female survivors of dating violence and their social networks.* Working paper.

Main, M. (1981). Avoidance in the service of attachment: A working paper. In K. Immelmann, G. Barlow, L. Petrenovich, & M. Main (Eds.), *Behavioral development: The Bielfield interdisciplinary project.* New York: Cambridge University Press.

Main, M., & George, C. (1985). Responses of abused and disadvantaged toddlers to distress in agemates: A study in the day-care setting. *Developmental Psychology, 21,* 407–412.

Maltz, D. N., & Borker, R. (1982). A cultural approach to male–female miscommunication. In J. J. Gumpertz (Ed.), *Language and social identity* (pp. 196–216). Cambridge, England: Cambridge University Press.

Margolin, L., & White, L. (1987). The continuing role of physical attractiveness in marriage. *Journal of Marriage and the Family, 49,* 21–28.

Markman, H. (1990). *Advances in understanding marital distress.* Unpublished manuscript, University of Denver.

Markman, H., Clements, M., & Wright, R. (1991, April). *Why father's pre-birth negativity and a first-born daughter predict marital problems: Results from a ten-year investigation.* Paper presented at a symposium at the biennial meeting of the Society for Research in Child Development, Seattle.

Marks, G., & Miller, N. (1982). Target attractiveness as a mediator of assumed attitude similarity. *Personality and Social Psychology Bulletin, 8,* 728–735.

Marriage builders get together. (1998, July 12). *Raleigh News and Observer,* p. 3B.

Martin, J., & Nakayama, T. (1997). *Intercultural communication in contexts.* Mountain View, CA: Mayfield.

Martin, R. W. (1991). Examining personal relationship thinking: The relational cognition complexity instrument. *Journal of Social and Personal Relationships, 8,* 467–480.

Martin, R. W. (1992). Relational cognition complexity and relational communication. *Communication Monographs, 59,* 150–163.

Maugh, T., II. (1998, 21 February). Happily ever after means doing things her way. *Raleigh News and Observer,* p. 11A.

May, R. (1969). *Love and will.* New York: Norton.

McCall, G. P (1970). The social organization of relationships. In G. J. McCall, M. M. McCall, N. K. Denzin, G. B. Suttles, & K. B. Kurth (Eds.), *Social relationships* (pp. 3–34). Chicago: Aldine.

McCall, G. J. (1982). Becoming unrelated: The management of bond dissolution. In S. Duck (Ed.), *Personal relationships 4: Dissolving personal relationships* (pp. 211–232). London: Academic Press.

McCall, G. J., & Simmons, J. L. (1966). *Identities and interactions.* New York: Free Press.

McCarthy, B. (1983, November). *Social cognition and personal relationships.* Paper presented to Lancaster University Relationships Group (cited in Duck, 1992).

McDonald, G. (1981). Structural exchange and marital interaction. *Journal of Marriage and the Family, 43,* 825–839.

McGee-Cooper, A., with Trammel, D., & Lau, B. (1992). *You don't have to go home from work exhausted!* New York: Bantam.

McGowen, K. R., & Hart, L. E. (1990). Still different after all these years: Gender differences in professional identity formation. *Professional Psychology. Research and Practice, 21,* 118–223.

Mead, G. H. (1934). *Mind, self, and society.* Chicago: University of Chicago Press.

Meerloo, J. A. M. (1952). *Conversation and communication.* New York: International Universities Press.

Mehrabian, A. (1976). *Public places, private spaces.* New York: Basic Books.

Mehrabian, A. (1981). *Silent messages: Implicit communication of emotion and attitudes* (2nd ed.). Belmont, CA: Wadsworth.

Meloy, R. (1998). *The psychology of stalking: Clinical and forensic perspectives.* New York: Academic Press.

Metts, S., & Cupach, W. (1990). The influence of relationship beliefs and problem-solving responses on satisfaction in romantic relationships. *Human Communication Research, 17,* 170–185.

Metts, S., Cupach, W., & Bejlovec, R. A. (1989). "I love you too much to ever start liking you": Redefining romantic relationships. *Journal of Social and Personal Relationships, 6,* 259–274.

Metts, S., Sprecher, S., & Cupach, W. R. (1991). Retrospective self-reports. In B. M. Montgomery & S. W. Duck (Eds.), *Studying interpersonal interaction* (pp. 162–178). New York: Guilford.

Miell, D. E. (1984). *Cognitive and communicative strategies in developing relationships.* Unpublished Ph.D. dissertation. University of Lancaster, England.

Miell, D. E. (1987). Remembering relationship development: Constructing a context for interactions. In R. Burnett, P. McGhee, & D. Clarke (Eds.), *Accounting for relationships.* London: Methuen.

Miell, D. E., & Duck, S. W. (1986). Strategies in developing friendship. In V. J.

Derlega & B. A. Winstead (Eds.), *Friendship and social interaction.* New York: Springer-Verlag.

Milardo, R. M., Johnson, M. P., & Huston, T. L. (1983). Developing close relationships: Changing patterns of interaction between pair members and social networks. *Journal of Personality and Social Psychology, 44,* 964–976.

Milbank, D. (1997, October 3). More dads raise families without mom. *Wall Street Journal,* pp. B1, B2.

Miller, J. B. (1986). *Toward a new psychology of women* (2nd ed.). Boston: Beacon.

Miller, J. B. (1993). Learning from early relationship experience. In S. W. Duck (Ed.), *Understanding relationship processes, 2: Learning about relationships* (pp. 1–29). Newbury Park, CA: Sage.

Miller, L., Berg, J., & Archer, R. (1983). Openers: Individuals who elicit intimate self-disclosure. *Journal of Personality and Social Psychology, 44,* 1234–1244.

Mills, J., & Clark, M. S. (1982). Communal and exchange relationships. In L. Wheeler (Ed.), *Review of personality and social psychology* (vol. 3, pp. 121–144). Beverly Hills, CA: Sage.

Mills, R. S. L., & Rubin, K. H. (1993). Parental ideas as influences on children's social competence. In S. W. Duck (Ed.), *Learning about relationships* (pp. 98–117). Newbury Park, CA: Sage.

Mirowsky, J., & Ross, C. E. (1986). Social patterns of distress. *Annual Review of Sociology, 12,* 23–45.

Monaghan, P. (1998, March 6). Beyond the Hollywood myths: Researchers examine stalkers and their victims. *Chronicle of Higher Education,* pp. A17, A20.

Monsour, M. (1992). Meanings of intimacy in cross- and same-sex friendships. *Journal of Social and Personal Relationships, 9,* 277–295.

Montgomery, B. (1992). Communication as the interface between couples and culture. In S. A. Deetz (Ed.), *Communication yearbook* (vol. 15, pp. 476–508). Newbury Park, CA: Sage.

Montgomery, B. (1993). Relationship maintenance versus relationship change: A dialectical dilemma. *Journal of Social and Personal Relationships, 10,* 205–224.

More fathers minding baby while mom works, study says. (1993, September 22). *Raleigh News and Observer,* p. 6A.

More women consider two kids just right. (1993, August 6). *Wall Street Journal,* p. B1.

Morrow, G., Clark, E., & Brock, K. (1995). Individual and partner love styles: Implications for the quality of romantic involvements. *Journal of Social and Personal Relationships, 12,* 363–387.

Muehlenhardt, C. L., & Linton, M. A. (1987). Date rape and sexual aggression in dating situations: Incidence and risk factors. *Journal of Counseling Psychology, 34,* 186–196.

Murphy-Milano, S. (1996). *Defending our lives.* New York: Anchor/Doubleday.

Murstein, B. (1997). On exchange theory, androcentrism, and sex stereotypy. *Psychological Reports, 81,* 1151–1162.

Naisbitt, J. (1982). *Megatrends: Ten new directions transforming our lives.* New York: Warner Publications.

Napier, A. Y. (1977). *The rejection-intrusion pattern: A central family dynamic.* Unpublished manuscript, University of Wisconsin-Madison, School of Family Resources.

National survey results of gay couples in long-lasting relationships. (1991). *Partners: Newsletter for Gay and Lesbian Couples,* pp. 1–16.

Neimeyer, G. J. (1984). Cognitive complexity and marital satisfaction. *Journal of Social and Clinical Psychology, 2,* 258–263.

Newcomb, T. M. (1961). *The acquaintance process.* New York: Holt, Rinehart & Winston.

Nias, D. K. B. (1979). Marital choice: Matching or complementation. In M. Cook & G. Wilson (Eds.), *Love and attraction* (pp. 151–155). Oxford, England: Pergamon.

Noller, P. (1982). Channel consistency and inconsistency in the communications of married couples. *Journal of Personality and Social Psychology, 43,* 732–741.

Noller, P. (1985). Negative communications in marriage. *Journal of Social and Personal Relationships, 2,* 289–301.

Norton, A. J. (1987, July–August). Families and children in the year 2000. *Children Today,* pp. 6–9.

Norton, A. J., & Mooman, J. E. (1987). Current trends in marriage and divorce among American women. *Journal of Marriage and the Family, 49,* 3–14.

Notarius, C. I. (1996). Marriage: Will I be happy or will I be sad? In N. Vanzetti & S. Duck (Eds.), *A lifetime of relationships* (pp. 265–289). Pacific Grove, CA: Brooks/Cole.

O'Connell, L. (1984). An exploration of exchange in three social relationships: Kinship, friendship, and the marketplace. *Journal of Social and Personal Relationships, 1,* 333–346.

O'Connor, P. (1992). *Friendships between women.* London: Harvester-Wheatsheaf.

Ognibene, T., & Collins, N. (1998). Adult attachment styles, perceived social support, and coping strategies. *Journal of Social and Personal Relationships, 15,* 323–345.

Okin, S. M. (1989). *Justice, gender, and the family.* New York: Basic Books.

Oring, E. (1984). Dyadic transitions. *Journal of Folklore Research, 21,* 19–28.

Orion, D. (1997). *I know you really love me: A psychiatrist's journal of erotomania, stalking, and obsessive love*. New York: Macmillan.

Orvis, B. R., Kelley, H. H., & Butler, D. (1976). Attributional conflict in young couples. In J. H. Harvey, W. J. Ickes, & R. E. Kidd (Eds.), *New directions in attribution research* (vol. 1, pp. 353–386). Hillsdale, NJ: Erlbaum.

Owen, W. F. (1984). Interpretive themes in relational communication. *Quarterly Journal of Speech, 70*, 274–387.

Parke, R., & Kellam, S. (Eds.). (1994). *Exploring family relationships with other social contexts*. Hillsdale, NJ: Erlbaum.

Parks, M. R., & Adelman, M. B. (1983). Communication networks and the development of romantic relationships: An expansion of uncertainty reduction theory. *Human Communication Research, 10*, 55–79.

Patterson, C. (1992). Children of gay and lesbian parents. *Child Development, 63*, 85–96.

Patterson, M. L. (1976). An arousal model of interpersonal intimacy. *Psychological Review, 83*, 235–245.

Patterson, M. L. (1984). Intimacy, social control, and nonverbal involvement: A functional approach. In V. J. Derlega (Ed.), *Communication, intimacy and close relationships* (pp. 105–132). Orlando, FL: Academic Press.

Patterson, M. L. (1988). Functions of nonverbal behavior in close relationships. In S. W. Duck, D. F. Hay, S. E. Hobfoll, W. J. Ickes, & B. M. Montgomery (Eds.), *Handbook of personal relationships* (pp. 467–486). Chichester, England: Wiley.

Patton, B. R., & Ritter, B. (1976). *Living together: Female–male communication*. Columbus, OH: Merrill.

Paul, E., & White, K. (1990). The development of intimate relationships in late adolescence. *Adolescence, 25*, 375–400.

Petronio, S. (1991). Communication boundary management: A theoretical model of managing disclosure of private information between married couples. *Communication Theory, 1*, 311–335.

Phillips, G. M., & Wood, J. T. (1983). *Communication and human relationships: The study of interpersonal communication*. New York: Macmillan.

Pike, G., & Sillars, A. (1985). Reciprocity of marital communication. *Journal of Social and Personal Relationships, 2*, 303–324.

Planalp, S. (1985). Relational schemata: A test of alternative forms of relational knowledge as guides to communication. *Human Communication Research, 12*, 3–29.

Planalp, S., Rutherford, D. K., & Honeycutt, J. M. (1988). Events that increase uncertainty in personal relationships II: Replication and extension. *Human Communication Research, 14*, 516–547.

Pleck, J. H. (1987). American fathering in historical perspective. In M. S. Kimmel (Ed.), *Changing men: New directions in research on men and masculinity* (pp. 83–97). Newbury Park, CA: Sage.

The power of invention. (1997–1998, Winter). *Newsweek Extra* (special edition).

Prins, K. S., Buunk, B. P., & VanYperen, N. W. (1993). Equity, normative disapproval, and extramarital relationships. *Journal of Social and Personal Relationships, 10*, 39–54.

Prusank, D. T., Duran, R. L., & DeLillo, D. A. (1993). Interpersonal relationships in women's magazines: Dating and relating in the 1970s and 1980s. *Journal of Social and Personal Relationships, 10*, 307–320.

Pryor, J. B., & Merluzzi, T. V. (1985). The role of expertise in processing social interaction scripts. *Journal of Experimental Social Psychology, 21*, 362–379.

Ptacek, J. (1988). Why do men batter their wives? In K. Yilo & M. Bograd (Eds.), *Feminist perspectives on wife abuse* (pp. 133–157). Newbury Park, CA: Sage.

Public pillow talk. (1987, October). *Psychology Today*, p. 18.

Putallaz, M., Costanzo, P. R., & Klein, P. K. (1993). Parental childhood social experiences and their effects on children's relationships. In S. W. Duck (Ed.), *Understanding relationship processes, 2: Learning about relationships* (pp. 63–97). Newbury Park, CA: Sage.

Ragan, S. L. (1989). Communication between the sexes: A consideration of differences in adult communication. In J. F. Nussbaum (Ed.), *Life-span communication: Normative processes* (pp. 179–193). Hillsdale, NJ: Erlbaum.

Rawlins, W. R. (1989). A dialectical analysis of the tensions, functions, and strategic challenges of communication in young adult friendships. In J. Anderson (Ed.), *Communication yearbook* (vol. 12, pp. 157–189). Newbury Park, CA: Sage.

Rawlins, W. R. (1992). *Friendship matters: Communication, dialectics, and the life course*. New York: de Gruyter.

Rechtschaffen, S. (1994, January–February). Why an empty hour scares us. *Utne Reader*, pp. 64–65.

Reis, H. T. (1984). Social interaction and well-being. In S. W. Duck (Ed.), *Personal relationships, 5: Repairing personal relationships*. London and New York: Academic Press.

Reis, H. T., & Shaver, P. (1988). Intimacy as an interpersonal process. In S. W. Duck (Ed.), *Handbook of personal relationships: Theory, research and interventions* (pp. 367–389). New York: Wiley.

Reissman, C., Aron, A., & Bergen, M. (1993). Shared activities and marital satisfaction: Causal direction and self-expansion versus boredom. *Journal of Social and Personal Relationships, 10*, 243–254.

Repetti, R. L. (1989). The effects of daily workload on subsequent behavior during marital interaction: The roles of social withdrawal and spouse support. *Journal of Personality and Social Psychology, 57*, 651–659.

Repetti, R. L. (1992). Social withdrawal as a short-term coping response to daily stressors. In H. S. Friedman (Ed.), *Hostility, coping and health*. Washington, DC: American Psychological Association.

Riessman, C. (1990). *Divorce talk: Women and men make sense of personal relationships*. New Brunswick, NJ: Rutgers University Press.

Risman, B. J. (1989). Can men mother? Life as a single father. In B. J. Risman & P. Schwartz (Eds.), *Gender in intimate relationships* (pp. 155–164). Belmont, CA: Wadsworth.

Roberts, L. J., & Krokoff, L. L. (1990). A time-series analysis of withdrawal, hostility, and displeasure in satisfied and dissatisfied marriages. *Journal of Marriage and the Family, 52*, 95–105.

Rohlfing, M. (1995). "Doesn't anybody stay in one place anymore?" An exploration of the understudied phenomenon of long-distance relationships. In J. Wood & S. Duck (Eds.), *Understanding relationship processes, 6: Understudied relationships: Off the beaten track* (pp. 173–196). Newbury Park, CA: Sage.

Roloff, M., & Cloven, D. (1994). When partners transgress: Maintaining violated relationships. In D. Canary & L. Stafford (Eds.), *Communication and relational maintenance* (pp. 23–44). New York: Academic Press.

Rook, K. S. (1987). Reciprocity of social exchange and social satisfaction among older women. *Journal of Personality and Social Psychology, 52*, 145–154.

Rose, S., & Frieze, I. H. (1989). Young singles' scripts for a first date. *Gender and Society*, 3, 258–268.

Rosenbaum, M. E. (1986). The repulsion hypothesis: On the nondevelopment of relationships. *Journal of Personality and Social Psychology*, 51, 1156–1166.

Rosewicz, B. (1996, September 10). Here comes the bride . . . and for the umpteenth time. *Wall Street Journal*, pp. B1, B14.

Rothenburg, P. (Ed.). (1995). *Race, class and gender in the United States*. New York: St. Martin's.

Rousar, E. E., III, & Aron, A. (1990, July). *Valuing, altruism, and the concept of love*. Paper presented at the Fifth International Conference on Personal Relationships, Oxford, England.

Routine of marriage seems part of positive bond. (1985, February 17). *Raleigh News and Observer*, p. 6C.

Rubin, L. (1985). *Just friends: The role of friendship in our lives*. New York: Harper & Row.

Rubin, Z., Peplau, L. A., & Hill, C. T. (1981). Loving and leaving: Sex differences in romantic attachments. *Sex Roles*, 7, 821–835.

Rubinson, L., & DeRubertis, L. (1991). Trends in sexual attitudes and behaviors of a college population over a 15-year period. *Journal of Sex Education and Therapy*, 17, 32–42.

Ruddick, S. (1989). *Maternal thinking. Toward a politics of peace*. New York: Ballantine.

Rusbult, C. (1980a). Commitment and satisfaction in romantic associations: A test of the investment model. *Journal of Experimental Social Psychology*, 16, 172–186.

Rusbult, C. (1980b). Satisfaction and commitment in friendships. *Representative Research in Social Psychology*, 11, 96–105.

Rusbult, C. (1987). Responses to dissatisfaction in close relationships: The exit-voice-loyalty-neglect model. In D. Perlman & S. W. Duck (Eds.), *Intimate relationships: Development, dynamics, deterioration* (pp. 209–238). London: Sage.

Rusbult, C. E. (1983). A longitudinal test of the investment model: The development (and deterioration) of satisfaction and commitment in heterosexual involvement. *Journal of Personality and Social Psychology*, 45, 101–117.

Rusbult, C., & Buunk, B. (1993). Commitment processes in close relationships: An interdependence analysis. *Journal of Social and Personal Relationships*, 10, 175–204.

Rusbult, C., Drigotas, S., & Verette, J. (1994). The investment model: An interdependence analysis of commitment processes and relationship maintenance phenomena. In D. Canary & L. Stafford (Eds.), *Communication and relational maintenance* (pp. 115–140). New York: Academic Press.

Rusbult, C. E., Johnson, D. J., & Morrow, G. D. (1986). Impact of couple patterns of problem solving on distress and nondistress in dating relationships. *Journal of Personality and Social Psychology*, 50, 744–753.

Rusbult, C. E., & Zembrodt, I. M. (1983). Responses to dissatisfaction in romantic involvement: A multidimensional scaling analysis. *Journal of Experimental Social Psychology*, 19, 274–293.

Rusbult, C. E., Zembrodt, I. M., & Gunn, L. K. (1982). Exit, voice, loyalty, and neglect: Responses to dissatisfaction in romantic involvements. *Journal of Personality and Social Psychology*, 43, 1230–1242.

Rusbult, C. E., Zembrodt, I. M., & Iwaniszek, J. (1986). The impact of gender and sex-role orientation on responses to dissatisfaction in close relationships. *Sex Roles*, 15, 1–20.

Rusk, T., & Rusk, N. (1988). *Mind traps: Change your mind, change your life.* Los Angeles: Price Stern Sloan.

Sachs, D. H. (1976). The effects of similarity, evaluation, and self-esteem on interpersonal attraction. *Representative Research in Social Psychology, 7,* 44–50.

Sadker, M., & Sadker, D. (1994). *Failing at fairness: How our schools cheat girls.* New York: Simon & Schuster.

Safran, I. C. (1979, January). Troubles that pull couples apart: A *Redbook* report. *Redbook,* pp. 138–141.

Sager, C. (1976). *Marriage contracts and couple therapy. Hidden forces in intimate relationships.* New York: Brunner/Mazel.

Sallinen-Kuparinen, A. (1992). Teacher communicator style. *Communication Education, 41,* 153–166.

Samovar, L., & Porter, R. (Eds.). (1997). *Intercultural communication: A reader* (8th ed.). Belmont, CA: Wadsworth.

Satir, V. (1967). *Conjoint family therapy.* Palo Alto, CA: Science and Behavior Books.

Scarf, M. (1987). *Intimate partners: Patterns in love and marriage.* New York: Random House.

Schaef, A. W. (1981). *Women's reality.* St. Paul, MN: West.

Schafer, R. B., & Keith, P. M. (1980). Equity and depression among married couples. *Social Psychology Quarterly, 43,* 430–435.

Schak, D. C. (1974). *Dating and mate selection in modern Taiwan.* Taipei, Taiwan: Orient Cultural Service.

Schank, R. C. (1982). *Dynamic memory. A theory of reminding and learning in computers and people.* Cambridge, England: Cambridge University Press.

Scharfe, E., & Bartholomew, K. (1995). Accommodation and attachment representations in young couples. *Journal of Social and Personal Relationships, 12,* 389–402.

Schneider, B. E., & Gould, M. (1987). Female sexuality: Looking back into the future. In B. B. Hess & M. M. Feree (Eds.), *Analyzing gender. A handbook of social science research* (pp. 120–153). Newbury Park, CA: Sage.

Schwartz, T. (1989, January–February). Acceleration syndrome: Does everyone live in the fast lane nowadays? *Utne Reader,* pp. 36–43.

Schwarzer, R., & Leppin, A. (1991). Social support and health: A theoretical and empirical overview. *Journal of Social and Personal Relationships, 8,* 99–128.

Searle, J. (1976). *Speech acts: An essay in the philosophy of language.* Cambridge, England: Cambridge University Press.

Segrin, C. (1993). Interpersonal reactions to dysphoria: The role of relationship with partner and perceptions of rejection. *Journal of Social and Personal Relationships, 10,* 83–97.

Seligman, M. E. P. (1990). *Learned optimism.* New York: Simon & Schuster/Pocket.

Seligmann, J. (1990, Winter–Spring). Variations on a theme. *Newsweek Special Edition,* pp. 38–46.

Senchak, M., & Leonard, K. E. (1992). Attachment styles and marital adjustment among newly-wed couples. *Journal of Social and Personal Relationships, 9,* 51–64.

Sexism in the schoolhouse. (1992, February 24). *Newsweek,* p. 62.

Shaver, K. G. (1985). *The attribution of blame.* New York: Springer-Verlag.

Shea, B. C., & Pearson, J. C. (1986). The effects of relationship type, partner intent, and gender on the selection of relationship maintenance strategies. *Communication Monographs, 53,* 352–364.

Sheehan, J. (1996, February). Kiss and well. *Longevity*, pp. 50–51, 93.

Shellenbarger, S. (1993a, December 6). As more pregnant women work, bias complaints rise. *Wall Street Journal*, pp. B1, B2.

Shellenbarger, S. (1993b, December 14). Some thrive, but many wilt working at home. *Wall Street Journal*, pp. B1, B6.

Shellenbarger, S. (1996, February 21). More men move past incompetence defense to share housework. *Wall Street Journal*, p. B1.

Sher, T. G. (1996). Courtship and marriage: Choosing a primary partner. In N. Vanzetti & S. Duck (Eds.), *A lifetime of relationships* (pp. 243–264). Pacific Grove, CA: Brooks/Cole.

Sherrod, D. (1989). The influence of gender on same-sex friendships. In C. Hendrick (Ed.), *Close relationships* (pp. 164–186). Newbury Park, CA: Sage.

Shotter, J. (1993). *Conversational realities: The construction of life through language.* Newbury Park, CA: Sage.

Siegert, J., & Stamp, G. (1994). "Our first big fight" as a milestone in the development of close relationships. *Communication Monographs, 61*, 345–360.

Silberstein, L. (1992). *Dual-career marriage: A system in transition.* Hillsdale, NJ: Erlbaum.

Sillars, A., Burggraf, C., Yost, S., & Zietlow, P. (1992). Conversational themes and marital relationship definitions. *Human Communication Research, 19*, 124–154.

Simon, E. P., & Baxter, L. A. (1993). Attachment style differences in relationship maintenance strategies. *Western Journal of Communication, 57*, 416–430.

Simpson, J. (1987). The dissolution of romantic relationships: Factors involved in relationship stability and emotional distress. *Journal of Personality and Social Psychology, 53*, 683–692.

Skolnick, A. (1981). *The intimate environment. Exploring marriage and the family* (2nd ed.). Boston: Little, Brown.

Smeaton, G., Byrne, D., & Murnen, S. K. (1989). The repulsion hypothesis revisited: Similarity irrelevance or dissimilarity bias? *Journal of Personality and Social Psychology, 56*, 54–59.

Snell, W. E., Jr., Hawkins, R. C., II, & Belk, S. S. (1988). Stereotypes about male sexuality and the use of social influence strategies in intimate relationships. *Journal of Clinical and Social Psychology, 7*, 42–48.

Snow, D., Robinson, C., & McCall, P. (1991, January). "Cooling out" men in singles bars and night clubs: Observations of the survival strategies of women in public places. *Journal of Contemporary Ethnography, 19*, 423–449.

Specialty magazines are hot issues today. (1993, September 6). *Raleigh News and Observer*, p. 10C.

Spelman, E. V. (1988). *Inessential woman: Problems of exclusion in feminist thought.* Boston: Beacon.

Spencer, T. (1994). Transforming relationships through ordinary talk. In S. W. Duck (Ed.), *Understanding relationship processes, 4: Dynamics of relationships* (pp. 58–85). Thousand Oaks, CA: Sage.

Spitzberg, B., Nicastro, A., & Cousins, A. (1998). Exploring the interactional phenomenon of stalking and obsessive relational intrusion. *Communication Reports, 11*, 33–47.

Sprecher, S. (1986). The relation between equity and emotions in close relationships. *Social Psychology Bulletin, 49*, 309–321.

Sprecher, S. (1987). The effects of self-disclosure given and received on affection for an intimate partner and stability of the relationship. *Journal of Social and Personal Relationships, 4*, 115–127.

Sprecher, S., & Metts, S. (1989). Development of the "Romantic Beliefs Scale" and examination of the effects of gender and gender-role orientation. *Journal of Social and Personal Relationships, 6,* 387–411.

Springen, K. (1998, July 13). Matchmaker, matchmaker, find me a web site . . . *Newsweek,* p. 12.

Stafford, L., & Canary, D. J. (1991). Maintenance strategies and romantic relationship type, gender, and relational characteristics. *Journal of Social and Personal Relationships, 8,* 217–242.

Stafford, L., & Kline, S. (1996). Women's surnames and titles: Men's and women's views. *Communication Research Reports, 13,* 214–224.

Stamp, G. H. (1992). *Toward generative family theory. Dialectical tensions within family life.* Paper presented at the Speech Communication Association Meeting, Chicago.

Stein, C. (1993). Felt obligation in adult family relationships. In S. Duck (Ed.), *Understanding relationship processes, 3: Social context and relationships* (pp. 78–99). Newbury Park, CA: Sage.

Steinberg, L., & Silverberg, S. B. (1987). Influences on marital satisfaction during the middle stages of the family life cycle. *Journal of Marriage and the Family, 49,* 751–760.

Stern, M., & Karraker, K. H. (1989). Sex stereotyping of infants: A review of gender labeling studies. *Sex Roles, 20,* 501–522.

Sternberg, R. J. (1986). A triangular theory of love. *Psychological Review, 93,* 119–135.

Sternberg, R. J. (1987). Liking versus loving: A comparative evaluation of theories. *Psychological Bulletin, 102,* 331–345.

Sternberg, R. J., & Barnes, M. (1985). Real and ideal others in romantic relationships: Is four a crowd? *Journal of Personality and Social Psychology, 49,* 1589–1596.

Sternberg, R., & Hojjat, M. (1997). (Eds.). *Satisfaction in close relationships.* New York: Guilford.

Stets, J. E. (1990). Verbal and physical aggression in marriage. *Journal of Marriage and the Family, 52,* 501–514.

Stets, J. E., & Straus, M. A. (1989). The marriage license as a hitting license: A comparison of assaults in dating, cohabiting, and married couples. *Journal of Family Violence, 41,* 33–52.

Stewart, A., Copeland, A., Chester, N., Malley, J., & Barenbaum, N. (1997). *Separating together.* New York: Guilford.

Strikwerda, R. A., & May, L. (1992). Male friendship and intimacy. In L. May & R. A. Strikwerda (Eds.), *Rethinking masculinity. Philosophical explorations in light of feminism* (pp. 95–110). Lanham, MD: Rowman & Littlefield.

Strong, S. R., Hills, H. J., Kilmartin, C. T., DeVries, H., Lanier, K., Nelson, B. N., Strickland, D., & Meyer, C. W., III (1988). The dynamic relations among interpersonal behaviors: A test of complementarity and anticomplementarity. *Journal of Personality and Social Psychology, 54,* 798–810.

Students provide pointers. (1983, February 17). *Daily Tarheel,* p. 7.

Suitor, J. J. (1991). Marital quality and satisfaction with the division of household labor across the family life cycle. *Journal of Marriage and the Family, 53,* 221–230.

Sunnafrank, M. (1991). Review of the attraction paradigm. In J. Anderson (Ed.), *Communication yearbook, 14,* 451–483. Newbury Park, CA: Sage.

Sunnafrank, M., & Miller, G. R. (1981). The role of initial conversations in determining attraction to similar and dissimilar strangers. *Human Communication Research, 8,* 16–25.

Surra, C. A. (1985). Courtship types: Variations in interdependence between partners and social networks. *Journal of Personality and Social Psychology, 49,* 357–375.

Surra, C. A. (1987). Reasons for changes in commitment: Variations by courtship style. *Journal of Social and Personal Relationships, 4,* 17–33.

Surra, C. A. (1990). Research and theory on mate selection and premarital relationships in the 1980s. *Journal of Marriage and the Family, 52,* 844–865.

Surra, C., Arizzi, P., & Asmussen, L. (1988). The association between reasons for commitment and the development and outcome of marital relationships. *Journal of Social and Personal Relationships, 5,* 47–64.

Surra, C. A., & Bohman, T. (1991). The development of close relationships: A cognitive perspective. In G. J. Fletcher & F. D. Fincham (Eds.), *Cognition in close relationships* (pp. 281–306). Hillsdale, NJ: Erlbaum.

Surra, C., & Huston, T. (1987). Mate selection as a social transition. In D. Perlman & S. Duck (Eds.), *Intimate relations* (pp. 88–120). Newbury Park, CA: Sage.

Surra, C., & Milardo, R. (1991). The social psychological context of developing relationships: Interactive and psychological networks. In W. H. Jones & D. Perlman (Eds.), *Advances in personal relationships* (vol. 3, pp. 1–36). London: Jessica Kingsley.

Swain, S. (1989). Covert intimacy: Closeness in men's friendships. In B. J. Risman & P. Schwartz (Eds.), *Gender in intimate relationships* (pp. 71–86). Belmont, CA: Wadsworth.

Swann, W. B. (1987). Identity negotiation: Where two roads meet. *Journal of Personality and Social Psychology, 53,* 1038–1051.

Szinovatz, M. E. (1984). Changing family roles and interactions. In B. B. Hess & M. B. Sussman (Eds.), *Women and the family. Two decades of change* (pp. 164–201). New York: Hawthorne.

Tannen, D. (1990). *You just don't understand: Women and men in conversation.* New York: Morrow.

Tavris, C. (1992). *The mismeasure of woman.* New York: Simon & Schuster.

Texier, C. (1990, April 22). Have women surrendered in MTV's battle of the sexes? *New York Times,* pp. H29, H31.

That loving feeling: It's all in your mind. (1993, July 27). *Raleigh News and Observer,* pp. 1E, 5E.

Thibaut, J. W., & Kelley, H. H. (1959). *The social psychology of groups.* New York: Wiley.

Thomas, E. (1977). *Marital communication and decision making.* New York: Free Press.

Thompson, E. H., Jr. (1991). The maleness of violence in dating relationships: An appraisal of stereotypes. *Sex Roles, 24,* 261–278.

Thompson, L., & Walker, A. J. (1989). Gender in families: Women and men in marriage, work, and parenthood. *Journal of Marriage and the Family, 51,* 845–871.

Titus, S. L. (1980). A function of friendship: Social comparisons as a frame of reference for marriage. *Human Relations, 33,* 409–431.

Toffler, A. (1970). *Future shock.* New York: Random House.

Toffler, A. (1980). *The third wave.* New York: Morrow.

Trenholm, S., & Jensen, A. (1992). *Interpersonal communication* (2nd ed.). Belmont, CA: Wadsworth.

Tucker, M. B., & Mitchell-Kernan, C. (1995). Social structural and psychological correlates of interethnic dating. *Jour-*

nal of Social and Personal Relationships, 12, 341–362.

Van Lear, C. A. (1987). The formation of social relationships: A longitudinal study of social penetration. *Human Communication Research, 13,* 310–322.

Van Lear, C. A. (1992). Testing a cyclical model of communicative openness in relationship development: Two longitudinal studies. *Communication Monographs, 58,* 337–361.

VanYperen, N., & Buunk, B. (1990). A longitudinal study of equity and satisfaction in intimate relationships. *European Journal of Social Psychology, 20,* 287–309.

Vuchinich, S. (1987). Starting and stopping spontaneous family conflicts. *Journal of Marriage and the Family, 43,* 785–788.

Wallerstein, J. (1995). *The good marriage: How and why love lasts.* Boston: Houghton Mifflin.

Walsh, F. (1993). Conceptualization of normal family processes. In F. Walsh (Ed.), *Normal family processes* (2nd ed., pp. 3–69). New York: Guilford.

Wamboldt, F. S., & Reiss, D. (1989). Defining a family heritage and a new relationship identity: Two central tasks in the making of a marriage. *Family Process, 28,* 317–335.

Watzlawick, P. J., Beavin, J., & Jackson, D. (1967). *Pragmatics of human communication: A study of interactional patterns, pathologies, and paradoxes.* New York: Norton.

Weber, A. (1983, May). *The breakdown of relationships.* Paper presented to the conference on Social Interaction and Relationships, Nags Head, NC.

Weedon, C. (1987). *Feminist practice and poststructuralist theory.* New York: Basil Blackwell.

Wegner, D., Raymond, P., & Erber, R. (1990). Transactive memory in personal

relationships. *Journal of Personality and Social Psychology, 61,* 923–929.

Weiss, R. S. (1969). The fund of sociability. *Transaction, 7,* 36–43.

Wegner, D. M., Erber, R., & Raymond, P. (1991). Transactive memory in close relationships. *Journal of Personality and Social Psychology, 61,* 923–929.

Wellman, B., & Wellman, B. (1992). Domestic affairs and network relations. *Journal of Social and Personal Relationships, 9,* 385–409.

Werman, R. (1992). *Notes from a sealed room.* Carbondale: Southern Illinois University Press.

Werner, C., Altman, I., Brown, B., & Ginat, J. (1993). Celebrations in personal relationships: A transactional/dialectical perspective. In S. Duck (Ed.), *Social contexts of relationships* (pp. 109–138). Newbury Park, CA: Sage.

Werner, C., Altman, I., & Oxley, D. (1985). Temporal·aspects of homes: A transactional perspective. In I. Altman & C. M. Werner (Eds.), *Home environments, Vol. 8: Human behavior and environment: Advances in theory and research* (pp. 1–32). Beverly Hills, CA: Sage.

Werner, C., Brown, B., Altman, I., & Staples, B. (1992). Close relationships in their physical and social contexts: A transactional perspective. *Journal of Social and Personal Relationships, 9,* 411–431.

Werner, C. M., & Haggard, I. M. (1985). Temporal qualities of interpersonal relationships. In G. R. Miller & M. L. Knapp (Eds.), *Handbook of interpersonal communication* (pp. 59–99). Beverly Hills, CA: Sage.

Werner, C. M., Peterson-Lewis, S., & Brown, B. B. (1989). Inferences about homeowners' sociability: Impact of Christmas decorations and other cues. *Journal of Environmental Psychology, 9,* 279–296.

West, C., & Zimmerman, D. (1983). Small insults: A study of interruptions in cross-sex conversations between unacquainted persons. In B. Thorne, C. Kramarae, & N. Henley (Eds.), *Language, gender, and society* (pp. 103–117). Rowley, MA: Newbury House.

West, J. T. (1995). Understanding how the dynamics of ideology influence violence between intimates. In S. W. Duck & J. T. Wood (Eds.), *Understanding relationship processes, 5: Confronting relationship challenges* (pp. 129–149). Newbury Park, CA: Sage.

Weston, K. (1991). *Families we choose.* New York: Columbia University Press.

Wexler, J., & Steidl, J. (1978). Marriage and the capacity to be alone. *Psychiatry, 41,* 72–82.

Whitbeck, L. B., & Hoyt, D. R. (1994). Social prestige and assortive mating: A comparison of students from 1956 and 1988. *Journal of Social and Personal Relationships, 11,* 137–145.

White, B. (1989). Gender differences in marital communication patterns. *Family Process, 28,* 89–106.

White, G. L. (1980). Physical attractiveness and courtship progress. *Journal of Personality and Social Psychology, 39,* 660–668.

White, J., & Bondurant, B. (1996). Gendered violence in intimate relationships. In J. T. Wood (Ed.), *Gendered relationships* (pp. 197–212). Mountain View, CA: Mayfield.

Wilkie, J. R. (1991). The decline in men's labor force participation and income and the changing structure of family economic support. *Journal of Marriage and the Family, 53,* 111–122.

Willis, L. (1994, January 25). Group will examine relationship violence. *Raleigh News and Observer,* p. 3B.

Wilmot, W. W. (1987). *Dyadic communication.* New York: Random House

Wilmot, W. W. (1994). Relationship rejuvenation. In D. Canary & L. Stafford (Eds.), *Communication and relational maintenance* (pp. 255–274). New York: Academic Press.

Wilmot, W. W., & Stevens, D. C. (1994). Relationship rejuvenation: Arresting decline in personal relationships. In D. Conville (Ed.), *Uses of structure in communication studies* (pp. 103–124). Westport, CT: Praeger.

Wiseman, J. P. (1986). Friendship: Bonds and binds in a voluntary relationship. *Journal of Social and Personal Relationships, 3,* 191–211.

Wood, J. T. (1982). Communication and relational culture: Bases for the study of human relationships. *Communication Quarterly, 30,* 75–84.

Wood, J. T. (1986). Different voices in relationship crises: An extension of Gilligan's theory. *American Behavioral Scientist, 29,* 273–301.

Wood, J. T. (1992). *Spinning the symbolic web: Human communication as symbolic interaction.* Norwood, NJ: Ablex.

Wood, J. T. (1993a). Diversity and commonality: Sustaining their tension in communication courses. *Western Journal of Communication, 57,* 367–380.

Wood, J. T. (1993b). Engendered relations: Interaction, caring, power, and responsibility in intimacy. In S. W. Duck (Ed.), *Understanding relationship processes, 3: Social context and relationships* (pp. 26–54). Newbury Park, CA: Sage.

Wood, J. T. (1993c). Enlarging conceptual boundaries: A critique of research on interpersonal communication. In S. P. Bowen & N. J. Wyatt (Eds.), *Transforming visions: Feminist critiques in communication studies* (pp. 19–49). Cresskill, NJ: Hampton.

Wood, J. T. (1993d). Gender and moral voice: From woman's nature to standpoint theory. *Women's Studies in Communication, 15,* 1–24.

Wood, J. T. (1994a). Engendered identities: Shaping voice and mind through gender. In D. Vocate (Ed.), *Intrapersonal communication: Different voices, different minds* (pp. 145–167). Hillsdale, NJ: Erlbaum.

Wood, J. T. (1994b). Gender and relationship crises: Contrasting reasons, responses, and relational orientations. In J. Ringer (Ed.), *Queer words, queer images: The construction of homosexuality* (pp. 238–264). New York: New York University Press.

Wood, J. T. (1994c). Gender, communication, and culture. In L. Samovar & R. Porter (Eds.), *Intercultural communication: A reader* (7th ed.) (pp. 155–164). Belmont, CA: Wadsworth.

Wood, J. T. (1994d). *Who cares? Women, care and culture.* Carbondale: Southern Illinois University Press.

Wood, J. T. (1995). Feminist scholarship and research on personal relationships. *Journal of Social and Personal Relationships, 12,* 103–120.

Wood, J. T. (Ed.). (1996). *Gendered relationships.* Mountain View, CA: Mayfield.

Wood, J. T. (1997). Diversity in dialogue: Communication between friends. In J. Makau & R. Arnett (Eds.), *Ethics of communication in an age of diversity* (pp. 5–26). Urbana: University of Illinois Press.

Wood, J. T. (1998a). An exchange about exchange: A reply to Bernard Murstein. *Psychological Reports, 82,* 1057–1058.

Wood, J. T. (1998b). *But I thought you meant . . . : Misunderstandings in human communication.* Mountain View, CA: Mayfield.

Wood, J. T. (1998c). Ethics, justice, and the "private sphere." *Women's Studies in Communication, 21,* 127–140.

Wood, J. T. (1999). *Gendered lives: Communication, gender and culture* (3rd ed). Belmont, CA: Wadsworth.

Wood, J. T., & Cox, J. R. (1993). Rethinking critical voice: Materiality and situated knowledges. *Western Journal of Communication, 57,* 278–287.

Wood, J. T., Dendy, L., Dordek, E., Germany, M., & Varallo, S. (1994). Dialectic of difference: A thematic analysis of intimates' meanings for differences. In K. Carter & M. Presnell (Eds.), *Interpretive approaches to interpersonal communication* (pp. 115–136). New York: SUNY Press.

Wood, J. T., & Duck, S. W. (Eds.). (1995). *Understanding relationship processes, 6: Understudied relationships: Off the beaten track.* Newbury Park. CA: Sage.

Wood, J. T., & Inman, C. C. (1993). In a different mode: Masculine styles of communicating closeness. *Journal of Applied Communication Research, 21,* 279–295.

Wood, J. T., & Lenze, L. F. (1991). Strategies to enhance gender sensitivity in communication education. *Communication Education, 40,* 16–21.

Wright, P. H. (1978). Toward a theory of friendship based on a conception of the self. *Human Communication Research, 4,* 196–207.

Wright, P. H. (1988). Interpreting research on gender differences in friendship: A case for moderation and a plea for caution. *Journal of Social and Personal Relationships, 5,* 367–373.

Wright, P., & Wright, K. (1995). Codependency: Personality syndrome or relational process? In J. T. Wood & S. W. Duck (Eds.), *Understanding relationship processes, 6: Understudied relationships: Off the beaten track* (pp. 109–128). Newbury Park, CA: Sage.

Yerby, J. (1992). *Family systems theory reconsidered. Integrating social construction theory and dialectical process into a sys-*

tems perspective of family communication. Paper presented at the Speech Communication Association Meeting, Chicago.

Yougev, S., & Brett, J. (1985). Perceptions of the division of housework and child care and marital satisfaction. *Journal of Marriage and the Family, 47,* 609–618.

Zarit, S., Pearlin, L., & Schaie, K. W. (Eds.). (1993). *Caregiving systems: Informal and formal helpers.* Hillsdale, NJ: Erlbaum.

Zietlow, P. H., & Sillars, A. L. (1988). Life-stage differences in communication during marital conflicts. *Journal of Social and Personal Relationships, 5,* 223–245.

Zimmer, T. (1986). Premarital anxieties. *Journal of Social and Personal Relationships, 3,* 149–159.

Index